Ending the Era

of

Dictatorships

Spiritualizing the World, vol 9

Ending the Era

of

Dictatorships

KIM MICHAELS

MORE TO LIFE PUBLISHING

www.morepublish.com

For foreign and translation rights,

contact: info@ morepublish.com

ISBN: 978-87-93297-68-5

Cover art by Sandra Singer

For more information: *www.ascendedmasterlight.com and*
www.transcendencetoolbox.com

Content

INTRODUCTION

This book belongs to the series *Spiritualizing the World*. The books in this series are given by the ascended masters as workbooks that provide the knowledge and practical tools we need in order to make a contribution to solving concrete world problems. This book contains the knowledge and the tools we need in order to end the era where we have dictators on earth. These books do not contain foundational knowledge about ascended masters and their teachings. In order to make the most efficient use of this book, you need to have a general knowledge of the following topics:

- You need to know who the ascended masters are, how they give their teachings and how you can make the best use of them on a personal and planetary level. You can find extensive teachings on this in the books: *How You Can Help Change the World* and *The Power of Self*.

- You need to know how the earth functions as a cosmic schoolroom. You need to know your own role and the authority you have as a spiritual being in embodiment. You need to know the role of the ascended masters and how only we who are in embodiment can give them the authority to use their unlimited power to affect change on earth. You can find more on these topics in the first book in this series: *How You Can Help Change the World*.

• You need to know how to use the practical tools given by the ascended masters. You can find more on this topic in: *How You Can Help Change the World* and on the website: *www.transcendencetoolbox.com.*

• You need to know about the existence and methods of the dark forces who are ultimately responsible for creating problems on earth. You can find foundational teachings on this in: *Cosmology of Evil.*

How to use this book

There is no one way of using the teachings and tools in this book. However, if you want to make a significant contribution to solving world problems, it is suggested that you start by following this program:

• You read one of the chapters in the book completely in order to increase your understanding of the topic.

• You give the invocation associated with that chapter once a day for nine days while studying the same chapter again.

The reasoning behind this program is that the chapters in the book form a progression. As you give an invocation for one chapter, you are also clearing your own consciousness from certain energies and illusions. This makes it easier for you to absorb and apply the teachings from the next chapter.

You can, of course, also read the book all the way through and then select one or more invocation(s) that you give several times. It is always more powerful to give an invocation once a day for nine or 33 days.

Because some of the invocations in this book are so long, they have been divided into two parts. It takes about 15-20 minutes to give each part. If you prefer, you can give both parts for one invocation in succession. In that case, you do not need to give the sealing after the first invocation or the preamble to the next. You give a preamble in the beginning, continue through the parts and give a sealing in the end.

If you feel burdened by fear-based energy

The purpose of this book is not to merely give you intellectual knowledge. The real purpose is that you give the invocations, whereby you give the ascended masters the authority to remove the dark forces and energies that are behind all problems on earth. These forces will not be happy that you contribute to the process of removing them from the earth. They may therefore seek to direct psychic energy at you that can make you feel burdened in various ways. Their purpose is to make you stop your efforts (or prevent you from starting).

If you feel burdened, please read the last chapter in the book and use the invocation associated with that chapter to make the calls for the protection of yourself and all people around you. As stated in that chapter, most people can quickly come to a point where they are no longer vulnerable to the attacks from the forces of darkness.

The dark forces will always seek to inflate any condition in our personal lives that makes us vulnerable. If you have particular issues, it may be helpful to use other tools that address those issues in a more direct manner. The ascended masters have given many invocations and decrees that can help you deal with specific topics, and you can find most of them on *www.transcendencetoolbox.com*. Some tools are found in the other books by Kim Michaels, and you can see them on *www.morepublish.com*.

It is important that a certain number of people give the invocations and transcend the consciousness behind the issue. It is highly recommended that you talk to other people about this book, including using social media. If enough people use this book and its invocations, it will be possible for the ascended masters to remove dictatorships from earth within the foreseeable future. *Isn't that a message worth spreading?*

1 | EVEN DICTATORS HAVE THE CONSENT OF THE GOVERNED

I AM Michael, the Archangel or if you prefer, the Ascended Master Archangel Michael. Why do we say that an archangel is an ascended master? Well, because we want you all to realize that there are no divisions in the ascended realm. I am not in any way different from or separated from or in opposition to any other being who is ascended because you ascend by overcoming all the divisions that are so common on earth.

We are very grateful for all of you who are part of this conference. Those of you who are physically here, those of you who are connected via the Internet and those who will later study and apply the teachings. Why have we chosen this topic of ending the era of dictatorships on earth? Well, because we intend to give a series of conferences that are focused on giving you the tools to raise the earth out of specific conditions that we have evaluated you are ready to begin to work on and that the planet is ready to begin to work on, given the state of the collective consciousness.

Raising the collective consciousness

What is the state of the collective consciousness? It is something that you who are ascended master students (and all who have been ascended master students now for nearly a century) have been helping to raise. We have from a very early stage in our revealing teachings through sponsored messengers, given the concept that our students can help raise the collective consciousness. We have given tools and decrees and invocations for this specific purpose. Therefore, it is natural that as a part of this raising of the collective consciousness, and as part of the progressive revelation that we are giving, that we will now step up and give a certain amount of tools that are meant to help the planet overcome certain conditions. This will be our focus for this year's conferences.

You will see that last year, we gave a different set of conferences where we gave you tools for raising your personal awareness, especially for healing the birth trauma and earth trauma [See the book *Healing Your Spiritual Traumas* and other books in that series]. These tools are of course still valid and will be valid for a long time to come, especially for when new people come in and find the teachings. You can resolve your own psychology to the highest possible degree before you start using these tools for transcending the planetary consciousness—for raising the planetary consciousness.

The tools we are going to give here (during this year's conferences and the other tools we have given for raising the earth) will be most effective if the people who give them have already raised their personal awareness and overcome, especially the birth trauma and the earth trauma, or at least begun to work on it. That way, you will have the greatest impact. That way, you will not be seeking to change the earth based on your birth or earth trauma. Therefore, you are not colored by that trauma so that you direct your energy into a vision that is a human vision, or that you do it with feelings that are human feelings. Naturally, the more neutral you are, the more effective you are in using these tools, giving the invocations and the decrees.

Truly, my beloved, we are not asking any of you to be perfect, to be enlightened, to be in some specific state of consciousness before you start using our tools. But we have now given you a set of tools that can help you truly resolve the deeper aspects of your psychology. We want you to know of course that the more you resolve, the more effective you will be. This is not to discourage anyone from using the tools at whatever level of consciousness you are at. But we do want to let you know that we have in previous ascended master dispensations seen that people have used our tools, used the decrees, with a certain fear-based state of consciousness, with a certain fear-based vision. We are encouraging you very strongly to recognize if you have this in yourself, and to use the tools for healing your psychology to overcome this so that you do not use our present tools with a fear-based state of mind.

Overcoming your fear of dark forces

We know, my beloved, that when we make you aware of many conditions that are going on here on this planet, it is unavoidable that some of you will react with a certain fear or trepidation. We have given many teachings on the fallen beings and the dark forces that are not commonly known by people. Naturally, as an ascended master student, when you first start to awaken to the reality that there is so much more to know here on earth than what you were told in kindergarten, then you will go through a period where you are somewhat fearful of this. You are somewhat fearful of the dark forces because you realize they are there and you realize that you have been personally attacked by dark forces, certainly in this embodiment but probably in many embodiments. Of course, this can give you a certain amount of fear when you realize that these dark forces are there and you do not know how you can protect yourself from them.

You understand, my beloved, that (as other masters have said during this last year) we are always facing a certain dilemma as ascended masters. The question is, how much can we reveal? How much teachings can we give you without overwhelming you and without having you plunge into fear? This is always a delicate balance we are walking. I trust that you all realize that with the tools for resolving psychology that we have given you over these last years (for that matter, these last many years), it is possible for you to free yourself of this fear-based reaction. Because the fear-based reaction naturally comes from your outer self (or selves) because your Christ Self, your I AM Presence, they have no fear.

I trust you can actually see (when you begin to lock in to what we have taught you about the Conscious You) that the Conscious You has no fear either. The Conscious You, when it is conscious of who and what it is, is simply observing life on earth in a neutral state of mind. Fear does not reside in the Conscious You. The Conscious You has no extension. There is no room for fear in the Conscious You so where can fear reside? Only in one of these separate selves, one of these external selves. It may be your primal self (which naturally reacted with fear to what you were exposed to by the fallen beings), but it may be also be any number of other separate selves. You now have the tools to work on this and I encourage you that if you look at yourself, and if you feel that you have a fear-based reaction to any teaching we give, then do not use these tools for trying to change the world right away. Instead, take a period of time, however long you need it individually, to free yourself from this fear-based self or these fear-based selves. For most of you, you probably have several based on the very turbulent history of this planet. Take some time to overcome the fear until you can give these tools for changing the world from a neutral state of mind. I of course, AM the Archangel of the First Ray and it is my task and my joy to help you overcome fear and the doubt that is always the starting point of fear. Therefore, you can of course use the invocations and the decrees to me but you can also simply ask me. Ask me to help you overcome the fear and ask me to help you see the selves that you have that are the repositories of fear in your being. You can ask me to help you see where the fear resides in your four lower bodies.

You will find that although most people would think of fear as a feeling that is associated with the emotional body, there is actually a mental fear and an identity level fear. You can ask me to help you see this, you can ask other masters to help you see this, so that you can come to the point where you are free from fear. You may not be totally free from fear for some time, but at least you can come to a point where you are not driven by fear, you are not colored by fear and you do not fear a particular response from the dark forces to you giving invocations. Naturally, you can give the decrees and invocations to me for your protection, and when you know and experience that my protection works, then you are not over-whelmed by fear.

How we become broadcast stations for the masters

Fear is of course the primary feeling that has been used by dictators throughout the ages to suppress the population. Therefore, if you are to be effective in helping raise the earth to the point where the era of dicta-torships will come to an end, you need to raise yourself above that fear. Naturally, we are not expecting that this conference will, in itself, end the era of dictators on earth, but we are very happy to see so many people who have chosen to attend this conference. We are very careful not to give you the sense that numbers are so important. But it is of course obvious that the more people you are, the more of a multiplication factor there will be.

Your decrees, your invocations will be multiplied by the number of people that are present. Therefore, we are gratified that so many of you are here so that this conference can be an important turning point towards that process where people use the invocations that will be based on the dictations, and then gradually this will end the era of dictatorships on earth.

Now, you realize I trust that even though you are now sitting, listening to me speak through the messenger, you are not passive participants of this conference. Each and every one of you is an active participant in this conference. You may be sitting, you may be taking in, but I trust you realize that as you are taking in the vibration, the light and the words we are releasing, you are at the same time, if you are willing, becoming a broadcast station. Your aura, your four lower bodies, your chakras are broadcast stations for sending our light and our vibration into the collective consciousness. Therefore, the more you can tune in to the Presence of the master who is speaking, the more effective you will be as a broadcast station.

You understand, my beloved, the basic equation. We of the ascended masters do not have authority to act in the physical realm. You who are embodied in the physical realm, you have authority by your free will to act. Now, of course the messenger has allowed us to speak through him and this has an effect, and in a sense we could have the messenger stand alone and take dictations and it would have an effect. But by you being here and also becoming broadcast stations in the physical octave, the effect is multiplied manifold and that is why it is important for you not to see yourselves as passive recipients of what we are releasing. You are active participants in this conference. There is a figure-eight flow from us Above to you below and back again.

This is guided by the eternal law that Jesus exposed when he was on earth 2,000 years ago, when he talked about the multiplication of the talents. As you become a broadcast station for what you receive from us, as you allow your chakras to radiate it into the collective consciousness, the more you radiate into the collective, the more is returned to us Above, whereby we can multiply what you have multiplied and thereby increase the figure-eight flow.

Therefore, the highest potential for any ascended master conference is that you allow yourselves to spiral upwards in these coming days. You focus your attention on us, on the Presence of the ascended masters. Naturally, you can sit at home, you can read our dictations, you can listen to them, you can give our invocations. But the value of coming together at a conference is that you are setting aside your normal daily activities, your normal daily life. This gives you (especially, my beloved, if you minimize the use of your smart phones over these next days) an opportunity to raise your consciousness beyond what you could do in your normal environment and your normal state of awareness.

You have the opportunity here that you can all spiral upwards. We are ready to help you spiral upwards. *We* are already up, but we are ready to help *you* spiral upwards and come as close to our vibration as you are willing to go. Because you are so many people together, you can collectively spiral much higher that you could do alone. This is the potential for any ascended master conference, but it is especially important when dealing with a heavy topic, such as the topic of dictatorships. I wish to give you some opening thoughts on dictators, and how we see it from the ascended realm.

A government with the consent of the governed

Now, there is a concept that was introduced by the founding fathers of America when they set, under our guidance, the pattern, the matrix, for modern democracies. The concept is that of a government that has the "consent of the governed." The founding fathers, and many people in the modern democracies around the world, see this concept as being very important for democracy. Many people have felt that one of the primary differences between a democracy and a more dictatorial form of government is that a democratic government has the consent of the governed. The people have given their consent to the government by voting the government into position.

Naturally, this is correct. I am not trying to in any way say that this is an incorrect assessment. What you need to understand as ascended master students is that any government, even the worst dictator you can imagine on earth, *any government* has the consent of the governed. Even the worst dictator on earth could not govern if he or she did not have the consent of the governed. The question is not whether a dictator has the consent of the governed, because he does. The question is: Is it *conscious* consent or *unconscious* consent?

This is a question that is also valid for democracy. You may say: "But in a democracy, people always give their conscious consent to the government because they are conscious of going to the voting booth, going in there, putting their mark in the box, and therefore voting for a particular political party or a particular political candidate." Of course, this is true. People are conscious of doing this act. But how conscious are they? What is their level of consciousness?

Naturally, in the first democracies that were created, such as the early American nation, people did not have a very high level of consciousness compared to what they have today in many modern democracies. How conscious were they of the consent that they gave to the government? What did they know about the government, about the candidates, about the political parties? What did they know about the public process or what was going on behind the scenes? The same can be applied today to any modern democracy. How much do the people know? What is their level of consciousness? How high are they on the scale of the 144 levels of consciousness?

How conscious is the consent people give?

There are some democracies where you could say that the average level of consciousness of the people in that nation is barely above the 48th level. Naturally, that is not as high of a level as some of the older democracies where people have grown to a higher level of consciousness. Still, you can go to any modern democracy and you can look at how much the people know about their political parties, the political candidates, the political process, about the bureaucracy, about corruption, about how big companies have an "in" with the government and can put various kinds of pressure on the government. How aware are people of what is going on in the corridors of power?

Naturally, the lower their awareness, the less they know about what is going on in the hidden compartments of the government, the less consent does that government have. It is also a matter of how engaged people are in the political process, how willing they are to inform themselves. In many of the older democracies, people have become so accustomed to going to the polling booth every four years or so and putting their mark that they hardly even think about it. They hardly even think about what they are doing and where they are going. In some of the democracies people have resigned themselves to thinking: "Well, this is all we can achieve, this is the kind of country we have, this is the kind of government we have."

You do see that in some nations, there is this growing dissatisfaction with the government, whether it is democratic or not democratic, and therefore people are becoming more and more active, more and more aware. You see how they are voting for candidates that do not represent politics as usual. You have seen this recently in Ukraine where they elected a president primarily because they saw him as not being part of the political machine, the political apparatus. Therefore, they hope that he can bring the change that they all realize is necessary.

You saw of course the situation a few years ago here in Korea where the people staged a peaceful demonstration that forced the president – that all knew was corrupt – to step down. You have seen in Korea where this brought new hope, a new sense of freedom. You have seen how the old established elites have tried to again restrict that freedom and get things back to politics as usual. But you also have the opportunity to give our invocations and decrees so that you can again create that upward momentum towards greater freedom, greater engagement by the people in the political process.

Any government fulfills the needs of the people

What you need to realize here is that a dictator has the consent of the governed, but it is largely an unconscious consent. Now, you may say, in order to understand this better, what is the purpose of any government? If you go back in time, you will see that there were societies where there was no real organized government, partly because of the poor communications at the time. For example, one thousand years ago or more, there was no real organized government. Then, there started to appear some form of government, such as a king for example, but there were many, many people who lived their lives without ever having anything to do with any kind of government.

Why have we seen this growth in the arising of governments that have become more and more organized, more and more efficient? What is the purpose of government? Well, naturally, it is to fulfill certain needs of the people. The people have certain needs, they realize they cannot fulfill them as individuals and they realize that by coming together, they can do something that they cannot do individually. My beloved, the purpose of government is to fulfill the needs of the population.

This is equally true for a democratic so-called free government, as it is for a dictatorship. The dictator can come to power and can take power only by fulfilling the needs of the people. Now, you may be surprised by this and you may look at many dictators throughout history, and you would say that they have taken power by force. They have somehow used violence, force or even the threat of violence and force to take the power and the authority of the government. You may even say that there are examples where this did not happen with a conscious consent of the people, it actually happened in a way where the people were consciously objecting to this.

You need to recognize here as ascended master students that all people have a conscious mind and a subconscious mind. The lower you go on the scale of the 144 levels of consciousness, the more you find people who are ruled by their subconscious minds. When you go below the 48th level of consciousness, people are dominated by their subconscious minds. They are not so conscious of what they are doing, how they are living their lives. They are ruled by the subconscious mind, and this means that even though the people might consciously object to a particular dictator taking power, they are not subconsciously objecting or the dictator would not be able to take power and hold on to power.

You may go to some of the examples of dictatorships you see around the world today or that you have seen in the past, even the distant past that you are not aware of. You may look at all of these and you may say: Well, did Stalin for example, who killed 21 million Soviet citizens in order to maintain power, did he have the consent of the Russian people? The fact is that he did. Not the *conscious* consent necessarily, but certainly the *subconscious* consent.

Dictators have a subconscious power apparatus

You have to recognize here that the fallen beings are not stupid. That is one thing you should never think about fallen beings. They have a very great awareness of how things work in the physical octave, but also in the emotional, the mental and, to some degree, the identity realm. They are not wise in the sense that they understand the ascended reality and the teachings we are giving from the ascended level. They know a lot more about how things work in the four levels of matter than most people do and that is why they know how to manipulate people. They know how to manipulate people at the identity level, at the mental level, and in the emotional level, and of course also in the physical.

You may look at a certain dictator, and you may look at his physical claim to power and the apparatus he has put in force in order to maintain that power. You may look at Stalin, for example, and the secret police and the death squads and what his physical apparatus was that allowed him to stay in power, but this is just the tip of the iceberg. You do not realize that there was also a very, very strong emotional component to his reign. There was a strong mental component, and there was a certain component even at the identity level. In many cases, a dictator himself of course has such a low level of consciousness that he is not really aware of what is happening at the identity level. Stalin is one of those dictators that were not quite as aware of what was happening at the mental level either, but he was very much aware of the emotional and physical. You will see other dictators, such as Mao Tse-Tung, who were much stronger at the mental level than, for example, Stalin.

What I am saying here is that a dictator is attuned to the consciousness of the people and understands what the people need at the identity, mental and emotional levels and so his physical power apparatus is very carefully designed to fulfill those needs. In some cases, the dictator may not be consciously aware of how his apparatus of power is designed, but those who are taking over the mind of the dictator and using him as a puppet, the fallen beings in the emotional, mental and identity realms, they are certainly aware.

This means that if you look at Stalin, the Russian people had a certain need at the identity level. You can see this in Russia today, you can see it in any other nation that has a dictatorial form of government. You can look across the border to North Korea and see that the North Korean people have a certain sense of identity as being apart from the rest of the world, and apart from their family members in South Korea. They have a certain sense of superiority and they have a need for that sense of superiority. Now, you can also see that this is based on a certain sense of insecurity, which has been covered over. This is exactly what the fallen beings are so good at tuning in to and exploiting.

Again, the Russian people under Stalin (and the Russian people today for that matter) have a need to have a sense of identity that they are different from the rest of the world. They also have a very deep sense of insecurity and this is covered over by this sense of superiority that somehow they need to feel superior. Vladimir Putin understands this to a certain degree. He is not even as aware of it, or as good as exploiting it, as Lenin and Stalin, who understood the need to give the Russian people that sense of superiority because of communism and the Soviet Union, and the sense of power that they were meant to rule the world. This then, is what causes certain people to get to the point where, in order to maintain that dream of being superior, they are willing to, not only submit to the dictator, but also sacrifice themselves, their lives or the lives of their sons, by going to war for the dictator.

A dictator is helping people transcend a need

You see that even though most people would not be consciously aware of this, the people have a need and the dictator is filling that need. Now, it may be a need that cannot last forever. It may be a need that the people can grow out of, but if you go back to the 1920s and the 1930s, you will see that Adolph Hitler actually was, even at the conscious level, quite aware of the German people's need for superiority. This was a need that goes back in time beyond Hitler entering the stage, but he understood that they had that need. He, and of course the fallen beings behind him, exploited that need to a very, very high degree. You also saw that because of what happened during the war, and what happened after the war, the German people have actually, to a very high degree, transcended that need to feel superior.

The German nation is one of these examples of a people who had the strong need for superiority, who therefore became ruled by a ruthless dictator who exploited that need, but a people who have been willing to learn from that lesson and overcome it, to a very large degree. What you of course can make the calls for is that all nations, all people who are ruled by dictators, will go through that process of becoming aware of what needs they have at the identity level, at the mental level, at the emotional level, that the dictator is fulfilling. You can make the calls for this so that these people can go through the transformation process, without having to go to war and be defeated in war in order to learn their lesson. You will see, again to use the example of the Russian people, that to this day they have not overcome it. Many among the younger generation have, but many among the older generation have not overcome the need to feel that they are special, that they are superior. Therefore, they have not learned the lesson and that is why, even though they had the opportunity to have a democratic form of government, they were not able to hold on to it. They were not willing to overcome that need and see themselves as being people just like all other people on earth, and therefore being willing to engage in the family of nations, rather than wanting to be special and stand outside of it.

If you look at the Soviet Union, what claim to fame, so to speak, did the Soviet Union have? Was it a humanitarian organization that went to other nations that were poor and sought to raise them up? Was it a creative, artistic culture that brought forth new art forms? Did they bring forth new inventions that helped humankind? The only claim to fame that the Soviet Union had was raw military power. The only real invention brought forth by the Soviet Union was the Kalashnikov assault rifle, which we do not consider a real high level of invention from the ascended realm. You see my beloved, the need of the Russian people to stand apart and be special was so strong that if they could not do it any other way, they were willing to do it through raw physical power. This is what you have seen in other nations as well throughout history. You have seen how Japan did the same thing, not only during the second world war but also in the occupation of Korea and other nations. It was again raw power. They thought they had a certain culture, but as most people realize, the Japanese people were not particularly creative and inventive. They were very good at following orders, but not inherently creative.

People who become subject to dictators

You see that the people who become subject to dictators are people who are not really creative, they are not inventive and they do not have a high level of what we have called this basic humanity that makes you realize that what you do to others, you are also doing to yourself. They are not humanitarian people. They are not seeking to help others. They are primarily concerned about themselves. They often have a certain insecurity and they have a high level of fear, and that is why they become subject to a dictator who is willing to use raw physical power.

It has been said, for example, about the Russian people, that they have had several leaders who have treated them very harshly and in a very raw, physically abusive manner, but that this is the only kind of power they respect. You see the same in the Chinese people, who also needed a certain raw physical power so that they would submit themselves and therefore feel a certain sense of security.

You understand that the lower you go on the levels of the 144 levels of consciousness, the more fear people have, the more threatened they feel, the more insecure they feel and the more they have a need for some sense of security. What was the Iron Curtain all about? Well, many things of course but one of them was that the Russian people felt secure by being behind that Iron Curtain where they could not easily be invaded, not just in a physical way, but they could not be invaded by new ideas that might force them to change. Why did the Chinese build the great wall? Well, the physical reason was to keep out invaders from the north, but the reason at the emotional, mental and identity level was partly to keep out ideas that might force Chinese society to change. That is why you see Chinese society for thousands of years having this policy of not allowing foreigners to enter. Even when they started having business dealings with the West, they would only allow a few little enclaves here and there to be occupied by the western trades people, they were not allowed to enter China as such. It was partly because the Chinese people were unwilling to change. They felt threatened by change, and therefore they had a need for a kind of government that would build a wall around China to keep change out. Of course, the price you pay then is that you are subject to this government that also keeps you at a certain station that you cannot go beyond.

What you actually saw before Mao took power in China was that the Chinese people had come to a point where they were not satisfied with their station of living in great poverty as peasants. They wanted change. On the one hand, Mao tuned in to this desire for change, and he used a communist ideology to promise them that change. On the other hand, he was also (or at least the fallen beings behind him in other realms) tuned in to that the Chinese people did not want too much change. Therefore, he created the Cultural Revolution that was basically an attempt to control the Chinese people at a certain level. In other words, he wanted to use their desire for change to overthrow the previous government in China, but not allow that desire for change to run too far—and the Chinese people were not ready for that either.

You see today in China where you still have a largely dictatorial form of government, but China has opened up so much that there is now a stronger desire for change, which cannot be turned back. Still, you have the tension between the old form of government and a desire for change and it all revolves around the people and their willingness to change.

The historical origin of dictatorships

My beloved, truly the topic of dictators is a very, very important topic because it says so many different things about the consciousness of the people that they have allowed this. If you go back and look at (in some parts of the world only 1000 years ago, in other parts of the world, such as Korea, you will have to go even further back) where you had these societies without any form of government. They were just hunter-gatherer cultures, they were agricultural people, they were nomads or whatever.

There was no strong form of government, and you see that if you look at the world scale, there were actually different ways for such people to start instituting various forms of government. It was not that they all had dictators, or kings that were acting like dictators. There are examples (not so many but they are there) of people who found an almost democratic form of government, a more cooperative form of government. Some of the Native American people had forms of government that could not in any way be described as dictatorships.

You need to look at why is it that, when people started feeling the need to have a government, in so many cases, they ended up with a government that was, or that became, a dictatorship? Why did that happen? You need to understand that it was because that form of government fulfilled the needs of the people at a certain level. It had a lot to do with people in previous ages having much more fear, feeling much more insecure, and therefore needing to have a sense of security. You see that in the beginning, it was mainly to give people security, and therefore they felt they needed to have a strong government that was willing to use raw physical power. You also had, for example in Europe, where you had the threat of the invasion from the East, from the Huns, and this gave this absolute need to defend yourself against a ruthless enemy. Therefore, the defenders had to be as ruthless as the enemy to turn back the enemy. You then had a situation where you had the emergence of these leaders who were willing to suppress their own people and demand that they go into military service in order to turn back the enemy that would otherwise have overrun their society.

This of course is a situation created by the fallen beings where, as soon as you saw that societies became more organized, you also saw that the fallen beings managed to use these very strong individuals, such as Genghis Khan and others, to amass large armies and attack other nations. Then, those nations that were attacked, the fallen beings used this to make them create a more centralized form of government, a stronger army. Therefore, you had this whole game where the fallen beings were able to become the government, to become the leaders of almost all societies on earth. It was a situation that they created entirely through this physical threat of invasion by these armies that were willing to kill any number of people in the invaded areas.

The fallen being used this threat of raw physical power, the abuse of power, the total perversion of the First Ray, to create the need for a strong government that could defend the people against a strong outside enemy. This is how they managed, over centuries, to create a situation where most nations on earth had a dictatorial form of government where one person was at the top of the pyramid. He had certain advisors, certain henchmen, a certain power apparatus but a very, very small group of people had unlimited power over the population, and that was how it was in most nations.

The purpose of war was to uphold the elite

What was the main purpose of war during that time? Well, it was to maintain that situation where a small elite of primarily fallen beings had unlimited power over the population. If you look at it on a world scale, a very small number of fallen beings in embodiment were the leaders who had control over the population of earth. Of course, the fallen beings in the emotional, mental and identity realms also had that control through those in embodiment, and so this is the primary reason for the evolution or the appearance of dictatorships.

The fallen beings today are maintaining dictatorial forms of government, partly because it creates that threat, the threat of invasion, the threat of warfare. This allows them to manipulate people and manipulate situations so that they can hold back the creativity that is always the greatest threat, the desire for freedom, the desire to just live your life.

Now, my beloved, as you were giving these affirmations before this dictation, the messenger was tuning in to the South Korean people. What he realized is that the reason he feels at home and welcome in South Korea is that the South Korean people are peaceful people who want to live their lives. They have no intention whatsoever of raising an army and invading other countries. This is the way it is with many people around the world, especially the ones who have democratic forms of government.

You see my beloved, there are many people around the world who have risen to a certain level of consciousness, to a certain level of humanity, where they would never even consider raising an army and forcefully taking over the territory of another nation. They simply would no longer consider this. They may have done so in the past, but they have grown out of it. It is no longer there in the collective consciousness of these people.

These people then, as you also see here in South Korea, they are content, and they are realizing that raising your nation is not a matter of expanding territory. It is not even a matter of physical resources. It is a matter of creativity, using what you have in better ways. This is what drives the modern democracies who have risen to a higher level of consciousness. You could not even conceive of these nations invading other nations.

Therefore, you have in these nations, and here in South Korea and many other nations around the world, this awareness that: "We are not aggressive. Why do we even need an army? We do not need it for our own sake because we would never use it aggressively." So why do you need an army? Well, only because there are these aggressive dictatorial nations in the world who might invade you. If you look at yourselves here in Korea and elsewhere, you will see that you have a very deep sense, a very deep desire, that you should not have to defend yourself against an invading force, that this is not the way things should be on earth. What you can learn from this is that you have risen to a level of consciousness – collectively and individually – where you are not aggressive but you still have a certain fear that those who are aggressive might take action against you.

Dictators serve as a threat to democracies

You see here that there is a certain relationship between dictatorial nations and democratic nations. The dictatorial nations are serving as the threat that actually validates the people in the democratic nations that they need to protect themselves. They need to have physical means of protection. You need to have a physical army.

What you can make the calls on, what you can work on in yourselves as well, is to overcome this sense that you need physical protection against a physical enemy. I understand very well that many nations, many people will say: "But look, there is a physical enemy right there across the border that is ready to invade us. If we didn't have an army, they would surely have invaded us already." Yes my beloved, that is true. But why is it so?

What have we told you as ascended master students now for many years in many different ways? We have told you one underlying truth about life on earth: Consciousness comes before the physical manifestation. The physical armies, the physical enemies could not exist if you did not have something in your consciousness that corresponded to that level of consciousness. In other words, you have risen in the democratic nations to a level where you are not aggressive but you have not risen to the level where you fully realize, acknowledge and accept that when you have risen above all aggression, no one can take aggressive action against you.

Now, you may say: "But does this not contradict what you just told us, that the fallen beings have manipulated life on earth—that they manipulated the threat that led to dictatorial governments?" Yes, they did, my beloved, but do you think that fallen beings wanted the emergence of democracy? Do you think that they manipulated people to create democracies? Nay, my beloved. The fallen beings would much have preferred that all nations on earth continued to have dictatorial forms of government indefinitely. Why have democracies emerged? Because people have risen to a higher level of consciousness. This meant that even though they had armies and even though they tried, they could not overrun the democratic nations.

Why do you think the Soviet Union could not overrun the West? Why do you think the North Korean nation and the Chinese helping them could not overrun South Korea? It was because of the level of consciousness. I know there was a tremendous struggle, both here in Korea and elsewhere. There were physical wars. Nevertheless, you need to recognize here that if it had been up to the fallen beings, then the Soviet Union and China would have taken over the world and made it entirely communist. That was their aim, their plan. They could not do this because so many people around the world had raised their level of consciousness to where it was not possible.

How to remove dictatorships

How are we going to get rid of the remaining dictatorships on earth? Well, it will have to happen both because the people who are under the dictators raise their consciousness, but it will also have to happen because people in the democratic nations raise their consciousness where they no longer see the dictatorships as a threat. They trust, they accept, that when you have raised your consciousness beyond aggression, your nation cannot be destroyed by these aggressive forces. Why not? Because when you are not aggressive, you have the protection of the Ascended Host, the ascended masters. You even have the protection of the law, the absolute spiritual law, even as an aspect of free-will.

Why did Jesus tell people to turn the other cheek? Because when you turn the other cheek to an aggressor, and when you do this with a neutral frame of mind, the aggressor's aggression is reflected back by the cosmic mirror upon himself. When people begin to trust, acknowledge and accept this, then you will see that the dictatorships will start losing power. As the people in those dictatorial nations raise their consciousness, the dictators will begin to fall one by one by one. There was a concept during the Cold War of the domino effect where the communist forces would take over one country after another, but I can assure you that there is a higher domino effect where the forces of light and freedom will take over one nation after another. This is what you have seen since the emergence of democracies.

There are various ways of determining whether a nation is a democracy or a dictatorship, but according to some estimates, there are around 200 nations in the world, and 50 of them are dictatorships. That means one quarter. But my beloved, go back 300 years and 100% of them were dictatorships. So is a 75% increase in democratic nations not a significant increase? Therefore, can you not see that there is a clear upward trend here? Dictatorships are in the process of becoming extinct, as were the dinosaurs. It did not happen overnight that the dinosaurs all died out, as some envision, just from one day to another. No, it happened because of a raising of consciousness, and it takes time because free will allows people to take some time to raise their consciousness.

How is the raising of consciousness accomplished? Only through free will—it cannot be forced. When you raise *your* consciousness, you are pulling up on the collective, but you are not *forcing* other people to raise their consciousness. What you are giving them is an opportunity to see more clearly, to see what they could not see before.

My beloved, you have the old story that if you are holding something you think is a rope and you suddenly see that what you are holding is a snake, you do not have to stand there and debate: "Should I let go or should I hold on to it?" You just instinctively – immediately – let go of the snake. The same thing with people in dictatorships. When they truly see what kind of government they have, and when they truly see what freedom is, they will let go of the snake and embrace the freedom.

You may say: "But then why have not the Chinese people or the North Korean people, or the Russian people let go?" Because they have not *seen* it. Most of them have not truly seen it. You may ask yourself how that can be, but it is simply that they are blinded by the level of the collective consciousness, they are blinded by certain lies, they are blinded by certain desires. In many cases, as I said, they are blinded by the desire for superiority, the desire to be special. They think that if they let go of this desire to be special, they will be nobody and nobody will respect them.

Making people think they cannot have more

Many, many people in Russia have felt that after the dissolution of the Soviet Union, they have lost respect. It is because they have not yet tuned in to their own humanity and started to express that humanity. When they do, they will find a new form of respect. Because when people rise in humanity, you respect each other for who you are, not for what you do, or the power you have, or the size of your army, or the size of certain body parts, or whatever people use to measure their status.

You see my beloved, these people have not yet seen it. They have not seen what freedom and democracy offer, they have not truly grasped it. As you raise your consciousness in the democratic nations, as you who are ascended master students make the calls, then there will come a point where they *will* see it. When they *do* see it, they will let go of the past, as you and the people in the democratic nations let go of the past when you saw something better. It is human nature, basic human nature to want more. You can come to a point where you accept that because of outer conditions, you cannot have more, and this is what the fallen beings and all dictatorships have used to suppress the people.

The people who are under a dictator, they accept that because of certain outer conditions (that they think cannot be changed), then they have to live this way—they cannot have greater freedom. These people have accepted that in order to get security, they have to give up part of their freedom. Security is still so important to them that they are willing to give up the freedom, and therefore they are trapped. When the consciousness is raised, and they can see that they can have more freedom and still have security (because they find a new level of security), then they will want the freedom, they will want the abundance, they will want material affluence.

Of course, the people in North Korea want greater freedom. They want the freedom that you have here in South Korea. Most of them do not know what kind of freedom you have because they have been so blinded by the propaganda, but they would want it if they knew. Of course, they want the greater material affluence that you have here. Of course, they want the freedom from aggression that you have here. Do you not realize that aggression is the most insidious prison on earth? Being in this aggressive state of mind where you feel you have to force other people, that you belong to this great Soviet Empire or this great Roman Empire that has to conquer the world. Or for that matter, this great American Empire that has to bring freedom and democracy to the world by force, as if that could ever be done. Having this aggressive mindset is the most restrictive and insidious prison ever invented by the fallen beings.

When people see that they can overcome that mindset, and let go of it and just live peaceful, normal, happy lives, they will want it. They will want it when they see it, and when they come to accept that they can have it.

My beloved, you recognize, of course, that as an ascended master, I am not bound by time and space and therefore I could go on indefinitely. I recognize that you are in time and space and so therefore, I shall save also some wisdom for the other ascended masters who wish to speak at this conference. I am very grateful for your willingness to be the broadcasting stations for this message to be sent from the level of the archangels into the collective consciousness on earth. With this, I seal this release. I seal you in the love of the First Ray.

2 | INVOKING FREEDOM FROM AGGRESSION

In the name of the I AM THAT I AM, Jesus Christ, I use the authority that I have as a being in embodiment on earth to call upon Archangel Michael to reinforce my calls and use my chakras to project the statements in this invocation into the collective consciousness and awaken people to the fact that only when we stop giving our consent, can be overcome dictatorships. Awaken people to the reality that we are spiritual beings and that we can co-create a new future by working with the ascended masters. I especially call for …

[Make your own calls here.]

Part 1

1. Archangel Michael, shatter the energetic matrix that prevents people from seeing that even the worst dictator on earth could not govern if he or she did not have the consent of the governed.

> Michael Archangel, in your flame so blue,
> there is no more night, there is only you.

In oneness with you, we're filled with your light,
what glorious wonder, revealed to our sight.

Michael Archangel, your Knowing so strong,
Michael Archangel, oh sweep us along.
Michael Archangel, we're singing your song,
Michael Archangel, with you we belong.

2. Archangel Michael, shatter the energetic matrix that prevents people from seeing that the question is not whether a dictator has the consent of the governed, but whether it is *conscious* consent or *unconscious* consent.

Michael Archangel, protection you give,
within your blue shield, we ever shall live.
Sealed from all creatures, roaming the night,
we remain in your sphere, of electric blue light.

Michael Archangel, your Knowing so strong,
Michael Archangel, oh sweep us along.
Michael Archangel, we're singing your song,
Michael Archangel, with you we belong.

3. Archangel Michael, shatter the energetic matrix that prevents people from seeing that even in a democracy we need to consider how much the people know about their political parties, the candidates, the political process, the bureaucracy, corruption and how big companies can put pressure on the government. How aware are people of what is going on in the corridors of power?

Michael Archangel, what power you bring,
as millions of angels, praises will sing.
Consuming the demons, of doubt and of fear,
we know that your Presence, will always be near.

Michael Archangel, your Knowing so strong,
Michael Archangel, oh sweep us along.
Michael Archangel, we're singing your song,
Michael Archangel, with you we belong.

4. Archangel Michael, shatter the energetic matrix that prevents people from seeing that the less people know about what is going on in the hidden compartments of the government, the less consent does that government have.

> Michael Archangel, God's will is your love,
> you bring to us all, God's light from Above.
> God's will is to see, all life taking flight,
> transcendence of self, our most sacred right.
>
> **Michael Archangel, your Knowing so strong,**
> **Michael Archangel, oh sweep us along.**
> **Michael Archangel, we're singing your song,**
> **Michael Archangel, with you we belong.**

5. Archangel Michael, shatter the energetic matrix that prevents people from seeing that the purpose of any government is to fulfill certain needs of the people. This is equally true for democratic so-called free governments as it is for a dictatorship.

> Michael Archangel, you are the best friend,
> from all worldly dangers you do us defend,
> the devil no match for your power of light,
> and therefore our souls can freely take flight.
>
> **Michael Archangel, your Knowing so strong,**
> **Michael Archangel, oh sweep us along.**
> **Michael Archangel, we're singing your song,**
> **Michael Archangel, with you we belong.**

6. Archangel Michael, shatter the energetic matrix that prevents people from seeing that a dictator can come to power only by fulfilling the needs of the people, but it may not be the conscious needs of the people.

> Michael Archangel, as children we play,
> we're bringing the earth into a new day,
> we raise it from all of the patterns so old,
> our planet's life story is by us retold.

Michael Archangel, your Knowing so strong,
Michael Archangel, oh sweep us along.
Michael Archangel, we're singing your song,
Michael Archangel, with you we belong.

7. Archangel Michael, shatter the energetic matrix that prevents people from seeing that all people have a conscious mind and a subconscious mind, and many people are dominated by their subconscious minds.

Michael Archangel, God's power you show,
that you are invincible, this we do know,
you are undivided and thus can withstand,
anything coming from serpentine band.

Michael Archangel, your Knowing so strong,
Michael Archangel, oh sweep us along.
Michael Archangel, we're singing your song,
Michael Archangel, with you we belong.

8. Archangel Michael, shatter the energetic matrix that prevents people from seeing that when they are ruled by the subconscious mind, the people might consciously object to a particular dictator taking power, but they are not subconsciously objecting or the dictator would not be able to hold on to power.

Michael Archangel, come raise now the earth,
giving her thus a complete rebirth,
collective the mind that we do now raise,
for this we do give our infinite praise.

Michael Archangel, your Knowing so strong,
Michael Archangel, oh sweep us along.
Michael Archangel, we're singing your song,
Michael Archangel, with you we belong.

9. Archangel Michael, shatter the energetic matrix that prevents people from seeing that a dictator has a physical claim to power and an apparatus that maintains that power, but this is just the tip of the iceberg. The dictator also has an emotional, mental and identity level component to his reign.

Michael Archangel, the earth is now new,
covered in Blue-flame as the morning dew,
our planet now sparkles throughout all of space,
as we are receiving your infinite Grace.

Michael Archangel, your Knowing so strong,
Michael Archangel, oh sweep us along.
Michael Archangel, we're singing your song,
Michael Archangel, with you we belong.

Part 2

1. Archangel Michael, shatter the energetic matrix that prevents people from seeing that a dictator is attuned to the consciousness of the people and understands what the people need at the identity, mental and emotional levels. The physical power apparatus is designed to fulfill those needs.

Michael Archangel, in your flame so blue,
there is no more night, there is only you.
In oneness with you, we're filled with your light,
what glorious wonder, revealed to our sight.

Michael Archangel, your Knowing so strong,
Michael Archangel, oh sweep us along.
Michael Archangel, we're singing your song,
Michael Archangel, with you we belong.

2. Archangel Michael, bind and consume the fallen beings and demons in the emotional, mental and identity realms who are taking over the mind of dictators and designing their power apparatus.

Michael Archangel, protection you give,
within your blue shield, we ever shall live.
Sealed from all creatures, roaming the night,
we remain in your sphere, of electric blue light.

**Michael Archangel, your Knowing so strong,
Michael Archangel, oh sweep us along.
Michael Archangel, we're singing your song,
Michael Archangel, with you we belong.**

3. Archangel Michael, shatter the energetic matrix that prevents people from seeing that people in a dictatorship have a certain sense of identity as being apart from the rest of the world, which gives them a sense of superiority.

Michael Archangel, what power you bring,
as millions of angels, praises will sing.
Consuming the demons, of doubt and of fear,
we know that your Presence, will always be near.

**Michael Archangel, your Knowing so strong,
Michael Archangel, oh sweep us along.
Michael Archangel, we're singing your song,
Michael Archangel, with you we belong.**

4. Archangel Michael, shatter the energetic matrix that prevents people from seeing that this is based on a sense of insecurity, which has been covered over. Bind the fallen beings who are exploiting this need.

Michael Archangel, God's will is your love,
you bring to us all, God's light from Above.
God's will is to see, all life taking flight,
transcendence of self, our most sacred right.

**Michael Archangel, your Knowing so strong,
Michael Archangel, oh sweep us along.
Michael Archangel, we're singing your song,
Michael Archangel, with you we belong.**

5. Archangel Michael, shatter the energetic matrix that prevents people from seeing that the fallen beings always exploit the need for security by giving people the sense that they are different from the rest of the world, that they are superior, that they have power and that they are meant to rule the world.

Michael Archangel, you are the best friend,
from all worldly dangers you do us defend,
the devil no match for your power of light,
and therefore our souls can freely take flight.

Michael Archangel, your Knowing so strong,
Michael Archangel, oh sweep us along.
Michael Archangel, we're singing your song,
Michael Archangel, with you we belong.

6. Archangel Michael, shatter the energetic matrix that prevents people from seeing that this is what causes certain people to get to the point where, in order to maintain the dream of being superior, they are willing to submit to the dictator and sacrifice their lives or the lives of their sons by going to war for the dictator.

Michael Archangel, as children we play,
we're bringing the earth into a new day,
we raise it from all of the patterns so old,
our planet's life story is by us retold.

Michael Archangel, your Knowing so strong,
Michael Archangel, oh sweep us along.
Michael Archangel, we're singing your song,
Michael Archangel, with you we belong.

7. Archangel Michael, shatter the energetic matrix that prevents people from seeing that Adolph Hitler was, even at the conscious level, quite aware of the German people's need for superiority. He, and the fallen beings behind him, exploited that need.

Michael Archangel, God's power you show,
that you are invincible, this we do know,
you are undivided and thus can withstand,
anything coming from serpentine band.

Michael Archangel, your Knowing so strong,
Michael Archangel, oh sweep us along.

Michael Archangel, we're singing your song,
Michael Archangel, with you we belong.

8. Archangel Michael, shatter the energetic matrix that prevents people from seeing that the German nation is an example of a people who had the strong need for superiority, who therefore became ruled by a ruthless dictator, but they have been willing to learn from that lesson and grow.

Michael Archangel, come raise now the earth,
giving her thus a complete rebirth,
collective the mind that we do now raise,
for this we do give our infinite praise.

Michael Archangel, your Knowing so strong,
Michael Archangel, oh sweep us along.
Michael Archangel, we're singing your song,
Michael Archangel, with you we belong.

9. I call for all nations, all people who are ruled by dictators to go through that process of becoming aware of what needs they have at the identity level, at the mental level, at the emotional level that the dictator is fulfilling.

Michael Archangel, the earth is now new,
covered in Blue-flame as the morning dew,
our planet now sparkles throughout all of space,
as we are receiving your infinite Grace.

Michael Archangel, your Knowing so strong,
Michael Archangel, oh sweep us along.
Michael Archangel, we're singing your song,
Michael Archangel, with you we belong.

Part 3

1. Archangel Michael, shatter the energetic matrix that prevents people from going through the transformation process, without having to go to war and be defeated in war in order to learn their lesson.

Michael Archangel, in your flame so blue,
there is no more night, there is only you.
In oneness with you, we're filled with your light,
what glorious wonder, revealed to our sight.

**Michael Archangel, your Knowing so strong,
Michael Archangel, oh sweep us along.
Michael Archangel, we're singing your song,
Michael Archangel, with you we belong.**

2. Archangel Michael, cut the Russian people free to overcome the need to feel that they are special, that they are superior. Cut them free to see themselves as being people like all other people on earth, and therefore being willing to engage in the family of nations, rather than wanting to be special and stand outside of it.

Michael Archangel, protection you give,
within your blue shield, we ever shall live.
Sealed from all creatures, roaming the night,
we remain in your sphere, of electric blue light.

**Michael Archangel, your Knowing so strong,
Michael Archangel, oh sweep us along.
Michael Archangel, we're singing your song,
Michael Archangel, with you we belong.**

3. Archangel Michael, cut the Russian people free from the need to stand apart and be special that made them willing to do it through raw physical power.

Michael Archangel, what power you bring,
as millions of angels, praises will sing.
Consuming the demons, of doubt and of fear,
we know that your Presence, will always be near.

**Michael Archangel, your Knowing so strong,
Michael Archangel, oh sweep us along.
Michael Archangel, we're singing your song,
Michael Archangel, with you we belong.**

4. Archangel Michael, shatter the energetic matrix that prevents people from seeing that those who become subject to dictators are people who are not creative and they do not have a high level of basic humanity that makes them realize that what they do to others, they are also doing to themselves.

Michael Archangel, God's will is your love,
you bring to us all, God's light from Above.
God's will is to see, all life taking flight,
transcendence of self, our most sacred right.

Michael Archangel, your Knowing so strong,
Michael Archangel, oh sweep us along.
Michael Archangel, we're singing your song,
Michael Archangel, with you we belong.

5. Archangel Michael, shatter the energetic matrix that prevents people from seeing that those who become subject to dictators are not humanitarian people and are primarily concerned about themselves. They often have insecurity and they have a high level of fear, and that is why they become subject to a dictator who is willing to use raw physical power.

Michael Archangel, you are the best friend,
from all worldly dangers you do us defend,
the devil no match for your power of light,
and therefore our souls can freely take flight.

Michael Archangel, your Knowing so strong,
Michael Archangel, oh sweep us along.
Michael Archangel, we're singing your song,
Michael Archangel, with you we belong.

6. Archangel Michael, cut free the Russian and the Chinese people from the need for a dictator who is using raw physical power, causing them to submit themselves and therefore feel a certain sense of security.

Michael Archangel, as children we play,
we're bringing the earth into a new day,
we raise it from all of the patterns so old,
our planet's life story is by us retold.

Michael Archangel, your Knowing so strong,
Michael Archangel, oh sweep us along.
Michael Archangel, we're singing your song,
Michael Archangel, with you we belong.

7. Archangel Michael, cut free the Russian and the Chinese people from the unwillingness to change and the need for a kind of government that would build a wall around them to keep change out.

Michael Archangel, God's power you show,
that you are invincible, this we do know,
you are undivided and thus can withstand,
anything coming from serpentine band.

Michael Archangel, your Knowing so strong,
Michael Archangel, oh sweep us along.
Michael Archangel, we're singing your song,
Michael Archangel, with you we belong.

8. Archangel Michael, bind the fallen beings in the identity, mental and emotional realms who are controlling the Russian people, the Russian leaders and the Russian government.

Michael Archangel, come raise now the earth,
giving her thus a complete rebirth,
collective the mind that we do now raise,
for this we do give our infinite praise.

Michael Archangel, your Knowing so strong,
Michael Archangel, oh sweep us along.
Michael Archangel, we're singing your song,
Michael Archangel, with you we belong.

9. Archangel Michael, bind the fallen beings in the identity, mental and emotional realms who are controlling the Chinese people, the Chinese leaders and the Chinese government.

Michael Archangel, the earth is now new,
covered in Blue-flame as the morning dew,

our planet now sparkles throughout all of space,
as we are receiving your infinite Grace.

**Michael Archangel, your Knowing so strong,
Michael Archangel, oh sweep us along.
Michael Archangel, we're singing your song,
Michael Archangel, with you we belong.**

Part 4

1. Archangel Michael, shatter the energetic matrix that prevents people from seeing that dictatorships have historically been based on people having fear, feeling insecure, and therefore needing to have a strong government that was willing to use raw physical power.

Michael Archangel, in your flame so blue,
there is no more night, there is only you.
In oneness with you, we're filled with your light,
what glorious wonder, revealed to our sight.

**Michael Archangel, your Knowing so strong,
Michael Archangel, oh sweep us along.
Michael Archangel, we're singing your song,
Michael Archangel, with you we belong.**

2. Archangel Michael, shatter the energetic matrix that prevents people from seeing that this is a situation created by the fallen beings who used individuals to amass large armies and attack other nations. In the nations that were attacked, the fallen beings used this to make them create a more centralized form of government, a stronger army.

Michael Archangel, protection you give,
within your blue shield, we ever shall live.
Sealed from all creatures, roaming the night,
we remain in your sphere, of electric blue light.

Michael Archangel, your Knowing so strong,
Michael Archangel, oh sweep us along.
Michael Archangel, we're singing your song,
Michael Archangel, with you we belong.

3. Archangel Michael, bind the fallen beings who used war to become the government, to become the leaders of almost all societies on earth.

Michael Archangel, what power you bring,
as millions of angels, praises will sing.
Consuming the demons, of doubt and of fear,
we know that your Presence, will always be near.

Michael Archangel, your Knowing so strong,
Michael Archangel, oh sweep us along.
Michael Archangel, we're singing your song,
Michael Archangel, with you we belong.

4. Archangel Michael, bind the fallen beings who created this situation through the physical threat of invasion by these armies that were willing to kill any number of people in the invaded areas.

Michael Archangel, God's will is your love,
you bring to us all, God's light from Above.
God's will is to see, all life taking flight,
transcendence of self, our most sacred right.

Michael Archangel, your Knowing so strong,
Michael Archangel, oh sweep us along.
Michael Archangel, we're singing your song,
Michael Archangel, with you we belong.

5. Archangel Michael, bind the fallen beings who used this threat of raw physical power, the abuse of power, the total perversion of the First Ray, to create the need for a strong government that could defend the people against a strong outside enemy.

Michael Archangel, you are the best friend,
from all worldly dangers you do us defend,

the devil no match for your power of light,
and therefore our souls can freely take flight.

Michael Archangel, your Knowing so strong,
Michael Archangel, oh sweep us along.
Michael Archangel, we're singing your song,
Michael Archangel, with you we belong.

6. Archangel Michael, bind the fallen beings who created a situation where most nations on earth had a dictatorial form of government where one person or a small group of people had unlimited power over the population.

Michael Archangel, as children we play,
we're bringing the earth into a new day,
we raise it from all of the patterns so old,
our planet's life story is by us retold.

Michael Archangel, your Knowing so strong,
Michael Archangel, oh sweep us along.
Michael Archangel, we're singing your song,
Michael Archangel, with you we belong.

7. Archangel Michael, bind the fallen beings who used war to maintain a situation where a small elite of primarily fallen beings had unlimited power over the population.

Michael Archangel, God's power you show,
that you are invincible, this we do know,
you are undivided and thus can withstand,
anything coming from serpentine band.

Michael Archangel, your Knowing so strong,
Michael Archangel, oh sweep us along.
Michael Archangel, we're singing your song,
Michael Archangel, with you we belong.

8. Archangel Michael, bind the small number of fallen beings in embodiment who were the leaders who had control over the population of earth.

Michael Archangel, come raise now the earth,
giving her thus a complete rebirth,
collective the mind that we do now raise,
for this we do give our infinite praise.

**Michael Archangel, your Knowing so strong,
Michael Archangel, oh sweep us along.
Michael Archangel, we're singing your song,
Michael Archangel, with you we belong.**

9. Archangel Michael, bind the fallen beings in the emotional, mental and identity realms who also had that control through those in embodiment.

Michael Archangel, the earth is now new,
covered in Blue-flame as the morning dew,
our planet now sparkles throughout all of space,
as we are receiving your infinite Grace.

**Michael Archangel, your Knowing so strong,
Michael Archangel, oh sweep us along.
Michael Archangel, we're singing your song,
Michael Archangel, with you we belong.**

Part 5

1. Archangel Michael, bind the fallen beings who today are maintaining dictatorial forms of government because it creates the threat of warfare that allows them to manipulate people.

Michael Archangel, in your flame so blue,
there is no more night, there is only you.
In oneness with you, we're filled with your light,
what glorious wonder, revealed to our sight.

**Michael Archangel, your Knowing so strong,
Michael Archangel, oh sweep us along.**

Michael Archangel, we're singing your song,
Michael Archangel, with you we belong.

2. Archangel Michael, shatter the energetic matrix that prevents people from seeing that they are peaceful people who want to live their lives. They have no intention of raising an army and invading other countries.

Michael Archangel, protection you give,
within your blue shield, we ever shall live.
Sealed from all creatures, roaming the night,
we remain in your sphere, of electric blue light.

Michael Archangel, your Knowing so strong,
Michael Archangel, oh sweep us along.
Michael Archangel, we're singing your song,
Michael Archangel, with you we belong.

3. Archangel Michael, shatter the energetic matrix that prevents people from rising to the level of consciousness, to the level of humanity, where they would never even consider raising an army and forcefully taking over the territory of another nation.

Michael Archangel, what power you bring,
as millions of angels, praises will sing.
Consuming the demons, of doubt and of fear,
we know that your Presence, will always be near.

Michael Archangel, your Knowing so strong,
Michael Archangel, oh sweep us along.
Michael Archangel, we're singing your song,
Michael Archangel, with you we belong.

4. Archangel Michael, shatter the energetic matrix that prevents people from seeing that raising your nation is not a matter of expanding territory. It is not even a matter of physical resources. It is a matter of creativity, using what you have in better ways.

Michael Archangel, God's will is your love,
you bring to us all, God's light from Above.

God's will is to see, all life taking flight,
transcendence of self, our most sacred right.

Michael Archangel, your Knowing so strong,
Michael Archangel, oh sweep us along.
Michael Archangel, we're singing your song,
Michael Archangel, with you we belong.

5. Archangel Michael, shatter the energetic matrix that prevents people from seeing that we have risen to a level of consciousness where we are not aggressive but we still have a fear that those who are aggressive might take action against us.

Michael Archangel, you are the best friend,
from all worldly dangers you do us defend,
the devil no match for your power of light,
and therefore our souls can freely take flight.

Michael Archangel, your Knowing so strong,
Michael Archangel, oh sweep us along.
Michael Archangel, we're singing your song,
Michael Archangel, with you we belong.

6. Archangel Michael, shatter the energetic matrix that prevents people from seeing that the dictatorial nations are serving as the threat that validates the people in the democratic nations who think they need to protect themselves and have a physical army.

Michael Archangel, as children we play,
we're bringing the earth into a new day,
we raise it from all of the patterns so old,
our planet's life story is by us retold.

Michael Archangel, your Knowing so strong,
Michael Archangel, oh sweep us along.
Michael Archangel, we're singing your song,
Michael Archangel, with you we belong.

7. Archangel Michael, cut people free from this sense that we need physical protection against a physical enemy so we can begin to see that it is our consciousness that attracts the external enemy.

> Michael Archangel, God's power you show,
> that you are invincible, this we do know,
> you are undivided and thus can withstand,
> anything coming from serpentine band.

> **Michael Archangel, your Knowing so strong,**
> **Michael Archangel, oh sweep us along.**
> **Michael Archangel, we're singing your song,**
> **Michael Archangel, with you we belong.**

8. Archangel Michael, shatter the energetic matrix that prevents people from seeing that the physical armies, the physical enemies could not exist if we did not have something in our consciousness that corresponded to that level of consciousness.

> Michael Archangel, come raise now the earth,
> giving her thus a complete rebirth,
> collective the mind that we do now raise,
> for this we do give our infinite praise.

> **Michael Archangel, your Knowing so strong,**
> **Michael Archangel, oh sweep us along.**
> **Michael Archangel, we're singing your song,**
> **Michael Archangel, with you we belong.**

9. Archangel Michael, shatter the energetic matrix that prevents people from seeing that in the democratic nations, we have risen to a level where we are not aggressive but we have not risen to the level where we fully realize, acknowledge and accept that when we have risen above all aggression, no one can take aggressive action against us.

> Michael Archangel, the earth is now new,
> covered in Blue-flame as the morning dew,
> our planet now sparkles throughout all of space,
> as we are receiving your infinite Grace.

**Michael Archangel, your Knowing so strong,
Michael Archangel, oh sweep us along.
Michael Archangel, we're singing your song,
Michael Archangel, with you we belong.**

Part 6

1. Archangel Michael, cut free the people who are still under dictators to raise their consciousness. Cut free the people in democratic nations to raise their consciousness to where they no longer see the dictatorships as a threat.

Michael Archangel, in your flame so blue,
there is no more night, there is only you.
In oneness with you, we're filled with your light,
what glorious wonder, revealed to our sight.

**Michael Archangel, your Knowing so strong,
Michael Archangel, oh sweep us along.
Michael Archangel, we're singing your song,
Michael Archangel, with you we belong.**

2. Archangel Michael, shatter the energetic matrix that prevents people from seeing that when we have raised our consciousness beyond aggression, our nation cannot be destroyed by these aggressive forces because we have the protection of the ascended masters. We have the protection of the absolute spiritual law.

Michael Archangel, protection you give,
within your blue shield, we ever shall live.
Sealed from all creatures, roaming the night,
we remain in your sphere, of electric blue light.

**Michael Archangel, your Knowing so strong,
Michael Archangel, oh sweep us along.
Michael Archangel, we're singing your song,
Michael Archangel, with you we belong.**

3. Archangel Michael, shatter the energetic matrix that prevents people from seeing that Jesus told people to turn the other cheek because when we turn the other cheek to an aggressor, the aggressor's aggression is reflected back upon itself by the cosmic mirror. When we begin to trust, acknowledge and accept this, then the dictators will fall.

Michael Archangel, what power you bring,
as millions of angels, praises will sing.
Consuming the demons, of doubt and of fear,
we know that your Presence, will always be near.

Michael Archangel, your Knowing so strong,
Michael Archangel, oh sweep us along.
Michael Archangel, we're singing your song,
Michael Archangel, with you we belong.

4. Archangel Michael, shatter the consciousness that is blinding the people in Russia, China, North Korea and other dictatorial nations so they can see the lies and overcome the desire for superiority, the desire to be special. Help them overcome the fear that if they let go of this desire to be special, they will be nobody, and nobody will respect them.

Michael Archangel, God's will is your love,
you bring to us all, God's light from Above.
God's will is to see, all life taking flight,
transcendence of self, our most sacred right.

Michael Archangel, your Knowing so strong,
Michael Archangel, oh sweep us along.
Michael Archangel, we're singing your song,
Michael Archangel, with you we belong.

5. Archangel Michael, cut free the people in Russia, China, North Korea and other dictatorial nations so they can tune in to their own humanity and start to express that humanity, thereby finding a new form of respect.

Michael Archangel, you are the best friend,
from all worldly dangers you do us defend,

the devil no match for your power of light,
and therefore our souls can freely take flight.

Michael Archangel, your Knowing so strong,
Michael Archangel, oh sweep us along.
Michael Archangel, we're singing your song,
Michael Archangel, with you we belong.

6. Archangel Michael, cut free the people in Russia, China, North Korea and other dictatorial nations so they can see what freedom and democracy have to offer, and thereby let go of the past because it is natural to want something better.

Michael Archangel, as children we play,
we're bringing the earth into a new day,
we raise it from all of the patterns so old,
our planet's life story is by us retold.

Michael Archangel, your Knowing so strong,
Michael Archangel, oh sweep us along.
Michael Archangel, we're singing your song,
Michael Archangel, with you we belong.

7. Archangel Michael, cut free the people in Russia, China, North Korea and other dictatorial nations from the consciousness of accepting that because of outer conditions, they cannot have more, causing them to give up freedom in order to have security.

Michael Archangel, God's power you show,
that you are invincible, this we do know,
you are undivided and thus can withstand,
anything coming from serpentine band.

Michael Archangel, your Knowing so strong,
Michael Archangel, oh sweep us along.
Michael Archangel, we're singing your song,
Michael Archangel, with you we belong.

8. Archangel Michael, cut free the people in Russia, China, North Korea and other dictatorial nations to see that they can have more freedom and still have security, setting them free to want the freedom, the abundance, the material affluence.

> Michael Archangel, come raise now the earth,
> giving her thus a complete rebirth,
> collective the mind that we do now raise,
> for this we do give our infinite praise.

> **Michael Archangel, your Knowing so strong,**
> **Michael Archangel, oh sweep us along.**
> **Michael Archangel, we're singing your song,**
> **Michael Archangel, with you we belong.**

9. Archangel Michael, cut free the people in Russia, China, North Korea and other dictatorial nations to see that having this aggressive mindset is the most restrictive and insidious prison ever invented by the fallen beings. Cut them free to see that by letting go of this mindset, they will be free to live the peaceful, normal, happy lives that they truly want.

> Michael Archangel, the earth is now new,
> covered in Blue-flame as the morning dew,
> our planet now sparkles throughout all of space,
> as we are receiving your infinite Grace.

> **Michael Archangel, your Knowing so strong,**
> **Michael Archangel, oh sweep us along.**
> **Michael Archangel, we're singing your song,**
> **Michael Archangel, with you we belong.**

Sealing

In the name of the I AM THAT I AM, I accept that Archangel Michael, Astrea and Shiva form an impenetrable shield around myself and all constructive people, sealing us from all fear-based energies in all four octaves. I accept that the Light of God is consuming and transforming all fear-based energies that make up the dark forces working against ending the era of dictatorships on earth!

3 | A BETTER SOCIETY, NOT BY FORCE BUT BY CHOICE

I AM the Ascended Master Surya. I want to continue on what Archangel Michael talked about earlier, about the fact that every dictator has at some level of consciousness the consent of the governed. Now, if you think about how most people in the world look at the topic of dictators, you will realize that it is very difficult for people to understand what a dictator is, why dictatorships have arisen, what kind of people are willing to be dictators. You can see that there is a certain element of denial in many people around the world.

For example, if you go to China you might know that even today they universally talk about the "Great Chairman Mao" and you are not allowed to say anything critical about Chairman Mao. It is almost unthinkable that the people would even dare to criticize what has become an idol for the nation. Likewise, in Russia you will see that many people, even though they know about what happened during Stalinist times, they are reluctant to criticize Stalin. It was only a few years ago that there was a public survey done in Russia where the Russian people could vote for the person they thought was the historically most significant person in Russia. For a long time Stalin was actually winning the contest, only in the end was he overtaken by a poet.

People deny the cruelty of the dictator

You will see that there is this tendency that the people will deny the cruelty of the dictator. What they will basically deny, is that the dictator did not care about them whatsoever. When you look at the reality, when you look at even what is known publicly about people like Mao or Stalin, you will see – if you look at it honestly and neutrally – that they did not care about their people, the people they were leading. They were willing to sacrifice any amount of those people for the cause, which basically was the cause of them staying in power. Chairman Mao had certain ideals that he was pursuing but Stalin had hardly any ideals other than him staying in power.

You will see that there is that element of denial that is still there in certain countries that either have a dictatorial form of government or have had it recently. You will see of course a difference when it comes to Hitler, who has for the most part been recognized as being universally evil. Of course, there are certain neo-Nazi groups that look at him with admiration but the vast majority of the people, both in Germany and elsewhere, have recognized and admitted the evil of Hitler. Of course, when they look at this, they cannot understand it. You will see the almost comical extent to which intellectuals will go when they attempt to analyze Hitler and explain how he could do what he did. They attempt to come up with rational, materialistic explanations: Whether it was his family background, his upbringing, his psychology, his genes or whatever.

Dictators are not normal human beings

My point for bringing this up, is that the world at large cannot understand why there are dictators. They cannot understand why there are a few people that are willing to step into this position of having unlimited power over a population of people. Then, once they have that power, they do absolutely anything they think necessary to maintain their power. They cannot understand and explain why there are some people that have held on to their power beyond all reasonability or rationality. They will not let go of their power, as you even saw with Hitler. When any rational person could see that the war was lost, he kept living in a fantasy world, moving around army units that did not exist except in his imagination. Always thinking about this super weapon that would be developed but which somehow never materialized. You see many other dictators like this.

Again, conventional science cannot explain this. Why is it that some dictators lose their minds to a point where they are out of touch with the real world, out of touch with their own people? They are blindly pursuing some kind of goal without any willingness to look at the practical reality of the situation. Naturally, we have given you very, very carefully (both through this messenger and also in previous ascended master dispensations) the knowledge that means that you can understand this at a deeper level. This of course is what we have attempted to condense in the "My Lives" book [*My Lives with Lucifer, Satan, Hitler and Jesus*] where in a concentrated form that is easier to read, people can get the knowledge that is the critical aspect to understanding dictators. That knowledge is of course that the reason why there is a few people that are willing to step into this position as dictators, is because there are a few people embodied on earth who are not normal human beings, they are different from the norm. This is what people in general have not been willing to recognize.

We must therefore logically ask ourselves why the world has not been willing to recognize this? Again, the only logical answer is that the major thought systems of the world have been influenced by (perhaps even in some cases generated by) certain forces that do not want people to understand the basic dynamic of earth, of how life works on earth. They do not want people in general to know that the earth is a planet with a very broad range of consciousness where many different lifestreams have embodied. This of course has its background in the fallen beings who do not want themselves to be known. They do not want the population to know that there is a specific group of people on earth who have no humanitarian ideals, who have no concerns whatsoever for human beings. These people do not see themselves as human beings, they see the population as human beings but they see themselves as being superior, as being in a special class of people.

This is something that the world is actually ready to recognize. It is almost like the old fairy tale about the Emperor's new clothes where the people who are closest to the Emperor are so concerned about maintaining their position that they are not willing to step back and look at the Emperor and see that he has nothing on. They are certainly not willing to speak out and say it. The world, the population, is ready to acknowledge that there is a certain group of people on the planet that have no respect, no caring, no love, no humanity when it comes to the population at large. They are willing to kill or sacrifice any number of human beings for whatever cause they have in their heads. It is a complete disrespect for life.

Deciding we want no more dictators

This is something the world is ready to recognize. They do not need to acknowledge ascended master teachings before they can recognize this. It is possible to have people who are creative thinkers, who can simply look at history, look at human psychology, what is already known in general psychology. They can put these together and draw this conclusion that we need to recognize that throughout history we have seen this special group of people, who have taken these positions of being dictators and who have no respect for life whatsoever. We need to recognize this openly, acknowledge it. Then we need to make a determination: "We do not want this kind of people to lead us anymore, we do not want this kind of people to attain any position in government, or any other position where they have power over the population on earth."

The collective consciousness has gradually been brought up to where it is ready to recognize this. What we need you to do as ascended master students is of course to make the calls so that, first of all, the people who can be the forerunners for this awareness will be cut free, will be awakened, will be inspired. They will be able to tune in to the ascended masters (even if they do not recognize us consciously) and receive these ideas where it suddenly snaps into focus, their consciousness shifts and they see: "Oh but the dictator has nothing on!" They see the naked truth of who these beings are.

They may not have the concept of fallen beings but they see they have no respect for life. This is what needs to be seen, because (especially in the modern democracies) most people have that respect for life. As Archangel Michael said, they have risen above this level of consciousness where they would ever dream of perpetrating some aggressive actions upon other people. They would never dream of assembling an army and conquering another nation, they have transcended that. Therefore, they are ready to see that it was never really the people as such who assembled armies and conquered territories. It was only that small group of people who had no respect for life.

All dictators are narcissists

Now, once this has been recognized (and it can be recognized based on the developments in psychology where you talk about narcissistic personality disorder, narcissists, you talk about sociopaths, psychopaths and so on) you can realize that basically all the dictators in history have had that kind of psychology, that kind of abnormal psychology. They have been narcissists or sociopaths or psychopaths or however psychology currently labels them. It is not difficult at all to see this. It is simply that the fallen beings have managed to create this cloud of ignorance that is still hanging there so that people have not been willing to step back and see it for what it is. They can, with your calls and our help, come to that point where they "see it." Suddenly, the public awareness shifts and there is now an awareness of this and an outcry for a better type of leadership. However, the Omega aspect of this is of course also that people come to understand why dictators arose in the first place and why there are still dictators in the world. Archangel Michael said: "A dictator has the consent of the governed because at some level (usually subconscious) the dictator is fulfilling the needs of the people." There are of course different needs as Archangel Michael talked about: the need for superiority, the need for security. There are other needs and the need that I wish to bring to your attention here, is a slightly different matter.

The dictator relieves people of personal responsibility

Now, if you look at the dynamic in a country. It can be North Korea today, it can be Communist China under Mao or even China as it is today to a large degree. It can be Russia under Stalin or even Russia under communism. It can be Germany during the Nazi era. What is it you see, what is the dynamic you see? Basically, you see that you have this very strong leader who has assumed, taken to himself forcefully, almost absolute power. The population, at least the majority of them, have come to accept (mind you) that this leader has some extraordinary power. Why is it that people in general are ready to see that there is a special group of people that have no respect for life?

Well, it is because in dictatorships they usually think that the dictator belongs to a special group of people, or at least he as an individual stands out from the rest of humanity. He is different. Therefore, he has this ability to lead, he has these special powers to lead. You already have the concept that the dictator is in a special category compared to the rest of the population. It is not so hard to connect that with the narcissistic personality disorder, with no empathy and no respect for life. People see that: "Yes, it is true, the dictator really was in a special category of people. It was not because he had superhuman powers, it was because he had a subhuman disrespect for life."

What is the dynamic, the psychological dynamic, that happens in a nation once it has accepted a dictator and elevated him to this superhuman status? The psychological dynamic that happens in the people is that they have accepted that the dictator is there, that he has power over them and they cannot stand up against it. It is perhaps futile, perhaps they do not have the power to stand up, or perhaps they do not even want to because they believe that he is taking them to this wonderful new world that he is promising them. They either believe in the dictators promises or they have submitted themselves to his power, thinking they can do nothing about it. What then happens in the psychology of people when they get to that point? What happens is this: They feel that as individuals, they no longer have any responsibility. They do not have personal responsibility for their lives or for their nation. They become followers of the dictator, mindless followers, even if they are very intelligent people.

You will know that in Nazi Germany many of the people who followed Hitler were actually very intelligent and well educated. Not all of them, but certainly some. What happens is that once they surrender that sense of personal responsibility, then even though they may be very well educated and very intelligent people, they have given up the responsibility to look at the dictator with critical eyes. They suspend all critical evaluation of the dictator and his actions. This means that they have basically said: "I have no personal responsibility."

What you see here is that in all nations that have or have had a dictator, the dictator fulfilled the need of a large part of the population, the need to feel that they are not responsible. They do not need to be responsible, they can focus on their daily lives, they do not need to think about the bigger more complicated matters of their nation, or this or that. They do not need to look with critical eyes at communist ideology, Nazi ideology or whatever you have.

What makes a nation ready for a dictatorship

What you realize here is that there is a certain portion of the human population who have this need to give up, to be free from, personal responsibility. If a majority of the people in a nation have this need at a subconscious level, then that nation is vulnerable to being taken over by a dictatorial form of government. This is how it has happened historically to a very large degree.

When you look at history over the last several thousand years, you can see that as you go further and further back, a greater and greater part of the population had this need to abandon personal responsibility. That is why in the past you had very few more democratic societies. People were not ready for them. What you have seen is that this has very slowly and very gradually been changed. I can assure you that we of the ascended masters have been working very actively to change the equation. We have found it very, very slow work.

We have had to be very, very patient and see many setbacks. Sometimes one step forward, two steps backwards. Sometimes one step backwards, one step forward and every once in a while a decisive step forward. This is how we very, very slowly, very gradually brought society forward to the point where the modern democracies could begin to emerge.

Naturally, we had that period in time that you all know about in ancient Greece where there was a form of democracy. Although it was not what we today consider a modern democracy, partly because it was only a small percentage of the population who actually had the right to vote. Women, slaves and others did not have the right to vote. This is not what we call a modern democracy where all men and women are created equal and all men and women are endowed by their Creator with inalienable rights.

What you see is again that the fallen beings are very adept at reading the collective consciousness and where that consciousness is at. Of course, one of the parameters they have is how many people are willing to take responsibility and how many people want to abandon personal responsibility. When there is a majority of those who want to give up the responsibility, that is when they attempt to move in and create some dictatorial form of government. Of course, it does not mean that once a nation has a democratic form of government, they stop trying to infiltrate it and bring it back down. They will of course work with any society, seeking to undermine the democratic rights and the democratic freedoms and create a government that takes on more and more power.

This is what you see outpictured in the United States, even going back to the time of the birth of the nation, of the discussions between those who were Federalists and wanted a strong federal government and those who were anti-Federalists and wanted a weak federal government. You see that in the United States today, you have a much stronger federal government than the Founding Fathers originally envisioned. This of course was brought about, as Archangel Michael talked about, by the fallen beings creating the communist threat, by creating a Russia that was taken over by a dictatorial form of government. Thereby spreading its powers to all of the Soviet Republics and creating the Soviet Union, which then became a direct physical threat to the freedom of the West and the democracies. This was one of the major justifications for strengthening the federal government in the United States, in order to stand up to this communist threat. This has to a large degree undermined some of these freedoms and rights that the Founding Fathers originally saw as necessary in the United States.

Democracy is a demanding form of government

You need to recognize here that even in democracies there can be a certain percentage of the people who still want to give up their personal responsibility. This is what the fallen beings will then take advantage of, by making people feel that as long as they read the news and know what is going on in their nation, then go to the polling stations every four years and vote for the government, then they have fulfilled their responsibility as democratic citizens and they do not need to do anymore actively. They can sit back and whine and complain about the government and why the government is not doing what it is supposed to be doing. They do not need to take responsibility for finding out why the government is not doing what it is doing. They do not need to educate themselves as to what is really going on behind the facade. They do not need to see the forces that are attempting to turn their democracy into a more totalitarian form of government.

This is something that we of course need you to be aware of as ascended master students. We first of all need you to make the calls on this as well so that you can help bring about a shift where a critical mass of people in the democratic nations will recognize that a democracy is a very demanding form of government. It is not so that once you have established democracy, you can sit back and relax. On the contrary, democracy demands constant vigilance, constant alertness, a constant willingness to educate yourself, to look at what is happening in your nation. You look at how the government is performing and look at, as we have talked about, the gap between what the government is supposed to be doing according to the Constitution and what they are actually doing. When you see too big of a gap, then you need to take action. Taking action does not mean sitting at some kind of gathering and drinking beer and whining and complaining. There is no way that you can fulfill your responsibility as democratic citizens by pouring words out of a beer can. It cannot be done. My beloved, this is what you need to make the calls on. This is why we have, over these last several years, talked about a more direct form of democracy where the people are much more involved. Instead of seeing a representative democracy, you now have the people being involved and the people are directly voting on major issues.

Now, this of course is a topic that I want to make some remarks on because you will see that there will be a tremendous opposition to this idea of direct democracy. It will come, at least part of it, from the modern democracies, the modern democratic nations. I wish to make you aware of why there is this opposition. It goes back to this very idea, that the fallen beings have inserted into the human population now for a very, very long time: There is a special group of people, a special elite of people, who have abilities beyond the general population. You will see that this very idea is, as I said, the foundational idea behind a dictatorship. When you have one person who has unlimited power, then unless that person has special abilities, how could he exercise that power and exercise it wisely?

The myth of the super leader

That is why you need to build up this myth that, for example, Adolph Hitler had some infallible ability to know exactly what was right for the nation. You will see how for a time, he did seem to have an uncanny ability to tell the armed forces where to attack and when, and they would be successful. For a time it looked like he could not fail and that the German forces could not fail when they followed the Führer. But then of course the tides started turning and suddenly the failure became even more spectacular than the early victories.

The fallen beings have, from the moment they started embodying on this planet, spread this idea that there are certain people that have special abilities compared to the population. As I said, one of the ways to combat the fallen beings, or at least expose them as we are really calling you to do, is to become aware of how they use ideas and then turn those ideas upon themselves. They have projected the idea that certain people have special abilities. You can turn that around and see that regardless of what abilities they may have, these people also have a complete disrespect for life and disrespect for the people that they are leading. Therefore, this is not the kind of leader we want anymore, especially not in a free democratic nation.

Now, what is it that happens? What have we told you so many times now about duality and the dualistic mindset where there are always two polarities. The fallen beings project the idea that there is a small group of people that have special abilities, but what is the (so to speak) omega aspect of that. Well, it is of course that the general population do not have special abilities. What have they said? There is a small group of people who have the abilities to rule, but the majority of the population do not have the ability to rule themselves. This is the two prongs of their strategy. They project that you, the people, you cannot rule yourselves, it will only lead to disaster. But we, we have the ability to rule you and our rule will not lead to disaster, it will lead you to the promised land, to this glorious future, to the Third Reich or the Communist Utopia.

Can you not see as ascended master students, my beloved, that the collective consciousness is ready for a shift? A very simple shift where you just look at history and you look at this claim: "There is a small elite that has the ability to rule, but the population does not have the ability to rule, because if they rule themselves it will lead to disaster." You just look at this objectively and say: "But what has the rule of the elite led us to? Has it not led us from one disaster to another? Is it really true that if the people rule themselves, it will lead to disaster? Even if it did lead to disaster, would it perhaps be a lesser disaster than what the elite has led us to?" It is right there under the surface, my beloved, it is right there where your calls can make the difference that you shift the collective consciousness and they suddenly see it: "We have allowed a small elite to rule us and it has led to disaster after disaster. This cannot go on—we want a different form of government."

Can the people rule themselves?

Now my beloved, there was a time, if you go back in history, where the people could not have ruled themselves. They were not able to rule themselves. Why were they not able to rule themselves? It was because the leadership of the fallen beings had over millennia and centuries brought the population to a much lower level of consciousness than is natural for them. You may say: "Why is it that so many people are not willing to take responsibility for themselves and make decisions for their nation." Well, it is because, my beloved, the fallen beings have manipulated people into making certain choices that led to a disaster. Then, they have made the people feel responsible for the disaster.

For example, you will see that the German people after the second world war acknowledged some degree of responsibility for the disaster created by Hitler because after all they had voted him into office. There was a certain willingness to take responsibility for this, but this was only because Hitler failed so spectacularly that there was no way of denying it. There was no way of re-writing history so that it looked like a good thing after all.

What have the Chinese done with Mao's cultural revolution, an agricultural revolution that caused millions of Chinese to starve to death? They have re-written history so that it after all looks like it was a forward step. What have the Russians done with communism and the reign of Stalin? They have re-written history even to this day where it looks like: "Oh, it wasn't so bad after all, maybe it was necessary, maybe the Russian people need the rod of iron to rule them." Well, maybe they need the rod of iron but that is because the fallen beings have, over a very long period of time, brought them down.

Do you see what the fallen beings did with Hitler and the German people? They made the German people take partial responsibility for the disaster created by Hitler. This causes some people to say: "Oh we can't make decisions. We do not want to make decisions." This is what you see repeated in past ages, that are not known in current history, where many, many people have been manipulated by the fallen beings into supporting the leadership of the fallen beings. Then, when it led to a disaster, the fallen beings have turned it around and made the people feel responsible for it. When the people have felt responsible for precipitating such a disaster, they have reacted by saying: "Oh we don't want to make decisions."

What is it that causes people to feel responsible for a disaster? It is that they have that level of humanity, they have that level of compassion for life, respect for life. When they see that something goes really wrong, that millions of people are killed, then they feel this should not have happened.

Now, the fallen beings, do they take responsibility? Nay, they never take responsibility when things go wrong. In some cases, as is described in the *My Lives* book with Hitler, they rejoice in disaster and catastrophe. The more chaos the better because it allows them to steal people's energy, or manipulate them into feeling guilty. Again, this is not something that the general public cannot understand. They can grasp this as general, universal ideas. They can see that they have been manipulated into this situation of not wanting to make decisions, wanting someone else to make decisions for them. They can also come to see that whenever they allow someone else to make decisions for them, it leads from one disaster to another.

Therefore, they can see that we need a new approach, the older democracies are getting ready for a new approach. They can be brought to see also that the whole idea of representative democracy, as benign as it might sound, is actually based on this age-old idea that there is an elite with special abilities to rule, whereas the general population do not the ability to rule themselves. Why else would you need to elect representatives? Yes, in the 1700's communication was so poor that you could not have a public debate about a certain issue. You could not bring it out to the people and let them vote on certain issues. You needed to have representatives that were elected, that traveled to Washington, D.C. and went into the Congress building and then voted on a certain issue.

Today, with the communication you have today with the Internet, this is no longer necessary. You do not need an elitist, top-down form of government, form of decision making. It is perfectly possible to have a debate. Today, this debate could be more open than ever because instead of the mainstream media, which are often manipulated by the power elite, you can have the free debate on the Internet, at least somewhat free debate on the Internet—even though that is being attempted to be manipulated as well by the power elite. But you still have more freedom there so that the people, if they are willing, can educate themselves and then they can vote based on that knowledge.

Direct democracy will not lead to disaster

I can assure you that this will give better results than what you have today. It will not lead to the kind of disasters that you saw in the past. Why is this? Because the collective consciousness has been raised. This does not mean that it has been raised beyond some natural level. What has happened is that after a long period of time where the fallen beings manipulated humanity into lowering the collective consciousness, it has gradually been raised to the point where people – at least most people in modern democracies – have connected to their basic humanity, they have that respect for life. Therefore, they will not make these kinds of decisions that are based on a total lack of respect for life.

My beloved, look at some of the worst disasters that have happened in the last century. Again, you have Hitler, you have Stalin or the Soviet Union, you have Mao, you have Pol Pot, you have North Korea, you have Japan under the emperors, you have so many examples of this. Look at what was the basis for the decision making of these dictators. It was a total lack of respect for human life. If Hitler had had a basic respect for human life, he would not have made some of the decisions he made. If Stalin or Mao had had that respect, how could they have killed so many of their own citizens? It simply is not possible.

Therefore, you see that the general population could never have made those decisions in a democratic manner. It simply could not have been done. People can quickly come to see that it is actually better that everybody votes. Now, I know that there are some who will object and they will say: "But what did the philosopher Plato say about government? Did he not call for a wise philosopher-king?" Have there not been ascended master students who thought this was the ideal form of government? You have a king who is anointed by the ascended masters, who has constant connection to the ascended masters, as the ideal given in previous dispensations about King Arthur and the Knights of the Round Table. Is this not the ideal form of government? It is *not* in this age, my beloved.

What is the goal of the ascended masters? We have said it many times in these last years, we do not have a particular outer goal, the overall goal is the raising of the awareness of all people. We are not elitists, contrary to what you might have concluded based on previous dispensations. We are *not* elitists.

Look at Jesus, was he an elitist? Look at the Buddha, can you possibly construe the Buddha as an elitist? They both attempted to give teachings for all people. Look how Jesus went out of his way to not be part of the religious elite in the Jewish religion. Look how he went to those who were outcasts of the Jewish Religion. Look at the parable of the Good Samaritan, a Samaritan who was looked down upon by the Jews. The Jewish priest ignored the man who was suffering but the Samaritan was willing to do something for him. Again and again, Jesus attempted to reach all people and actually helped people connect to what we have called the basic humanity that gives you the respect for other people because you have respect for yourself.

The downfall of ascended master students

You look at it historically, you look at it today, we of the ascended masters have been given the task to raise up *all* people. We are sometimes working with select groups of people who have a higher level of consciousness than the general population because we recognize that if we can get a small group of people to raise their consciousness, it will pull up on the collective consciousness. That is why we talk about the top ten percent, the bottom ten percent and the eighty percent in the middle.

Nevertheless, let me say this from the level of consciousness of the God Star Sirius. The biggest downfall of ascended master students over this last century has been when they have gone into the state of superiority and felt that because they are ascended master students, because they recognize these high teachings from the ascended masters, they are better than others on a dualistic scale.

This has been the downfall of ascended master students and what has prevented them from having the impact that they could have had. We have very, very carefully given you the teachings and tools to avoid falling into this trap. My beloved, when you resolve the birth trauma, when you get rid of these outer selves, all of this desire to be better than others falls away and you are free to be who you really are. You are free to recognize that you have a basic humanity in yourself but it is the same basic humanity that is in everyone else. How could you be better, or more important, or higher than others? You may have a higher level of consciousness, but the higher you go towards the 144th level, the more you feel oneness with all life. The more oneness you feel, the less you can be special, the less you can feel better than others. These two things, feeling better than others and feeling one with all life, are not compatible. The beings who feel the most better than others are the fallen beings. I trust you can see that you do not want to be like them. My beloved, it is not possible to go towards the 144th level and have a sense of superiority and a need for superiority. It just is not possible.

What you need to recognize here is that we want to raise up all life, all people. That is why we do not want a form of government where a wise philosopher-king rules the population. It is no longer the time for this kind of government. We are not seeking to have a king who could (so to speak) do the bidding of the ascended masters and thereby manifest some ideal society. We are seeking to raise the consciousness of all of the people. In the modern democracies nothing would raise the consciousness more at this level than if we had a direct form of democracy where the people had to vote on the major issues and therefore had to educate themselves in order to get the best possible result.

The unreal dream of an ideal society

You see that we do not have in our vision, and Saint Germain does not have in his plans for the Golden Age, to raise up a few select people who could be in connection with Saint Germain and do whatever he wanted and then get the people to accept this, the population to accept this. Saint Germain's vision of the Golden Age is to have the people make decisions and see the outcome. Even if it leads to certain undesirable outcomes, that is still something they learn more from than by having a small elite of representatives make decisions for them. It is not a matter of achieving certain results in the physical but of raising the collective consciousness.

Why is this so my beloved? Because there may be some futurists, some spiritual people, some ascended master students who have certain visions and ideas of a golden future. Since we started giving these concepts of a Golden Age of Saint Germain, many ascended students have had these visions, as Saint Germain himself has commented on, of seeing this ideal society. Although you may sometimes have glimpses that are true, I can tell you that at the present level of the collective consciousness, it is not possible to even give a teaching with words about how the Golden Age will be. The collective consciousness is so low that people would not be able to accept the changes that Saint Germain envisions. Again, as we have said many times, this needs to be taken step by step by step so that people gradually come to accept it.

Now, we may give teachings on the future but what we will give, will be based on the collective consciousness as it is today. What often happens is that ascended master students, futurists, other spiritual people, they will take certain elements of the consciousness, the collective consciousness. They will use those to project a vision of how they would like the future to be, what they think the Golden Age *should* be like. But my beloved, if you would use the same amount of mental effort that you use to imagine what the Golden Age could be like and instead of imagining, tune in to Saint Germain, then you would get an entirely different perspective.

The dream of enlightenment

Now, this messenger was reading in the little book on Buddhism that is in every hotel room in this hotel. He came upon an excerpt from the Buddha's teachings where he talks about enlightenment. What he read there was quite significant to him because he realized that this is what he has been going through himself and what he has been sensing over the last few years. What the Buddha was saying is that people today are in ignorance. It is because of this that it was necessary to give the concept that there is a way out of ignorance. The Buddha had to name it something so he named it "enlightenment." He wanted the people to be aware that they were currently in ignorance but that there is something to strive for where you escape ignorance, and it is enlightenment.

However, what the Buddha was saying in this quote is that enlightenment is necessary only because people are in ignorance. Therefore, enlightenment to the ignorant mind becomes just another concept. When you actually, when the mind that is ignorant actually escapes from ignorance and becomes enlightened, that mind disappears. We may say that (with the terminology we are using today) when the Conscious You shifts from the state of ignorance to the state of enlightenment, all of the outer selves die. What has happened historically, and what even happens today, is that people are in ignorance and now they hear of the concept of enlightenment. Now they take their ignorance and they use their ignorance to project what it will be like to be enlightened. The ignorant self imagines what it would be like to be enlightened but it cannot fathom what it is like to be enlightened because of its ignorance.

What we are telling you, who have all these teachings, is: "Take this next step. Recognize that as long as you have a primal self and many of these other selves, you cannot actually even imagine what the Golden Age of Saint Germain will be like." What you do is, you take the filter of these outer selves and you think: "Well, the Golden Age will be so much better than what we have today." You take the desires of the outer selves and you project that the Golden Age will fulfill all of those desires. This is what many, many people throughout the ages have done with the whole idea that we are in a lower state of consciousness but we can reach a higher state of consciousness by following the spiritual path, whether you call it enlightenment or the ascension or something else. They use the current desires of their outer selves to project what it will be like when they reach enlightenment.

For example, many people dream of having special powers so that they could awaken people to the reality of the spiritual path. They think: "When I am enlightened, I will have these powers. Then I will exercise these powers the way I want to do it today." They do not realize that the way they want to exercise power today is based on the needs of the outer selves. Those outer selves will never gain the power. Therefore, it is a completely empty dream.

The dilemma of ascended masters

What the messenger realized here is that this is the dilemma of the ascended masters. People are in ignorance. You have to show them there is a way out of ignorance. You have to define that there is a state of ignorance and there is a state outside of ignorance. As soon as you do this, people use their ignorance to turn the state of enlightenment into just another concept. Why is it that people are ignorant? This is also explained by the Buddha. It is because they have created mental concepts and they believe those mental concepts are reality. This is ignorance! Ignorance is not that you do not know anything. It is that you think that what you know is reality. *That* is ignorance.

People take the word "enlightenment" and they use their ignorance to project on it what it is like. Thereby, they turn enlightenment into another concept. Now they are chasing after that concept, which has nothing to do with enlightenment. The harder they push to get there, the more they push it away from them, like the donkey with a stick hanging in front of it with a bunch of carrots and it thinks it can reach them and it is just pulling the cart. Just like humanity has been pulling the cart of the fallen beings, and the fallen beings are sitting on the cart laughing all the way.

This is what we are calling you, as ascended master students, to realize, to step beyond. Listen! Read what Saint Germain has said about the Golden Age in the last few years. Truly, lock in to it. Make an effort to see that you have certain outer selves that have certain needs that you have projected onto it. Then, be willing to let those selves die. It is not a matter of creating a wonderful society by *force*. It is a matter of raising the collective consciousness so that people create this wonderful society by *choice*. By aware choice, by connecting to their humanity, by connecting to their spirituality and choosing this higher society, rather than having it forced upon them either by the fallen beings, or by a benevolent philosopher-king in the fashion of Plato. The people are perfectly capable of making decisions, seeing the result and then learning from the outcome. This is what the fallen beings will deny as long as they are on the planet. You of course have the authority and the ability to make the calls for these fallen beings to be taken off the planet, and all of those who are spreading these ideas that I have exposed in this dictation and that we will expose in others.

With this, my beloved, I have reached the end of what I wanted to give you. Again, I can only express my gratitude for you being willing to be the broadcasting stations for this long release. I realize that it seems long to some of you whereas in reality to me, well, I have barely gotten started. Again, other masters will surely pick up on it. Therefore, we will accomplish what we have set out to accomplish for this conference. We look forward, all of us, to being with you throughout these next days.

4 | TRANSCENDING THE CAUSE OF DICTATORSHIPS

In the name of the I AM THAT I AM, Jesus Christ, I use the authority that I have as a being in embodiment on earth to call upon Surya to reinforce my calls and use my chakras to project the statements in this invocation into the collective consciousness and awaken people to the real cause behind dictatorships. Awaken people to the reality that we are spiritual beings and that we can co-create a new future by working with the ascended masters. I especially call for ...

[Make your own calls here.]

Part 1

1. Surya, shatter the energetic matrix that prevents the Chinese people from thinking and talking openly about Chairman Mao.

> Surya, cosmic being bright,
> your balance is my pure delight,
> I am in orbit round God Star,
> in perfect unity we are.

Surya, banish all extremes,
Surya, shatter Serpent's schemes,
Surya, balance to me bring,
Surya, making my heart sing.

2. Surya, shatter the energetic matrix that prevents the Russian people from thinking and talking openly about Stalin and Putin.

Surya, there is more to life,
than human conflict, war and strife,
your balance gives me inner peace,
all outer conflicts do now cease.

Surya, banish all extremes,
Surya, shatter Serpent's schemes,
Surya, balance to me bring,
Surya, making my heart sing.

3. Surya, shatter the energetic matrix that causes people to deny the cruelty of a dictator and to deny that the dictator did not care about them whatsoever.

Surya, what a wondrous sight,
from Sirius you send the light,
of one mind, I now call to thee,
for your apprentice I would be.

Surya, banish all extremes,
Surya, shatter Serpent's schemes,
Surya, balance to me bring,
Surya, making my heart sing.

4. Surya, shatter the energetic matrix that causes people to deny that dictators like Mao or Stalin did not care about their people and were willing to sacrifice any amount of those people for the cause, which basically was the cause of them staying in power.

Surya, radiate your light,
with balance you set all things right,

consuming energetic dross,
my letting go is not a loss.

Surya, banish all extremes,
Surya, shatter Serpent's schemes,
Surya, balance to me bring,
Surya, making my heart sing.

5. Surya, shatter the energetic matrix of denial that is still there in countries that either have a dictatorial form of government or have had it recently.

Surya, your light is alive,
for inner balance I do strive,
the alchemy is now begun,
my heart transformed into a sun.

Surya, banish all extremes,
Surya, shatter Serpent's schemes,
Surya, balance to me bring,
Surya, making my heart sing.

6. Surya, shatter the energetic matrix that causes people to attempt to analyze Hitler and explain his behavior based on his family background, upbringing, psychology or genes, attempting to give a rational explanation.

Surya, come enlighten me,
duality you help me see,
extremes they cannot pull me in,
on Middle Way I always win.

Surya, banish all extremes,
Surya, shatter Serpent's schemes,
Surya, balance to me bring,
Surya, making my heart sing.

7. Surya, shatter the energetic matrix that prevents people from seeing that dictators are not normal human beings because normal people do not want unlimited power and will not do absolutely anything to maintain their power.

Surya, in your cosmic sphere,
with Cuzco I your light revere,
from your perspective o so grand,
life finally I understand.

**Surya, banish all extremes,
Surya, shatter Serpent's schemes,
Surya, balance to me bring,
Surya, making my heart sing.**

8. Surya, shatter the energetic matrix that prevents people from seeing that some dictators have held on to their power beyond all reasonability or rationality.

Surya, show me God's design,
I see that God is all benign,
you calm my feeling body's storm,
I know the God beyond all form.

**Surya, banish all extremes,
Surya, shatter Serpent's schemes,
Surya, balance to me bring,
Surya, making my heart sing.**

9. Surya, shatter the energetic matrix that prevents people from seeing that the critical aspect to understanding dictators is that there are a few people embodied on earth who are not normal human beings, they are different from the norm.

Surya, I come from afar,
and as you show me my home star,
I see now my internal light,
a star I am in my own right.

**Surya, banish all extremes,
Surya, shatter Serpent's schemes,
Surya, balance to me bring,
Surya, making my heart sing.**

Part 2

1. Surya, shatter the energetic matrix that prevents people from seeing that the major thought systems of the world have been influenced by certain forces that do not want people to understand the basic dynamic of how life works on earth.

> Surya, cosmic being bright,
> your balance is my pure delight,
> I am in orbit round God Star,
> in perfect unity we are.
>
> **Surya, banish all extremes,**
> **Surya, shatter Serpent's schemes,**
> **Surya, balance to me bring,**
> **Surya, making my heart sing.**

2. Surya, shatter the energetic matrix that prevents people from seeing that the earth is a planet with a very broad range of consciousness where many different lifestreams have embodied.

> Surya, there is more to life,
> than human conflict, war and strife,
> your balance gives me inner peace,
> all outer conflicts do now cease.
>
> **Surya, banish all extremes,**
> **Surya, shatter Serpent's schemes,**
> **Surya, balance to me bring,**
> **Surya, making my heart sing.**

3. Surya, shatter the energetic matrix that prevents people from seeing that there is a specific group of people on earth who have no humanitarian ideals, who have no concerns whatsoever for human beings.

> Surya, what a wondrous sight,
> from Sirius you send the light,

of one mind, I now call to thee,
for your apprentice I would be.

Surya, banish all extremes,
Surya, shatter Serpent's schemes,
Surya, balance to me bring,
Surya, making my heart sing.

4. Surya, shatter the energetic matrix that prevents people from seeing that these people do not see themselves as human beings, they see the population as human beings but they see themselves as being superior, as being in a special class of beings.

Surya, radiate your light,
with balance you set all things right,
consuming energetic dross,
my letting go is not a loss.

Surya, banish all extremes,
Surya, shatter Serpent's schemes,
Surya, balance to me bring,
Surya, making my heart sing.

5. Surya, shatter the energetic matrix that prevents people from seeing that there is a certain group of people on the planet that have no respect, no caring, no love, no humanity when it comes to the population. They are willing to kill or sacrifice any number of human beings for whatever cause they have in their heads. It is a complete disrespect for life.

Surya, your light is alive,
for inner balance I do strive,
the alchemy is now begun,
my heart transformed into a sun.

Surya, banish all extremes,
Surya, shatter Serpent's schemes,
Surya, balance to me bring,
Surya, making my heart sing.

6. Surya, shatter the energetic matrix that prevents people from seeing that throughout history there has been this special group of people who have taken positions of being dictators and who have no respect for life whatsoever.

Surya, come enlighten me,
duality you help me see,
extremes they cannot pull me in,
on Middle Way I always win.

Surya, banish all extremes,
Surya, shatter Serpent's schemes,
Surya, balance to me bring,
Surya, making my heart sing.

7. Surya, shatter the energetic matrix that prevents people from masking the determination: "We do not want this kind of people to lead us anymore, we do not want this kind of people to attain any position in government, or any other position where they have power over the population on earth."

Surya, in your cosmic sphere,
with Cuzco I your light revere,
from your perspective o so grand,
life finally I understand.

Surya, banish all extremes,
Surya, shatter Serpent's schemes,
Surya, balance to me bring,
Surya, making my heart sing.

8. Surya, shatter the energetic matrix so that the people who can be the forerunners for this awareness will be cut free, will be awakened, will be inspired so their consciousness shifts and they see: "Oh but the dictator has nothing on!"

Surya, show me God's design,
I see that God is all benign,

you calm my feeling body's storm,
I know the God beyond all form.

Surya, banish all extremes,
Surya, shatter Serpent's schemes,
Surya, balance to me bring,
Surya, making my heart sing.

9. Surya, shatter the energetic matrix that prevents people from seeing that it was never the people who assembled armies and conquered territories. It was only that small group of people who have no respect for life.

Surya, I come from afar,
and as you show me my home star,
I see now my internal light,
a star I am in my own right.

Surya, banish all extremes,
Surya, shatter Serpent's schemes,
Surya, balance to me bring,
Surya, making my heart sing.

Part 3

1. Surya, shatter the energetic matrix that prevents people from seeing that all the dictators in history have had an abnormal psychology. They have been narcissists or sociopaths or psychopaths.

Surya, cosmic being bright,
your balance is my pure delight,
I am in orbit round God Star,
in perfect unity we are.

Surya, banish all extremes,
Surya, shatter Serpent's schemes,
Surya, balance to me bring,
Surya, making my heart sing.

2. Surya, shatter the cloud of ignorance created by the fallen beings so that people can "see it," and suddenly the public awareness shifts and there is an awareness of this and an outcry for a better type of leadership.

Surya, there is more to life,
than human conflict, war and strife,
your balance gives me inner peace,
all outer conflicts do now cease.

Surya, banish all extremes,
Surya, shatter Serpent's schemes,
Surya, balance to me bring,
Surya, making my heart sing.

3. Surya, shatter the energetic matrix that prevents people from seeing that in dictatorships people usually think that the dictator belongs to a special group of people. He is different and therefore, he has the ability to lead.

Surya, what a wondrous sight,
from Sirius you send the light,
of one mind, I now call to thee,
for your apprentice I would be.

Surya, banish all extremes,
Surya, shatter Serpent's schemes,
Surya, balance to me bring,
Surya, making my heart sing.

4. Surya, shatter the energetic matrix that prevents people from connecting the concept that the dictator is in a special category with the narcissistic personality disorder with no empathy and no respect for life.

Surya, radiate your light,
with balance you set all things right,
consuming energetic dross,
my letting go is not a loss.

Surya, banish all extremes,
Surya, shatter Serpent's schemes,

Surya, balance to me bring,
Surya, making my heart sing.

5. Surya, shatter the energetic matrix that prevents people from seeing that a dictator really was in a special category of people. It was not because he had superhuman powers, it was because he had a subhuman disrespect for life.

Surya, your light is alive,
for inner balance I do strive,
the alchemy is now begun,
my heart transformed into a sun.

Surya, banish all extremes,
Surya, shatter Serpent's schemes,
Surya, balance to me bring,
Surya, making my heart sing.

6. Surya, shatter the energetic matrix that prevents people from seeing that once people have accepted a dictator and elevated him to this superhuman status, they either believe in the dictators promises or they have submitted themselves to his power, thinking they can do nothing about it.

Surya, come enlighten me,
duality you help me see,
extremes they cannot pull me in,
on Middle Way I always win.

Surya, banish all extremes,
Surya, shatter Serpent's schemes,
Surya, balance to me bring,
Surya, making my heart sing.

7. Surya, shatter the energetic matrix that prevents people from seeing that what happens in the psychology of people is that they feel that as individuals, they no longer have any responsibility. They do not have personal responsibility for their lives or for their nation. They become followers of the dictator, mindless followers, even if they are very intelligent people.

Surya, in your cosmic sphere,
with Cuzco I your light revere,
from your perspective o so grand,
life finally I understand.

Surya, banish all extremes,
Surya, shatter Serpent's schemes,
Surya, balance to me bring,
Surya, making my heart sing.

8. Surya, shatter the energetic matrix that prevents people from seeing that once people surrender that sense of personal responsibility, then even though they may be very intelligent, they have given up the responsibility to look at the dictator with critical eyes. They suspend all critical evaluation of the dictator and his actions.

Surya, show me God's design,
I see that God is all benign,
you calm my feeling body's storm,
I know the God beyond all form.

Surya, banish all extremes,
Surya, shatter Serpent's schemes,
Surya, balance to me bring,
Surya, making my heart sing.

9. Surya, shatter the energetic matrix that prevents people from seeing that a dictator fulfilled the need of a large part of the population, the need to feel that they are not responsible. They can focus on their daily lives and do not need to think about the bigger more complicated issues.

Surya, I come from afar,
and as you show me my home star,
I see now my internal light,
a star I am in my own right.

Surya, banish all extremes,
Surya, shatter Serpent's schemes,

Surya, balance to me bring,
Surya, making my heart sing.

Part 4

1. Surya, shatter the energetic matrix that prevents people from seeing that a certain portion of the human population have a need to give up personal responsibility. If a majority of the people in a nation have this need at a subconscious level, then that nation is vulnerable to being taken over by a dictatorial form of government.

> Surya, cosmic being bright,
> your balance is my pure delight,
> I am in orbit round God Star,
> in perfect unity we are.

> **Surya, banish all extremes,**
> **Surya, shatter Serpent's schemes,**
> **Surya, balance to me bring,**
> **Surya, making my heart sing.**

2. Surya, shatter the energetic matrix that prevents people from seeing that the fallen beings will work with any society, seeking to undermine the democratic rights and the democratic freedoms and create a government that takes on more and more power.

> Surya, there is more to life,
> than human conflict, war and strife,
> your balance gives me inner peace,
> all outer conflicts do now cease.

> **Surya, banish all extremes,**
> **Surya, shatter Serpent's schemes,**
> **Surya, balance to me bring,**
> **Surya, making my heart sing.**

3. Surya, shatter the energetic matrix that prevents people from seeing that even in democracies there can be a certain percentage of the people who still want to give up their personal responsibility.

Surya, what a wondrous sight,
from Sirius you send the light,
of one mind, I now call to thee,
for your apprentice I would be.

Surya, banish all extremes,
Surya, shatter Serpent's schemes,
Surya, balance to me bring,
Surya, making my heart sing.

4. Surya, shatter the energetic matrix that prevents people from seeing that the fallen beings will take advantage of this, by making people feel that as long as they read the news and vote every four years, they have fulfilled their responsibility as democratic citizens.

Surya, radiate your light,
with balance you set all things right,
consuming energetic dross,
my letting go is not a loss.

Surya, banish all extremes,
Surya, shatter Serpent's schemes,
Surya, balance to me bring,
Surya, making my heart sing.

5. Surya, shatter the energetic matrix that prevents people from bringing about a shift where a critical mass of people in the democratic nations will recognize that a democracy is a very demanding form of government. It is not so that once we have established democracy, we can sit back and relax.

Surya, your light is alive,
for inner balance I do strive,
the alchemy is now begun,
my heart transformed into a sun.

Surya, banish all extremes,
Surya, shatter Serpent's schemes,
Surya, balance to me bring,
Surya, making my heart sing.

6. Surya, shatter the energetic matrix that prevents people from seeing that a democracy demands constant vigilance, a constant willingness to educate ourselves about what is happening in our nation.

Surya, come enlighten me,
duality you help me see,
extremes they cannot pull me in,
on Middle Way I always win.

Surya, banish all extremes,
Surya, shatter Serpent's schemes,
Surya, balance to me bring,
Surya, making my heart sing.

7. Surya, shatter the energetic matrix that prevents people from seeing that for a long time the fallen beings have inserted the idea into the human population that there is a special group of people who have abilities beyond the general population.

Surya, in your cosmic sphere,
with Cuzco I your light revere,
from your perspective o so grand,
life finally I understand.

Surya, banish all extremes,
Surya, shatter Serpent's schemes,
Surya, balance to me bring,
Surya, making my heart sing.

8. Surya, shatter the energetic matrix that prevents people from seeing that this is the foundational idea behind a dictatorship. When one person has unlimited power, then unless that person has special abilities, how could he exercise that power and exercise it wisely?

Surya, show me God's design,
I see that God is all benign,
you calm my feeling body's storm,
I know the God beyond all form.

Surya, banish all extremes,
Surya, shatter Serpent's schemes,
Surya, balance to me bring,
Surya, making my heart sing.

9. Surya, shatter the energetic matrix that prevents people from seeing that the fallen beings have spread this idea that there are certain people that have special abilities compared to the population.

Surya, I come from afar,
and as you show me my home star,
I see now my internal light,
a star I am in my own right.

Surya, banish all extremes,
Surya, shatter Serpent's schemes,
Surya, balance to me bring,
Surya, making my heart sing.

Part 5

1. Surya, shatter the energetic matrix that prevents people from seeing that regardless of what abilities such people may have, they also have a complete disrespect for life and disrespect for the people they are leading. Therefore, this is not the kind of leader we want anymore, especially not in a free democratic nation.

Surya, cosmic being bright,
your balance is my pure delight,
I am in orbit round God Star,
in perfect unity we are.

Surya, banish all extremes,
Surya, shatter Serpent's schemes,
Surya, balance to me bring,
Surya, making my heart sing.

2. Surya, shatter the energetic matrix that prevents people from seeing that the fallen beings project the idea that there is a small group of people that have special abilities, and therefore the general population do not have special abilities. A small group of people have the abilities to rule, but the majority of the population do not have the ability to rule themselves.

Surya, there is more to life,
than human conflict, war and strife,
your balance gives me inner peace,
all outer conflicts do now cease.

Surya, banish all extremes,
Surya, shatter Serpent's schemes,
Surya, balance to me bring,
Surya, making my heart sing.

3. Surya, shatter the energetic matrix that prevents people from seeing that the fallen beings project that we cannot rule ourselves, it will only lead to disaster. But they have the ability to rule us and their rule will not lead to disaster, it will lead us to the promised land.

Surya, what a wondrous sight,
from Sirius you send the light,
of one mind, I now call to thee,
for your apprentice I would be.

Surya, banish all extremes,
Surya, shatter Serpent's schemes,
Surya, balance to me bring,
Surya, making my heart sing.

4. Surya, shatter the energetic matrix that prevents people from seeing that the rule of the elite has led us from one disaster to another. Therefore, if

the people rule themselves it could not possibly be worse than being ruled by the elite.

Surya, radiate your light,
with balance you set all things right,
consuming energetic dross,
my letting go is not a loss.

Surya, banish all extremes,
Surya, shatter Serpent's schemes,
Surya, balance to me bring,
Surya, making my heart sing.

5. Surya, shatter the energetic matrix that prevents people from seeing: "We have allowed a small elite to rule us and it has led to disaster after disaster. This cannot go on—we want a different form of government."

Surya, your light is alive,
for inner balance I do strive,
the alchemy is now begun,
my heart transformed into a sun.

Surya, banish all extremes,
Surya, shatter Serpent's schemes,
Surya, balance to me bring,
Surya, making my heart sing.

6. Surya, shatter the energetic matrix that prevents people from seeing that the fallen beings have manipulated people into making certain choices that led to a disaster. Then they have made the people feel responsible for the disaster, making people believe they cannot rule themselves.

Surya, come enlighten me,
duality you help me see,
extremes they cannot pull me in,
on Middle Way I always win.

Surya, banish all extremes,
Surya, shatter Serpent's schemes,

Surya, balance to me bring,
Surya, making my heart sing.

7. Surya, shatter the energetic matrix that prevents people from seeing that the Chinese and the Russian leaders have rewritten history to make it seem like Mao and Stalin did not create disasters.

Surya, in your cosmic sphere,
with Cuzco I your light revere,
from your perspective o so grand,
life finally I understand.

Surya, banish all extremes,
Surya, shatter Serpent's schemes,
Surya, balance to me bring,
Surya, making my heart sing.

8. Surya, shatter the energetic matrix that prevents people from seeing that in past ages many people have been manipulated by the fallen beings into supporting the leadership of the fallen beings. Then, when it led to a disaster, the fallen beings have turned it around and made the people feel responsible for it, making them feel: "Oh we do not want to make decisions."

Surya, show me God's design,
I see that God is all benign,
you calm my feeling body's storm,
I know the God beyond all form.

Surya, banish all extremes,
Surya, shatter Serpent's schemes,
Surya, balance to me bring,
Surya, making my heart sing.

9. Surya, shatter the energetic matrix that prevents people from seeing that what causes people to feel responsible for a disaster is that they have a level of humanity, they have compassion for life. The fallen beings never take responsibility because they have no respect for life.

Surya, I come from afar,
and as you show me my home star,
I see now my internal light,
a star I am in my own right.

Surya, banish all extremes,
Surya, shatter Serpent's schemes,
Surya, balance to me bring,
Surya, making my heart sing.

Part 6

1. Surya, shatter the energetic matrix that prevents people from seeing that we need a new approach. The idea of representative democracy is based on this age-old idea that there is an elite with special abilities to rule, whereas the general population do not the ability to rule themselves.

Surya, cosmic being bright,
your balance is my pure delight,
I am in orbit round God Star,
in perfect unity we are.

Surya, banish all extremes,
Surya, shatter Serpent's schemes,
Surya, balance to me bring,
Surya, making my heart sing.

2. Surya, shatter the energetic matrix that prevents people from seeing that with the communication technology we have today, we do not need an elitist, top-down form of government. It is perfectly possible to have a free debate on the Internet, so that the people can educate themselves and vote based on that knowledge.

Surya, there is more to life,
than human conflict, war and strife,
your balance gives me inner peace,
all outer conflicts do now cease.

Surya, banish all extremes,
Surya, shatter Serpent's schemes,
Surya, balance to me bring,
Surya, making my heart sing.

3. Surya, shatter the energetic matrix that prevents people from seeing that direct democracy will give better results than what we have today. It will not lead to the kind of disasters that we saw in the past because the collective consciousness has been raised.

Surya, what a wondrous sight,
from Sirius you send the light,
of one mind, I now call to thee,
for your apprentice I would be.

Surya, banish all extremes,
Surya, shatter Serpent's schemes,
Surya, balance to me bring,
Surya, making my heart sing.

4. Surya, shatter the energetic matrix that prevents people from seeing that people have connected to our basic humanity, we have respect for life. Therefore, we will not make the kind of decisions that are based on a total lack of respect for life.

Surya, radiate your light,
with balance you set all things right,
consuming energetic dross,
my letting go is not a loss.

Surya, banish all extremes,
Surya, shatter Serpent's schemes,
Surya, balance to me bring,
Surya, making my heart sing.

5. Surya, shatter the energetic matrix that prevents people from seeing that the basis for the decision making of dictators is a total lack of respect for human life. Therefore, the general population could never have made those decisions in a democratic manner.

Surya, your light is alive,
for inner balance I do strive,
the alchemy is now begun,
my heart transformed into a sun.

Surya, banish all extremes,
Surya, shatter Serpent's schemes,
Surya, balance to me bring,
Surya, making my heart sing.

6. Surya, shatter the energetic matrix that prevents ascended master students from overcoming the mindset that they are better than the general population.

Surya, come enlighten me,
duality you help me see,
extremes they cannot pull me in,
on Middle Way I always win.

Surya, banish all extremes,
Surya, shatter Serpent's schemes,
Surya, balance to me bring,
Surya, making my heart sing.

7. Surya, shatter the energetic matrix that prevents people from seeing that we have a basic humanity in ourselves but it is the same basic humanity that is in everyone else. Therefore, how could we be better or more important than others.

Surya, in your cosmic sphere,
with Cuzco I your light revere,
from your perspective o so grand,
life finally I understand.

Surya, banish all extremes,
Surya, shatter Serpent's schemes,
Surya, balance to me bring,
Surya, making my heart sing.

8. Surya, shatter the energetic matrix that prevents people from seeing that the ascended masters want to raise up all people. They do not want a form of government where a wise philosopher-king rules the population.

Surya, show me God's design,
I see that God is all benign,
you calm my feeling body's storm,
I know the God beyond all form.

**Surya, banish all extremes,
Surya, shatter Serpent's schemes,
Surya, balance to me bring,
Surya, making my heart sing.**

9. Surya, shatter the energetic matrix that prevents people from seeing that in the modern democracies nothing would raise the consciousness more than if we had a direct form of democracy where the people had to vote on the major issues and therefore had to educate themselves in order to get the best possible result.

Surya, I come from afar,
and as you show me my home star,
I see now my internal light,
a star I am in my own right.

**Surya, banish all extremes,
Surya, shatter Serpent's schemes,
Surya, balance to me bring,
Surya, making my heart sing.**

Sealing

In the name of the I AM THAT I AM, I accept that Archangel Michael, Astrea and Shiva form an impenetrable shield around myself and all constructive people, sealing us from all fear-based energies in all four octaves. I accept that the Light of God is consuming and transforming all fear-based energies that make up the dark forces working against ending the era of dictatorships on earth!

5 | EXPOSING THE ILLUSION BEHIND ALL DICTATORS

I AM the Ascended Master Sanat Kumara. I greet you in the flame of love. Not only the flame of love that we have brought from Venus, but the flame of love of the Third Ray.

I wish to speak about how dictators pervert love. They do not pervert the flame of love as it cannot be perverted, but they pervert love, and how do they do it? Well, many people would say that love is a feeling. The reason they say this is that a concept has been created by the fallen beings that has reduced love to a feeling, because love is a spiritual flame. A spiritual flame has nothing to do with what human beings on earth call feelings. They are divine qualities: love, wisdom, purity, and so forth. But divine qualities are not human feelings.

How love has been perverted

Now, what happens on earth is that you have a need—human beings have a need to name and label everything. When you create a label expressed in words, then the fallen beings can take those words and create a man-made concept, a dualistic, relative concept. That is how they take divine qualities and reduce them to human feelings. You have the concept of a human feeling named love. You have a divine quality, which can also be named love but of course is much more than any name that can be expressed in words. What the fallen beings have done is they have taken this word and they have perverted it so that it now describes both what is supposedly a divine quality (even though they cannot see a divine quality) but also a human feeling.

Many people think that it might be the same thing. They think that human love and divine love are the same thing, which of course they are not. It is not simply that you can set up a scale for love and you can say that at the lower levels this is human love and as you go gradually higher, you reach divine love. This is a false image. There is a fundamental difference between human love and divine love. You cannot go from one to the other. You cannot cultivate and perfect human love, and thereby reach divine love.

This is a mistake made by so many Christians, and other spiritual and religious people throughout the ages, where they think that if they are loving enough in a human way, then they will eventually become loving in a divine way. But it cannot be done. You cannot be an open door for divine love unless you have transcended the human love, or rather transcended the self that can only deal with human love. You see that self for what it is, a separate self in your being, and you let it die. Then, you can be an open door for divine love.

People love the dictator and hate the scapegoat

What you see in many dictatorships is that there is this entire consciousness created that people are supposed to love the dictator. You see this across the border in North Korea. You saw it in Nazi Germany. You have seen it in China even today where they glorify and supposedly love Chairman Mao. You see it in Russia with Stalin. You saw it with Pol Pot. You have seen it with other dictators. You can go back to medieval Europe and see how they were supposed to love the kings and so forth and so on. How do you have a situation where you have a brutal dictator, who is oppressing the people, and yet the people, or at least a sizable portion of them, love that dictator?

Well, this is what the fallen beings are able to accomplish when they pervert things into human love, for example. They take this human feeling, and then they are able to get people to go into this very strange state of mind where they have both the human feeling and its opposite at the same time. This is what we have explained about the duality consciousness: It is polarized. There are always two polarizations, two opposite polarities. There is human love and there is hatred. Now, there is of course no divine hatred. But you could say that what the fallen beings have is a hatred that is actually beyond human hatred because they have had it for so long. They have cultured it for so long that it has taken on a quality and a proportion that is beyond what human beings on earth are capable of producing.

They have managed to get people on earth to go into this polarized state where they have the love, the human love, and the human hatred at the same time. This is how it is always expressed in a dictatorship. They manage to get people to love the dictator, but this can only be done because there is a scapegoat towards which people can direct the human hatred. They loved Adolph Hitler. They hated the Jews. This is what you see over and over again. There has to be a scapegoat. It has to be somebody where people can feel justified in directing the hatred that is the inevitable companion of human love. You cannot have human love without having hatred. When you go into this very unbalanced state that you have in a dictatorship, the people cannot avoid feeling both the intensity of the human love and the intensity of the human hatred.

Now, what you see in many of the modern democracies is that people have risen higher than this unbalanced state. Therefore, they do not have the strong emotions. They do not have this need to love their leader, or even love their country, as you see in all dictatorships. As a result of that, they do not have as strong of a hatred. Therefore, they do not need to direct that hatred against either a group in their own country or another country. It is not that people have transcended human feelings, but they have become more balanced. Therefore, they are not expressed in such an extreme way as you see in a dictatorship.

A very unbalanced form of government

By understanding this dynamic, you see that a dictatorship is a very, very unbalanced form of government. It is a very unbalanced state of mind that people go into when they are subject to a dictator. Of course, the dictator himself goes into an extremely unbalanced state of mind in order to become a dictator, do what he needs to do to gain power, and then be willing to do what he needs to do to maintain that power. That is why you see that all dictators go too far. They actually do more than they need to do in order to maintain power. The reason is that they become so unbalanced that they go into a state of paranoia where they see dangers and opposition everywhere. They see even their own people as enemies. They see even the very people who helped them gain power as threats. Therefore, they see anybody who gains influence in the government as a threat. And that is why you will see that they will sometimes cleanse them out as both Mao, Stalin and Hitler did at certain times.

What you realize here is that love is a feeling that does not stand still. We have said before that love flows, but in reality all divine qualities flow. Love has this special dynamic where even the perversion of the divine quality of love, namely human love, has a certain intensity. This means that it is very difficult for people to remain in one state. When they claim to be loving something from a human perspective, their love is possessive. Human love is possessive. This means in a sense that you are always striving to have some ultimate state of love. In love relationships you see many people who are looking for the perfect love partner. They find one person they think is the perfect love partner. They go into a relationship. When they discover that the person is not the perfect partner after all, then they often seek another partner. Or they seek to change their partner and mold that person into the perfect partner. It is difficult for even human love to stand still.

This is also what you see when people are manipulated by the fallen beings into loving a dictator and loving their country. You will see how in Nazi Germany, for example, they had a love for Hitler, they had a love for their nation. But it was not enough for them to just love their own nation and be content by sitting in their own nation and loving their nation and feeling superior. They had to export their view of life to other countries. They could not stay within their own borders. You see the Soviet Union where there was this desire to go beyond the borders. This is what leads to that unbalanced state where you engage in more and more ambitious measures. You can see, as we have mentioned before, that Adolph Hitler went into such an unbalanced state of mind that he wanted to conquer the entire world. Therefore, from the very beginning his defeat was assured, as the world is simply too big to be conquered by one power.

What is it that really happens when you reach this unbalanced state? Well, when you go into love and the state of love, you have this very special dynamic where people feel completely justified in doing what they are doing because they think they are doing it out of love. In other words, there is a certain state of consciousness, a certain illusion that has been projected by the fallen beings, that love is the ultimate human emotion.

Love is the ultimate feeling and there is nothing higher than being loving. Therefore, when people feel that they are doing something out of love, they feel justified in forcing this upon others because it is for the good of these other people. If you really love your country and if your country is being threatened by another group of people, whether inside the country or outside, then is it not justified, by the very fact that you love your country so much, that you kill and eradicate those other people? This is how love can be perverted.

Perverting what it means to be a loving person

Now, you see it even in relationships between humans, how two people can enter this very possessive love of seeking to own and control each other, seeking to change each other, or even seeking to blame each other if they are not living up to their expectations. This is certainly one aspect of how a dictatorship perverts love. Behind this is of course an even deeper perversion. This springs from the fact that the fallen beings have been very careful in creating this perversion of love. Now, why have they been able to do this? Well, in a sense, because we of the ascended masters have given them the opportunity to pervert love. You see, this is one of the dilemmas we face when we are dealing with a planet like earth.

What have we talked about in recent years that can help people overcome their divisions? It is what we have called your basic humanity. Well, in previous times, we have (both in Buddhism, Christianity and other religions) talked about love—that you love other people. If you really love other people, you also care for them. You respect them and therefore you will not harm them. You cannot harm people that you truly love. What we were really trying to help people connect to is the basic humanity that binds people together. Because you cannot hurt other people, if you feel connected to them. You can only hurt them, if you see them as separate from yourself. This was just saying that the basic humanity is another way of talking about love, as we talked about in the past.

What the fallen beings do is that every time we give a concept that is meant to help people, then they of course seek to pervert it so that they can use it to bind people—whereas we give it to set people free. We have given the concept that you love one another in order to set people free. But the fallen beings have perverted this so that you think that when you are a truly loving person, then it is justified to do things that you actually know are not love. You know it is not loving to kill other people. What do the fallen beings have to do to override this knowledge? Well, they have to get you to a point where you have perverted love so you think that by loving your country, by loving your dictator, then it is acceptable that you do to other people what you know is not loving, what you know is not up to the standard of love.

Getting people to love the fallen beings

The real goal of the fallen beings here is actually to get human beings on earth to love the fallen beings. You see, what happens here is this: When you have come to a point where you have decided that you love someone or something, then you are setting aside normal carefulness, normal restraints, normal restrictions. You are unconditionally or openly giving of yourself, your attention, your energy to that person or to that cause. The fallen beings naturally want to steal your energy and when you love them (or love some institution they have created, or love an idea), then you are voluntarily giving your energy to them. You can see if you watch these movies about the old rallies where Adolph Hitler was speaking from the stage and where the people were screaming: "Heil Hitler," and you can see on the faces of the people how they were totally hypnotized. They were totally in love with Hitler and his ideas. Therefore, they, in an unrestricted way, gave their energy to him and to the fallen beings in the identity, mental and emotional realms that were directing him. This is of course what the fallen beings love to do.

With this we can then take a look at other institutions, other examples of dictatorships. So far we have talked about one person who is at the head of a government of a nation, the leader of a nation, and we have used this as an example. We can say that people are then manipulated into giving their loyalty. Because when you love somebody, you feel loyal towards them. If you love the dictator, you are loyal to the dictator. You do not question it.

What happens here is that people's normal discernment, discrimination, is suspended. Therefore, as I said, people feel they have to love the dictator, they have to be loyal to the dictator. That means they have to do what the dictator tells them to do and therefore, they are not evaluating in their hearts: "Is what the dictator tells me to do right? Or is it a violation of love? Is what he is telling me in accordance with love or in violation of love?" Even human love can be used to have a certain standard for evaluating what is loving, what is unloving behavior. You know of course that killing other people is not loving behavior.

The Catholic church is a dictatorship

With this I want to turn to another form of dictatorship that has much the same dynamic. Now, you may say we have given you these historical examples of Nazi Germany, the Soviet Union, and Mao's China. And yes, there was almost a billion people in Mao's China. But was China under Mao actually the largest dictatorship on earth? Nay, my beloved. You have a dictatorship today that is much older than Mao's China, that has lasted much longer and has more members, more people, 1.3 billion people. That dictatorship is what you normally call the Catholic church.

Is not the Pope essentially a dictator? Now, you see here how the Catholic church has taken the teachings of Jesus, and the teachings of Jesus were an expression of the divine quality of love. They have created a false religion, based on the teachings of Jesus where they have perverted them into a human quality of love. This has resulted in a culture where Catholics feel they have to "love" the church. They have associated the divine love that Jesus expressed with an earthly, human institution. The fallen beings have manipulated people into feeling human love for the institution of the Catholic church, and for the Pope, and for their local priest.

What you see here is that people have, throughout the history of the Catholic church, gone into this exact dynamic that I described. They have felt they had to be loving towards the church. Therefore, they have given loyalty to the church. They have done what the church told them to do. They have suspended their normal discernment, even the discernment based on human love. They have therefore done what they normally would not have done. They have allowed the church to do what they normally would not have allowed. You can go back in history and see the Crusades, the Inquisition. Were they acts of love? There is no way that you can actually construe human love to make it loving to kill other people or to torture them. There is no way you can see this as an expression of human love.

How did the Catholic church manage to make people accept that it was an institution based on the teachings of Christ, and an institution devoted to the love of Christ, while at the same time people did not object to the completely anti-loving acts, such as torture, burning witches, killing

Muslim men, women and children and so on? Well, it was because people had felt they had to be loyal, and therefore they suspended their judgment.

Now, what have we talked about with these dictators who were leaders of nations? Sometimes they had to be defeated in a very harsh manner for the people to wake up. We have talked about people in Germany waking up because Hitler was defeated. But this is not likely to happen with the Catholic church, because the Catholic church is no longer a warring organization like it was during the Crusades. What needs to happen for the dictatorship of the Catholic church to be overthrown? Well, it is that people switch back into using even human love to evaluate: Are the actions of the church loving, even according to a human standard?

Loving the church and child abuse

Now, take the dynamic I have described. You have been manipulated into thinking you have to feel love for an earthly institution, the Catholic church. You are suspending your normal critical judgment of what is loving and not. You think you have to love your local priest. You are a young boy who loves the church, loves Jesus, loves your priest and you love to do service in the church. Now, the priest approaches you and wants to touch you in inappropriate ways or wants to have sex with you. How do you deal with this? Well, if you have suspended your normal judgment, you might submit to it. But you cannot avoid feeling that this was wrong, that you were violated. This is what creates these deep traumas, these deep scars in the psyche of these children who have been violated this way. Because they are pulled apart in different directions by their loyalty to the outer organization and their inner knowing of what is loving and what is not.

There is no way whatsoever, even with human love, that you can construct a philosophy that says that a priest violating a young child is acting out of love. It makes no sense whatsoever. Why can people not see this? Because their loyalty to the outer organization overrides what they know in their hearts. That is why they do not speak out and say: "The Pope has nothing on. The priest has nothing on. They are exposed. We see them for what they are. They are at best hypocrites and at worst they are as bad as the worst dictator we have seen throughout history."

You see my beloved, we have talked about how, over time, there can be a building tension in the collective consciousness. You have all probably as children (or at least you can do it as adults, if you have not done it) taken a glass of water. You can take a pitcher and you can pour water into the glass. As you pour it in carefully, you can come to a point where you can see that at the top of the glass the water is bulging upwards. There is more water in the glass than the glass can hold, but it is not overflowing because of the surface tension of the water. It is holding it, even though it cannot fit into the glass. Then, as you pour in a little more, there comes a point where suddenly the tension is broken. Now, the water overflows. Well, this is what can happen in the collective consciousness and is happening all the time.

The Catholic church cannot represent Christ

Right now, there is such a tension in the collective consciousness, not only among Catholics, but also among people in general. There have been so many exposures of the pedophilia in the Catholic church in various countries that the tension has been building. By you making the calls for the judgment of Christ upon this, for the exposure of this, there can be that shift in the collective consciousness where suddenly the tension is released and people see.

What do they see? Well, at the very least, they can see that these actions of the Catholic priests are not according to even a human standard of love. But they can also see that the actions of the church, where they have so often denied this and tried to cover it over, they are not according to a human standard of love either because they are setting the image of the institution higher than the lives of people. This is not love. This is not caring. This is not loving your neighbor as yourself. What can actually happen beyond this is that more and more people come to realize that the actions of the Catholic priests who are violating children, and the actions of the church seeking to cover it up, cannot in any way be construed to be justified by Jesus.

In other words, you can look at a single priest who continually over many years violates one child after another. You can look at the church who has covered it up. You can ask yourself: "How could this happen?" You can even ask yourself: "How can there be so many Catholic priests who are pedophiles?" Of course, you can see that you also find pedophiles in other areas of society. But you must be willing to acknowledge that the Catholic church has a higher concentration of them than many other organizations. Then, you must ask yourself: "Why is this happening?" It can only be happening because there are certain institutions in the Catholic church that have been taken over by a mindset that actually pulls new priests into this abuse. They are abused, and therefore they become abusers and it promotes the abuse. It spreads the abuse.

When people see this and acknowledge that this is happening (that the church has created an institution that actually educates, not priests but pedophiles), then they can see that there is no way you can believe that this is justified or approved by Jesus. If an institution over centuries has systematically violated children and therefore done things that cannot be approved by Jesus, then how on earth can we uphold the belief that this institution represents Christ? Therefore, the shift that can happen, the shift you can make the calls for, is that people wake up from this hypnotic state they have been in where they realize the Catholic church cannot represent Christ.

Then, they can take that further step of realizing: "What are we loyal to? Are we loyal to an earthly and therefore fallible institution? Or are we loyal to Christ? Are we loyal to Jesus as an ascended being who exists today? Or are we loyal to some human institution?" Once that awareness begins to spread, you can see that there will be an enormous shift.

Now, we do not foresee, as we have said before, that the Catholic church will be able to transform itself, because it is so ingrained. There are people in the Catholic church, in the church hierarchy, whose minds are so taken over by the fallen beings that they will continue to be in a state of denial, just as Hitler and at least some of his generals were in a state of denial until the end of the war.

We are not concerned about preserving a human institution. We are concerned about the people. The people who have been traumatized by the abuse of the priests, but also Catholics in general, who are being held in this hypnotic state, in this "no gods land" where they are trapped by the fallen beings in this web of lies and illusions. We are looking for you to make the calls to shatter this web of illusions that envelops the entire Catholic church, which truly is, as I have said, the primary, the largest, and in a sense the most powerful dictatorship left on earth today.

Religious dictatorships

Now, you may think that I have been radical enough already by exposing the Catholic church. But I do wish to go a step further and talk about other examples of dictatorships on earth. You can say of course that a religious dictatorship is, in a sense, the most insidious example of a dictatorship. It is truly that the fallen beings have created an institution that claims to represent spirit, represent God, or a divine being. Yet, that institution is taken over by the fallen beings so that when people love the institution, or even love the divine being that they think the institution represents, they are giving their love to the fallen beings.

Of course, there have been other examples of how a religious dictatorship has been used by the fallen beings. You can look at Islam today and you can see that it has also been turned into a religious dictatorship that is holding millions of Muslims in this exact same state. They feel they have to love Allah, they have to love Mohammed, they have to love the Koran, they have to love the institution of Islam. They have to be loyal because if you love somebody, you are loyal. Therefore, they suspend their judgment. They are not willing to see that what Islam has come to represent, what they have promoted with this Sharia law, with many other institutions they have created, this is not according to even a human standard of love. Nor is it according to the original revelations given in the Koran. They have deviated from this.

Naturally, you can make the calls also that this will be exposed. You can say there has been exposure upon exposure over the last several decades of the pedophilia in the Catholic church, and this has built a tension. Well, since 9-11, 2001, and the exposure of more and more extremist forms of Muslim fanaticism and radicalism, again, a tension has been building. There is right now a tension in the collective consciousness among Muslim people where they realize there is something here that just is not right. But because of their loyalty, they have suspended their judgment, their discernment, their discrimination. They are not willing, they are not able, to see it. Again, you can make the calls for a shift so that the tension will be released and people will see this.

Corporations are dictatorships

Now, let me shift away from religious institutions and talk about other institutions in society. You can of course see that military institutions also require a high degree of loyalty, but they do not generally claim to be expressions of love. What you do see is that there is another type of organization that you find on earth. Even though they do not directly claim to be an expression of love, they do claim to be beneficial for individuals and for society. That type of organization is what you call business corporations.

Many business corporations are essentially a dictatorship that has a pyramidal structure with one person at the very top. You still see examples of businesses started by one person, owned by that one person and controlled by that one person. You see other corporations that have a board of directors with a CEO, and that CEO is essentially a dictator. The board of directors may guide or support the CEO, just as a dictator of a nation may have a board of people that councils him or carries out his orders. Nevertheless, in many corporations the person at the top is essentially a dictator whose word is the law. Whatever he says, the organization will carry out.

You will see many of these western corporations who have morphed into multinational conglomerates. They claim to be for the benefit of society. They claim that they are doing good. They are providing jobs. They are providing economic growth. They will even claim that, for example, after the fall of the iron curtain these corporations went into former Soviet republics, or the other states of Eastern Europe, for example, and they helped the economy grow by bringing jobs and bringing investment. Of course, what they have done ever since is extract money and profits from those countries that actually should have stayed in those countries. The question is really: "Have they helped the economy in these nations grow?" Well, they did for a certain time, but it was only out of self-interest so that they could now extract more from these countries than they ever put into them.

This is a perversion of love. Because what is love based on? Love is based on giving. The essence of love is giving. If you take more than you give, you are not expressing love. It is that simple. In the true sense of the word, the divine sense of the word, love is what Jesus expressed when he said: "Freely you have received, freely give," multiply the talents, and so on. You receive divine love from Above. You give that to others and then you receive more from Above. When you are in a state of true love, you are not giving in order to get. You are not having the possessive love that says that the object of your love now becomes obligated towards you and has to give back to you. If you are in the flow of love, you are giving out horizontally. The more you give out horizontally, the more you receive vertically because the talents are multiplied. You receive more as a result of having multiplied the love.

Well, this is not what you see in these corporations. They are all about profit. They are all about taking from the population and concentrating it in the hands of a small elite that become richer and richer. While the people actually, after a certain period of growth, stagnate and perhaps even go backwards. This is also an expression of anti-love, and again the tension has been building in the collective consciousness. People are ready to see this and see that you cannot allow the unrestricted growth of these multinational corporations. Because, as we have said before, the ultimate outcome of capitalism is that one corporation owns the means of production and therefore owns the state. You have much the same centralized economy as you have in a communist country.

As we have said, capitalism and communism are simply two ways that the fallen beings have designed to accomplish the same end and completely centralize society where the fallen beings have absolute, unrestricted power. Now naturally, this can never be achieved because of the second law of thermodynamics, as the fall of communism demonstrates. Nevertheless, many people still believe that this can be achieved. Or they are not aware of the outcome of capitalism so they still think that it is a free society, a free economy, and it is beneficial. You can make the calls for people to see that it is not beneficial whatsoever.

Having given you this long discourse (that I realize has tested your endurance) I wish to end by anchoring a certain flame from my heart on earth. It is not anchored in a specific location but it is anchored so that anyone who makes the calls, the invocation based on this dictation, can tap into this flame. You will receive both a personal benefit from making these calls, but you will also receive a reinforcement, a multiplication of your calls for the resolution of these issues that I have brought to your attention.

With the fire and the power of the Ruby Ray, I, Sanat Kumara, therefore anchor this flame in the identity level, the mental level, the emotional level and the physical level on planet earth. This flame now seals this release, seals you who are here, and it will seal all of those who read or listen to this dictation from this point on. Therefore, it is finished.

6 | EXPOSING THE ILLUSION BEHIND DICTATORSHIPS (PART 1)

In the name of the I AM THAT I AM, Jesus Christ, I use the authority that I have as a being in embodiment on earth to call upon Sanat Kumara to reinforce my calls and use my chakras to project the statements in this invocation into the collective consciousness and awaken people from the illusion that supports all dictatorships. Awaken people to the reality that we are spiritual beings and that we can co-create a new future by working with the ascended masters. I especially call for …

[Make your own calls here.]

Part 1

1. Sanat Kumara, shatter the energetic matrix that prevents people from seeing that love is not a feeling. It is a spiritual flame.

> Sanat Kumara, Ruby Fire,
> I seek my place in love's own choir,

with open hearts we sing your praise,
together we the earth do raise.

Sanat Kumara, Ruby Ray,
bring to earth a higher way,
light this planet with your fire,
clothe her in a new attire.

2. Sanat Kumara, shatter the energetic matrix that prevents people from seeing that the fallen beings take a label expressed with words and create a man-made concept, a dualistic, relative concept. That is how they take divine qualities and reduce them to human feelings.

Sanat Kumara, Ruby Fire,
initiations I desire,
I am for you an electrode,
Shamballa is my true abode.

Sanat Kumara, Ruby Ray,
bring to earth a higher way,
light this planet with your fire,
clothe her in a new attire.

3. Sanat Kumara, shatter the energetic matrix that prevents people from seeing that the fallen beings have taken the word "love" and they have perverted it so that it now describes both a divine quality and a human feeling. Many people think it is the same thing.

Sanat Kumara, Ruby Fire,
I follow path that you require,
initiate me with your love,
the open door for Holy Dove.

Sanat Kumara, Ruby Ray,
bring to earth a higher way,
light this planet with your fire,
clothe her in a new attire.

4. Sanat Kumara, shatter the energetic matrix that prevents people from seeing that we cannot set up a scale for love and say that at the lower levels is human love and as we go gradually higher, we reach divine love. This is a false image.

Sanat Kumara, Ruby Fire,
your great example all inspire,
with non-attachment and great mirth,
we give the earth a true rebirth.

Sanat Kumara, Ruby Ray,
bring to earth a higher way,
light this planet with your fire,
clothe her in a new attire.

5. Sanat Kumara, shatter the energetic matrix that prevents people from seeing that there is a fundamental difference between human love and divine love. We cannot go from one to the other. We cannot cultivate and perfect human love, and thereby reach divine love.

Sanat Kumara, Ruby Fire,
you are this planet's purifier,
consume on earth all spirits dark,
reveal the inner Spirit Spark.

Sanat Kumara, Ruby Ray,
bring to earth a higher way,
light this planet with your fire,
clothe her in a new attire.

6. Sanat Kumara, shatter the energetic matrix that prevents people from seeing that we cannot be an open door for divine love unless we have transcended the human love, or rather transcended the self that can only deal with human love.

Sanat Kumara, Ruby Fire,
you are a cosmic amplifier,
the lower forces can't withstand,
vibrations from Venusian band.

**Sanat Kumara, Ruby Ray,
bring to earth a higher way,
light this planet with your fire,
clothe her in a new attire.**

7. Sanat Kumara, shatter the energetic matrix that prevents people from seeing that in many dictatorships there is a consciousness saying that people are supposed to love the dictator.

Sanat Kumara, Ruby Fire,
I am on earth your magnifier,
the flow of love I do restore,
my chakras are your open door.

**Sanat Kumara, Ruby Ray,
bring to earth a higher way,
light this planet with your fire,
clothe her in a new attire.**

8. Sanat Kumara, shatter the energetic matrix that prevents people from seeing that it makes no sense that there is a brutal dictator, who is oppressing the people, and yet the people love that dictator.

Sanat Kumara, Ruby Fire,
Venusian song the multiplier,
as we your love reverberate,
the densest minds we penetrate.

**Sanat Kumara, Ruby Ray,
bring to earth a higher way,
light this planet with your fire,
clothe her in a new attire.**

9. Sanat Kumara, shatter the energetic matrix that prevents people from seeing that the fallen beings are able to get people to go into this state of mind where they have both the human feeling and its opposite at the same time. There is human love, and there is hatred.

Sanat Kumara, Ruby Fire,
you are for all the sanctifier,
the earth is now a holy place,
purified by cosmic grace.

Sanat Kumara, Ruby Ray,
bring to earth a higher way,
light this planet with your fire,
clothe her in a new attire.

Part 2

1. Sanat Kumara, shatter the energetic matrix that prevents people from seeing that the fallen beings have a hatred that is beyond human hatred because they have had it for so long. They have cultured it for so long that it has taken on a quality and a proportion that is beyond what human beings on earth are capable of producing.

Sanat Kumara, Ruby Fire,
I seek my place in love's own choir,
with open hearts we sing your praise,
together we the earth do raise.

Sanat Kumara, Ruby Ray,
bring to earth a higher way,
light this planet with your fire,
clothe her in a new attire.

2. Sanat Kumara, shatter the energetic matrix that prevents people from seeing that the fallen beings have managed to get people to go into this polarized state where they have the human love and the human hatred at the same time.

Sanat Kumara, Ruby Fire,
initiations I desire,
I am for you an electrode,
Shamballa is my true abode.

**Sanat Kumara, Ruby Ray,
bring to earth a higher way,
light this planet with your fire,
clothe her in a new attire.**

3. Sanat Kumara, shatter the energetic matrix that prevents people from seeing that people love the dictator, but this can only be done because there is a scapegoat towards which people can direct the human hatred.

Sanat Kumara, Ruby Fire,
I follow path that you require,
initiate me with your love,
the open door for Holy Dove.

**Sanat Kumara, Ruby Ray,
bring to earth a higher way,
light this planet with your fire,
clothe her in a new attire.**

4. Sanat Kumara, shatter the energetic matrix that prevents people from seeing that in a dictatorship there has to be a scapegoat where people can feel justified in directing the hatred that is the inevitable companion of human love.

Sanat Kumara, Ruby Fire,
your great example all inspire,
with non-attachment and great mirth,
we give the earth a true rebirth.

**Sanat Kumara, Ruby Ray,
bring to earth a higher way,
light this planet with your fire,
clothe her in a new attire.**

5. Sanat Kumara, shatter the energetic matrix that prevents people from seeing that we cannot have human love without having hatred. When we go into this very unbalanced state that we have in a dictatorship, the people cannot avoid feeling both the intensity of the human love and the intensity of the human hatred.

Sanat Kumara, Ruby Fire,
you are this planet's purifier,
consume on earth all spirits dark,
reveal the inner Spirit Spark.

**Sanat Kumara, Ruby Ray,
bring to earth a higher way,
light this planet with your fire,
clothe her in a new attire.**

6. Sanat Kumara, shatter the energetic matrix that prevents people from seeing that in many of the modern democracies people have risen higher than this unbalanced state. They do not have this need to love their leader and they do not have as strong of a hatred.

Sanat Kumara, Ruby Fire,
you are a cosmic amplifier,
the lower forces can't withstand,
vibrations from Venusian band.

**Sanat Kumara, Ruby Ray,
bring to earth a higher way,
light this planet with your fire,
clothe her in a new attire.**

7. Sanat Kumara, shatter the energetic matrix that prevents people from seeing that a dictatorship is a very unbalanced form of government. It is a very unbalanced state of mind that people go into when they are subject to a dictator.

Sanat Kumara, Ruby Fire,
I am on earth your magnifier,
the flow of love I do restore,
my chakras are your open door.

**Sanat Kumara, Ruby Ray,
bring to earth a higher way,
light this planet with your fire,
clothe her in a new attire.**

8. Sanat Kumara, shatter the energetic matrix that prevents people from seeing that the dictator himself goes into an extremely unbalanced state of mind in order to become a dictator, do what he needs to do to gain power and to maintain that power.

Sanat Kumara, Ruby Fire,
Venusian song the multiplier,
as we your love reverberate,
the densest minds we penetrate.

Sanat Kumara, Ruby Ray,
bring to earth a higher way,
light this planet with your fire,
clothe her in a new attire.

9. Sanat Kumara, shatter the energetic matrix that prevents people from seeing that this is why all dictators go too far. They do more than they need to do in order to maintain power. They are so unbalanced that they go into a state of paranoia where they see dangers and opposition everywhere.

Sanat Kumara, Ruby Fire,
you are for all the sanctifier,
the earth is now a holy place,
purified by cosmic grace.

Sanat Kumara, Ruby Ray,
bring to earth a higher way,
light this planet with your fire,
clothe her in a new attire.

Part 3

1. Sanat Kumara, shatter the energetic matrix that prevents people from seeing that dictators often see their own people as enemies. They see the people who helped them gain power as threats. They see anybody who gains influence in the government as a threat.

Sanat Kumara, Ruby Fire,
I seek my place in love's own choir,
with open hearts we sing your praise,
together we the earth do raise.

Sanat Kumara, Ruby Ray,
bring to earth a higher way,
light this planet with your fire,
clothe her in a new attire.

2. Sanat Kumara, shatter the energetic matrix that prevents people from seeing that love is a feeling that does not stand still. Love has this special dynamic where even the perversion of the divine quality of love, namely human love, has a certain intensity, making it difficult for people to remain in one state.

Sanat Kumara, Ruby Fire,
initiations I desire,
I am for you an electrode,
Shamballa is my true abode.

Sanat Kumara, Ruby Ray,
bring to earth a higher way,
light this planet with your fire,
clothe her in a new attire.

3. Sanat Kumara, shatter the energetic matrix that prevents people from seeing that when we claim to be loving something from a human perspective, love is possessive. We are always striving to have some ultimate state of love.

Sanat Kumara, Ruby Fire,
I follow path that you require,
initiate me with your love,
the open door for Holy Dove.

Sanat Kumara, Ruby Ray,
bring to earth a higher way,

light this planet with your fire,
clothe her in a new attire.

4. Sanat Kumara, shatter the energetic matrix that prevents people from seeing that when people are manipulated by the fallen beings into loving a dictator and loving their country, it is not enough in itself. They have to export their view of life to other countries.

Sanat Kumara, Ruby Fire,
your great example all inspire,
with non-attachment and great mirth,
we give the earth a true rebirth.

Sanat Kumara, Ruby Ray,
bring to earth a higher way,
light this planet with your fire,
clothe her in a new attire.

5. Sanat Kumara, shatter the energetic matrix that prevents people from seeing that this desire to go beyond the borders leads to an unbalanced state where people engage in more and more ambitious measures.

Sanat Kumara, Ruby Fire,
you are this planet's purifier,
consume on earth all spirits dark,
reveal the inner Spirit Spark.

Sanat Kumara, Ruby Ray,
bring to earth a higher way,
light this planet with your fire,
clothe her in a new attire.

6. Sanat Kumara, shatter the energetic matrix that prevents people from seeing that when people have unbalanced love, they feel completely justified in doing what they are doing, because they think they are doing it out of love.

Sanat Kumara, Ruby Fire,
you are a cosmic amplifier,

the lower forces can't withstand,
vibrations from Venusian band.

**Sanat Kumara, Ruby Ray,
bring to earth a higher way,
light this planet with your fire,
clothe her in a new attire.**

7. Sanat Kumara, shatter the energetic matrix that prevents people from seeing that there is a certain illusion that has been projected by the fallen beings, saying that love is the ultimate human emotion. Love is the ultimate feeling and there is nothing higher than being loving.

Sanat Kumara, Ruby Fire,
I am on earth your magnifier,
the flow of love I do restore,
my chakras are your open door.

**Sanat Kumara, Ruby Ray,
bring to earth a higher way,
light this planet with your fire,
clothe her in a new attire.**

8. Sanat Kumara, shatter the energetic matrix that prevents people from seeing that when people feel that they are doing something out of love, they feel justified in forcing this upon others because it is for the good of those people.

Sanat Kumara, Ruby Fire,
Venusian song the multiplier,
as we your love reverberate,
the densest minds we penetrate.

**Sanat Kumara, Ruby Ray,
bring to earth a higher way,
light this planet with your fire,
clothe her in a new attire.**

9. Sanat Kumara, shatter the energetic matrix that prevents people from seeing that people are manipulated into thinking that if they really love their country and if it is being threatened by another group of people, whether inside the country or outside, then is justified that they kill those other people.

Sanat Kumara, Ruby Fire,
you are for all the sanctifier,
the earth is now a holy place,
purified by cosmic grace.

Sanat Kumara, Ruby Ray,
bring to earth a higher way,
light this planet with your fire,
clothe her in a new attire.

Part 4

1. Sanat Kumara, shatter the energetic matrix that prevents people from seeing that every time the ascended masters give a concept that is meant to help people, the fallen beings seek to pervert it so that they can use it to entrap people.

Sanat Kumara, Ruby Fire,
I seek my place in love's own choir,
with open hearts we sing your praise,
together we the earth do raise.

Sanat Kumara, Ruby Ray,
bring to earth a higher way,
light this planet with your fire,
clothe her in a new attire.

2. Sanat Kumara, shatter the energetic matrix that prevents people from seeing that the fallen beings have perverted love so that people think that when we are truly loving persons, then it is justified to do things that we actually know are not loving.

Sanat Kumara, Ruby Fire,
initiations I desire,
I am for you an electrode,
Shamballa is my true abode.

Sanat Kumara, Ruby Ray,
bring to earth a higher way,
light this planet with your fire,
clothe her in a new attire.

3. Sanat Kumara, shatter the energetic matrix that prevents people from seeing that because people know it is not loving to kill other people, the fallen beings have to pervert love so people think that by loving their country, by loving their dictator, then it is acceptable that they do to other people what they know is not loving.

Sanat Kumara, Ruby Fire,
I follow path that you require,
initiate me with your love,
the open door for Holy Dove.

Sanat Kumara, Ruby Ray,
bring to earth a higher way,
light this planet with your fire,
clothe her in a new attire.

4. Sanat Kumara, shatter the energetic matrix that prevents people from seeing that the real goal of the fallen beings is to get human beings to love the fallen beings.

Sanat Kumara, Ruby Fire,
your great example all inspire,
with non-attachment and great mirth,
we give the earth a true rebirth.

Sanat Kumara, Ruby Ray,
bring to earth a higher way,
light this planet with your fire,
clothe her in a new attire.

5. Sanat Kumara, shatter the energetic matrix that prevents people from seeing that when we love someone or something, then we are setting aside normal carefulness. We are unconditionally giving our energy to that person or to that cause. The fallen beings want to steal our energy and when we love them, we are voluntarily giving our energy to them.

Sanat Kumara, Ruby Fire,
you are this planet's purifier,
consume on earth all spirits dark,
reveal the inner Spirit Spark.

**Sanat Kumara, Ruby Ray,
bring to earth a higher way,
light this planet with your fire,
clothe her in a new attire.**

6. Sanat Kumara, shatter the energetic matrix that prevents people from seeing that the people who were hypnotized by Adolph Hitler, gave their energy to him and to the fallen beings in the identity, mental and emotional realms that were directing him. This is what the fallen beings love to do.

Sanat Kumara, Ruby Fire,
you are a cosmic amplifier,
the lower forces can't withstand,
vibrations from Venusian band.

**Sanat Kumara, Ruby Ray,
bring to earth a higher way,
light this planet with your fire,
clothe her in a new attire.**

7. Sanat Kumara, shatter the energetic matrix that prevents people from seeing that through perverted love, people's normal discernment and discrimination, is suspended. People feel they have to love the dictator, they have to be loyal to the dictator and not question him.

Sanat Kumara, Ruby Fire,
I am on earth your magnifier,

the flow of love I do restore,
my chakras are your open door.

**Sanat Kumara, Ruby Ray,
bring to earth a higher way,
light this planet with your fire,
clothe her in a new attire.**

8. Sanat Kumara, shatter the energetic matrix that prevents people from seeing that when people are loyal to a dictator, they are not evaluating in their hearts: "Is what the dictator tells me to do right? Is what he is telling me in accordance with love or in violation of love?"

Sanat Kumara, Ruby Fire,
Venusian song the multiplier,
as we your love reverberate,
the densest minds we penetrate.

**Sanat Kumara, Ruby Ray,
bring to earth a higher way,
light this planet with your fire,
clothe her in a new attire.**

9. Sanat Kumara, I invoke the flame that you have anchored on earth, and I call forth both a personal benefit, but also a reinforcement and multiplication of my calls for the resolution of the issues mentioned in this invocation. I accept this manifest right now in the identity realm, the mental realm, the emotional realm and the physical realm. It is finished.

Sanat Kumara, Ruby Fire,
you are for all the sanctifier,
the earth is now a holy place,
purified by cosmic grace.

**Sanat Kumara, Ruby Ray,
bring to earth a higher way,
light this planet with your fire,
clothe her in a new attire.**

Sealing

In the name of the I AM THAT I AM, I accept that Archangel Michael, Astrea and Shiva form an impenetrable shield around myself and all constructive people, sealing us from all fear-based energies in all four octaves. I accept that the Light of God is consuming and transforming all fear-based energies that make up the dark forces working against ending the era of dictatorships on earth!

7 | EXPOSING THE ILLUSION BEHIND DICTATORSHIPS (PART 2)

In the name of the I AM THAT I AM, Jesus Christ, I use the authority that I have as a being in embodiment on earth to call upon Sanat Kumara to reinforce my calls and use my chakras to project the statements in this invocation into the collective consciousness and awaken people from the illusion that supports all dictatorships. Awaken people to the reality that we are spiritual beings and that we can co-create a new future by working with the ascended masters. I especially call for ...

[Make your own calls here.]

Part 1

1. Sanat Kumara, shatter the energetic matrix that prevents people from seeing that the largest and oldest dictatorship on earth is the Catholic church. The church has taken the teachings of Jesus that were an expression of the divine quality of love and created a false religion where they have perverted them into a human quality of love.

Sanat Kumara, Ruby Fire,
I seek my place in love's own choir,
with open hearts we sing your praise,
together we the earth do raise.

Sanat Kumara, Ruby Ray,
bring to earth a higher way,
light this planet with your fire,
clothe her in a new attire.

2. Sanat Kumara, shatter the energetic matrix that prevents people from seeing that Catholics feel they have to "love" the church. They have associated the divine love that Jesus expressed with an earthly, human institution. The fallen beings have manipulated people into feeling human love for the institution of the Catholic church, the Pope and the local priest.

Sanat Kumara, Ruby Fire,
initiations I desire,
I am for you an electrode,
Shamballa is my true abode.

Sanat Kumara, Ruby Ray,
bring to earth a higher way,
light this planet with your fire,
clothe her in a new attire.

3. Sanat Kumara, shatter the energetic matrix that prevents people from seeing that people have given loyalty to the church, and they have suspended their normal discernment, allowing the church to do what they normally would not have allowed.

Sanat Kumara, Ruby Fire,
I follow path that you require,
initiate me with your love,
the open door for Holy Dove.

Sanat Kumara, Ruby Ray,
bring to earth a higher way,

light this planet with your fire,
clothe her in a new attire.

4. Sanat Kumara, shatter the energetic matrix that prevents people from seeing that the Catholic church managed to make people accept that it was an institution based on the teachings of Christ, and an institution devoted to the love of Christ, while at the same time people did not object to the completely anti-loving acts, such as torture, burning witches and killing Muslims.

Sanat Kumara, Ruby Fire,
your great example all inspire,
with non-attachment and great mirth,
we give the earth a true rebirth.

Sanat Kumara, Ruby Ray,
bring to earth a higher way,
light this planet with your fire,
clothe her in a new attire.

5. Sanat Kumara, shatter the energetic matrix that prevents people from seeing that in order for the dictatorship of the Catholic church to be overthrown, people must use even human love to evaluate whether the actions of the church are loving according to a human standard.

Sanat Kumara, Ruby Fire,
you are this planet's purifier,
consume on earth all spirits dark,
reveal the inner Spirit Spark.

Sanat Kumara, Ruby Ray,
bring to earth a higher way,
light this planet with your fire,
clothe her in a new attire.

6. Sanat Kumara, shatter the energetic matrix that prevents people from seeing that the fact that people have suspended normal critical judgment is what has allowed the sexual abuse of children by priests to go on for so long and reach such a large scale.

Sanat Kumara, Ruby Fire,
you are a cosmic amplifier,
the lower forces can't withstand,
vibrations from Venusian band.

**Sanat Kumara, Ruby Ray,
bring to earth a higher way,
light this planet with your fire,
clothe her in a new attire.**

7. Sanat Kumara, shatter the energetic matrix that prevents people from seeing that when people suspend normal judgment, they submit to abuse but they cannot avoid feeling that this was wrong, that they were violated. This creates deep traumas in the psyche of these children.

Sanat Kumara, Ruby Fire,
I am on earth your magnifier,
the flow of love I do restore,
my chakras are your open door.

**Sanat Kumara, Ruby Ray,
bring to earth a higher way,
light this planet with your fire,
clothe her in a new attire.**

8. Sanat Kumara, shatter the energetic matrix that prevents people from seeing that there is no way, even with human love, that one can construct a philosophy that says that a priest violating a young child is acting out of love. Yet people cannot see this if their loyalty to the outer organization overrides what they know in their hearts.

Sanat Kumara, Ruby Fire,
Venusian song the multiplier,
as we your love reverberate,
the densest minds we penetrate.

**Sanat Kumara, Ruby Ray,
bring to earth a higher way,**

**light this planet with your fire,
clothe her in a new attire.**

9. Sanat Kumara, shatter the energetic matrix that prevents people from waking up and saying: "The Pope has nothing on. The priest has nothing on. They are exposed. We see them for what they are. They are at best hypocrites and at worst they are as bad as the worst dictator we have seen throughout history."

Sanat Kumara, Ruby Fire,
you are for all the sanctifier,
the earth is now a holy place,
purified by cosmic grace.

**Sanat Kumara, Ruby Ray,
bring to earth a higher way,
light this planet with your fire,
clothe her in a new attire.**

Part 2

1. Sanat Kumara, I call forth the judgment of Christ upon the Catholic church and the pedophilia in the church. I demand an exposure of the hidden forces behind this so there will be a shift in the collective consciousness where suddenly the tension is released and people see the Church for what it is.

Sanat Kumara, Ruby Fire,
I seek my place in love's own choir,
with open hearts we sing your praise,
together we the earth do raise.

**Sanat Kumara, Ruby Ray,
bring to earth a higher way,
light this planet with your fire,
clothe her in a new attire.**

2. Sanat Kumara, shatter the energetic matrix that prevents people from seeing that the actions of the Catholic priests are not according to even a human standard of love.

Sanat Kumara, Ruby Fire,
initiations I desire,
I am for you an electrode,
Shamballa is my true abode.

Sanat Kumara, Ruby Ray,
bring to earth a higher way,
light this planet with your fire,
clothe her in a new attire.

3. Sanat Kumara, shatter the energetic matrix that prevents people from seeing that the actions of the church seeking to deny or cover it over are not according to a human standard of love.

Sanat Kumara, Ruby Fire,
I follow path that you require,
initiate me with your love,
the open door for Holy Dove.

Sanat Kumara, Ruby Ray,
bring to earth a higher way,
light this planet with your fire,
clothe her in a new attire.

4. Sanat Kumara, shatter the energetic matrix that prevents people from seeing that setting the image of the institution higher than the lives of people is not love. This is not caring. This is not loving your neighbor as yourself.

Sanat Kumara, Ruby Fire,
your great example all inspire,
with non-attachment and great mirth,
we give the earth a true rebirth.

Sanat Kumara, Ruby Ray,
bring to earth a higher way,
light this planet with your fire,
clothe her in a new attire.

5. Sanat Kumara, shatter the energetic matrix that prevents people from seeing that the actions of the Catholic priests who are violating children, and the actions of the church seeking to cover it up, cannot in any way be construed to be justified by Jesus.

Sanat Kumara, Ruby Fire,
you are this planet's purifier,
consume on earth all spirits dark,
reveal the inner Spirit Spark.

Sanat Kumara, Ruby Ray,
bring to earth a higher way,
light this planet with your fire,
clothe her in a new attire.

6. Sanat Kumara, shatter the energetic matrix that prevents people from seeing that there are certain institutions in the Catholic church that have been taken over by a mindset that pulls new priests into this abuse. They are abused, and therefore they become abusers and it promotes the abuse. It spreads the abuse.

Sanat Kumara, Ruby Fire,
you are a cosmic amplifier,
the lower forces can't withstand,
vibrations from Venusian band.

Sanat Kumara, Ruby Ray,
bring to earth a higher way,
light this planet with your fire,
clothe her in a new attire.

7. Sanat Kumara, shatter the energetic matrix that prevents people from seeing that the church has created an institution that educates not priests, but pedophiles, and this cannot be justified or approved by Jesus.

Sanat Kumara, Ruby Fire,
I am on earth your magnifier,
the flow of love I do restore,
my chakras are your open door.

**Sanat Kumara, Ruby Ray,
bring to earth a higher way,
light this planet with your fire,
clothe her in a new attire.**

8. Sanat Kumara, shatter the energetic matrix that prevents people from seeing that if an institution over centuries has systematically violated children and therefore done things that cannot be approved by Jesus, then we cannot uphold the belief that this institution represents Christ.

Sanat Kumara, Ruby Fire,
Venusian song the multiplier,
as we your love reverberate,
the densest minds we penetrate.

**Sanat Kumara, Ruby Ray,
bring to earth a higher way,
light this planet with your fire,
clothe her in a new attire.**

9. Sanat Kumara, shatter the energetic matrix that prevents people from waking up from the hypnotic state they have been in so they realize the Catholic church cannot represent Christ.

Sanat Kumara, Ruby Fire,
you are for all the sanctifier,
the earth is now a holy place,
purified by cosmic grace.

**Sanat Kumara, Ruby Ray,
bring to earth a higher way,
light this planet with your fire,
clothe her in a new attire.**

Part 3

1. Sanat Kumara, shatter the energetic matrix that prevents people from realizing: "What are we loyal to? Are we loyal to an earthly and therefore fallible institution? Or are we loyal to Christ? Are we loyal to Jesus as an ascended being who exists today? Or are we loyal to some human institution?"

> Sanat Kumara, Ruby Fire,
> I seek my place in love's own choir,
> with open hearts we sing your praise,
> together we the earth do raise.
>
> **Sanat Kumara, Ruby Ray,**
> **bring to earth a higher way,**
> **light this planet with your fire,**
> **clothe her in a new attire.**

2. Sanat Kumara, shatter the energetic matrix that prevents people from seeing that there are people in the Catholic church, in the church hierarchy, whose minds are so taken over by the fallen beings that they will continue to be in a state of denial, just as Hitler was in a state of denial until the end of the war.

> Sanat Kumara, Ruby Fire,
> initiations I desire,
> I am for you an electrode,
> Shamballa is my true abode.
>
> **Sanat Kumara, Ruby Ray,**
> **bring to earth a higher way,**
> **light this planet with your fire,**
> **clothe her in a new attire.**

3. Sanat Kumara, shatter the energetic matrix that prevents people from escaping this web of illusions that envelops the entire Catholic church, which truly is the primary, the largest, and in a sense the most powerful dictatorship left on earth today.

Sanat Kumara, Ruby Fire,
I follow path that you require,
initiate me with your love,
the open door for Holy Dove.

Sanat Kumara, Ruby Ray,
bring to earth a higher way,
light this planet with your fire,
clothe her in a new attire.

4. Sanat Kumara, shatter the energetic matrix that prevents people from seeing that a religious dictatorship is the most insidious example of a dictatorship. The fallen beings have created an institution that claims to represent God, yet that institution is taken over by the fallen beings so that people give their love to the fallen beings.

Sanat Kumara, Ruby Fire,
your great example all inspire,
with non-attachment and great mirth,
we give the earth a true rebirth.

Sanat Kumara, Ruby Ray,
bring to earth a higher way,
light this planet with your fire,
clothe her in a new attire.

5. Sanat Kumara, shatter the energetic matrix that prevents people from seeing that Islam has also been turned into a religious dictatorship that is holding millions of Muslims in a hypnotic state.

Sanat Kumara, Ruby Fire,
you are this planet's purifier,
consume on earth all spirits dark,
reveal the inner Spirit Spark.

Sanat Kumara, Ruby Ray,
bring to earth a higher way,
light this planet with your fire,
clothe her in a new attire.

6. Sanat Kumara, shatter the energetic matrix that prevents people from seeing that Muslims feel they have to love Allah and the institution of Islam. Therefore, they suspend their judgment and will not see that Islam is not in accordance with a human standard of love or the original revelations in the Koran.

Sanat Kumara, Ruby Fire,
you are a cosmic amplifier,
the lower forces can't withstand,
vibrations from Venusian band.

Sanat Kumara, Ruby Ray,
bring to earth a higher way,
light this planet with your fire,
clothe her in a new attire.

7. Sanat Kumara, shatter the energetic matrix that prevents an exposure of the extremist forms of Muslim fanaticism and radicalism. I call forth a shift so that the tension will be released and Muslims will see the need for change.

Sanat Kumara, Ruby Fire,
I am on earth your magnifier,
the flow of love I do restore,
my chakras are your open door.

Sanat Kumara, Ruby Ray,
bring to earth a higher way,
light this planet with your fire,
clothe her in a new attire.

8. Sanat Kumara, shatter the energetic matrix that prevents people from seeing that many business corporations are essentially dictatorships that have a pyramidal structure with one person at the very top.

Sanat Kumara, Ruby Fire,
Venusian song the multiplier,
as we your love reverberate,
the densest minds we penetrate.

**Sanat Kumara, Ruby Ray,
bring to earth a higher way,
light this planet with your fire,
clothe her in a new attire.**

9. Sanat Kumara, shatter the energetic matrix that prevents people from seeing that many Western corporations have morphed into multinational conglomerates. They claim to be for the benefit of society, but they are based on a perversion of love because they are taking instead of giving.

Sanat Kumara, Ruby Fire,
you are for all the sanctifier,
the earth is now a holy place,
purified by cosmic grace.

**Sanat Kumara, Ruby Ray,
bring to earth a higher way,
light this planet with your fire,
clothe her in a new attire.**

Part 4

1. Sanat Kumara, shatter the energetic matrix that prevents people from seeing that the essence of love is giving. If you take more than you give, you are not expressing love.

Sanat Kumara, Ruby Fire,
I seek my place in love's own choir,
with open hearts we sing your praise,
together we the earth do raise.

**Sanat Kumara, Ruby Ray,
bring to earth a higher way,
light this planet with your fire,
clothe her in a new attire.**

2. Sanat Kumara, shatter the energetic matrix that prevents people from seeing that love is what Jesus expressed when he said: "Freely you have received, freely give," thereby multiplying the talents.

Sanat Kumara, Ruby Fire,
initiations I desire,
I am for you an electrode,
Shamballa is my true abode.

**Sanat Kumara, Ruby Ray,
bring to earth a higher way,
light this planet with your fire,
clothe her in a new attire.**

3. Sanat Kumara, shatter the energetic matrix that prevents people from seeing that we receive divine love from Above. We give that to others and then we receive more from Above. When we are in a state of true love, we are not giving in order to get or in order to make other people obligated towards us.

Sanat Kumara, Ruby Fire,
I follow path that you require,
initiate me with your love,
the open door for Holy Dove.

**Sanat Kumara, Ruby Ray,
bring to earth a higher way,
light this planet with your fire,
clothe her in a new attire.**

4. Sanat Kumara, shatter the energetic matrix that prevents people from seeing that when we are in the flow of love, we are giving out horizontally. The more we give out horizontally, the more we receive vertically because the talents are multiplied. We receive more as a result of having multiplied the love.

Sanat Kumara, Ruby Fire,
your great example all inspire,

with non-attachment and great mirth,
we give the earth a true rebirth.

**Sanat Kumara, Ruby Ray,
bring to earth a higher way,
light this planet with your fire,
clothe her in a new attire.**

5. Sanat Kumara, shatter the energetic matrix that prevents people from seeing that corporations are all about profit. They are all about taking from the population and concentrating it in the hands of a small elite that becomes richer and richer.

Sanat Kumara, Ruby Fire,
you are this planet's purifier,
consume on earth all spirits dark,
reveal the inner Spirit Spark.

**Sanat Kumara, Ruby Ray,
bring to earth a higher way,
light this planet with your fire,
clothe her in a new attire.**

6. Sanat Kumara, shatter the energetic matrix that prevents people from seeing that this is an expression of anti-love, and we cannot allow the unrestricted growth of these multinational corporations.

Sanat Kumara, Ruby Fire,
you are a cosmic amplifier,
the lower forces can't withstand,
vibrations from Venusian band.

**Sanat Kumara, Ruby Ray,
bring to earth a higher way,
light this planet with your fire,
clothe her in a new attire.**

7. Sanat Kumara, shatter the energetic matrix that prevents people from seeing that the ultimate outcome of capitalism is that one corporation

owns the means of production and therefore owns the state. We then have much the same centralized economy as in a communist country.

Sanat Kumara, Ruby Fire,
I am on earth your magnifier,
the flow of love I do restore,
my chakras are your open door.

Sanat Kumara, Ruby Ray,
bring to earth a higher way,
light this planet with your fire,
clothe her in a new attire.

8. Sanat Kumara, shatter the energetic matrix that prevents people from seeing that capitalism and communism are simply two ways that the fallen beings have designed to accomplish the same end and completely centralize society where the fallen beings have absolute, unrestricted power.

Sanat Kumara, Ruby Fire,
Venusian song the multiplier,
as we your love reverberate,
the densest minds we penetrate.

Sanat Kumara, Ruby Ray,
bring to earth a higher way,
light this planet with your fire,
clothe her in a new attire.

9. Sanat Kumara, I invoke the flame that you have anchored on earth, and I call forth both a personal benefit, but also a reinforcement and multiplication of my calls for the resolution of the issues mentioned in this invocation. I accept this manifest right now in the identity realm, the mental realm, the emotional realm and the physical realm. It is finished.

Sanat Kumara, Ruby Fire,
you are for all the sanctifier,
the earth is now a holy place,
purified by cosmic grace.

Sanat Kumara, Ruby Ray,
bring to earth a higher way,
light this planet with your fire,
clothe her in a new attire.

Sealing

In the name of the I AM THAT I AM, I accept that Archangel Michael, Astrea and Shiva form an impenetrable shield around myself and all constructive people, sealing us from all fear-based energies in all four octaves. I accept that the Light of God is consuming and transforming all fear-based energies that make up the dark forces working against ending the era of dictatorships on earth!

8 | DIVERSITY AS THE KEY TO SURVIVAL AND PROGRESS

I AM the Ascended Master, the Elohim Astrea. My task is to give you some teachings on a characteristic of dictatorships that you can see throughout history.

A dictator always takes power by force. It may be that the dictator inherited this from his predecessor, but nevertheless, the power was originally taken by force and it is upheld by force. You know from your physics lessons as a child that for every action, there is an opposite and equal reaction. Or at least that is what Newtonian science says. You know that when you take power by force, by the mere act of doing this, you will create a reaction from the universe.

You are projecting with force into the cosmic mirror and what you are essentially saying to the cosmic mirror is that you want opposition because, by the mere fact that you are using force, you are demonstrating that your mindset operates with opposites. If you did not think there was resistance and opposition, why would you need to take power by force? Therefore, the message you are subconsciously sending into the cosmic mirror is that you want to be in a situation where there is an opposition to you that you constantly need to resist and defend yourselves from.

This is the mindset of every dictator and of course the fallen beings behind every dictator. Which is why you see that dictatorships and dictators always need to have a scapegoat, there needs to be an enemy that is a threat. You can see in every dictatorship how there is that concept of the threat, the enemy, the scapegoat. It is sometimes an external enemy, another group of people, but it is often also some of the people that are in the same nation.

The dictator's attempt to purify humanity

In other words, the dictator feels threatened from within and from without. This is why the dictator then sets up a system that is meant to essentially purify the nation from all who might oppose or threaten the dictator. In many cases, also, the dictator then creates the system that is meant to purify the world from all that might oppose the dictator.

You can see of course that given that I am the Elohim of the Fourth Ray of Purity, how this is a perversion of the Fourth Ray, or the God-quality of Purity, or at least the human derivative of purity, that is a perversion of the God flame. You will see an extreme outcome of this of course in Hitler's attempt to purify the human race and create this Aryan super-race by eliminating all unwanted elements. You might know, if you have studied history, that it was not just the Jews that Hitler attempted to eradicate. He also had an internal program of purification where all those with mental illnesses or unwanted genetic traits were euthanized. It was clearly an extreme perversion of the Fourth Ray, an extreme attempt to use force to purify the race, so to speak.

You will see, if you look across the border to North Korea, how there has been (not only during the current dictator, but going back to when North Korea originated) this need to purify the population from a political viewpoint so that those who are not true believers in the system and the dictator are cleansed out. You can see how this also was the case under Mao and it was the case under Stalin. Even after Stalin, to some degree, in the Soviet Union there was this need to imprison or even execute and torture those who opposed the system.

Now my beloved, why is it that these unbalanced regimes believe they need to purify the people, to create this purification process that weeds out those that they consider unwanted? Well, it is of course because they feel threatened. There is a deeper reality here, in the sense that the fallen beings have, ever since they fell, built this greater and greater intolerance of differences.

Fallen beings and intolerance of differences

You must understand that, as a fallen being goes through the fall and the period of embodying in a new sphere after the fall, perhaps even going through this several times, that fallen being gains a more and more narrow mind, a more and more narrow vision. It feels more and more threatened by anything that could upset the vision of the world that the fallen being has built. This leads to that extreme intolerance where the fallen beings are attempting to destroy all those who do not accept or submit to their vision of how the world works.

This is why you see that communism is an extreme example of how the fallen beings inspired a certain ideology. Then, other fallen beings used that ideology to create an actual regime, a communist regime. They felt so threatened, those in embodiment, that they had to seek to eradicate anyone who would not accept that ideology. You have seen the same in other dictatorships that have had other thought systems, other ideologies they have been based on. They have all attempted to cleanse out those who did not accept the world view upon which the dictatorship was based.

What you need to then realize is that any ideology, any thought system, that is based on this need to purify humanity, this need to limit diversity, is not only against the laws of nature, it is actually against the spiritual laws as well. The primary spiritual law that governs life on earth is, as we have said many times, the Law of Free Will. What does the Law of Free Will encourage? It encourages individual experimentation. What will individual experimentation lead to? Diversity.

Now, you can see from this that many other religions you know in the world have been out of touch with this spiritual law. You can see how Christianity has gone through a period where it also felt the need to purify the population. They created the Crusades in an attempt to destroy Islam and kill the Muslims. They had the Massacre of the Cathars, the Inquisition, the witch hunts as an internal "purification process" where they attempted to weed out those who did not accept official doctrines. You can see that the same thing has been happening in Islam and is going on in Islam today. In a sense, the extreme Islamic movements, such as ISIS, are also obsessed with this need to purify the faith, and even to kill those Muslims who do not accept the imbalanced fanatical version that they have built.

Diversity and the laws of genetics

Now, if you look at what you know about physical science, you will see that the science of biology has developed the science of genetics. You know, for example, that if a population becomes isolated, it will gradually lead to a very narrow gene pool that will then lead to various birth defects. You have seen examples of this in history, such as after the Viking Age when there was a Viking settlement in Greenland. It survived for two to three hundred years, whereupon the gene pool became so narrow, that it deteriorated, in large part due to the birth defects that showed up. You have seen other examples of this in both animal and human populations.

Based on this, you can also see that the attempt to purify the race, so to speak, is in opposition to the very laws of nature. If you take Adolph Hitler and if you project imaginatively that he had accomplished his goals of purifying the entire human race by eradicating all who were not of Aryan descent and did not have the Aryan characteristics (presumably eradicating himself as part of this process, given that he was not a true Aryan), what would have happened? Well, within just a few generations, the gene pool would have become so narrow that the race would have started deteriorating.

What you see is that the entire dream of purifying the human race by destroying diversity and creating uniformity is against both the laws of nature and the spiritual laws. This is easy enough to understand when you know about fallen beings, but it is actually possible for people in general to realize that this is not a realistic scenario. Therefore, we need to realize here that anything that happens on earth is an opportunity for humankind to learn certain lessons. You can make the calls that there will be a shift in the collective consciousness, and again this is one of those things that people are ready for. The shift can be that people start looking at the situation of dictatorships. They have become willing to look at history, and they become willing to consider: "What can we learn from this?" This can begin with certain scientists, certain historians, even writers who look at this, and say: "What is the lesson we can learn? Why have we had these dictatorial forms of government and what does it show us about ourselves?"

Intolerance is not a survival strategy

Naturally, as the other masters have talked about, there are many lessons to learn from this, such as people not wanting to take responsibility. The lesson I am concerned about in this release is that people actually learn that the only way to survive is through diversity and that destroying diversity threatens your own survival in the long run, and often even in the short run. Intolerance is not a survival strategy. Purification, uniformication, as you might say, is not a survival strategy. You cannot survive by destroying diversity. What can you then do? You can do what many of the modern democracies have already started doing—you can *embrace* diversity.

This of course is the major challenge, the major initiation, in a sense, that the Fourth Ray is presenting to humanity. It is also an initiation for spiritual people to deal with this. You need to of course find some balance here. If you look at it realistically, you can see that what we have told you is that there was, in previous ages, a situation where the earth had a very sophisticated civilization. It was based on this desire to create harmony and peace by making people, not necessarily the same in all ways, but making them accept the same view of life. In other words, it was based on creating uniformity, rather than embracing diversity. We have explained to you that this had reached a point where we could see that the planet would go into a self-destructive downward spiral. As an attempt to avoid this, we allowed the fallen beings to embody on earth because they created so much chaos that it became impossible to hold on to this very uniform worldview. This is an example of how the fallen beings were, in a way, used to create diversity and to shatter this uniformity that had been artificially created.

Now, you realize of course that the fallen beings are a two-edged sword. It is true that they will go in and create diversity by creating chaos and upsetting the existing structures on any planet where they are allowed to embody. Some of the fallen beings will do this, as we have explained, just in order to create chaos. There are other fallen beings that do this because they have an agenda of setting themselves up in positions of power. In order to do this, they will start working against diversity. You can see that when the fallen beings first were allowed to embody on earth, they did generate diversity, but there came a point where at least certain fallen beings then attempted to go the other way by destroying diversity. They were the ones who have created these dictatorships, not only individual dictatorships, but also the dictatorship of communism, the dictatorship of the Catholic church, and other similar ones you have seen, both in known history and before.

The challenge, the very delicate challenge, that you face is embracing diversity without going to an extreme. The only way to resolve this challenge is to realize what we have given you: the teachings on duality and how there are always the two extremes. We have also told you that the solution is not a compromise between the extremes. The Middle Way that the Buddha promoted did not mean that you go to the midpoint between the two extremes, it means that you transcend the two extremes, you transcend the consciousness that generates the two extremes, the two polarities.

Diversity does not mean tolerating anything

You could say that if you embrace diversity that means you need to tolerate anything and everything. There are some of the modern democracies that have gotten to this point where they feel that in order to uphold their democratic ideals and be a free society, they have to let people do almost anything they want to do. This of course can also lead to the downfall of a society by creating so much chaos and turmoil that a society cannot sustain itself over time.

For example, you will see in Italy today (and in the last several centuries) that if you allow the mafia to take over and run the economy, then the economy will gradually go down and cannot maintain a high level of growth. Essentially, what the mafia is creating is an economy that is as controlled by a centralized authority as the economy in a communist nation. It is not possible and realistic in a democratic nation that you allow free reign to those who are actually undermining democracy. You see here that this presents another aspect of this challenge because some people would say: "But you are saying that the dictatorships have an extreme form of intolerance and they are trying to forcefully destroy any opposition, anyone who has a diverting viewpoint. And now you're saying that the free democracies who are the opposite of dictatorships cannot have complete tolerance because that will also destroy them?" The resolution of this is of course to realize that when you transcend duality, you rise to a state of consciousness where you do not have two opposite polarities and therefore, you are able to discern more clearly and see both extremes. What you will see if you look at history is that (for the last couple of centuries, perhaps even a little bit beyond in some nations) the nations who have now become democracies have been in the situation where they have come to clearly see one dualistic polarity and see it as unbalanced. They saw this in the dictatorial nations. Many of the modern democracies saw it in their own nations when they had a king or an emperor in previous times.

They did see that a dictatorship is an unbalanced polarity. Now, they have thought that they need to go to the opposite extreme where instead of restricting freedom, you have to allow freedom and you have to allow freedom in the sense that anything goes. What they are ready to see (and can come to see when you make the calls on this) is that this is just going from one extreme to another, and you are still in a force-based mindset. Whether you *use* force or *ban* force, you are still thinking in terms of force. When you transcend duality, you gain a new vision, a new way of thinking, where you realize that there is not necessarily a balance to be found between the extremes, but it is possible to find a state that is not pulled towards the extremes. You might say it is a balanced state, but it is not balanced in the sense that it is in between the extremes. You have transcended the pull of the extremes.

Democracy is not in opposition to dictatorships

What you realize here is that there is right now that tension in the collective consciousness where people are beginning to, or they are very close to being ready to, see that there is an alternative to duality. This will begin with certain of the more evolved people, the more aware people, those who have perhaps some education in history, psychology, political science, and what have you, who are able to break through and see this. They are able to see that the modern democracies have to stop seeing themselves as being the opposite polarity to a dictatorship. They have to see that despite their history, they are not in opposition to dictatorships.

Democracy, especially when it steps up to this next level of becoming a more direct democracy, has transcended the mindset that created dictatorships. This is the next logical step for that part of human civilization, which has now for some time had democratic nations, democratic societies. This will of course require a major shift. It is not a shift that just happens by a few people seeing this. It is a shift that requires a longer process where you go into even the educational system, and at a relatively early age, start educating children about some of these basic things: duality, non-duality, the two polarities, how they have outplayed themselves in history. This is something that people are quite capable of understanding, and especially the younger generation that are embodying and have embodied. They are fully capable of understanding this, but it will require a process whereby the modern democracies can begin to see that they do not need to see themselves as being in opposition to dictatorships and therefore, they do not need to see themselves as being threatened by dictatorships.

The challenge for the United States

You can see in this invocation you were giving before this dictation, how there is a call for a shift even in the South Korean nation, but also in a unified Korea, where you stop seeing yourself as being threatened by outside nations and therefore, you do not need to build an army to defend a unified Korea. There is also the call made that this would require South Korea to make the shift where they also ask the Americans to withdraw their military presence from the Korean Peninsula. This is because we see that there is a certain potential that the Korean nation could challenge the superpowers to say: "Step back, draw your militaries back and stop seeing these smaller nations as a tool you can use in your internal rivalry between these supposedly superpowers."

I do not foresee that this change I am talking about will happen first in the United States. It could happen in Korea, it could happen in many of the other modern democracies, but it is more likely to happen in smaller nations before the larger nations. As it begins to happen, it is clear that the present world order, so to speak, where there are a few nations who consider themselves superpowers and who think they have a right to rule the world, they will be challenged. Especially those of them who claim to be democracies will be challenged to live up to their democratic ideals.

The United States, as we have said before, has a military that is way beyond what is mandated by the Constitution and envisioned by the Founding Fathers. It is not completely unwarranted that there are nations in the world who consider the United States an aggressive, imperialist power. It is clear that this needs to be challenged before the United States can make that shift of rising above this dualistic polarity. How can the United States uphold this military and justify it to the American people? Well, they must project that there is a threat out there. Whether it is Russia or China or the "Axis of Evil," they need the threat. This is what people in other nations can begin to see and they can then begin to challenge the United States and say: "Are you truly the kind of democratic, free, peaceful nation that you claim to be? Why do you not bring your actions into alignment with your ideals?"

Nations in an in-between state

This of course is a very important step in this process we talk about of overcoming this perversion of purity where people think everything has to be the same and that differences and diversity are a threat. You see my beloved, when you are in a dualistic state of consciousness, there will always be opposite polarities and one of those will be seen as a threat. When you are in a dualistic state of consciousness, you see two polarities, but you also apply the value judgment that one is right, one is wrong, one is good, one is evil. Naturally, you align yourself with the one that you think is good. Therefore, you must label the opposite as evil. This is a state of consciousness that the world needs to begin to transcend in order to reach the age where dictatorships become obsolete and they fade away, they lose their influence.

Now, you see my beloved, that many nations around the world are in this in-between state. For example, you will see in China how the current president has, in recent years, changed the system to the point where he has set himself up as having larger power than any Chinese leader since Chairman Mao—larger personal power. In a sense, then we could say that China has moved towards a more dictatorial form of government than it has had in recent decades. Not saying that it had a free government but less dictatorial than under Chairman Mao, for example. On the other hand, you also see that China has the realization that it wants to trade with the world and it first of all wants to trade with the more affluent nations of the world, meaning the democratic nations. Therefore, it cannot revert back to the state of dictatorial government that it had under Mao. It is recognized even by the Chinese President that this is not a realistic scenario. This is not the path that China wants to go down.

There is some realization in Chinese leadership that they need to gradually give more and more freedom inside the nation. You see that there are the two opposing forces that are working in Chinese leadership: a concentration of power yet the realization of the need to give more freedom. You can make the calls that China will be able to make a transition and get on a path that leads towards greater and greater freedom for the population. Now my beloved, I have said that if you look at history, both natural history and human history, you will see that diversity is the road to survival. The same goes for nations. China will not survive unless it allows freedom and diversity.

Freedom is the key to prosperity

What is the lesson you can learn from the history of the past 200 years? Well, which are the most affluent nations in the world? They are the ones who have given the greatest amount of freedom to their citizens: the democracies. Why did the Soviet Union collapse? Primarily because the economy could not sustain itself and why not? Because there was too many restrictions. Russia under Putin has moved back towards the state where the economy is less free and this will surely have ramifications in the coming years and decades.

You will see that the lesson of history is clear: Give freedom, and a nation prospers. Therefore, it is possible again to make the calls that there will be this shift in the collective consciousness where even many of the nations who are currently dictatorships will realize that the only way to have more affluence, more prosperity in their nation, is to give more freedom. Of course, the more aware dictators can see that the people want better economic conditions and that they cannot allow themselves to hold this back.

Now, you see an example of this in the nation of Kazakhstan that has had a dictator for the entire time since the collapse of the Soviet Union where it became an independent nation again. You have recently seen this dictator step down, as we actually predicted in some dictations in Kazakhstan could happen, and you saw that this was because he had, the President had, a higher awareness than what you might call the average dictator. He could see that the people wanted and needed better economic conditions. He attempted to create this within the system that was in place but after several years of this, he was willing to recognize that it had not produced the desired results. Therefore, he recognized that the only way to provide the prosperity was to also give the freedom, but that required a fundamental change in the government, in the form of government. This of course can happen in many other nations who are on the verge of this. There are even nations in the Middle East who are on the verge of this awareness shifting. You saw it some years ago with what happened in Egypt but now Egypt has gone backwards. Still, there is enormous pressure because in some of the Middle Eastern nations, you have a youth unemployment of over 25%, or even higher, where a very large part of young people cannot find a job. But it is the young people who are more aware and who know how people in other nations have more affluence, and they want this, but they see that they cannot have it in their own country the way the system is. Therefore, there is tremendous pressure in the collective consciousness.

Iran is another nation where you have the same dynamic. People want that economic affluence. They see that they cannot have it with a restricted system and it creates a tension. It is possible that this can shift in many nations where there does not have to be a violent revolution because the leaders become aware enough to look at history, to see what has happened in other nations and say: "If we don't do something, there's going to be some violent uprising and we will then face the choice that Assad faced in Syria, that in order to maintain our power, we will have to bomb our own nation back to the Stone Age. And is that really what we want?"

Dictators voluntarily giving up power

You can see how these pressures can actually have the effect of having people who are in a dictatorial form of government voluntarily give up their power. Now, you may look at some of the democracies in Europe and you can see that not so long ago they had a dictatorial form of government. They had a king who had all power in that nation and you can see how some of these kings were able to realize that times have changed. Why did they realize this? Partly because they saw the example of France where the king resisted change and there was a violent revolution. Some of the other leaders, some of the other kings in Europe, said: "Well, if we don't want the guillotine to take over in our nation, we better give some concessions and create a more free form of government."

You also saw that, with the advent of the Soviet Union, there were people in the West who said that unless we want a communist revolution in our countries, we better give the workers better working conditions and more affluence. You can see how there are many, many examples from history of how the transition from a dictatorial form of government to a more free form of government has happened without war, without revolution, without bloodshed, but simply because there was a shift in the mind of the dictator, as you here in Korea have been calling for since you received that invocation, based on our dictations.

This concludes the teachings I want to give you, and I want to express the gratitude of all of us for your presence here, for your willingness to be the broadcast stations, for sending this into the collective consciousness. I am sure that those of you who are from Korea realize that this conference, we are not talking so much about Korea. This is because we realize that you are fully aware and willing to also serve as the broadcasting stations to broadcast this into the collective consciousness of the entire world. This is of course to your credit and we are grateful for your willingness to serve this way.

With this, I seal you in the love of the Fourth Ray, the pure love of the Fourth Ray. Of course, the love of all of the rays is pure, but nevertheless, I could not resist that play on words.

9 | INVOKING A TOLERANCE FOR DIVERSITY AS THE KEY TO PROGRESS

In the name of the I AM THAT I AM, Jesus Christ, I use the authority that I have as a being in embodiment on earth to call upon Elohim Astrea to reinforce my calls and use my chakras to project the statements in this invocation into the collective consciousness and awaken people to the fact that diversity is the key to both survival and progress. Awaken people to the reality that we are spiritual beings and that we can co-create a new future by working with the ascended masters. I especially call for …

[Make your own calls here.]

Part 1

1. Astrea, shatter the energetic matrix that prevents people from seeing that a dictator always takes power by force and this will create a reaction from the universe.

Astrea, loving Being white,
your Presence is my pure delight,

your sword and circle white and blue,
the astral plane is cutting through.

Astrea, come accelerate,
with purity I do vibrate,
release the fire so blue and white,
my aura filled with vibrant light.

2. Astrea, shatter the energetic matrix that prevents people from seeing that a dictator is saying to the cosmic mirror that he wants opposition because, by the fact that he is using force, he is demonstrating that his mindset operates with opposites.

Astrea, calm the raging storm,
so purity will be the norm,
my aura filled with blue and white,
with shining armor, like a knight.

Astrea, come accelerate,
with purity I do vibrate,
release the fire so blue and white,
my aura filled with vibrant light.

3. Astrea, shatter the energetic matrix that prevents people from seeing that the message a dictator is subconsciously sending into the cosmic mirror is that he wants to be in a situation where there is an opposition to him so he constantly needs to defend himself.

Astrea, come and cut me free,
from every binding entity,
let astral forces all be bound,
true freedom I have surely found.

Astrea, come accelerate,
with purity I do vibrate,
release the fire so blue and white,
my aura filled with vibrant light.

4. Astrea, shatter the energetic matrix that prevents people from seeing that this is the mindset of every dictator and the fallen beings behind every dictator. Dictators always need to have a scapegoat, there needs to be an enemy that is a threat.

Astrea, I sincerely urge,
from demons all, do me purge,
consume them all and take me higher,
I will endure your cleansing fire.

**Astrea, come accelerate,
with purity I do vibrate,
release the fire so blue and white,
my aura filled with vibrant light.**

5. Astrea, shatter the energetic matrix that prevents people from seeing that in every dictatorship there is a concept of the threat, the enemy, the scapegoat. It is often an external enemy, but it is often also people from the same nation.

Astrea, do all spirits bind,
so that I am no longer blind,
I see the spirit and its twin,
the victory of Christ I win.

**Astrea, come accelerate,
with purity I do vibrate,
release the fire so blue and white,
my aura filled with vibrant light.**

6. Astrea, shatter the energetic matrix that prevents people from seeing that a dictator feels threatened from within and from without and must set up a system that is meant to purify the nation from all who might oppose or threaten the dictator, even purify the world from all that might oppose the dictator.

Astrea, clear my every cell,
from energies of death and hell,

my body is now free to grow,
each cell emits an inner glow.

Astrea, come accelerate,
with purity I do vibrate,
release the fire so blue and white,
my aura filled with vibrant light.

7. Astrea, shatter the energetic matrix that prevents people from seeing that the deeper reality behind dictators is that ever since they fell, the fallen beings have built this greater and greater intolerance of differences.

Astrea, clear my feeling mind,
in purity my peace I find,
with higher feeling you release,
I co-create in perfect peace.

Astrea, come accelerate,
with purity I do vibrate,
release the fire so blue and white,
my aura filled with vibrant light.

8. Astrea, shatter the energetic matrix that prevents people from seeing that fallen beings have a very narrow vision and feel threatened by anything that could upset the vision of the world that the fallen beings have built.

Astrea, clear my mental realm,
my Christ self always at the helm,
I see now how to manifest,
the matrix that for all is best.

Astrea, come accelerate,
with purity I do vibrate,
release the fire so blue and white,
my aura filled with vibrant light.

9. Astrea, shatter the energetic matrix that prevents people from seeing that fallen beings are using dictators to destroy all those who do not accept or submit to their vision of how the world works.

Astrea, with great clarity,
I claim a new identity,
etheric blueprint I now see,
I co-create more consciously.

Astrea, come accelerate,
with purity I do vibrate,
release the fire so blue and white,
my aura filled with vibrant light.

Part 2

1. Astrea, shatter the energetic matrix that prevents people from seeing that fallen beings inspired communist ideology and created a communist regime. They then sought to eradicate anyone who would not accept that ideology.

Astrea, loving Being white,
your Presence is my pure delight,
your sword and circle white and blue,
the astral plane is cutting through.

Astrea, come accelerate,
with purity I do vibrate,
release the fire so blue and white,
my aura filled with vibrant light.

2. Astrea, shatter the energetic matrix that prevents people from seeing that any ideology, any thought system, that is based on this need to purify humanity, this need to limit diversity, is against the laws of nature and the spiritual laws.

Astrea, calm the raging storm,
so purity will be the norm,
my aura filled with blue and white,
with shining armor, like a knight.

Astrea, come accelerate,
with purity I do vibrate,
release the fire so blue and white,
my aura filled with vibrant light.

3. Astrea, shatter the energetic matrix that prevents people from seeing that the primary spiritual law that governs life on earth is the Law of Free Will, and it encourages individual experimentation. Experimentation will lead to diversity.

Astrea, come and cut me free,
from every binding entity,
let astral forces all be bound,
true freedom I have surely found.

Astrea, come accelerate,
with purity I do vibrate,
release the fire so blue and white,
my aura filled with vibrant light.

4. Astrea, shatter the energetic matrix that prevents people from seeing that many religions have been and are out of touch with this spiritual law and also seek to make everyone believe in their religion.

Astrea, I sincerely urge,
from demons all, do me purge,
consume them all and take me higher,
I will endure your cleansing fire.

Astrea, come accelerate,
with purity I do vibrate,
release the fire so blue and white,
my aura filled with vibrant light.

5. Astrea, shatter the energetic matrix that prevents people from seeing that the attempt to purify the race is in opposition to the laws of nature because if the gene pool becomes too narrow, a population will start deteriorating.

> Astrea, do all spirits bind,
> so that I am no longer blind,
> I see the spirit and its twin,
> the victory of Christ I win.
>
> **Astrea, come accelerate,**
> **with purity I do vibrate,**
> **release the fire so blue and white,**
> **my aura filled with vibrant light.**

6. Astrea, shatter the energetic matrix that prevents people from seeing that anything that happens on earth is an opportunity for humankind to learn certain lessons.

> Astrea, clear my every cell,
> from energies of death and hell,
> my body is now free to grow,
> each cell emits an inner glow.
>
> **Astrea, come accelerate,**
> **with purity I do vibrate,**
> **release the fire so blue and white,**
> **my aura filled with vibrant light.**

7. Astrea, shatter the energetic matrix that prevents a shift in the collective consciousness so people start considering what we can learn from dictatorships.

> Astrea, clear my feeling mind,
> in purity my peace I find,
> with higher feeling you release,
> I co-create in perfect peace.
>
> **Astrea, come accelerate,**
> **with purity I do vibrate,**

**release the fire so blue and white,
my aura filled with vibrant light.**

8. Astrea, shatter the energetic matrix that prevents scientists, historians and writers from considering: "What is the lesson we can learn? Why have we had these dictatorial forms of government and what does it show us about ourselves?"

Astrea, clear my mental realm,
my Christ self always at the helm,
I see now how to manifest,
the matrix that for all is best.

**Astrea, come accelerate,
with purity I do vibrate,
release the fire so blue and white,
my aura filled with vibrant light.**

9. Astrea, shatter the energetic matrix that prevents people from seeing that the only way to survive is through diversity and that destroying diversity threatens our own survival in the long run, and often even in the short run.

Astrea, with great clarity,
I claim a new identity,
etheric blueprint I now see,
I co-create more consciously.

**Astrea, come accelerate,
with purity I do vibrate,
release the fire so blue and white,
my aura filled with vibrant light.**

Part 3

1. Astrea, shatter the energetic matrix that prevents people from seeing that intolerance is not a survival strategy. Purification, uniformication is not a survival strategy. We cannot survive by destroying diversity.

> Astrea, loving Being white,
> your Presence is my pure delight,
> your sword and circle white and blue,
> the astral plane is cutting through.

> **Astrea, come accelerate,**
> **with purity I do vibrate,**
> **release the fire so blue and white,**
> **my aura filled with vibrant light.**

2. Astrea, shatter the energetic matrix that prevents people from seeing that we must continue what many of the modern democracies have already started doing, namely embrace diversity.

> Astrea, calm the raging storm,
> so purity will be the norm,
> my aura filled with blue and white,
> with shining armor, like a knight.

> **Astrea, come accelerate,**
> **with purity I do vibrate,**
> **release the fire so blue and white,**
> **my aura filled with vibrant light.**

3. Astrea, shatter the energetic matrix that prevents people from seeing that the very delicate challenge we face is embracing diversity without going to an extreme.

> Astrea, come and cut me free,
> from every binding entity,
> let astral forces all be bound,
> true freedom I have surely found.

Astrea, come accelerate,
with purity I do vibrate,
release the fire so blue and white,
my aura filled with vibrant light.

4. Astrea, shatter the energetic matrix that prevents people from seeing that the only way to resolve this challenge is to realize that there are always two extremes. The solution is not a compromise between the extremes, but that we transcend the consciousness that generates the two polarities.

Astrea, I sincerely urge,
from demons all, do me purge,
consume them all and take me higher,
I will endure your cleansing fire.

Astrea, come accelerate,
with purity I do vibrate,
release the fire so blue and white,
my aura filled with vibrant light.

5. Astrea, shatter the energetic matrix that prevents people from seeing that upholding democratic ideals and being a free society does not mean we have to let people do anything they want to do.

Astrea, do all spirits bind,
so that I am no longer blind,
I see the spirit and its twin,
the victory of Christ I win.

Astrea, come accelerate,
with purity I do vibrate,
release the fire so blue and white,
my aura filled with vibrant light.

6. Astrea, shatter the energetic matrix that prevents people from seeing that when we transcend duality, we rise to a state of consciousness where we do not have two opposite polarities and therefore, we are able to discern more clearly and see both extremes.

Astrea, clear my every cell,
from energies of death and hell,
my body is now free to grow,
each cell emits an inner glow.

Astrea, come accelerate,
with purity I do vibrate,
release the fire so blue and white,
my aura filled with vibrant light.

7. Astrea, shatter the energetic matrix that prevents people from seeing that dictatorships represent one extreme where they use force to limit freedom. Some democratic nations think they need to allow freedom in the sense that anything goes. Yet this is just going from one extreme to another.

Astrea, clear my feeling mind,
in purity my peace I find,
with higher feeling you release,
I co-create in perfect peace.

Astrea, come accelerate,
with purity I do vibrate,
release the fire so blue and white,
my aura filled with vibrant light.

8. Astrea, shatter the energetic matrix that prevents people from seeing that we are still in a force-based mindset. Whether we *use* force or *ban* force, we are still thinking in terms of force. When we transcend duality, we gain a new vision, a new way of thinking.

Astrea, clear my mental realm,
my Christ self always at the helm,
I see now how to manifest,
the matrix that for all is best.

Astrea, come accelerate,
with purity I do vibrate,
release the fire so blue and white,
my aura filled with vibrant light.

9. Astrea, shatter the energetic matrix that prevents people from seeing that there is not necessarily a balance to be found between the extremes, but it is possible to find a state that is not pulled towards the extremes. It is a balanced state, but not balanced in the sense that it is in between the extremes, we have transcended the pull of the extremes.

> Astrea, with great clarity,
> I claim a new identity,
> etheric blueprint I now see,
> I co-create more consciously.
>
> **Astrea, come accelerate,**
> **with purity I do vibrate,**
> **release the fire so blue and white,**
> **my aura filled with vibrant light.**

Part 4

1. Astrea, shatter the energetic matrix that prevents the more evolved people, those who have some education in history, psychology, political science, from seeing that there is an alternative to duality.

> Astrea, loving Being white,
> your Presence is my pure delight,
> your sword and circle white and blue,
> the astral plane is cutting through.
>
> **Astrea, come accelerate,**
> **with purity I do vibrate,**
> **release the fire so blue and white,**
> **my aura filled with vibrant light.**

2. Astrea, shatter the energetic matrix that prevents people from seeing that the modern democracies have to stop seeing themselves as being the opposite polarity to a dictatorship. They are not in opposition to dictatorships.

Astrea, calm the raging storm,
so purity will be the norm,
my aura filled with blue and white,
with shining armor, like a knight.

Astrea, come accelerate,
with purity I do vibrate,
release the fire so blue and white,
my aura filled with vibrant light.

3. Astrea, shatter the energetic matrix that prevents people from seeing that a more direct democracy has transcended the mindset that created dictatorships.

Astrea, come and cut me free,
from every binding entity,
let astral forces all be bound,
true freedom I have surely found.

Astrea, come accelerate,
with purity I do vibrate,
release the fire so blue and white,
my aura filled with vibrant light.

4. Astrea, shatter the energetic matrix that prevents people from seeing the need to educate children about duality, non-duality, the two polarities and how they have outplayed themselves in history.

Astrea, I sincerely urge,
from demons all, do me purge,
consume them all and take me higher,
I will endure your cleansing fire.

Astrea, come accelerate,
with purity I do vibrate,
release the fire so blue and white,
my aura filled with vibrant light.

5. Astrea, shatter the energetic matrix that prevents people from seeing that the modern democracies do not need to see themselves as being in opposition to dictatorships and therefore, they do not need to see themselves as being threatened by dictatorships.

Astrea, do all spirits bind,
so that I am no longer blind,
I see the spirit and its twin,
the victory of Christ I win.

Astrea, come accelerate,
with purity I do vibrate,
release the fire so blue and white,
my aura filled with vibrant light.

6. Astrea, shatter the energetic matrix that prevents people from seeing that this shift will challenge the superpowers, especially the United States, to live up to their democratic ideals.

Astrea, clear my every cell,
from energies of death and hell,
my body is now free to grow,
each cell emits an inner glow.

Astrea, come accelerate,
with purity I do vibrate,
release the fire so blue and white,
my aura filled with vibrant light.

7. Astrea, shatter the energetic matrix that prevents people from seeing that the United States has a military that is beyond what is mandated by the Constitution, and this needs to be challenged before the United States can rise above the dualistic polarities.

Astrea, clear my feeling mind,
in purity my peace I find,
with higher feeling you release,
I co-create in perfect peace.

**Astrea, come accelerate,
with purity I do vibrate,
release the fire so blue and white,
my aura filled with vibrant light.**

8. Astrea, shatter the energetic matrix that prevents people from seeing that in order to justify the military to the American people, there must be a threat. But is this the kind of democratic, free, peaceful nation that it claims to be?

Astrea, clear my mental realm,
my Christ self always at the helm,
I see now how to manifest,
the matrix that for all is best.

**Astrea, come accelerate,
with purity I do vibrate,
release the fire so blue and white,
my aura filled with vibrant light.**

9. Astrea, shatter the energetic matrix that prevents people from seeing that when we are in a dualistic state of consciousness, we see two polarities, but we also apply the value judgment that one is right, one is wrong, one is good, one is evil.

Astrea, with great clarity,
I claim a new identity,
etheric blueprint I now see,
I co-create more consciously.

**Astrea, come accelerate,
with purity I do vibrate,
release the fire so blue and white,
my aura filled with vibrant light.**

Part 5

1. Astrea, shatter the energetic matrix that prevents people from seeing that the world needs to transcend this dualistic consciousness in order to reach the age where dictatorships become obsolete and lose their influence.

> Astrea, loving Being white,
> your Presence is my pure delight,
> your sword and circle white and blue,
> the astral plane is cutting through.

> **Astrea, come accelerate,**
> **with purity I do vibrate,**
> **release the fire so blue and white,**
> **my aura filled with vibrant light.**

2. Astrea, shatter the energetic matrix that prevents the Chinese leadership from dealing with the two opposing forces that are working in China: a concentration of power yet the realization of the need to give more freedom.

> Astrea, calm the raging storm,
> so purity will be the norm,
> my aura filled with blue and white,
> with shining armor, like a knight.

> **Astrea, come accelerate,**
> **with purity I do vibrate,**
> **release the fire so blue and white,**
> **my aura filled with vibrant light.**

3. Astrea, shatter the energetic matrix that prevents China from making a transition and getting on a path that leads towards greater and greater freedom for the population. China will not survive unless it allows freedom and diversity.

> Astrea, come and cut me free,
> from every binding entity,

let astral forces all be bound,
true freedom I have surely found.

Astrea, come accelerate,
with purity I do vibrate,
release the fire so blue and white,
my aura filled with vibrant light.

4. Astrea, shatter the energetic matrix that prevents people from seeing that the most affluent nations in the world are the ones who have given the greatest amount of freedom to their citizens. The lesson of history is clear: Give freedom, and a nation prospers.

Astrea, I sincerely urge,
from demons all, do me purge,
consume them all and take me higher,
I will endure your cleansing fire.

Astrea, come accelerate,
with purity I do vibrate,
release the fire so blue and white,
my aura filled with vibrant light.

5. Astrea, shatter the energetic matrix that prevents a shift in the collective consciousness where many of the nations that are currently dictatorships will realize that the only way to have more affluence and prosperity is to give more freedom.

Astrea, do all spirits bind,
so that I am no longer blind,
I see the spirit and its twin,
the victory of Christ I win.

Astrea, come accelerate,
with purity I do vibrate,
release the fire so blue and white,
my aura filled with vibrant light.

6. Astrea, shatter the energetic matrix that prevents nations in the Middle East from shifting so there does not have to be a violent revolution because the leaders become aware enough to look at history and learn from what has happened in other nations.

    Astrea, clear my every cell,
from energies of death and hell,
my body is now free to grow,
each cell emits an inner glow.

**Astrea, come accelerate,
with purity I do vibrate,
release the fire so blue and white,
my aura filled with vibrant light.**

7. Astrea, shatter the energetic matrix that prevents people who are in a dictatorial form of government from voluntarily giving up their power in order to avoid a violent revolution.

    Astrea, clear my feeling mind,
in purity my peace I find,
with higher feeling you release,
I co-create in perfect peace.

**Astrea, come accelerate,
with purity I do vibrate,
release the fire so blue and white,
my aura filled with vibrant light.**

8. Astrea, shatter the energetic matrix that prevents people from learning from the examples from history of how the transition from a dictatorial form of government to a more free form of government has happened without war or revolution.

    Astrea, clear my mental realm,
my Christ self always at the helm,
I see now how to manifest,
the matrix that for all is best.

Astrea, come accelerate,
with purity I do vibrate,
release the fire so blue and white,
my aura filled with vibrant light.

9. Astrea, shatter the energetic matrix that prevents people from seeing that giving the population the freedom to think freely without religious or political constraints is the only way to bring about the inventiveness that leads to economic prosperity.

Astrea, with great clarity,
I claim a new identity,
etheric blueprint I now see,
I co-create more consciously.

Astrea, come accelerate,
with purity I do vibrate,
release the fire so blue and white,
my aura filled with vibrant light.

Sealing

In the name of the I AM THAT I AM, I accept that Archangel Michael, Astrea and Shiva form an impenetrable shield around myself and all constructive people, sealing us from all fear-based energies in all four octaves. I accept that the Light of God is consuming and transforming all fear-based energies that make up the dark forces working against ending the era of dictatorships on earth!

10 | BEHIND EVERY DICTATOR THERE IS A VISION

I AM the Ascended Master the Elohim Cyclopea. Now my beloved, some decades ago, there was a common saying in the United States of America that said: "Behind every great man, there is a woman." The fact that this joke has become obsolete shows that society has made *some* progress, at least, in recognizing the absolute equality of men and women. Nevertheless, I would like to begin with a statement that: "Behind every great man, there is a *woman,* and "behind every 'great dictator,' there is a *vision."*

This of course introduces the concept of "great dictator." It gives me the opportunity to at least talk about the fact that there are two different types of dictators: those who consider themselves great because they have some kind of agenda, some kind of overall vision, that they believe will actually improve the conditions on this planet, improve conditions for humanity. Then, there are those who do not particularly consider themselves great because they are only focused on themselves and getting power and position for themselves. You want examples of the two? You can look at the Soviet Union of how Stalin was clearly the kind of dictator who was focused on himself and his own power whereas Lenin was the visionary who had an agenda that he thought would improve the world.

Perverted vision behind all dictators

Naturally, you see that behind dictators, there is a perversion of vision, there is a perverted vision. This is something that originates with the fallen beings who are experts at perverting vision. Of course, I do not think that it is a good quality to be an expert on perverting anything, but the fallen beings disagree with me. I of course allow them to do so because it has no impact on me as an ascended being. Nevertheless, it does have a great impact on the un-ascended beings on earth, and that is why we need to discuss it.

Now my beloved, if you could step back and see what I can see from the ascended level, you would see that the fallen beings have created, in the physical realm, in the emotional realm, in the mental realm and in the lower identity realm, an incredibly complex apparatus and machine that is aimed at producing false and distorted visions and spreading them on earth. The purpose is to get people to believe in something that is false, obscuring the truth, taking any higher statement and perverting it, or coming up with an opposite that seems to challenge it.

This apparatus is so elaborate and so complex that if people could see it, they would be overwhelmed by the aggressive intent behind it. It is, in a small way, comparable to what you can see, for example, from the Cold War where both sides had a very elaborate machine aimed at directing propaganda at the people on the other side. You can also see the spy networks and how elaborate they were. They are of course even more elaborate today, but this is not as known as what you at least know from the Cold War days.

This machinery created by the fallen beings is more elaborate than anything on earth, anything in the physical octave, because the physical octave is like the tip of the iceberg, and what happens in the other three realms is much more complex and much more vast. If people could at least see it and see the aggressive intent behind it, they would be so shocked that they might actually be awakened to the need to purify their vision, to raise their vision, and to come to be able to see through these elaborate deceptions created by the fallen beings throughout the ages.

Vision that leads to di-vision

Now, if you go back to when the first beings fell in the fourth sphere and trace how they have built illusion after illusion, you would again be overwhelmed at the complexity. Nevertheless, you can also look at the complexity, and you can begin to see patterns. Therefore, you can gradually reduce the complexity to something that is manageable to the human mind where you can see what they are actually trying to do. If you reduce it to the most simple level, you can say that the purpose behind the false vision created by the fallen beings is the divide-and-conquer strategy.

They are always trying to create a *vision* that creates *di-vision*. This is really the essence of what they are trying to do: vision leading to division. Once you understand this, you have at least a foundation, a starting point, for looking at what is happening in the world. You can see how the fallen beings have used anything that happens in an attempt to create division.

Division through religion

You can see, as we have already talked about with the Catholic church, how religion throughout the ages has been used to create division. Ask yourself this, my beloved: Why is it necessary that a particular religion defines a clear dividing line between those who are followers of that religion, those who are inside the religion, and those who are outside? Why is that necessary?

The claim that many religions have based their existence on is that they have a truth given directly from God. They claim that the God who has given them this truth is the ultimate God, the superior God of the universe. Well, if that claim was true, would it not stand to reason that the ultimate God of the universe would be able to create a universe where all people would be saved? Why would an ultimate God create different groups of people, and some would be saved and some would not? Would it not stand to reason that the ultimate God would have the ultimate vision of what kind of universe he is creating, and therefore would be able to set up a universe that had a set of universal laws that would bring people towards salvation, if they need that, but that would bring growth. In other words, the ultimate God should be able to create a universe where there is a set of universal principles and laws that causes that universe to unfold as that God envisions. Why would that God need religion on earth?

Why would the ultimate God need a religion that claims to represent this ultimate God on earth if the God has already defined certain universal principles that are causing the universe to grow as the God wants it to grow? In other words, you will see that the claim behind most religions is that something went wrong with God's creation, and therefore as an emergency measure, as a stopgap measure, people need to be saved. In order to be saved, they have to follow the one and only true religion, and those who follow that religion are guaranteed to be saved, and those who do not follow that religion are guaranteed *not* to be saved—possibly ending up in a fiery hell for all eternity.

Now, why an ultimate God would find it necessary to create a fiery hell, and why he would want to punish those who do not follow his one true religion for all eternity, is a question rarely asked by these people. Nevertheless, what you can see here is that many religions create, by the very essence of their teachings, this fundamental division between those who will be saved and those who will not.

Division through political ideologies

You will see that many political ideologies also have this division. Communism is based on a definition of two opposite polarities, capitalism, and the opposite is communism. There is supposedly some historical necessity that will bring societies towards a state of communism. If there was some law of nature (given that the communists do not recognize any God) that inevitably would bring society towards a communist state, why does that law of nature need help from people who are willing to kill other people in order to force them to become communists? Why is it necessary for human beings to intervene and force other human beings in order to achieve something that these human beings claim is based on either the laws of nature, or the existence of some superior God?

If there is a superior God, why would that God need help from human beings on earth? Why would he need some human beings on earth to force other human beings to come into that religion? If there is a law of nature that inevitably moves human society towards communism, why does that law of nature need help from violent revolutionaries? It makes no sense when you see it. Of course, most people do not see it because of the distortion created by the fallen beings over time, and because of the duality consciousness that causes people to suspend their better judgment, to suspend their discernment, because they are focused on one polarity being good, which automatically makes the opposite polarity evil.

Now my beloved, you can look back at the world and world history, and you can see that the religions, the political ideologies, many of the philosophies that were created, were created by the fallen beings in order to manipulate, deceive and control human beings, the human population. This is true for the Catholic religion, Islam and many other religions. It is true for Marxism, but even so for what you might call a capitalist ideology. It is certainly true for many of the philosophers you have seen out there, even though not all of them have been completely blinded by the fallen beings.

Escaping the propaganda apparatus

What is it that can help people escape this? There are two main movements in the world that can help people escape this propaganda of the fallen beings, this deception of the fallen beings. The one that has always been available has been mysticism. Mysticism is not religion, mysticism is a direct experience of something that is beyond the dualistic state of consciousness. We have given you teachings that you have a Conscious You that is able to step outside of your four lower bodies, and therefore have an experience of some higher reality. Throughout the ages, even without having this concept, various people have had mystical experiences, and these mystical experiences are neutral, they are not dualistic.

Now, as we have just said, it is possible that people can come back from a mystical experience, start interpreting it with their outer minds, and therefore even claim that they have had some genuine revelation from God that shows that their religion is the true one, and that God wants them to kill all non-believers. This has happened in a few cases, although I would say that in these cases, these people did not have a true mystical experience. They did have an experience of something beyond their normal level of consciousness, but it did not come from the ascended realm, it came from the mental realm or the lower identity realm. These people had an experience of contacting what we might call the false hierarchy impostors of ascended masters instead of the genuine ascended masters. We of course never have and never will encourage violence, and will never ever give anybody an experience, teaching or interpretation that can be used to justify the killing of other human beings.

Mysticism has been one way to escape the propaganda, the deception of the fallen beings. Another one that has been released by us in modern times, and that has been available in past ages, is science. Science, in its pure original form, is an attempt to go beyond all theories, all religions, all ideologies, all philosophies. In other words, you are not looking at a theory of how the world *should* work, or how you would like the world to work. You are looking at concrete, practical observations and you are trying to find out: "How does the world *actually* work?" This is science in its pure form. This is what Saint Germain released as Francis Bacon, Roger Bacon and from the ascended state.

Of course, the fallen beings are always quick to take anything that catches on and seek to pervert it. They have attempted to pervert science by creating this quasi-religious, quasi-political overlay called materialism. Materialism has nothing more to do with pure science than organized religion has to do with pure mysticism. We can say that organized religion is the fallen beings' attempting to pervert the mystical aspect of life and materialism is the fallen beings' attempt to pervert the scientific aspects.

If you have a combination of mysticism and scientific observation, then you actually have a quite powerful method for freeing yourself from the illusions of the fallen beings. This is what a growing number of people are beginning to realize. They may not call it mysticism, they may call it intuition, they may say that human beings have two faculties, two abilities, that allow them to go beyond the ideologies, the theories.

Freeing people from division

If you look at the ideologies and the theories, whether they are religious, political or philosophical, they are in most cases based on what we have called the rational mind, the linear mind, the intellectual mind. This is the mind that is a comparative mind. It always wants to compare anything new to something known. On top of that, you have the mind that is not rational in a neutral way, but imposes that value judgment where what is known is true or good; and that which differs from what is known and accepted is therefore false, bad or evil.

By using a combination of intuitive insights, intuitive flashes, and the scientific observations of how the world seems to work, you have a powerful process for raising society beyond all of these illusions that have been created. It is not necessary that people know about fallen beings because there are enough people already who have sensed that there are illusions in the world. There are people who are beginning to realize that, even though they have so far been focused on how the Catholic church during the Middle Ages created all of these erroneous and superstitious doctrines, religion is not the only source of such superstition. Philosophies and ideologies can also be erroneous and out of touch with how the world actually works.

There are many people, and there is this tension in the collective consciousness that has been building, where the calls of a relative small number of ascended masters students can trigger a shift so that people become aware that it is necessary to step up and become more conscious of how we use this process of combining scientific observation with intuitive insights. We need to figure out how the world actually works, not only the material world, but also how the world is actually constructed.

As Saint Germain talked about in one of the answers to your questions, scientific observations have already been made that demonstrate that there must be a realm beyond the material world, that there must be energy in this realm and that this energy can enter the material world. Right there, you see the need to have a combination of neutral scientific observation (what they call "objective" scientific observation) combined with these intuitive insights in order to bring forth the technology that will free humanity from this lower form of energy that can so easily be monopolized by corporations, or even a state, and therefore used as a weapon to restrict the people.

Free energy technology

My beloved, let me give you a vision of what will happen in a matter of decades, perhaps only a few decades, when there is a breakthrough in what they call free energy but which I would prefer to call non-material energy. Imagine that you have a society where energy is completely free, there is no cost associated with obtaining energy. Every house has a little box that is hooked up to the electrical system, and that box produces electricity. There is a cost associated with producing the box, but it can be produced in such a way that it will last a long time. Once you have bought that box, there is no ongoing cost of producing the energy. It simply just appears. It comes out of the box, it is an out-of-the-box experience as a result of out-of-box thinking. Imagine what that will do. Do you remember, some of you, your parents telling you to turn off the light when you leave your room? Well, that will not be necessary in the future. You can leave the light on night and day. You can keep the temperature in your house constant summer and winter because there is no cost of heating or air conditioning. More than that, do you need to live in an area where they have run electrical lines to your house? No, you do not, so you can move anywhere you want.

You can, for that matter, build a house that floats on the water and you still have electricity in that house. You can build a boat that has an electrical generator that runs an electrical motor that powers the propeller, and you can sail around the world at no cost. You can have Internet connection wherever you are because that will also be the new technology. You can sit in your boat out on the ocean somewhere while you are doing your work on the Internet and making a living that way.

Now, imagine how you have cars that also have a small box that produces electricity that drives an electric engine. Therefore, you can go anywhere you want. There is no cost associated with transportation. This would mean that you could, for example, live out in the countryside and still work in the city because there would not be any cost of going back and forth. Even more than that, people would have a whole new view of their possibilities. Travel would become much less expensive.

Of course, when you have free energy, you will also, very shortly afterwards, have the release of technology whereby the free energy can actually be used to create devices that can suspend gravity. Therefore, you do not need a car that drives on the road. You can have a car where you push a button, and the free energy drives a device that makes the car float into the air, and it can now travel through the air.

Imagine that the main transportation vehicle that people have does not have to drive on the surface of the earth. You do not need roads, you do not have congestion because vehicles can travel at multiple levels. If it is too congested at the level of 10 to 15 meters above the surface, you just go up to 20 to 25 meters and there is much less traffic there.

Imagine also that you have vehicles that are of course driver-less as what they are experimenting on now with cars. Because these vehicles can move up and down, not just back and forth, it is much easier to avoid collisions. You can get in your car, enter on a screen your destination, and then you can sit back and do whatever you want to do while you are being transported there. You can take a nap, you can work on your Internet even though computers will also be much more sophisticated.

Therefore, vast new opportunities open up. Look at the city of Seoul where you have these high-rise buildings where people work in offices.

They live in other high-rise buildings that, for some reason that no one really understands, are located many kilometers from the high rises where people work. This means that people have to travel back and forth with the congestion either in trains or subways or in cars, and so much time is spent on going back and forth from home to work. Imagine that this has been replaced by first of all better transportation that makes it easier to travel to your workplace. In the longer run, societies will be much more spread out. There will not be the large cities you have today where it is necessary to build up, because people can live either further from their work because of easier transportation, or their workplaces can be decentralized so that people can actually live closer to their workplace. These are just some examples of what will happen, not what *can* happen, but what *will* happen as humanity begins to rise above the vision of the fallen beings.

Nothing has gone wrong with the universe

Now, I said that the modus operandi of the fallen beings is to create a vision that creates division, but the division has many levels. Division is not just that you create a division between different groups of people. You also create a division between the individual and his or her higher self, and of course, between human beings in embodiment and the ascended masters. This division is actually what creates limitations. Do you understand that, as I said in the beginning, the Creator of this universe was indeed able to create a universe that has a set of universal principles or laws that are guiding this universe in the direction that the Creator envisioned and defined. The universe works perfectly well.

We know very well that we are always facing the delicate balance of what kind of revelation people are ready for. We know that when we started giving direct revelation through messengers in earlier decades, people were still so attached to the old ways of looking at life. They thought that the current conditions on earth, the warfare, the poverty, the disease, the limited lifespan, that all of these conditions showed that something must have gone wrong somewhere. We have talked about how avatars from a natural planet looked upon earth and reasoned that something must have gone wrong and someone needed to go to earth to help improve conditions.

Many, many people on earth have also been subject to this illusion created by the fallen beings that the current misery and suffering on earth proves that something has gone wrong with God's plan for the universe.

That is precisely why these people who claim to have a connection to the one true God are the ones who need to help humanity get out of the misery and correct what has gone wrong, using force if necessary. Because when something has gone wrong, it is justified to kill the people who are opposing the move back towards the way God wants it to be.

The universe is self-correcting

This of course is a complete illusion. The reality is that God has created, as we have explained to you many times now, a universe that has a certain set of laws that are self-correcting. The universe is self-correcting. God has created an un-ascended sphere (or at least the ascended masters in the previous sphere created this un-ascended sphere) and sent people in there with a limited self-awareness but unlimited free-will. It was foreseeable that, at least on some planets in this sphere, people would take the planet into a downward spiral. That is why there is defined a set of laws, and one of the obvious ones is what we have called the second law of thermodynamics (because we refer to science, even though there is much more to this law). One of these self-correcting laws is the principle described by the second law of thermodynamics where a closed system breaks down.

Humankind, with the manipulation of the fallen beings, but even before the advent of the fallen beings, had turned the earth into a closed system and that is why things have broken down on earth. It is not God's design that there is misery, warfare, suffering and disease on earth. It is a result of the collective consciousness becoming a closed system, and therefore activating the self-correcting law of the universe, which breaks down that which is created in an imbalanced state.

You understand that there is a worldly view of balance and there is a higher view of balance. As we have said, duality divides everything into two polarities. There are some people who have risen in awareness where they have become aware that it is not right that there are always two polarities that are opposing each other. As they begin to see this, they do not quite see beyond the dualistic consciousness so they think that balance means to find some midpoint between the two extremes.

The higher view of balance is that you transcend the dualistic consciousness so that you are not pulled in opposite directions by the dualistic polarities. This is what the Buddha taught 2,500 years ago, as it could be taught back then based on the collective consciousness. There are people who are beginning to realize the need to step up to a higher level, to go beyond these opposites. There is a tension in the collective consciousness where people can quickly rise. They can make the shift and recognize that when you use scientific observation (*neutral* scientific observation) and intuitive insight, you can realize that there is a law (whether you call it a law of God or law of nature is immaterial because the law is immaterial), and it has an effect in the material universe of causing that which is unbalanced to break down.

This law was activated by the Soviet Union and caused it to break down. This law was activated by the Catholic church and caused it to break down, although it took a long time. The same law was activated by the Roman Empire and caused it to break down. The same law has been activated by a capitalist economy that allows these corporations to grow larger and larger. The same law has been activated by materialist science, which has produced nuclear weapons but not really solved any of the basic issues facing humanity.

An objective look at history

It is possible, within a short time span, for people to make the shift and realize that any society that is based on an unbalanced vision will self-destruct. Therefore, we need to take a neutral, objective look at our societies and at history. We need to look at what it is that causes a civilization or society to break down. What are the mechanisms?

We need to then look neutrally at our own societies and use scientific observation and intuitive insights to see where we have those same characteristics that we can see in the dictatorships that have already broken down, or that even exist today but have various issues. Do we have some of the same mechanisms in our society? Then, we can neutrally observe that if we allow these mechanisms to continue, then our societies will break down. It is inevitable because we are dealing with a law of nature.

Again, people do not have to recognize the presence of ascended masters. They do not have to believe in all of the many things that you have come to accept. They just have to observe: "How does life actually work?" What we are saying is that right now, the tension has been built to a critical point in the collective consciousness. There is still that surface tension that is preventing the water from spilling over the edge of the glass. That surface tension is the elaborate deception of the fallen beings that has hypnotized most people so they cannot – even though they are looking straight at the naked emperor – they cannot see that he has nothing on.

This can shift almost in the blink of an eye. One of the factors that can cause it to shift is that you make the calls based on these dictations and teachings we have given. When more and more people start using these tools, then it can produce these shifts. All of a sudden, as we have explained to you before has happened many times in history, there is a shift where first, the top ten percent of the people start recognizing it, and then gradually it spreads until most of the people have recognized the new reality. They see the deception, they see how completely unreal it was. They see a higher understanding that can take society to the next step up.

Producing a shift in people's awareness

Now my beloved, one of the main perversions put out by the fallen beings throughout the ages is that they define a certain thought system—a religion, a political ideology, a philosophy or scientific materialism. Then, they say that this now represents the ultimate truth, the ultimate knowledge, the ultimate understanding of how the world works. We have not claimed, at least in this dispensation, through this messenger, that we of the ascended masters have given you the ultimate truth with the teachings we have given you and the teachings we are giving you today. We are giving you what we evaluate can be given based on the present level of the collective consciousness. We are not concerned about giving an ultimate truth that can be expressed in words because no ultimate truth could ever be expressed in words. The ultimate truth can only be gained as a result of an intuitive experience, but it cannot be truly gained until you approach the 144th level of consciousness. Even then, you will not have the same kind of vision that you will have when you ascend.

We are not concerned about ultimate truth here. We are not concerned about society coming to recognize some ultimate truth, even an ascended master teaching. We are concerned about producing a series of shifts so that people come up to a higher awareness that brings life forward. We have told you before there was a shift that ended slavery. There was a shift that ushered in the democratic era. There was a shift that caused people to stop believing in Catholic doctrines about the earth being the center of the universe, and instead accepting that the earth is not flat, the earth is round, it revolves on its axis, and it revolves around the sun. These are the kind of shifts we are looking to produce. Therefore, we are asking you as ascended masters students, to focus your attention and your energy on producing those kind of shifts.

In previous ascended master dispensations we have seen how people became fixated on this vision that one day, the world would acknowledge their particular ascended master messenger and teaching as the ultimate truth. Therefore, they themselves would be looked at as the heroes that brought in a new age, as they think people today look at the disciples of Jesus as being so special. My beloved, if you have any trace of this consciousness in your being, you should know that it comes from a separate self. You should know that this separate self will prevent you from being the open door for bringing forth the change we are wanting to bring forth. Therefore, let that self die. I challenge you, ascended master students, to realize that this consciousness comes from a separate self.

It does not matter where it came from, it does not matter how long you have had it, it eventually traces back to your birth trauma. The fact is that you can come to see that it is a separate self. You can come to look at it, and see that it is not the real you, that it limits you. It limits what you can do for the ascended masters because you cannot be an open door as long as you have that separate self. Therefore, you can come to see: "I no longer want this self in my life experience." You can spontaneously come to feel, as many of you have already experienced with other separate selves, that you are just letting it go, you are just giving that up, you are just letting that separate self die. You are realizing that the problem that the separate self projects is not a real problem, that the solution that the separate self projects is not a real solution.

The problem in the world is not that people are not students of the ascended masters. The solution to the world's problems is not that all people become conscious students of the ascended masters. The problem in the world is a lower state of consciousness. The solution is a shift to a higher state of consciousness, which will happen gradually.

The claim to have the ultimate truth

My beloved, look at all the religions created by the fallen beings. Look how they have made the claim that they have the ultimate truth. Well, if they had the ultimate truth, should they not have been able to solve all of the world's problems? The Catholic church dominated the life of Europe for almost a thousand years. If they had the ultimate truth, should they not have solved all of your problems in that time? But did they? Nay! They only made those problems worse, which anyone can see by looking at history.

Do you really think that we of the ascended masters are as ignorant as the fallen beings? Do you really think that we want to create the same kind of religion as the fallen beings have created many times? Do you really think that we look at the world's problems and the solution the same way as the fallen beings do? Well, of course you do not. But many of you have a separate self that does think that way because you have been so affected over many lifetimes by the deceptions of the fallen beings.

Therefore, I simply say, it is time for you as ascended master students to step up and to let go of these dreams. This is something that actually has been created over the last decades by ascended master students who have fed their energy and attention into this, creating a beast. It is not nearly as powerful as the Catholic beast, but nevertheless, it is a beast that prevents many ascended master students from stepping up to the higher level and grasping our true vision of how change can happen. Let go of it in yourself, make the calls for the shattering of these illusions.

If you go beyond the ascended master students, you see how many people in the world have created other beasts that are programmed from the belief that there is one solution to all problems, and that solution is to spread a particular religion, a particular ideology, or scientific materialism. My beloved, there is a huge beast (or rather, a conglomerate of beasts) in the world, based on this very idea that there is one solution, one truth, and the solution to all of the world's problems is to get all people to accept that truth by following this outer thought system.

Anchoring a Flame of Vision

I, Cyclopea, am anchoring a flame of the Fifth Ray in the physical octave in no specific location, because it is omnipresent in the physical octave. It is a flame that will, as people are willing to step up and as you make the calls, shatter this matrix, consume these beasts in the collective consciousness, so that humankind can be free of this entire idea that there is one solution to all problems—and it is to make all people come into a specific thought system, whether by hook or by crook, or by force, or by persuasion, or deception, or whatever they use to justify it.

There is no need to force other people. It is only people who do not have truth who think there is a need to force others. Because when you have truth, you realize what we have told you, that change on earth can be produced without forcing other people. It can be produced by making use of free will and the laws that are set up to make the universe a self-correcting entity, a self-correcting being. You have proven as ascended masters students that you individually have been willing to self-correct. That is why you have embraced these teachings that are in their essence, all about helping you self-correct.

With this, I take great joy in having been able to deliver this address. I am grateful that you have been willing to be here, and I am grateful that even though this is in the late afternoon, you have still been willing to listen, to serve as the broadcast stations, even though I know that your stomachs have been projecting at you: "When is dinner coming? When is he going to stop talking so we can get dinner? I am empty. I want to be filled." Well, my beloved. Your spirits have been filled, now go and fill your bellies as well.

11 | INVOKING A VISION OF WHAT IS BEHIND DICTATORS

In the name of the I AM THAT I AM, Jesus Christ, I use the authority that I have as a being in embodiment on earth to call upon Cyclopea to reinforce my calls and use my chakras to project the statements in this invocation into the collective consciousness and awaken people to the perverted vision behind all dictators. Awaken people to the reality that we are spiritual beings and that we can co-create a new future by working with the ascended masters. I especially call for …

[Make your own calls here.]

Part 1

1. Cyclopea, shatter the energetic matrix that prevents people from seeing that some dictators consider themselves great because they have an agenda that they believe will improve conditions for humanity.

Cyclopea so dear, the truth you reveal,
the truth that duality's ailments will heal,

your Emerald Light is like a great balm,
our emotional bodies are perfectly calm.

Cyclopea so dear, in Emerald Sphere,
in raising perception we shall persevere,
as deep in our hearts your truth we revere,
to immaculate vision the earth does adhere.

2. Cyclopea, shatter the energetic matrix that prevents people from seeing that some dictators are focused on themselves and getting power and position for themselves.

Cyclopea so dear, with you we unwind,
all negative spirals clouding the mind,
we know pure awareness is truly our core,
the key to becoming the wide-open door.

Cyclopea so dear, in Emerald Sphere,
in raising perception we shall persevere,
as deep in our hearts your truth we revere,
to immaculate vision the earth does adhere.

3. Cyclopea, shatter the energetic matrix that prevents people from seeing that behind dictators, there is a perversion of vision, there is a perverted vision.

Cyclopea so dear, clear our inner sight,
empowered, we pierce the soul's fearful night,
we now see our life through your single eye,
beyond all disease we're ready to fly.

Cyclopea so dear, in Emerald Sphere,
in raising perception we shall persevere,
as deep in our hearts your truth we revere,
to immaculate vision the earth does adhere.

4. Cyclopea, shatter the energetic matrix behind the machine that the fallen beings have created in the physical, emotional, mental and identity

realm, this complex apparatus that is aimed at producing false and distorted visions and spreading them on earth.

Cyclopea so dear, life can only reflect,
the images that the mind does project,
the key to our healing is clearing the mind,
from the images the ego is hiding behind.

Cyclopea so dear, in Emerald Sphere,
in raising perception we shall persevere,
as deep in our hearts your truth we revere,
to immaculate vision the earth does adhere.

5. Cyclopea, shatter the energetic matrix behind the machine that is designed to get people to believe in something that is false, obscure the truth, take any higher statement and perverting it, or coming up with an opposite that seems to challenge it.

Cyclopea so dear, we want to aim high,
to your healing flame we ever draw nigh,
through veils of duality we now take flight,
bathed in your penetrating Emerald Light.

Cyclopea so dear, in Emerald Sphere,
in raising perception we shall persevere,
as deep in our hearts your truth we revere,
to immaculate vision the earth does adhere.

6. Cyclopea, shatter the energetic matrix behind this elaborate, and complex apparatus and the aggressive intent behind it.

Cyclopea so dear, your Emerald Flame,
exposes every subtle, dualistic power game,
including the game of wanting to say,
that truth is defined in only one way.

Cyclopea so dear, in Emerald Sphere,
in raising perception we shall persevere,

as deep in our hearts your truth we revere,
to immaculate vision the earth does adhere.

7. Cyclopea, shatter the energetic matrix that prevents people from seeing this machinery and the aggressive intent behind it, so they can be awakened to the need to purify their vision and see through the elaborate deceptions created by the fallen beings throughout the ages.

> Cyclopea so dear, we're feeling the flow,
> as your Living Truth upon us you bestow,
> from all dual vision we are now set free,
> planet earth in immaculate matrix will be.

> **Cyclopea so dear, in Emerald Sphere,**
> **in raising perception we shall persevere,**
> **as deep in our hearts your truth we revere,**
> **to immaculate vision the earth does adhere.**

8. Cyclopea, shatter the energetic matrix that prevents people from seeing that the purpose behind the false vision created by the fallen beings is the divide-and-conquer strategy.

> Cyclopea so dear, the truth is now clear,
> we see higher purpose for which we are here
> we know truth transcends all systems below,
> immersed in your light, we continue to grow.

> **Cyclopea so dear, in Emerald Sphere,**
> **in raising perception we shall persevere,**
> **as deep in our hearts your truth we revere,**
> **to immaculate vision the earth does adhere.**

9. Cyclopea, shatter the energetic matrix that prevents people from seeing that the fallen beings are always trying to create a *vision* that creates *di-vision*. The fallen beings have used anything that happens in an attempt to create division.

> Cyclopea so dear, we're feeling your joy,
> as creative vision we now do employ,

in lifting earth out of serpentine cage,
to manifest Saint Germain's Golden Age.

**Cyclopea so dear, in Emerald Sphere,
in raising perception we shall persevere,
as deep in our hearts your truth we revere,
to immaculate vision the earth does adhere.**

Part 2

1. Cyclopea, shatter the energetic matrix that prevents people from seeing that religion throughout the ages has been used to create division.

Cyclopea so dear, the truth you reveal,
the truth that duality's ailments will heal,
your Emerald Light is like a great balm,
our emotional bodies are perfectly calm.

**Cyclopea so dear, in Emerald Sphere,
in raising perception we shall persevere,
as deep in our hearts your truth we revere,
to immaculate vision the earth does adhere.**

2. Cyclopea, shatter the energetic matrix that prevents people from seeing that it is not necessary that a particular religion defines a clear dividing line between those who are followers of that religion and those who are outside.

Cyclopea so dear, with you we unwind,
all negative spirals clouding the mind,
we know pure awareness is truly our core,
the key to becoming the wide-open door.

**Cyclopea so dear, in Emerald Sphere,
in raising perception we shall persevere,
as deep in our hearts your truth we revere,
to immaculate vision the earth does adhere.**

3. Cyclopea, shatter the energetic matrix that prevents people from seeing that many religions have claimed they have a truth given directly by the ultimate God, the superior God of the universe.

Cyclopea so dear, clear our inner sight,
empowered, we pierce the soul's fearful night,
we now see our life through your single eye,
beyond all disease we're ready to fly.

**Cyclopea so dear, in Emerald Sphere,
in raising perception we shall persevere,
as deep in our hearts your truth we revere,
to immaculate vision the earth does adhere.**

4. Cyclopea, shatter the energetic matrix that prevents people from seeing that the ultimate God is able to create a universe where all people would be saved.

Cyclopea so dear, life can only reflect,
the images that the mind does project,
the key to our healing is clearing the mind,
from the images the ego is hiding behind.

**Cyclopea so dear, in Emerald Sphere,
in raising perception we shall persevere,
as deep in our hearts your truth we revere,
to immaculate vision the earth does adhere.**

5. Cyclopea, shatter the energetic matrix that prevents people from seeing that an ultimate God would not create different groups of people, and some would be saved and some would not.

Cyclopea so dear, we want to aim high,
to your healing flame we ever draw nigh,
through veils of duality we now take flight,
bathed in your penetrating Emerald Light.

**Cyclopea so dear, in Emerald Sphere,
in raising perception we shall persevere,**

as deep in our hearts your truth we revere,
to immaculate vision the earth does adhere.

6. Cyclopea, shatter the energetic matrix that prevents people from seeing that the ultimate God should be able to create a universe where there is a set of universal laws that causes the universe to unfold as God envisions.

Cyclopea so dear, your Emerald Flame,
exposes every subtle, dualistic power game,
including the game of wanting to say,
that truth is defined in only one way.

Cyclopea so dear, in Emerald Sphere,
in raising perception we shall persevere,
as deep in our hearts your truth we revere,
to immaculate vision the earth does adhere.

7. Cyclopea, shatter the energetic matrix that prevents people from seeing that the ultimate God does not need a religion on earth if the God has already defined universal principles that are causing the universe to grow as God wants it to grow.

Cyclopea so dear, we're feeling the flow,
as your Living Truth upon us you bestow,
from all dual vision we are now set free,
planet earth in immaculate matrix will be.

Cyclopea so dear, in Emerald Sphere,
in raising perception we shall persevere,
as deep in our hearts your truth we revere,
to immaculate vision the earth does adhere.

8. Cyclopea, shatter the energetic matrix that prevents people from seeing that the claim behind most religions is that something went wrong with God's creation, and therefore as an emergency measure, people need to be saved. In order to be saved, they have to follow the one and only true religion.

Cyclopea so dear, the truth is now clear,
we see higher purpose for which we are here
we know truth transcends all systems below,
immersed in your light, we continue to grow.

Cyclopea so dear, in Emerald Sphere,
in raising perception we shall persevere,
as deep in our hearts your truth we revere,
to immaculate vision the earth does adhere.

9. Cyclopea, shatter the energetic matrix that prevents people from seeing that an ultimate God would not need to create a fiery hell in order to punish people. Many religions create, by the very essence of their teachings, this fundamental division between those who will be saved and those who will not.

Cyclopea so dear, we're feeling your joy,
as creative vision we now do employ,
in lifting earth out of serpentine cage,
to manifest Saint Germain's Golden Age.

Cyclopea so dear, in Emerald Sphere,
in raising perception we shall persevere,
as deep in our hearts your truth we revere,
to immaculate vision the earth does adhere.

Part 3

1. Cyclopea, shatter the energetic matrix that prevents people from seeing that many political ideologies also create a fundamental division. Communism is based on a definition of two opposite polarities, capitalism and communism.

Cyclopea so dear, the truth you reveal,
the truth that duality's ailments will heal,
your Emerald Light is like a great balm,
our emotional bodies are perfectly calm.

Cyclopea so dear, in Emerald Sphere,
in raising perception we shall persevere,
as deep in our hearts your truth we revere,
to immaculate vision the earth does adhere.

2. Cyclopea, shatter the energetic matrix that prevents people from seeing that if there was some law of nature that inevitably would bring society towards a communist state, why does that law of nature need help from people who are willing to kill other people in order to force them to become communists?

Cyclopea so dear, with you we unwind,
all negative spirals clouding the mind,
we know pure awareness is truly our core,
the key to becoming the wide-open door.

Cyclopea so dear, in Emerald Sphere,
in raising perception we shall persevere,
as deep in our hearts your truth we revere,
to immaculate vision the earth does adhere.

3. Cyclopea, shatter the energetic matrix that prevents people from seeing that it is not necessary for some people to intervene and force others in order to achieve something that these people claim is based on either the laws of nature or the existence of some superior God.

Cyclopea so dear, clear our inner sight,
empowered, we pierce the soul's fearful night,
we now see our life through your single eye,
beyond all disease we're ready to fly.

Cyclopea so dear, in Emerald Sphere,
in raising perception we shall persevere,
as deep in our hearts your truth we revere,
to immaculate vision the earth does adhere.

4. Cyclopea, shatter the energetic matrix that prevents people from seeing that if there is a law of nature that inevitably moves human society towards communism, why does that law need help from violent revolutionaries?

Cyclopea so dear, life can only reflect,
the images that the mind does project,
the key to our healing is clearing the mind,
from the images the ego is hiding behind.

Cyclopea so dear, in Emerald Sphere,
in raising perception we shall persevere,
as deep in our hearts your truth we revere,
to immaculate vision the earth does adhere.

5. Cyclopea, shatter the energetic matrix of distortion created by the fallen beings based on the duality consciousness that causes people to suspend their better judgment because they are focused on one polarity being good, which automatically makes the opposite polarity evil.

Cyclopea so dear, we want to aim high,
to your healing flame we ever draw nigh,
through veils of duality we now take flight,
bathed in your penetrating Emerald Light.

Cyclopea so dear, in Emerald Sphere,
in raising perception we shall persevere,
as deep in our hearts your truth we revere,
to immaculate vision the earth does adhere.

6. Cyclopea, shatter the energetic matrix that prevents people from seeing that religions, political ideologies and many philosophies were created by the fallen beings in order to manipulate, deceive and control the human population.

Cyclopea so dear, your Emerald Flame,
exposes every subtle, dualistic power game,
including the game of wanting to say,
that truth is defined in only one way.

Cyclopea so dear, in Emerald Sphere,
in raising perception we shall persevere,
as deep in our hearts your truth we revere,
to immaculate vision the earth does adhere.

7. Cyclopea, shatter the energetic matrix that prevents people from seeing that one of the two main movements that can help people escape this propaganda of the fallen beings is mysticism.

> Cyclopea so dear, we're feeling the flow,
> as your Living Truth upon us you bestow,
> from all dual vision we are now set free,
> planet earth in immaculate matrix will be.

> **Cyclopea so dear, in Emerald Sphere,**
> **in raising perception we shall persevere,**
> **as deep in our hearts your truth we revere,**
> **to immaculate vision the earth does adhere.**

8. Cyclopea, shatter the energetic matrix that prevents people from seeing that mysticism is not religion, mysticism is a direct experience of something that is beyond the dualistic state of consciousness.

> Cyclopea so dear, the truth is now clear,
> we see higher purpose for which we are here
> we know truth transcends all systems below,
> immersed in your light, we continue to grow.

> **Cyclopea so dear, in Emerald Sphere,**
> **in raising perception we shall persevere,**
> **as deep in our hearts your truth we revere,**
> **to immaculate vision the earth does adhere.**

9. Cyclopea, shatter the energetic matrix that prevents people from seeing that it is possible that people can come back from a so-called mystical experience, start interpreting it with their outer minds, and therefore claim God said their religion is the true one and that he wants them to kill all non-believers.

> Cyclopea so dear, we're feeling your joy,
> as creative vision we now do employ,
> in lifting earth out of serpentine cage,
> to manifest Saint Germain's Golden Age.

**Cyclopea so dear, in Emerald Sphere,
in raising perception we shall persevere,
as deep in our hearts your truth we revere,
to immaculate vision the earth does adhere.**

Part 4

1. Cyclopea, shatter the energetic matrix that prevents people from seeing that the other way to escape the propaganda of the fallen beings is science. Science, in its original form, is an attempt to go beyond all theories, religions, ideologies and philosophies.

Cyclopea so dear, the truth you reveal,
the truth that duality's ailments will heal,
your Emerald Light is like a great balm,
our emotional bodies are perfectly calm.

**Cyclopea so dear, in Emerald Sphere,
in raising perception we shall persevere,
as deep in our hearts your truth we revere,
to immaculate vision the earth does adhere.**

2. Cyclopea, shatter the energetic matrix that prevents people from seeing that through pure science we are not looking at a theory of how the world *should* work, or how we would like the world to work. We are looking at concrete, practical observations, and we are trying to find out how the world actually works.

Cyclopea so dear, with you we unwind,
all negative spirals clouding the mind,
we know pure awareness is truly our core,
the key to becoming the wide-open door.

**Cyclopea so dear, in Emerald Sphere,
in raising perception we shall persevere,
as deep in our hearts your truth we revere,
to immaculate vision the earth does adhere.**

3. Cyclopea, shatter the energetic matrix that prevents people from seeing that the fallen beings have attempted to pervert science by creating this quasi-religious, quasi-political overlay called materialism.

> Cyclopea so dear, clear our inner sight,
> empowered, we pierce the soul's fearful night,
> we now see our life through your single eye,
> beyond all disease we're ready to fly.

> **Cyclopea so dear, in Emerald Sphere,**
> **in raising perception we shall persevere,**
> **as deep in our hearts your truth we revere,**
> **to immaculate vision the earth does adhere.**

4. Cyclopea, shatter the energetic matrix that prevents people from seeing that materialism has nothing more to do with pure science than organized religion has to do with pure mysticism. Organized religion is the fallen beings' attempting to pervert the mystical aspect of life, and materialism is their attempt to pervert the scientific aspect.

> Cyclopea so dear, life can only reflect,
> the images that the mind does project,
> the key to our healing is clearing the mind,
> from the images the ego is hiding behind.

> **Cyclopea so dear, in Emerald Sphere,**
> **in raising perception we shall persevere,**
> **as deep in our hearts your truth we revere,**
> **to immaculate vision the earth does adhere.**

5. Cyclopea, shatter the energetic matrix that prevents people from seeing that through a combination of mysticism and scientific observation, we have a powerful method for freeing ourselves from the illusions of the fallen beings. We have two faculties that allow us to go beyond ideologies and theories.

> Cyclopea so dear, we want to aim high,
> to your healing flame we ever draw nigh,

through veils of duality we now take flight,
bathed in your penetrating Emerald Light.

Cyclopea so dear, in Emerald Sphere,
in raising perception we shall persevere,
as deep in our hearts your truth we revere,
to immaculate vision the earth does adhere.

6. Cyclopea, shatter the energetic matrix that prevents people from seeing that most ideologies and theories are based on the rational, linear, intellectual mind.

Cyclopea so dear, your Emerald Flame,
exposes every subtle, dualistic power game,
including the game of wanting to say,
that truth is defined in only one way.

Cyclopea so dear, in Emerald Sphere,
in raising perception we shall persevere,
as deep in our hearts your truth we revere,
to immaculate vision the earth does adhere.

7. Cyclopea, shatter the energetic matrix that prevents people from seeing that the rational mind is a comparative mind. It always wants to compare anything new to something known.

Cyclopea so dear, we're feeling the flow,
as your Living Truth upon us you bestow,
from all dual vision we are now set free,
planet earth in immaculate matrix will be.

Cyclopea so dear, in Emerald Sphere,
in raising perception we shall persevere,
as deep in our hearts your truth we revere,
to immaculate vision the earth does adhere.

8. Cyclopea, shatter the energetic matrix that prevents people from seeing that the relative mind is not rational in a neutral way. It imposes a value

judgment where what is known is true or good; and anything different from what is accepted is false, bad or evil.

Cyclopea so dear, the truth is now clear,
we see higher purpose for which we are here
we know truth transcends all systems below,
immersed in your light, we continue to grow.

Cyclopea so dear, in Emerald Sphere,
in raising perception we shall persevere,
as deep in our hearts your truth we revere,
to immaculate vision the earth does adhere.

9. Cyclopea, shatter the energetic matrix that prevents people from seeing that by using a combination of intuitive insights and scientific observations of how the world seems to work, we have a powerful process for raising society beyond all of the illusions that have been created.

Cyclopea so dear, we're feeling your joy,
as creative vision we now do employ,
in lifting earth out of serpentine cage,
to manifest Saint Germain's Golden Age.

Cyclopea so dear, in Emerald Sphere,
in raising perception we shall persevere,
as deep in our hearts your truth we revere,
to immaculate vision the earth does adhere.

Part 5

1. Cyclopea, shatter the energetic matrix that prevents people from seeing that even though the Catholic church during the Middle Ages created all of these erroneous and superstitious doctrines, religion is not the only source of such superstition. Philosophies and ideologies can also be erroneous and out of touch with how the world actually works.

Cyclopea so dear, the truth you reveal,
the truth that duality's ailments will heal,
your Emerald Light is like a great balm,
our emotional bodies are perfectly calm.

**Cyclopea so dear, in Emerald Sphere,
in raising perception we shall persevere,
as deep in our hearts your truth we revere,
to immaculate vision the earth does adhere.**

2. Cyclopea, shatter the energetic matrix that prevents people from seeing that it is necessary to become more conscious of how we use the process of combining scientific observation with intuitive insights. We need to figure out how the world actually works, not only the material world, but also how the entire world is constructed.

Cyclopea so dear, with you we unwind,
all negative spirals clouding the mind,
we know pure awareness is truly our core,
the key to becoming the wide-open door.

**Cyclopea so dear, in Emerald Sphere,
in raising perception we shall persevere,
as deep in our hearts your truth we revere,
to immaculate vision the earth does adhere.**

3. Cyclopea, shatter the energetic matrix that prevents people from seeing that scientific observations have already demonstrated that there must be a realm beyond the material world, that there must be energy in this realm and that this energy can enter the material world.

Cyclopea so dear, clear our inner sight,
empowered, we pierce the soul's fearful night,
we now see our life through your single eye,
beyond all disease we're ready to fly.

**Cyclopea so dear, in Emerald Sphere,
in raising perception we shall persevere,**

as deep in our hearts your truth we revere,
to immaculate vision the earth does adhere.

4. Cyclopea, shatter the energetic matrix that prevents people from seeing that we need to use a combination of neutral scientific observation combined with intuitive insights in order to bring forth the technology that will free humanity from this lower form of energy that can so easily be monopolized by corporations, or even a state, and therefore used as a weapon to restrict the people.

Cyclopea so dear, life can only reflect,
the images that the mind does project,
the key to our healing is clearing the mind,
from the images the ego is hiding behind.

Cyclopea so dear, in Emerald Sphere,
in raising perception we shall persevere,
as deep in our hearts your truth we revere,
to immaculate vision the earth does adhere.

5. Cyclopea, shatter the energetic matrix that prevents people from seeing that it is possible to have a society where energy is completely free, there is no cost associated with obtaining energy. Every house has a little box that is hooked up to the electrical system, and that box produces electricity.

Cyclopea so dear, we want to aim high,
to your healing flame we ever draw nigh,
through veils of duality we now take flight,
bathed in your penetrating Emerald Light.

Cyclopea so dear, in Emerald Sphere,
in raising perception we shall persevere,
as deep in our hearts your truth we revere,
to immaculate vision the earth does adhere.

6. Cyclopea, shatter the energetic matrix that prevents people from seeing that free energy can be used to create devices that can suspend gravity. The main transportation vehicle that people will have in the future does not have to drive on the surface of the earth.

Cyclopea so dear, your Emerald Flame,
exposes every subtle, dualistic power game,
including the game of wanting to say,
that truth is defined in only one way.

Cyclopea so dear, in Emerald Sphere,
in raising perception we shall persevere,
as deep in our hearts your truth we revere,
to immaculate vision the earth does adhere.

7. Cyclopea, shatter the energetic matrix that prevents people from seeing that with such technology, societies will be much more spread out. There will not be the large cities because people can live either further from their work or their workplaces can be decentralized.

Cyclopea so dear, we're feeling the flow,
as your Living Truth upon us you bestow,
from all dual vision we are now set free,
planet earth in immaculate matrix will be.

Cyclopea so dear, in Emerald Sphere,
in raising perception we shall persevere,
as deep in our hearts your truth we revere,
to immaculate vision the earth does adhere.

8. Cyclopea, shatter the energetic matrix that prevents people from seeing through the illusion created by the fallen beings that the current misery and suffering on earth proves that something has gone wrong with God's plan for the universe.

Cyclopea so dear, the truth is now clear,
we see higher purpose for which we are here
we know truth transcends all systems below,
immersed in your light, we continue to grow.

Cyclopea so dear, in Emerald Sphere,
in raising perception we shall persevere,
as deep in our hearts your truth we revere,
to immaculate vision the earth does adhere.

9. Cyclopea, shatter the energetic matrix that prevents people from seeing that this is why some people claim they need to help humanity get out of the misery and correct what has gone wrong, using force if necessary. When something has gone wrong, it is justified to kill the people who are opposing the move back towards an ideal state.

> Cyclopea so dear, we're feeling your joy,
> as creative vision we now do employ,
> in lifting earth out of serpentine cage,
> to manifest Saint Germain's Golden Age.

> **Cyclopea so dear, in Emerald Sphere,**
> **in raising perception we shall persevere,**
> **as deep in our hearts your truth we revere,**
> **to immaculate vision the earth does adhere.**

Part 6

1. Cyclopea, shatter the energetic matrix that prevents people from seeing that God has created a universe that has a certain set of laws that are self-correcting. The universe is self-correcting.

> Cyclopea so dear, the truth you reveal,
> the truth that duality's ailments will heal,
> your Emerald Light is like a great balm,
> our emotional bodies are perfectly calm.

> **Cyclopea so dear, in Emerald Sphere,**
> **in raising perception we shall persevere,**
> **as deep in our hearts your truth we revere,**
> **to immaculate vision the earth does adhere.**

2. Cyclopea, shatter the energetic matrix that prevents people from seeing that one such law is the second law of thermodynamics, saying that a closed system will break down.

Cyclopea so dear, with you we unwind,
all negative spirals clouding the mind,
we know pure awareness is truly our core,
the key to becoming the wide-open door.

Cyclopea so dear, in Emerald Sphere,
in raising perception we shall persevere,
as deep in our hearts your truth we revere,
to immaculate vision the earth does adhere.

3. Cyclopea, shatter the energetic matrix that prevents people from seeing that humankind, with the manipulation of the fallen beings, has turned the earth into a closed system and that is why things have broken down on earth.

Cyclopea so dear, clear our inner sight,
empowered, we pierce the soul's fearful night,
we now see our life through your single eye,
beyond all disease we're ready to fly.

Cyclopea so dear, in Emerald Sphere,
in raising perception we shall persevere,
as deep in our hearts your truth we revere,
to immaculate vision the earth does adhere.

4. Cyclopea, shatter the energetic matrix that prevents people from seeing that it is not God's design that there is misery, warfare, suffering and disease on earth. It is a result of the collective consciousness becoming a closed system, and therefore activating the self-correcting law of the universe that breaks down what is created in an imbalanced state.

Cyclopea so dear, life can only reflect,
the images that the mind does project,
the key to our healing is clearing the mind,
from the images the ego is hiding behind.

Cyclopea so dear, in Emerald Sphere,
in raising perception we shall persevere,

as deep in our hearts your truth we revere,
to immaculate vision the earth does adhere.

5. Cyclopea, shatter the energetic matrix that prevents people from seeing that balance does not mean to find some midpoint between two extremes. The higher view of balance is that we transcend the dualistic consciousness so that we are not pulled in opposite directions by opposing polarities.

Cyclopea so dear, we want to aim high,
to your healing flame we ever draw nigh,
through veils of duality we now take flight,
bathed in your penetrating Emerald Light.

Cyclopea so dear, in Emerald Sphere,
in raising perception we shall persevere,
as deep in our hearts your truth we revere,
to immaculate vision the earth does adhere.

6. Cyclopea, shatter the energetic matrix that prevents people from seeing that when we use *neutral* scientific observation and intuitive insight, we see that there is a law, and it has an effect in the material universe of causing that which is unbalanced to break down.

Cyclopea so dear, your Emerald Flame,
exposes every subtle, dualistic power game,
including the game of wanting to say,
that truth is defined in only one way.

Cyclopea so dear, in Emerald Sphere,
in raising perception we shall persevere,
as deep in our hearts your truth we revere,
to immaculate vision the earth does adhere.

7. Cyclopea, shatter the energetic matrix that prevents people from seeing that any society that is based on an unbalanced vision, will self-destruct. Therefore, we need to take a neutral, objective look at our societies and at history. We need to look at what causes a civilization or society to break down.

Cyclopea so dear, we're feeling the flow,
as your Living Truth upon us you bestow,
from all dual vision we are now set free,
planet earth in immaculate matrix will be.

**Cyclopea so dear, in Emerald Sphere,
in raising perception we shall persevere,
as deep in our hearts your truth we revere,
to immaculate vision the earth does adhere.**

8. Cyclopea, shatter the energetic matrix that prevents people from seeing that we need to look neutrally at our own societies and use scientific observation and intuitive insights to see where we have the same characteristics that we can see in the dictatorships that have already broken down.

Cyclopea so dear, the truth is now clear,
we see higher purpose for which we are here
we know truth transcends all systems below,
immersed in your light, we continue to grow.

**Cyclopea so dear, in Emerald Sphere,
in raising perception we shall persevere,
as deep in our hearts your truth we revere,
to immaculate vision the earth does adhere.**

9. Cyclopea, shatter the energetic matrix that prevents people from seeing that if we allow these mechanisms to continue, then our societies will break down. It is inevitable because we are dealing with a law of nature.

Cyclopea so dear, we're feeling your joy,
as creative vision we now do employ,
in lifting earth out of serpentine cage,
to manifest Saint Germain's Golden Age.

**Cyclopea so dear, in Emerald Sphere,
in raising perception we shall persevere,
as deep in our hearts your truth we revere,
to immaculate vision the earth does adhere.**

Part 7

1. Cyclopea, shatter the energetic matrix behind the deception of the fallen beings that has hypnotized most people so they cannot see that the emperor has nothing on.

> Cyclopea so dear, the truth you reveal,
> the truth that duality's ailments will heal,
> your Emerald Light is like a great balm,
> our emotional bodies are perfectly calm.

> **Cyclopea so dear, in Emerald Sphere,**
> **in raising perception we shall persevere,**
> **as deep in our hearts your truth we revere,**
> **to immaculate vision the earth does adhere.**

2. Cyclopea, shatter the energetic matrix that prevents people from making the shift of seeing the deception, seeing how completely unreal it is, seeing a higher understanding that can take society to the next step up.

> Cyclopea so dear, with you we unwind,
> all negative spirals clouding the mind,
> we know pure awareness is truly our core,
> the key to becoming the wide-open door.

> **Cyclopea so dear, in Emerald Sphere,**
> **in raising perception we shall persevere,**
> **as deep in our hearts your truth we revere,**
> **to immaculate vision the earth does adhere.**

3. Cyclopea, shatter the energetic matrix that prevents people from seeing that one of the main perversions used by the fallen beings is to define a certain thought system and then saying that this now represents the ultimate truth, the ultimate knowledge, the ultimate understanding of how the world works.

> Cyclopea so dear, clear our inner sight,
> empowered, we pierce the soul's fearful night,

we now see our life through your single eye,
beyond all disease we're ready to fly.

Cyclopea so dear, in Emerald Sphere,
in raising perception we shall persevere,
as deep in our hearts your truth we revere,
to immaculate vision the earth does adhere.

4. Cyclopea, shatter the energetic matrix that prevents people from seeing that what we currently know is dependent upon the state of the collective consciousness. Only by going through a series of shifts so we come up to a higher awareness, will we bring life forward.

Cyclopea so dear, life can only reflect,
the images that the mind does project,
the key to our healing is clearing the mind,
from the images the ego is hiding behind.

Cyclopea so dear, in Emerald Sphere,
in raising perception we shall persevere,
as deep in our hearts your truth we revere,
to immaculate vision the earth does adhere.

5. Cyclopea, shatter the energetic matrix that prevents people from seeing that the solution to the world's problems is not that all people become followers of a particular thought system. The problem in the world is a lower state of consciousness, and the solution is a shift to a higher state of consciousness.

Cyclopea so dear, we want to aim high,
to your healing flame we ever draw nigh,
through veils of duality we now take flight,
bathed in your penetrating Emerald Light.

Cyclopea so dear, in Emerald Sphere,
in raising perception we shall persevere,
as deep in our hearts your truth we revere,
to immaculate vision the earth does adhere.

6. Cyclopea, shatter the energetic matrix that prevents people from seeing that if a thought system has the ultimate truth, it should have been able to solve all of the world's problems. The Catholic church dominated the life of Europe for almost a thousand years, but it did not solve all of our problems.

Cyclopea so dear, your Emerald Flame,
exposes every subtle, dualistic power game,
including the game of wanting to say,
that truth is defined in only one way.

**Cyclopea so dear, in Emerald Sphere,
in raising perception we shall persevere,
as deep in our hearts your truth we revere,
to immaculate vision the earth does adhere.**

7. Cyclopea, shatter the energetic matrix that has been created by ascended master students who have fed their energy and attention into creating a beast about ascended masters having the ultimate truth. This beast prevents many ascended master students from grasping the true vision of how change can happen.

Cyclopea so dear, we're feeling the flow,
as your Living Truth upon us you bestow,
from all dual vision we are now set free,
planet earth in immaculate matrix will be.

**Cyclopea so dear, in Emerald Sphere,
in raising perception we shall persevere,
as deep in our hearts your truth we revere,
to immaculate vision the earth does adhere.**

8. Cyclopea, shatter the energetic matrix behind the conglomerate of beasts based on the idea that there is one solution, one truth, and the solution to all of the world's problems is to get all people to accept that truth by following this outer thought system.

Cyclopea so dear, the truth is now clear,
we see higher purpose for which we are here

we know truth transcends all systems below,
immersed in your light, we continue to grow.

**Cyclopea so dear, in Emerald Sphere,
in raising perception we shall persevere,
as deep in our hearts your truth we revere,
to immaculate vision the earth does adhere.**

9. Cyclopea, I invoke the flame of the Fifth Ray that you have anchored in the physical octave, and I call for it to shatter this matrix, consume these beasts in the collective consciousness, so that humankind can be free of this entire idea that there is one solution to all problems. Help people see that change on earth can be produced without forcing other people.

Cyclopea so dear, we're feeling your joy,
as creative vision we now do employ,
in lifting earth out of serpentine cage,
to manifest Saint Germain's Golden Age.

**Cyclopea so dear, in Emerald Sphere,
in raising perception we shall persevere,
as deep in our hearts your truth we revere,
to immaculate vision the earth does adhere.**

Sealing

In the name of the I AM THAT I AM, I accept that Archangel Michael, Astrea and Shiva form an impenetrable shield around myself and all constructive people, sealing us from all fear-based energies in all four octaves. I accept that the Light of God is consuming and transforming all fear-based energies that make up the dark forces working against ending the era of dictatorships on earth!

12 | WHY THE ENDS REALLY CANNOT JUSTIFY THE MEANS

I AM the Ascended Master Archangel Uriel. Why is it that almost every dictator you have seen on earth has claimed to be working for the cause of peace, while at the same time preparing to kill or actually killing other human beings? How can killing lead to peace? How can violence lead to peace? This is not logical, unless you use the logic of the fallen beings based on the duality consciousness. Naturally, you will see in the history of the world and in the world today, how many, many people, millions of people, have been pulled into thinking that they could promote the cause of peace through violence and killing. Indeed, they have been led to believe that it was *necessary* for promoting the cause of peace to kill other human beings.

How did the fallen beings achieve this? Well, of course in various ways, as my brothers have explained, through division and in other ways setting the stage. Truly, the basis for this deception is to define a certain standard, which says there are some things that *should* happen on earth and there are some things that *should not* happen on earth.

In past ages you have seen many examples of how a religion has defined a certain standard or a certain goal and then defined that this could only happen if all people became members of that religion. What the religion has claimed is that their standard, the standard they are promoting, is defined by God himself and therefore it is the will of God that this should happen. Therefore, it is the will of God that other people must be converted to the one true religion and if they will not be converted, then it is the will of God that they be forced. If they will not be forced, it is the will of God that they be killed because when all those who oppose the manifestation of God's kingdom on earth have been killed, then supposedly God's kingdom will be manifest on earth.

You have also seen how a political ideology, supposedly based on scientific materialism, has been used to justify the killing of people. As we have already said, if communism, if Marxist ideology, was truly based on some inevitable historic necessity, how could it be necessary to kill those who oppose communism, when it is inevitable anyway? Of course, the logic of the fallen beings has distorted this in such a way that people have been led to believe that in order to bring about this communist utopia, then it is necessary to kill other people.

The ends cannot justify the means

The underlying principle that has been spread by the fallen beings for a very, very long time on earth, from the moment they first set foot here by taking embodiment here, is simply this: "The ends can justify the means." The goal is so important that even the means of forcing or killing other human beings are justified by the importance of the goal. Do you see, as we said yesterday, that when you apply even simple logic, you see that if Marxist utopia is a historical necessity, no help should be needed from human beings? If an almighty God has created a universe that is perfect, then why do human beings on earth need to help this almighty God by killing their brothers and sisters?

The fallen beings of course do not want people to reason this way. They want people to be blinded by this fog of dualistic logic. One claim *here,* an opposite claim *there,* until people do not know what to believe in themselves. What is, many would say, the opposite of peace? It is chaos. A state where there is total confusion where people are being bombarded with so many impressions that they cannot deal with them all. They are overwhelmed. They go into a state of overload where they do not know how to sort this out by themselves.

The fog of war between ideas

There is a concept in military terminology of the "fog of war." When people are in battle, they are so completely overwhelmed by everything that is happening, the noise, the explosions, the killing, the just total confusion of the battlefield that it is impossible to predict what will happen. Well, this does not just happen on a physical battlefield because life on earth could be considered a battlefield. At least, the fallen beings have attempted to turn it into a battlefield and envelop all people in this fog of war, this fog of war between ideas, between claims and counter claims. The fallen beings have for a long time put out many, many ideas. As Cyclopea said yesterday, they have an entire machine created for the purpose of deception. They have put out many ideas that have only one purpose: to create confusion. They have managed to create such a state of confusion on earth that people do not know what to believe.

Therefore, many people have come to a point where they do not dare to decide on their own what is true, what is right. They abandon their responsibility to discern and therefore they become vulnerable to someone who comes in with a very strong claim to having the truth, having authority. This is how millions of people, *billions* of people, have been pulled into supporting, for example, the Catholic church or a communist ideology. This is the basis for many dictatorships. Some have been established through raw violence. But in most cases, there is some claim to why the dictator is right, why the dictator has some specific authority. It is of course all a lie. You who are ascended master students can see this very clearly. Many, many people in the modern democracies can see it also. Unfortunately, there are many, many people in the modern democracies who have not truly seen the lie behind this idea that the ends can justify the means.

The United States and black-and-white thinking

This is especially true in the United States, which is more prone to black-and-white thinking than many of the smaller democracies. If you (you in general) could compare the mindset of the collective consciousness in

America or the average American, to the mindset you find in some of the smaller democratic nations around the world, such as South Korea or the Scandinavian nations, then I think most Americans would be shocked to realize how much more they are trapped in this black-and-white thinking, how much more they have been deceived into thinking that the ends can justify the means. Therefore, it is fully justified that America, which claims to be a peaceful democratic nation, a free society, maintains the largest military machine on the planet. How is this logical? How do you get away with making the claim to be a peaceful nation, a free nation, an example of a democratic society, yet you maintain the largest military in the world, a military that is capable of striking anywhere on the planet with short notice?

Well, of course the outer claim is that America, because of its special status, must defend freedom and democracy around the globe and therefore must be able to move out and defend South Korea from an invasion from the North, other countries from an invasion from this or that enemy. But this is the outer claim. It seems logical only because of the fog of war created by the fallen beings. A fog of war that has enveloped the American nation and the American people so they do not see how illogical that claim is. They do not see, as we said in the United States last year, how often the American military and the lives of American servicemen and -women have been used to further the cause of huge multinational corporations that are not loyal to America whatsoever and certainly not loyal to the cause of freedom.

As we have said, they indeed are examples of dictatorships. So how does it make sense that dictatorial corporations can manipulate this supposedly free democratic nation of America into sacrificing the lives of its young men and women for the cause of increasing profit for a few shareholders? Is this a military *of* the people, *by* the people and *for* the people? Or is it a military *of* the elite, *by* the elite, *for* the elite? Or I should actually say that the military is not *of* the elite, because it is not the children of the elite that are being sacrificed on a battlefield. They usually find a way to avoid military service.

Overcoming the view that the end justifies the means

You see my beloved, there is, as other masters have said, a tension in the collective consciousness that has been building for a long time. It is this tension where people, more and more people, are becoming ready to see that the end cannot justify the means. Again, if you could compare the consciousness of Americans to the consciousness of South Koreans, Danes or Swedes, you would see that these smaller democratic nations have long ago given up their ambition of forcing people in other nations to conform to their view of life. They have long ago given up this. That is why you see these nations have a military that is strictly for defense of the nation itself. You will also see that they do not have that aggressive intent. They do not have a need to project – to force people outside their borders – to conform to a particular view. Naturally, people in many democratic nations wish that all people on earth lived in democratic societies but that is because they have experienced how much better it is for themselves to live in a free democratic nation that increases material prosperity and hopefully also psychological well-being and so, they wish that other people had the same lifestyle that they have.

This is fundamentally different from having an epic mindset that your nation has a special role to play in promoting, in spreading, freedom and democracy around the world. You will see this back when President George Bush decided (President George Bush the younger, but for that matter also the older) decided to invade Iraq and how he had set up the situation that freeing Iraq from the dictator and establishing a free democratic society was only the first step. Then, there was Iran and there was North Korea on the axis of evil. Well, if that had been successful, would the axis of evil have ended in North Korea? Or would the people behind George Bush, the fallen beings in higher realms and the demons in the astral plane, would they have found some way to justify going further because: "Oh, there is also *that* dictatorship that we need to take down. Then, there is that one and the next." When would it have stopped? It might have gone on to a point where you could say that now the United States of America has used its military to take down every dictator around the earth. But what would have been the result? There would have been one dictatorship left because in the process of taking down the other dictators, the United States itself would have become a dictatorship.

You see my beloved, the major shift that needs to happen before the era of dictatorships can end on earth is that a critical mass of the people throughout the earth wake up, have that shift of awareness where they realize, where they *see*, they suddenly see it: The emperor has nothing on and therefore the goal cannot justify the means. This is what people in most democratic nations have seen.

America blocking an end to dictatorships

Many Americans have seen it as well but not a critical mass of Americans and that is why hardly anyone objected when Bush decided to invade Iraq. Hardly anyone stood up and said: "How can you spread freedom and democracy through warfare?" Do you see it in the American nation even today? Do you see any analysts who have questioned this? Do you see anybody questioning why do we maintain the largest military in the world? Why do we spend more on the military in the United States than most of the other big nations that we claim could be a threat taken together?

Imagine what could be done with that money. You could provide the best health care system in the world for free or rather, for the taxpayer money that is now being spent on the military. This is what many democratic nations have already done—made that transition. Certainly, it can be done in the United States. You do not need to have people pay higher taxes to provide universal health care. You just need to reallocate the means that are now being used to pay for military hardware. This is a step that is close to breaking through to where a critical mass of Americans can see it, and I can tell you right now that when it comes to this philosophy of the ends can justify the means, America, the American people, are the major block to ending the era of dictatorships.

You may say: "But isn't it necessary that people in the nations that are still under dictators will see it?" Of course, it is necessary but as other masters have explained, the democratic nations also have a role to play in ending the era of dictatorships. Because as long as you feel that you have an enemy you need to defend yourself from, and that this justifies you having a military and using it at your discretion, then you are projecting into the cosmic mirror that you want a situation on earth where there are dictatorships that you can see as a threat to democracy.

This is the basic dynamic, seen from the Sixth Ray of Peace, that is preventing the end of the era of dictatorships. People need to see that the ends cannot justify the means and the people who need to see it first are the people in the democratic part of the world, for they have the highest level of consciousness. The people in many democratic nations have already seen it, some of them decades ago. But the Americans are behind. You Americans who are so obsessed with winning and always being in front, you are behind on this point. You are decades behind other democracies when it comes to escaping the black-and-white thinking of the epic mindset.

Democracy is not the opposite of dictatorship

You see my beloved, most people in the world would say that the alternative, perhaps even the opposite of a dictatorship is a democracy. I would not say that a democracy is the *opposite* of a dictatorship. The opposite of a dictatorship is another dictatorship. Democracy, in its ideal form, has no opposition because when you truly rise to the democratic mindset, you are going beyond dualism and therefore there is no opposite anymore. Truly, the epic mindset, the idea that there is some epic cause that must be fulfilled and that this justifies the killing of other human beings, this epic mindset is completely and utterly anti-democratic.

What does it say in the American constitution? All men and women are created equal and endowed by their Creator with inalienable rights. What does that mean? It means there is no power, no authority, on earth that has the right to violate the rights of the people because the rights of the people are given by an authority that is not on earth, that is not of the earth—it is beyond earth.

What is a dictatorship? It is one person or a small group of people who claim that they are the ultimate authority, not just on earth, but sometimes even in the universe. Whenever a government claims to have some epic authority, some epic cause, that it must promote, then that government cannot be fully democratic. It may not be as dictatorial as Hitler, Stalin or Mao but it has dictatorial tendencies because this government, if it believes in the epic cause, if it has the epic mindset, then it believes that there are certain circumstances where it is justified to violate the rights of your own people in order to promote the epic cause.

Do you not see in the United States how the NSA and other agencies are spying on Americans in complete violation of the Constitution? But it is justified by the epic cause of defending the free democratic society from outside enemies. Anything, my beloved, any justification, any excuse, whereby a so-called self-proclaimed democratic government violates the rights of its own citizens is anti-democratic. It is a dictatorial element in those democratic societies. For that matter, if you take the American Constitution and the constitutions of many other democratic nations, they talk about all people having rights, all people having inalienable rights, not just the citizens of that nation. The American constitution does not say all *American* men, it says all men, meaning all human beings on earth have these rights.

The circular logic of the epic mindset

If the democratic government does not have the right to use force against its own people, then neither does the democratic government have the right to use force against people in other nations. This is what dictatorships do. They go into other nations and use force, and I know, many, many people will say: "Well, what about the remaining dictatorships? Who is going to stand up against them? Could South Korea defend itself against North Korea without the Americans being here to save the day?" No, they could not. From a certain worldly logic they could not. But the question that is not asked by the epic mindset, because the epic mindset cannot fathom it, is: "Would the South Korean people *have* to defend themselves against the North Koreans if the United States was not militarily present in South Korea?" In other words, if the epic mindset was not present, would there be a war?

You see again, if you go back, my beloved, if you use this logic that free democratic nations have to defend themselves against dictatorships and be ready to do so with violent means, if you take this logic and go back in time, you must ask yourself: "How did democracies ever arise?" I know Americans will say: "Well, we had a violent revolution or we would never have been free from England." But as we said before, it could have happened in a non-violent way. People at the time could not see how to make it happen but it could have been done.

What you see in many of the democratic nations around the world is that it was not necessary to have a violent revolution, or to have a war with other countries, in order to establish democracy. What led to the establishment of democracy, even in America? It was a raising of awareness. A raising of the collective awareness was what caused the first democracies to appear. What will it take for democracy to survive? That people in democratic nations continue to raise their awareness, and as they raise their awareness, the threats to democracy will gradually fall away. They will not be destroyed. They will not be conquered. They will be transcended.

Do you not see, my beloved, the very fact that you have democratic nations in the world actually proves the process that Cyclopea talked about? When you use scientific observation, neutral scientific observation, combined with intuitive insight, you can see how the world really works. The advent of democratic nations, the fact that you have democratic nations, proves that a raising of awareness is the first step in any kind of progress. It also proves that you cannot solve a problem, as Einstein said, with the same state of consciousness, from the same level of consciousness, that created the problem. If there had not been a raising of awareness, there would have been no democracies in the world.

The advent of democracy was not inevitable. If the awareness had not been raised, you would still have 150-200 dictatorial nations where the dictators would have been fighting amongst each other. The advent of democracy proves that the only real way to solve a problem is not to destroy the problem or the cause of the problem, but to transcend the consciousness of the problem, to transcend both of the dualistic polarities that give rise to the problem.

What is it that dictatorships always claim? They claim: "Here is a problem, it is epically important that this problem be solved. How can we solve the problem? By identifying the cause of the problem, which is always another group of people and then destroying those people." Hitler defined an epic cause—the purification of the human race. "How do we solve the problem? We identify another group of people as the core of the problem: the Jews. Then, we kill all the Jews, and we will automatically have the Aryan master race step forward and create utopia on earth." Everybody can see it was a lie, well, everybody except a few neo-Nazis.

How difficult is it to make the switch, to just turn the dial of consciousness those few degrees and see that Hitler was just one expression among many of the epic mindset? The epic mindset says that there is a cause so important that it justifies the use of force and the killing of other human beings. It justifies the violation of inalienable rights. It justifies that some authority on earth sets itself up as a god, or as the highest authority in the universe and therefore violates the rights that have been given to people from an authority that is beyond earth.

How fallen beings destroy inalienable rights

There are two ways that the fallen beings attempt to destroy these rights, this concept that human beings have rights that are given by a higher authority. One is to deny that there is any higher authority through materialism, such as you see in the communist nations, the communist dictatorships. Another is to set themselves up so that they are the only link between the people and that higher authority. This is what you see in the Catholic church, in Islam and in other religions that have this pattern where they claim that the leaders of the religion on earth are the intermediaries between God and the people. The people do not have the ability or the right to go within their own hearts and contact the spiritual realm and therefore come to know what is the higher reality.

I said earlier that there is a fog of war created by the fallen beings so that people do not know and do not even dare to decide what is right, what is true, but that is because they are using their outer minds. By using their intuitive faculties, people, *all* people, can go within their hearts and know what a higher vibration is and therefore use that higher vibration to discern anything on earth that does not resonate with that vibration. It is only through your intuitive faculties that you can know that you are not a human being who originated on earth. You originated in a higher realm, your source is in a higher realm. Because you were created from a higher source, a source that is beyond earth, you have rights that are beyond what can be defined or taken away by any authority on earth.

No authority on earth has the right to override what was given to you by your source, by your Creator. You can know this only by going within and having that experience of a connection, a sense of oneness with your source, which is your I AM Presence. However people can see it, they can still have that experience. That is how people in democratic nations knew that they have these rights. That is how people in the emerging democracies raised their awareness so that they were firm in demanding democratic rights. They were so firm in doing this that the leaders of their society realized that they could not hold back the change because the people demanded it.

Do you not realize (and of course you do as ascended master students, but the people in general do not realize) that when the people are united, are of one mind because they know in their hearts what is real and what rights they have, then the dictators must give way. How did the Soviet Union collapse? Well, there was a raising of awareness on a world level but also in all of the Soviet republics where the leaders of the Soviet Union realized that they could no longer maintain the illusion upon which the Soviet Union was built. The same can happen in other dictatorships, such as the invocation you have just given, calling for a shift in the mind of the dictator of North Korea where he realizes that he can no longer maintain the illusion of his father and grandfather, that it does not work anymore and therefore there must be some kind of change.

Once the dictator sees the need for change and decides to implement it, then what often will happen is that the dictator's vision does not go far enough. He thinks he can implement a change and still maintain control, just as Gorbachev thought he could implement economic reforms and maintain control of the Soviet Union and maintain the Soviet Union. It ran away from him, as it can run away from all dictators. This is how a peaceful transition can happen, by the dictator coming to see that he can no longer maintain the illusion that some changes are needed. Then, once you unleash, you open, the Pandora's box of change, it does not stop until the people have the democratic rights that they know they are entitled to from a higher authority than any dictator on earth. This is how change happens.

Democracy requires a higher authority

Right now, the need of the hour, so to speak, is that people in democratic nations, especially in the United States, come to see the utter illusion behind the philosophy that the ends can justify the means. Black-and-white thinking needs to be transcended. The epic mindset needs to be transcended. The tension is already created, but it has not been released and so, the waters of understanding cannot overflow the glass and water the people. Therefore, your calls, the calls of a relatively small number of people, in coming years can make that difference. It can be the trigger that triggers the shift in the collective awareness.

In order for this to happen, you who decide to give these invocations will have to know in yourselves that because you are in embodiment on earth, you have a right to call forth these changes. You are not forcing anyone to accept this, you are cutting them free to see it and once they see it, they will accept it voluntarily. Right now, they cannot accept it voluntarily because they cannot see it, because they have been forced into blindness by the fallen beings. Your calls are freeing them from that forced blindness and, my beloved, when they see that the epic mindset is like holding a poisonous snake, they will instinctively let go of the snake. They will let go of that serpent in the garden that tempted them into thinking that they could be as gods, knowing good and evil on earth, that they could define good and evil with the outer mind, the dualistic mind. Ttherefore, they could be as gods and they did not need the teacher who is just a symbol for their own intuitive awareness, their own connection to the source.

Do you not see that the entire idea behind democracy is that there is a higher authority in a higher realm? That higher authority is the source of all human beings on earth. It is because you came from that higher source that you have these inalienable rights defined by the source in the Law of Free Will, and it is only by maintaining your connection to that source that you can maintain a democratic society. Once that connection goes, a democracy is on the slide towards becoming more and more dictatorial because the people do not have that inner frame of reference where they know: "This is the vibration of oneness, this is the vibration of division. I do not want division because I know this is not who I am. This is not where I came from. I did not come from the vibration of division, I came from the vibration of oneness."

The key to establishing peace is for people individually to connect to that vibration of oneness in themselves whereby they realize that they came from a source that is beyond any division on earth, and so did all of their brothers and sisters. If you all came from a source that is beyond division, what sense does it make that you have allowed the fallen beings to divide you here on earth and to create conflict between the divisions? Why should there be war between men and women if you came from the same source? Why should there be war between North and South Koreans, between communists, capitalists, Russians, Americans—why, if you all came from the same source? Connecting to that source, that vibration of oneness, is the key to overcoming division, the key to establishing peace.

I, Uriel, am the Archangel who represents to all people on earth that vibration of oneness that leads to peace. Call to me, *call to me!* Invoke my flame of peace and I will respond with a greater measure than you can even imagine with the outer mind. The flame that I hold for earth is capable of consuming those demons of division that have lingered on this planet for far too long. But it cannot do so against the free will of the people, so someone on earth must make the call and say: "We have had enough of the era of division on earth. We want a higher form of government that is not based on the epic mindset, on black-and-white thinking and on the consciousness of division, or the belief that the ends can justify the means. We want that kind of government on earth and we demand it with one voice, and one heart, and one mind and one being."

13 | INVOKING A GOVERNMENT BASED ON ONENESS

In the name of the I AM THAT I AM, Jesus Christ, I use the authority that I have as a being in embodiment on earth to call upon Archangel Uriel to reinforce my calls and use my chakras to project the statements in this invocation into the collective consciousness and awaken people to the potential for a government based on oneness instead of division. Awaken people to the reality that we are spiritual beings and that we can co-create a new future by working with the ascended masters. I especially call for …

[Make your own calls here.]

Part 1

1. Uriel, shatter the energetic matrix that prevents people from seeing that most dictators claim to be working for the cause of peace, while at the same time preparing to kill or actually killing other human beings.

Uriel Archangel, immense is the power,
of angels of peace, all war to devour.

The demons of war, no match for your light,
consuming them all, with radiance so bright.

Uriel Archangel, use your great sword,
Uriel Archangel, consume all discord,
Uriel Archangel, we're of one accord,
Uriel Archangel, we walk with the Lord.

2. Uriel, shatter the energetic matrix that prevents people from seeing that killing cannot lead to peace, that violence cannot lead to peace. This is not logical, unless we use the logic of the fallen beings based on the duality consciousness.

Uriel Archangel, intense is the sound,
when millions of angels, their voices compound.
They build a crescendo, piercing the night,
life's glorious oneness revealed to our sight.

Uriel Archangel, use your great sword,
Uriel Archangel, consume all discord,
Uriel Archangel, we're of one accord,
Uriel Archangel, we walk with the Lord.

3. Uriel, shatter the energetic matrix that has pulled people into thinking that they can promote the cause of peace through violence and killing, even thinking it is *necessary* for promoting the cause of peace to kill other human beings.

Uriel Archangel, from out the Great Throne,
your millions of trumpets, sound the One Tone.
Consuming all discord with your harmony,
the sound of all sounds will set all life free.

Uriel Archangel, use your great sword,
Uriel Archangel, consume all discord,
Uriel Archangel, we're of one accord,
Uriel Archangel, we walk with the Lord.

4. Uriel, shatter the energetic matrix that prevents people from seeing that the basis for this deception is to define a certain standard, which says there are some things that *should* happen on earth and there are some things that *should not* happen on earth.

> Uriel Archangel, all war is now done,
> for you bring a message, from heart of the One.
> The hearts of all men, now singing in peace,
> the spirals of love, forever increase.

> **Uriel Archangel, use your great sword,**
> **Uriel Archangel, consume all discord,**
> **Uriel Archangel, we're of one accord,**
> **Uriel Archangel, we walk with the Lord.**

5. Uriel, shatter the energetic matrix that keeps people trapped in the illusion that the standard of their religion is defined by God, and therefore it is the will of God that other people must be converted to the one true religion.

> Uriel Archangel, your infinite peace,
> from all warring beings our planet release,
> war is a prison from which we are free,
> embracing the peace of true unity.

> **Uriel Archangel, use your great sword,**
> **Uriel Archangel, consume all discord,**
> **Uriel Archangel, we're of one accord,**
> **Uriel Archangel, we walk with the Lord.**

6. Uriel, shatter the energetic matrix that keeps people trapped in the illusion that if other people will not be converted, then they must be forced. If they will not be forced, they must be killed because when all those who oppose their religion have been killed, then God's kingdom will be manifest on earth.

> Uriel Archangel, we send forth the call,
> reveal now the oneness that unifies all,

help us the vision of peace now to see,
so we from all conflicts and struggles are free.

Uriel Archangel, use your great sword,
Uriel Archangel, consume all discord,
Uriel Archangel, we're of one accord,
Uriel Archangel, we walk with the Lord.

7. Uriel, shatter the energetic matrix that keeps people trapped in the illusion that in order to bring about a communist utopia, it is necessary and justified to kill other people.

Uriel Archangel, in service to life,
you give us release from struggle and strife,
forgetting the self is truly the key,
to living a life in true harmony.

Uriel Archangel, use your great sword,
Uriel Archangel, consume all discord,
Uriel Archangel, we're of one accord,
Uriel Archangel, we walk with the Lord.

8. Uriel, shatter the energetic matrix that keeps people trapped in the illusion that the ends can justify the means, that the goal is so important that even the means of forcing or killing other human beings are justified by the importance of the goal.

Uriel Archangel, the earth now you raise,
out of duality's death-bringing haze,
we call now upon your great Flame of Peace,
commanding that all petty squabbles do cease.

Uriel Archangel, use your great sword,
Uriel Archangel, consume all discord,
Uriel Archangel, we're of one accord,
Uriel Archangel, we walk with the Lord.

9. Uriel, shatter the energetic matrix that keeps people blinded by this fog of dualistic logic. One claim *here,* an opposite claim *there,* until people do not know what to believe in themselves.

Uriel Archangel, as peace is the norm,
to your higher vision the earth does conform,
as people have found your peace from within,
a Golden Age is the prize that we win.

Uriel Archangel, use your great sword,
Uriel Archangel, consume all discord,
Uriel Archangel, we're of one accord,
Uriel Archangel, we walk with the Lord.

Part 2

1. Uriel, shatter the energetic matrix that keeps people trapped in a state of chaos, a state of total confusion where they are being bombarded with so many impressions that they go into overload where they do not know what to accept.

Uriel Archangel, immense is the power,
of angels of peace, all war to devour.
The demons of war, no match for your light,
consuming them all, with radiance so bright.

Uriel Archangel, use your great sword,
Uriel Archangel, consume all discord,
Uriel Archangel, we're of one accord,
Uriel Archangel, we walk with the Lord.

2. Uriel, shatter the energetic matrix that prevents people from seeing that life on earth could be considered a battlefield. The fallen beings have attempted to turn it into a battlefield and envelop all people in this fog of war between ideas, between claims and counter claims.

Uriel Archangel, intense is the sound,
when millions of angels, their voices compound.
They build a crescendo, piercing the night,
life's glorious oneness revealed to our sight.

**Uriel Archangel, use your great sword,
Uriel Archangel, consume all discord,
Uriel Archangel, we're of one accord,
Uriel Archangel, we walk with the Lord.**

3. Uriel, shatter the energetic matrix that prevents people from seeing that the fallen beings have put out many ideas. They have created a machine for the purpose of deceiving and confusing people.

Uriel Archangel, from out the Great Throne,
your millions of trumpets, sound the One Tone.
Consuming all discord with your harmony,
the sound of all sounds will set all life free.

**Uriel Archangel, use your great sword,
Uriel Archangel, consume all discord,
Uriel Archangel, we're of one accord,
Uriel Archangel, we walk with the Lord.**

4. Uriel, shatter the energetic matrix that keeps people trapped in a state where they do not dare to decide on their own what is true or right. They abandon their responsibility to discern and therefore they become vulnerable to someone with a strong claim to having the truth, having authority.

Uriel Archangel, all war is now done,
for you bring a message, from heart of the One.
The hearts of all men, now singing in peace,
the spirals of love, forever increase.

**Uriel Archangel, use your great sword,
Uriel Archangel, consume all discord,
Uriel Archangel, we're of one accord,
Uriel Archangel, we walk with the Lord.**

5. Uriel, shatter the energetic matrix that prevents people from seeing that this is the basis for many dictatorships. Some have been established through raw violence, but in most cases, there is some claim to why the dictator is right, why the dictator has some specific authority.

Uriel Archangel, your infinite peace,
from all warring beings our planet release,
war is a prison from which we are free,
embracing the peace of true unity.

Uriel Archangel, use your great sword,
Uriel Archangel, consume all discord,
Uriel Archangel, we're of one accord,
Uriel Archangel, we walk with the Lord.

6. Uriel, shatter the energetic matrix that prevents people in the modern democracies from truly seeing the lie behind the idea that the ends can justify the means.

Uriel Archangel, we send forth the call,
reveal now the oneness that unifies all,
help us the vision of peace now to see,
so we from all conflicts and struggles are free.

Uriel Archangel, use your great sword,
Uriel Archangel, consume all discord,
Uriel Archangel, we're of one accord,
Uriel Archangel, we walk with the Lord.

7. Uriel, shatter the energetic matrix that keeps people in the United States trapped in black-and-white thinking and in the belief that the ends can justify the means, making them think it is fully justified that America, which claims to be a peaceful democratic nation, maintains the largest military machine on the planet.

Uriel Archangel, in service to life,
you give us release from struggle and strife,
forgetting the self is truly the key,
to living a life in true harmony.

Uriel Archangel, use your great sword,
Uriel Archangel, consume all discord,
Uriel Archangel, we're of one accord,
Uriel Archangel, we walk with the Lord.

8. Uriel, shatter the energetic matrix that prevents people from seeing that it is not logical that you claim to be a peaceful nation, a free nation, an example of a democratic society, yet you maintain the largest military in the world, a military that is capable of striking anywhere on the planet with short notice.

Uriel Archangel, the earth now you raise,
out of duality's death-bringing haze,
we call now upon your great Flame of Peace,
commanding that all petty squabbles do cease.

Uriel Archangel, use your great sword,
Uriel Archangel, consume all discord,
Uriel Archangel, we're of one accord,
Uriel Archangel, we walk with the Lord.

9. Uriel, shatter the energetic matrix that makes up the fog of war that has enveloped the American nation and the American people so they do not see how often the American military and the lives of American servicemen and -women have been used to further the cause of multinational corporations that are not loyal to America.

Uriel Archangel, as peace is the norm,
to your higher vision the earth does conform,
as people have found your peace from within,
a Golden Age is the prize that we win.

Uriel Archangel, use your great sword,
Uriel Archangel, consume all discord,
Uriel Archangel, we're of one accord,
Uriel Archangel, we walk with the Lord.

Part 3

1. Uriel, shatter the energetic matrix that prevents people from seeing that it makes no sense that dictatorial corporations can manipulate the supposedly free democratic nation of America into sacrificing the lives of its young men and women for the cause of increasing profit for a few shareholders.

> Uriel Archangel, immense is the power,
> of angels of peace, all war to devour.
> The demons of war, no match for your light,
> consuming them all, with radiance so bright.

> **Uriel Archangel, use your great sword,**
> **Uriel Archangel, consume all discord,**
> **Uriel Archangel, we're of one accord,**
> **Uriel Archangel, we walk with the Lord.**

2. Uriel, shatter the energetic matrix that prevents people from seeing that this not a military *of* the people, *by* the people and *for* the people. It is a military *of* the elite, *by* the elite and *for* the elite.

> Uriel Archangel, intense is the sound,
> when millions of angels, their voices compound.
> They build a crescendo, piercing the night,
> life's glorious oneness revealed to our sight.

> **Uriel Archangel, use your great sword,**
> **Uriel Archangel, consume all discord,**
> **Uriel Archangel, we're of one accord,**
> **Uriel Archangel, we walk with the Lord.**

3. Uriel, shatter the energetic matrix that keeps people trapped in the epic mindset that their nation has a special role to play in promoting freedom and democracy around the world.

> Uriel Archangel, from out the Great Throne,
> your millions of trumpets, sound the One Tone.

Consuming all discord with your harmony,
the sound of all sounds will set all life free.

Uriel Archangel, use your great sword,
Uriel Archangel, consume all discord,
Uriel Archangel, we're of one accord,
Uriel Archangel, we walk with the Lord.

4. Uriel, I call forth the judgment of Christ upon the fallen beings in higher realms and the demons in the astral plane, who seek to justify that democratic nations use violence to overthrow dictators.

Uriel Archangel, all war is now done,
for you bring a message, from heart of the One.
The hearts of all men, now singing in peace,
the spirals of love, forever increase.

Uriel Archangel, use your great sword,
Uriel Archangel, consume all discord,
Uriel Archangel, we're of one accord,
Uriel Archangel, we walk with the Lord.

5. Uriel, shatter the energetic matrix that prevents people from seeing that if the United States used its military to take down every dictator on earth, there would still be one dictatorship left because in the process of taking down the other dictators, the United States itself would have become a dictatorship.

Uriel Archangel, your infinite peace,
from all warring beings our planet release,
war is a prison from which we are free,
embracing the peace of true unity.

Uriel Archangel, use your great sword,
Uriel Archangel, consume all discord,
Uriel Archangel, we're of one accord,
Uriel Archangel, we walk with the Lord.

6. Uriel, shatter the energetic matrix that prevents people from seeing that the major shift that needs to happen before the era of dictatorships can end is that a critical mass of people wake up and realize: The emperor has nothing on and therefore the goal cannot justify the means.

Uriel Archangel, we send forth the call,
reveal now the oneness that unifies all,
help us the vision of peace now to see,
so we from all conflicts and struggles are free.

Uriel Archangel, use your great sword,
Uriel Archangel, consume all discord,
Uriel Archangel, we're of one accord,
Uriel Archangel, we walk with the Lord.

7. Uriel, shatter the energetic matrix that prevents Americans from questioning why the United States maintains the largest military in the world and spends more on the military than most of the nations that could be a threat taken together.

Uriel Archangel, in service to life,
you give us release from struggle and strife,
forgetting the self is truly the key,
to living a life in true harmony.

Uriel Archangel, use your great sword,
Uriel Archangel, consume all discord,
Uriel Archangel, we're of one accord,
Uriel Archangel, we walk with the Lord.

8. Uriel, shatter the energetic matrix that prevents people from seeing that America could provide the best health care system in the world for the taxpayer money that is now being spent on the military.

Uriel Archangel, the earth now you raise,
out of duality's death-bringing haze,
we call now upon your great Flame of Peace,
commanding that all petty squabbles do cease.

Uriel Archangel, use your great sword,
Uriel Archangel, consume all discord,
Uriel Archangel, we're of one accord,
Uriel Archangel, we walk with the Lord.

9. Uriel, shatter the energetic matrix that prevents a critical mass of Americans from seeing that it is not necessary to have people pay higher taxes to provide universal health care. It can be done by reallocating the means that are now being used to pay for military hardware.

Uriel Archangel, as peace is the norm,
to your higher vision the earth does conform,
as people have found your peace from within,
a Golden Age is the prize that we win.

Uriel Archangel, use your great sword,
Uriel Archangel, consume all discord,
Uriel Archangel, we're of one accord,
Uriel Archangel, we walk with the Lord.

Part 4

1. Uriel, shatter the energetic matrix that prevents people from seeing that when it comes to the philosophy of the ends can justify the means, America, the American people, are the major block to ending the era of dictatorships.

Uriel Archangel, immense is the power,
of angels of peace, all war to devour.
The demons of war, no match for your light,
consuming them all, with radiance so bright.

Uriel Archangel, use your great sword,
Uriel Archangel, consume all discord,
Uriel Archangel, we're of one accord,
Uriel Archangel, we walk with the Lord.

2. Uriel, shatter the energetic matrix that prevents people from seeing that the democratic nations also have a role to play in ending the era of dictatorships. As long as we feel that we have an enemy, and that this justifies us having a military, then we are projecting into the cosmic mirror that we want dictatorships that we can see as a threat to democracy.

Uriel Archangel, intense is the sound,
when millions of angels, their voices compound.
They build a crescendo, piercing the night,
life's glorious oneness revealed to our sight.

Uriel Archangel, use your great sword,
Uriel Archangel, consume all discord,
Uriel Archangel, we're of one accord,
Uriel Archangel, we walk with the Lord.

3. Uriel, shatter the energetic matrix that prevents people from seeing that in order to end the era of dictatorships, people need to see that the ends cannot justify the means and the people who need to see it first are the people in the democratic nations.

Uriel Archangel, from out the Great Throne,
your millions of trumpets, sound the One Tone.
Consuming all discord with your harmony,
the sound of all sounds will set all life free.

Uriel Archangel, use your great sword,
Uriel Archangel, consume all discord,
Uriel Archangel, we're of one accord,
Uriel Archangel, we walk with the Lord.

4. Uriel, shatter the energetic matrix that prevents people from seeing that the opposite of a dictatorship is not a democracy; it is another dictatorship.

Uriel Archangel, all war is now done,
for you bring a message, from heart of the One.
The hearts of all men, now singing in peace,
the spirals of love, forever increase.

Uriel Archangel, use your great sword,
Uriel Archangel, consume all discord,
Uriel Archangel, we're of one accord,
Uriel Archangel, we walk with the Lord.

5. Uriel, shatter the energetic matrix that prevents people from seeing that democracy has no opposition because when we rise to the democratic mindset, we are going beyond dualism and therefore there is no opposite anymore.

Uriel Archangel, your infinite peace,
from all warring beings our planet release,
war is a prison from which we are free,
embracing the peace of true unity.

Uriel Archangel, use your great sword,
Uriel Archangel, consume all discord,
Uriel Archangel, we're of one accord,
Uriel Archangel, we walk with the Lord.

6. Uriel, shatter the energetic matrix that prevents people from seeing that the epic mindset, the idea that there is some epic cause that must be fulfilled and that this justifies the killing of other human beings, this mindset is completely and utterly anti-democratic.

Uriel Archangel, we send forth the call,
reveal now the oneness that unifies all,
help us the vision of peace now to see,
so we from all conflicts and struggles are free.

Uriel Archangel, use your great sword,
Uriel Archangel, consume all discord,
Uriel Archangel, we're of one accord,
Uriel Archangel, we walk with the Lord.

7. Uriel, shatter the energetic matrix that prevents people from seeing that inalienable rights means there is no power or authority on earth that has the right to violate the rights of the people because the rights of the people are given by an authority that is not on earth.

Uriel Archangel, in service to life,
you give us release from struggle and strife,
forgetting the self is truly the key,
to living a life in true harmony.

Uriel Archangel, use your great sword,
Uriel Archangel, consume all discord,
Uriel Archangel, we're of one accord,
Uriel Archangel, we walk with the Lord.

8. Uriel, shatter the energetic matrix that prevents people from seeing that a dictatorship is one person or a small group of people who claim that they are the ultimate authority, not just on earth, but sometimes even in the universe.

Uriel Archangel, the earth now you raise,
out of duality's death-bringing haze,
we call now upon your great Flame of Peace,
commanding that all petty squabbles do cease.

Uriel Archangel, use your great sword,
Uriel Archangel, consume all discord,
Uriel Archangel, we're of one accord,
Uriel Archangel, we walk with the Lord.

9. Uriel, shatter the energetic matrix that prevents people from seeing that whenever a government claims to have some epic authority, some epic cause, then that government cannot be fully democratic. It believes that there are certain circumstances where it is justified to violate the rights of its own people in order to promote the epic cause.

Uriel Archangel, as peace is the norm,
to your higher vision the earth does conform,
as people have found your peace from within,
a Golden Age is the prize that we win.

Uriel Archangel, use your great sword,
Uriel Archangel, consume all discord,

Uriel Archangel, we're of one accord,
Uriel Archangel, we walk with the Lord.

Part 5

1. Uriel, shatter the energetic matrix that prevents people from seeing that any excuse whereby a self-proclaimed democratic government violates the rights of its own citizens is anti-democratic. It is a dictatorial element in those democratic societies.

Uriel Archangel, immense is the power,
of angels of peace, all war to devour.
The demons of war, no match for your light,
consuming them all, with radiance so bright.

Uriel Archangel, use your great sword,
Uriel Archangel, consume all discord,
Uriel Archangel, we're of one accord,
Uriel Archangel, we walk with the Lord.

2. Uriel, shatter the energetic matrix that prevents people from seeing that if a democratic government does not have the right to use force against its own people, then neither does it have the right to use force against people in other nations. This is what dictatorships do.

Uriel Archangel, intense is the sound,
when millions of angels, their voices compound.
They build a crescendo, piercing the night,
life's glorious oneness revealed to our sight.

Uriel Archangel, use your great sword,
Uriel Archangel, consume all discord,
Uriel Archangel, we're of one accord,
Uriel Archangel, we walk with the Lord.

3. Uriel, shatter the energetic matrix that prevents people from seeing that if the epic mindset was not present, then democratic nations would not

have to defend themselves against dictatorships because there would be no war.

> Uriel Archangel, from out the Great Throne,
> your millions of trumpets, sound the One Tone.
> Consuming all discord with your harmony,
> the sound of all sounds will set all life free.
>
> **Uriel Archangel, use your great sword,**
> **Uriel Archangel, consume all discord,**
> **Uriel Archangel, we're of one accord,**
> **Uriel Archangel, we walk with the Lord.**

4. Uriel, shatter the energetic matrix that prevents people from seeing that what led to the establishment of democracy was a raising of awareness. For democracy to survive, people in democratic nations must continue to raise their awareness.

> Uriel Archangel, all war is now done,
> for you bring a message, from heart of the One.
> The hearts of all men, now singing in peace,
> the spirals of love, forever increase.
>
> **Uriel Archangel, use your great sword,**
> **Uriel Archangel, consume all discord,**
> **Uriel Archangel, we're of one accord,**
> **Uriel Archangel, we walk with the Lord.**

5. Uriel, shatter the energetic matrix that prevents people from seeing that as people in democracies raise their awareness, the threats to democracy will gradually fall away. They will not be destroyed, they will not be conquered. They will be transcended.

> Uriel Archangel, your infinite peace,
> from all warring beings our planet release,
> war is a prison from which we are free,
> embracing the peace of true unity.

Uriel Archangel, use your great sword,
Uriel Archangel, consume all discord,
Uriel Archangel, we're of one accord,
Uriel Archangel, we walk with the Lord.

6. Uriel, shatter the energetic matrix that prevents people from seeing that the advent of democratic nations proves that a raising of awareness is the first step in any kind of progress. We cannot solve a problem from the same level of consciousness that created the problem.

Uriel Archangel, we send forth the call,
reveal now the oneness that unifies all,
help us the vision of peace now to see,
so we from all conflicts and struggles are free.

Uriel Archangel, use your great sword,
Uriel Archangel, consume all discord,
Uriel Archangel, we're of one accord,
Uriel Archangel, we walk with the Lord.

7. Uriel, shatter the energetic matrix that prevents people from seeing that the advent of democracy proves that the only real way to solve a problem is not to destroy the problem or the cause of the problem, but to transcend the consciousness of the problem, to transcend both of the dualistic polarities that give rise to the problem.

Uriel Archangel, in service to life,
you give us release from struggle and strife,
forgetting the self is truly the key,
to living a life in true harmony.

Uriel Archangel, use your great sword,
Uriel Archangel, consume all discord,
Uriel Archangel, we're of one accord,
Uriel Archangel, we walk with the Lord.

8. Uriel, shatter the energetic matrix that prevents people from seeing that dictatorships always claim: "Here is a problem, it is epically important that

this problem be solved, and we do this by destroying the people who are the cause of the problem."

Uriel Archangel, the earth now you raise,
out of duality's death-bringing haze,
we call now upon your great Flame of Peace,
commanding that all petty squabbles do cease.

Uriel Archangel, use your great sword,
Uriel Archangel, consume all discord,
Uriel Archangel, we're of one accord,
Uriel Archangel, we walk with the Lord.

9. Uriel, shatter the energetic matrix that prevents people from seeing that Hitler was just one expression among many of the epic mindset, which says that there is a cause so important that it justifies killing other human beings or violating their inalienable rights.

Uriel Archangel, as peace is the norm,
to your higher vision the earth does conform,
as people have found your peace from within,
a Golden Age is the prize that we win.

Uriel Archangel, use your great sword,
Uriel Archangel, consume all discord,
Uriel Archangel, we're of one accord,
Uriel Archangel, we walk with the Lord.

Part 6

1. Uriel, shatter the energetic matrix that prevents people from seeing that there are two ways that the fallen beings attempt to destroy the concept that human beings have rights that are given by a higher authority. One is to deny that there is any higher authority through materialism, such as in the communist dictatorships.

Uriel Archangel, immense is the power,
of angels of peace, all war to devour.
The demons of war, no match for your light,
consuming them all, with radiance so bright.

Uriel Archangel, use your great sword,
Uriel Archangel, consume all discord,
Uriel Archangel, we're of one accord,
Uriel Archangel, we walk with the Lord.

2. Uriel, shatter the energetic matrix that prevents people from seeing that another way is to set themselves up so that they are the only link between the people and that higher authority, such as in the Catholic church, Islam and other religions.

Uriel Archangel, intense is the sound,
when millions of angels, their voices compound.
They build a crescendo, piercing the night,
life's glorious oneness revealed to our sight.

Uriel Archangel, use your great sword,
Uriel Archangel, consume all discord,
Uriel Archangel, we're of one accord,
Uriel Archangel, we walk with the Lord.

3. Uriel, shatter the energetic matrix that prevents people from seeing that by using our intuitive faculties, we can go within our hearts and know what a higher vibration is and therefore use it to discern anything on earth that does not resonate with that vibration.

Uriel Archangel, from out the Great Throne,
your millions of trumpets, sound the One Tone.
Consuming all discord with your harmony,
the sound of all sounds will set all life free.

Uriel Archangel, use your great sword,
Uriel Archangel, consume all discord,
Uriel Archangel, we're of one accord,
Uriel Archangel, we walk with the Lord.

4. Uriel, shatter the energetic matrix that prevents people from seeing that it is only through our intuitive faculties that we can know that we are not human beings who originated on earth. We originated from a source that is beyond earth, and therefore we have rights that are beyond what can be defined or taken away by any authority on earth.

Uriel Archangel, all war is now done,
for you bring a message, from heart of the One.
The hearts of all men, now singing in peace,
the spirals of love, forever increase.

Uriel Archangel, use your great sword,
Uriel Archangel, consume all discord,
Uriel Archangel, we're of one accord,
Uriel Archangel, we walk with the Lord.

5. Uriel, shatter the energetic matrix that prevents people from seeing that no authority on earth has the right to override what was given to us by our source. We can know this only by going within and connecting to our source.

Uriel Archangel, your infinite peace,
from all warring beings our planet release,
war is a prison from which we are free,
embracing the peace of true unity.

Uriel Archangel, use your great sword,
Uriel Archangel, consume all discord,
Uriel Archangel, we're of one accord,
Uriel Archangel, we walk with the Lord.

6. Uriel, shatter the energetic matrix that prevents people from seeing that when the people are united, are of one mind because they know in their hearts what is real and what rights they have, then the dictators must give way.

Uriel Archangel, we send forth the call,
reveal now the oneness that unifies all,

help us the vision of peace now to see,
so we from all conflicts and struggles are free.

Uriel Archangel, use your great sword,
Uriel Archangel, consume all discord,
Uriel Archangel, we're of one accord,
Uriel Archangel, we walk with the Lord.

7. Uriel, shatter the energetic matrix that prevents the shift in the minds of the remaining dictators on earth, so they see the need for change and decide to implement it.

Uriel Archangel, in service to life,
you give us release from struggle and strife,
forgetting the self is truly the key,
to living a life in true harmony.

Uriel Archangel, use your great sword,
Uriel Archangel, consume all discord,
Uriel Archangel, we're of one accord,
Uriel Archangel, we walk with the Lord.

8. Uriel, shatter the energetic matrix that prevents people from seeing that a dictator often thinks he can implement a change and still maintain control, but it can run away from all dictators.

Uriel Archangel, the earth now you raise,
out of duality's death-bringing haze,
we call now upon your great Flame of Peace,
commanding that all petty squabbles do cease.

Uriel Archangel, use your great sword,
Uriel Archangel, consume all discord,
Uriel Archangel, we're of one accord,
Uriel Archangel, we walk with the Lord.

9. Uriel, shatter the energetic matrix that prevents people from seeing that a peaceful transition can happen by the dictator coming to see that he can no longer prevent change. Once change is allowed, it does not stop until

the people have the democratic rights that they know they are entitled to
from a higher authority than any dictator on earth.

Uriel Archangel, as peace is the norm,
to your higher vision the earth does conform,
as people have found your peace from within,
a Golden Age is the prize that we win.

Uriel Archangel, use your great sword,
Uriel Archangel, consume all discord,
Uriel Archangel, we're of one accord,
Uriel Archangel, we walk with the Lord.

Part 7

1. Uriel, shatter the energetic matrix that prevents people in democratic
nations, especially in the United States, from seeing the utter illusion
behind the philosophy that the ends can justify the means, thereby transcending black-and-white thinking and the epic mindset.

Uriel Archangel, immense is the power,
of angels of peace, all war to devour.
The demons of war, no match for your light,
consuming them all, with radiance so bright.

Uriel Archangel, use your great sword,
Uriel Archangel, consume all discord,
Uriel Archangel, we're of one accord,
Uriel Archangel, we walk with the Lord.

2. Uriel, shatter the energetic matrix that prevents people from seeing that
the tension is already created, and therefore the calls of a relatively small
number of people can make the difference. It can be the trigger that produces a shift in the collective awareness.

Uriel Archangel, intense is the sound,
when millions of angels, their voices compound.

They build a crescendo, piercing the night,
life's glorious oneness revealed to our sight.

Uriel Archangel, use your great sword,
Uriel Archangel, consume all discord,
Uriel Archangel, we're of one accord,
Uriel Archangel, we walk with the Lord.

3. Uriel, shatter the energetic matrix that prevents people from seeing that because we are in embodiment on earth, we have a right to call forth these changes. We are not forcing anyone to accept this, we are cutting them free to see it and once they see it, they will accept it voluntarily.

Uriel Archangel, from out the Great Throne,
your millions of trumpets, sound the One Tone.
Consuming all discord with your harmony,
the sound of all sounds will set all life free.

Uriel Archangel, use your great sword,
Uriel Archangel, consume all discord,
Uriel Archangel, we're of one accord,
Uriel Archangel, we walk with the Lord.

4. Uriel, shatter the energetic matrix created by the fallen beings, the matrix of forced blindness, so people can let go of that serpent in the garden that tempted them into thinking that they could be as gods, knowing good and evil on earth, that they could define good and evil with the outer, dualistic mind.

Uriel Archangel, all war is now done,
for you bring a message, from heart of the One.
The hearts of all men, now singing in peace,
the spirals of love, forever increase.

Uriel Archangel, use your great sword,
Uriel Archangel, consume all discord,
Uriel Archangel, we're of one accord,
Uriel Archangel, we walk with the Lord.

5. Uriel, shatter the energetic matrix that prevents people from seeing that the entire idea behind democracy is that there is a higher authority in a higher realm. That higher authority is the source of all human beings on earth. It is because we came from that higher source that we have inalienable rights defined in the Law of Free Will.

Uriel Archangel, your infinite peace,
from all warring beings our planet release,
war is a prison from which we are free,
embracing the peace of true unity.

Uriel Archangel, use your great sword,
Uriel Archangel, consume all discord,
Uriel Archangel, we're of one accord,
Uriel Archangel, we walk with the Lord.

6. Uriel, shatter the energetic matrix that prevents people from seeing that it is only by maintaining our connection to that source that we can maintain a democratic society. Once that connection goes, a democracy is on the slide towards becoming more and more dictatorial because the people do not have an inner sense of oneness.

Uriel Archangel, we send forth the call,
reveal now the oneness that unifies all,
help us the vision of peace now to see,
so we from all conflicts and struggles are free.

Uriel Archangel, use your great sword,
Uriel Archangel, consume all discord,
Uriel Archangel, we're of one accord,
Uriel Archangel, we walk with the Lord.

7. Uriel, shatter the energetic matrix that prevents people from seeing that the key to establishing peace is for people individually to connect to that vibration of oneness in themselves whereby they realize that they came from a source that is beyond any division on earth, and so did all of their brothers and sisters.

Uriel Archangel, in service to life,
you give us release from struggle and strife,
forgetting the self is truly the key,
to living a life in true harmony.

Uriel Archangel, use your great sword,
Uriel Archangel, consume all discord,
Uriel Archangel, we're of one accord,
Uriel Archangel, we walk with the Lord.

8. Uriel, shatter the energetic matrix that prevents people from seeing that if we all came from a source that is beyond division, what sense does it make that we have allowed the fallen beings to divide us and to create conflict between the divisions? Connecting to our source, the vibration of oneness, is the key to overcoming division, the key to establishing peace.

Uriel Archangel, the earth now you raise,
out of duality's death-bringing haze,
we call now upon your great Flame of Peace,
commanding that all petty squabbles do cease.

Uriel Archangel, use your great sword,
Uriel Archangel, consume all discord,
Uriel Archangel, we're of one accord,
Uriel Archangel, we walk with the Lord.

9. Uriel, I invoke your flame of peace to consume those demons of division that have lingered on this planet for far too long. On behalf of all people, I say: "We have had enough of the era of division on earth. We want a higher form of government that is not based on the epic mindset, on black-and-white thinking and on the consciousness of division, or the belief that the ends can justify the means. We want that kind of government on earth and we demand it with one voice, and one heart, and one mind and one being."

Uriel Archangel, as peace is the norm,
to your higher vision the earth does conform,
as people have found your peace from within,
a Golden Age is the prize that we win.

**Uriel Archangel, use your great sword,
Uriel Archangel, consume all discord,
Uriel Archangel, we're of one accord,
Uriel Archangel, we walk with the Lord.**

Sealing

In the name of the I AM THAT I AM, I accept that Archangel Michael, Astrea and Shiva form an impenetrable shield around myself and all constructive people, sealing us from all fear-based energies in all four octaves. I accept that the Light of God is consuming and transforming all fear-based energies that make up the dark forces working against ending the era of dictatorships on earth!

14 | FREEDOM FROM THE NEED TO BE SPECIAL

I AM the Ascended Master Saint Germain. You may look at a dictatorship and say that the dictator is restricting the freedom of the people. Yes, certainly he is. But why? Why is it that a dictator has come to see freedom as a threat? This cannot be understood by anyone, unless you have the knowledge we have given you of the fallen beings and their modus operandi.

Why do the fallen beings see freedom as a threat? Because they see individuality and individual creativity as a threat. They see it as a threat because they do not have it. You cannot be creative in a horizontal way—*truly* creative. Certainly, you can generate new ideas, new inventions, new ways of torturing or imprisoning other people, new instruments of deception in a horizontal way. But in order to be truly creative, you need to have a connection to your I AM Presence because it is through your I AM Presence, and what we have described as your intuitive faculties, that you are creative.

Does that mean that the Conscious You is not a creative being? Well, in a sense, you could say that the Conscious You is not inherently creative because the Conscious You does not have enough structure to be creative. It can be an open door for the creativity of the I AM Presence to flow through it but it is not creative in itself.

There are many people who would object to this statement because they would feel that they *are* creative. There are many artists, writers, philosophers, who will say that they have been creative in bringing forth new ideas. Nevertheless, those same artists, writers or philosophers will also say that they have received inspiration. Most people are aware that your conscious mind is focused at a certain level, focused on certain topics, and in order to bring forth a new idea in a certain area, you are seeking some inspiration. Even scientists, at least the more creative of them, are seeking inspiration. They are studying a certain topic through the scientific method that is somewhat mechanical. Nevertheless, in order to understand the deeper connections, such as Einstein's theory of relativity, they need that flash of inspiration. Most people actually realize that creativity is a matter of getting inspiration because what is the nature of creativity? It is that you get an idea you did not already have, you suddenly see something that you did not see before.

How creativity produces progress

Most people realize that in your present state of awareness, if you look at an individual, you see that this person is in a particular state of awareness. His outer conscious mind is focused on certain aspects of life, certain topics. It may be, for example, a scientist who is focused on subatomic particles. The person has a certain state of outer conscious awareness of a particular topic. He may have studied it for many years, and he may have great expertise, great knowledge that he can draw upon. Nevertheless, the knowledge that he already has sets certain parameters for how he thinks about the topic. His mind normally will not go beyond those parameters.

If the person is a good scientist, he may make certain observations or experiments that there is either something lacking in his current understanding or there is a contradiction in his current understanding. He may then become aware that there is a need for a new way to look at the topic, a new understanding of the issue. How does he bring forth that new idea? It is simple—you cannot bring forth a new idea with the awareness and the knowledge that you currently have. That is why Einstein was inspired to say that you cannot solve a problem with the same state of consciousness that created the problem. You need something new and where is that new going to come from? It is going to come from outside your present level of awareness, your present knowledge of the topic. For the vast majority of people, unless they are very spiritual and mystically inclined, their Conscious You will be so to speak trapped in, limited by, their normal state of awareness. Therefore, the Conscious You cannot be creative within the parameters of that state of awareness.

How can you then be creative and come up with a new idea? Only by reaching beyond your normal state of awareness. Throughout the ages, many people have attempted to do this, and they have done it in various ways, even using psychedelic drugs or other forceful means. You see people who have been creative in reaching beyond their normal state of awareness, but they have not reached the ascended realm or their I AM Presences. They have reached, for example, the astral plane, or the mental realm or the lower identity realm where some lower force (that is not ascended) has then given them some new idea.

This is what most people call creativity. They say that if they receive an idea from outside their normal state of awareness, they are being creative. This is not what I call creative because true creativity is that you establish a connection to your I AM Presence and you receive an idea from your I AM Presence or from an ascended master. *That* is true creativity. This is the kind of creativity that the fallen beings cannot have. Even the fallen beings in the identity realm do not have any connection to the ascended realm, and they are not willing to receive any ideas from us, even if we were willing to give it to the fallen beings, which of course we are not. We would be willing to give them ideas that could help them transcend their current level of consciousness, if they were willing to do so. You have fallen beings in embodiment who will claim that they can be creative, but that is because they receive ideas from fallen beings in the three other realms. But as I said, that is not creativity.

Fighting the battles of the fallen beings

What is it that the fallen beings are afraid of? They are afraid of any human being who establishes a connection to their I AM Presence and the ascended realm. Because when you do this, you can be the open door for bringing forth ideas that can overthrow the status quo. The status quo is what the fallen beings always seek to maintain, at least those who are part of what I have called the established power elite. The established power elite wants to maintain status quo, which gives them control. They often want to expand certain things, they might want to expand their power, they might want to expand communism to the entire world, but they are still seeking to maintain status quo in the sense that they are in control of the system.

There may be an aspiring power elite who are seeking to overthrow the established power elite. They are also fallen beings, and they might seek some ideas from fallen beings in, for example, the identity realm who are seeking to create chaos and therefore are willing to use the fallen beings and the aspiring power elite to overthrow the fallen beings in the established power elite. What you see so many times in history is that warfare and conflict has been between two groups of fallen beings who are simply fighting for who is going to be in control, who is going to have power.

This is precisely the outcome of the duality consciousness, the epic mindset. Many, many times, the fallen beings have managed to define an epic cause in such a way that it either keeps the established power elite in power, or that it seeks to overthrow the established elite because the aspiring elite claims that they have the new truth. Naturally, there was an established power elite who had control of the Catholic church. The first scientists, who were actually mystical scientists, were seeking to bring forth genuine creative ideas. That is why science in its pure form truly is a way out of the duality consciousness. But science quickly became dominated by materialism, which was simply an aspiring power elite seeking to take the power that was held by the power elite that was in control of the church. You see this over and over and over again. Right now, you see in China the struggle between an established power elite who is in control of the Communist Party, and an aspiring power elite who wants to take economic control and use the economy to take away the power of the established elite.

A new definition of freedom

Back to the issue of creativity. Creativity is when the Conscious You connects to its I AM Presence and the ascended realm and receives an idea that is not in your present awareness. This is what the fallen beings cannot do. That is why they are afraid of it. They have throughout the ages, since they first embodied here, attempted to break the connection between people's conscious minds and their I AM Presences. They have attempted to stop that flow of creative ideas from the ascended realm into and through the Conscious You to the conscious mind. We can therefore say that the definition of freedom is that you have a conscious connection to your higher self, to your I AM Presence, to the ascended realm. If we build upon what Archangel Uriel talked about, we see that the essence of democracy is that there is a higher realm, there is a source in that realm that is the source of all people and has therefore given all people certain rights. Therefore, you can see that already in the democratic nations, there is (or at least there *can* be) the awareness that democracy has no meaning unless there is something beyond the material world that has given people rights that no power on earth should be allowed to take away.

Therefore, it is not so difficult for people to make the switch and realize that true creativity also comes from beyond the material world. This is something that can be established, as Cyclopea said, by actually performing neutral scientific observation, combined with intuitive insights. Once you start actually looking at the reality of what has already been discovered by science, you see that there must be energy coming from a realm beyond the material, which means there must be a realm beyond the material.

When you then use intuition, you can start wondering, where does intuition come from? It also comes from beyond the material and that means what? It means that in that realm beyond the material, there must be some form of consciousness. Maybe actually there is a higher form of consciousness, a higher self, that each individual has access to in a realm beyond the material. This does not mean that people need to believe in ascended master teachings in order to recognize this because all the pieces of the puzzle are already there, they just have not been put together so people can see the big picture. This is what you can make the calls for so that suddenly there is that shift to where people realize that true creativity and intuition actually comes from beyond the material world. This means that if each person was created from a source beyond the material, perhaps each person has a connection to a part of its own higher being that is beyond the material world.

These are very general, very universal ideas that we have gradually prepared people to accept and understand. There are philosophies that talk about this. There are certain psychologists who are beginning to think in these terms because they have adapted a positive psychology. Instead of looking at anomalies in the psychology, they look at what actually are the positive aspects of the psychology, what is the higher potential of human beings. There is a large movement that is exploring the higher potentials of the mind and the powers of the mind. It is not so far-fetched, that these people can suddenly have that shift where they see that: "We must have a higher aspect of our beings."

Ultimate bondage

What we can say is that ultimate freedom is when you have that awareness, you have that connection. What is then ultimate bondage, the ultimate anti-freedom? It is when that connection is broken. Now, you can begin to look at this historically. Why has that connection been broken? How has it been broken? You can see that you can actually go all the way back to the very primitive version that you find in Genesis, of the story of Adam and Eve in the Garden of Eden and eating the apple that was offered by the serpent. The serpent can actually be seen as a symbol for the dualistic consciousness where people become as gods and they think they can define good and evil with the outer mind.

What have I just said? True creativity is reaching beyond your present mind, reaching for something from a source that is beyond the material. What does it mean? What is the value of having a source that is beyond the material? It is that it cannot be manipulated by any force on earth.

It is not difficult for people to see that throughout recorded history, people have been manipulated by a small elite. Elitism is a phenomenon that will be more and more recognized in coming years. That is why we have our conference coming up about elitism. It is not that far away that people will recognize that the major issue in history has been a small power elite attempting to take control of the population by manipulating them. How have they manipulated people? They have manipulated people by claiming that it is possible to create some ideology, some system in this world, that is defined based on the knowledge we have in this world without any regard to a higher authority or a higher source. They have of course also attempted to create religions that claim to be from a higher source. As you can see, in many examples, these religions have still set up an earthly, human hierarchy that are supposedly the intermediaries between the people and their source.

What you can very quickly come to see is that there is a tendency in the world of defining ideologies, religions, systems, political philosophies, that claim that we can know everything we need to know based on the knowledge that is available in this world. You can see for example how the Greek philosopher Plato claimed that there is a higher realm of ideal forms. In order to know reality, you need to see those ideal forms instead of seeing the shadows that people see with their present level of consciousness. You can see that Plato's own student, Aristotle, took a different approach and said that we can understand how the world works by looking at the world and what we can observe in the world. Right there, was a shift, and you can see similar shifts throughout history. You might say that Plato had not eaten the apple, the fruit of the knowledge of good and evil, but Aristotle had swallowed it, hook, line, and sinker.

Defining good and evil is the root of all evil

It is not difficult for people to come to see that there is a certain level of consciousness where we believe that we have the power to define good and evil, truth and untruth. It is not difficult to see that this is what has been done, by all or at least most dictatorial systems. Some dictatorial systems have been based on raw power but many of them have been based on a certain idea. It can be, as we have said, the communist ideology. It can be the Catholic church, which of course started with the true teachings of Jesus but perverted them. It can be many other examples of this.

You have in the world two tendencies. One is: "We human beings are capable of defining absolute truth in some system." Or you can have the other tendency: "We human beings are not capable of defining absolute truth. We need to reach for a higher source." Then, it is not so difficult for people in the modern democracies to make that switch and say: "Well, a democracy is based on the concept of inalienable rights, meaning rights given from a source that is beyond anything on earth and therefore cannot be manipulated by anything on earth. So isn't it clear, that if we take the approach that we human beings can define truth, this actually works against democracy?"

Because the very founding idea of democracy is that we human beings are not capable of defining our own rights. We cannot allow a dictator or a government, or any other authority to define the rights of the population. The rights of the population are not defined by a small elite. They are not defined by the population. They are defined by an authority that is beyond the level where it can be manipulated either by the elite or by the people themselves. In other words, our rights do not come from our present level of consciousness, they come from a higher level. That is why they are *rights,* that is why they should be *inalienable* because no authority on earth should take them away. If we do not acknowledge this, how can we hope to maintain democracy? How can we for that matter hope to create a true democracy, which we do not currently have in the highest potential. These are ideas that people can come to recognize. They can come to recognize that there has always been that tendency for a small elite to want to control the population and how do they do it? They claim that they have the ability to define absolute truth whereas the people, the general population, do not have that ability.

The people need to be governed

Now, you may say (and there are people, there are philosophers who have said this throughout the ages) that the people do not have the ability to define truth, therefore they cannot govern themselves. They need somebody who is wiser, who has a higher ability to govern the people. If you do not do this, chaos ensues, anarchy ensues. They will point to all kinds of examples of anarchy.

What have we told you before about the fallen beings? They first create a problem that results in chaos or other unwanted consequences and then they offer themselves as the solution to the problem. Why do not the people in general have a connection to their higher selves? Because they have been manipulated by the fallen beings. The fallen beings first manipulated people into the dualistic state of consciousness. They allow the rising of various kinds of chaos and anarchy and all kinds of unrest and un-peace. Then, they come in and say: "In order to avoid this kind of chaos, we need to have a firm government, we need to have a strong leader who can whip the people into shape, otherwise they will destroy themselves." People will not destroy themselves because, as we have said, even though people are in the duality consciousness, they still have a certain basic humanity, they still have a certain respect for life. The chaos that you see in various societies at various times was not created by the people. It was not created by human nature. It was created by the power elite of fallen beings who have no respect for life and have no basic humanity.

Now, why is it that dictators can make people believe this, believe that they have the ability to define truth and that the people should follow them? Well, it is partly, as we have said, because people have been afraid to make decisions, to take responsibility for themselves but there is more to it. The one aspect I want to bring to your attention here is that when you lose your connection, your conscious connection, to your I AM Presence, you lose the most important aspect of being a co-creator—namely your ability to co-create. *Co-create.*

How we co-create

In the original design, the Conscious You descends into physical embodiment. It has a point-like sense of awareness but it has an awareness that there is a part of its own mind that is beyond itself. Therefore, it has the awareness that Jesus expressed when he said: "I can of my own self do nothing, it is the I AM Presence within me that is the true doer."

The Conscious You, even if it has a very narrow, limited sense of self, it knows that it cannot create out of its own power. It can only create because it receives energy from a higher source. It receives ideas and impressions from that higher source. Once you break that connection by going into the duality consciousness, you cannot be a co-creator. You experience this as a sense of loss. You can see even in the story of the Garden of Eden—it describes how Adam and Eve after they were cast out, clearly experienced a sense of loss. They had to work at the sweat of their brow, they saw that they were naked and all of these things that are just primitive symbols for what actually happened. The psychological effect of leaving the Garden and going into the duality consciousness is that you suddenly feel that you are not connected to anything outside yourself. What you actually lose is your basic sense of individuality, your basic sense of creativity.

Now, we have said that the Conscious You first descends with a point-like sense of self, a very narrow sense of self. Most of you find it difficult to envision this because you have been in embodiment for a long time and you have expanded your sense of self immensely, compared to when you first started. Nevertheless, even when you have this very narrow sense of self, you still have a desire to express yourself. The basic driving force behind life is the desire to express yourself, the desire for self-expression. This is the true source of creativity, the driving force of creativity. This desire for self-expression comes from the I AM Presence. The I AM Presence desired to express itself in the material world and therefore it sent an extension of itself, the Conscious You, into this world.

What does the Conscious You come in with? It comes in with a very limited sense of self but a strong desire for self-expression. That is why it has a desire to expand its sense of self. You now break the connection to the I AM Presence and the Conscious You now loses the sense it had before—and what was the sense it had? I said it had a limited sense of self. From a certain worldly perspective, you can say that the Conscious You when it started out did not have a strong personality—to use a concept that you are familiar with. Nevertheless, the Conscious You had a sense that it was a unique being. It had a sense of uniqueness but where did that sense come from? It did not come from its outer personality because it was very narrow. It came from whatever connection the Conscious You had to the I AM Presence. The Conscious You did not see the fullness of its I AM Presence, but it did sense that it was the extension of a complex being that had a unique individuality.

The quest for uniqueness

We have said that your divine individuality, your spiritual individuality, is defined in your I AM Presence—that is what makes you unique. There are billions of I AM Presences but each one is completely unique. The I AM Presence is such a complex structure that you can scarcely fathom it, or rather, you cannot fathom it with the mind you have in embodiment. It is so complex that each I AM Presence is absolutely unique. That is why in the spiritual realm there is no competition here. Because in uniqueness, how can there be competition? How can there be comparison between two aspects, two I AM Presences that are unique? There is no room for comparison, there is no need for comparison in uniqueness. Each I AM Presence has a drive to expand and express its own unique individuality. That is what is embedded in the Conscious You.

Now, the Conscious You loses its connection to the I AM Presence and it feels this as a loss: "I have lost my uniqueness. Who am I now?" What then happens? Well, the Conscious You still has this drive to express itself. It now gets a desire, it creates an intention, to define a self in this world that can give it a sense of being unique. Do you understand? There is a drive to express a unique individuality, it truly comes from the I AM Presence. The Conscious You loses this and now it must build an outer personality in this world that can give it that sense of being unique.

You will see that even the fallen beings went through this process when they fell. They lost the connection to their I AM Presences and now they attempted to create a unique outer personality, worldly personality, and this is what they have done ever since. That is why you can see that the fallen beings have had such a long history of doing this that they have created this very, very strong outer personality that makes them feel very, very special and much, much better than the original inhabitants of the earth, who have not had nearly as long of a time after they fell into duality to create this outer personality. That is why you see on planet earth that after the fallen beings started embodying here, the original inhabitants of the earth took one of two approaches. Some people still continued to try to develop their outer personality. The majority of the people on earth actually gave up doing this. They were, as Nada so eloquently expressed it in her book, "hammered down by the fallen beings" to the point where they accepted: "Oh, I am not a unique being. I am not creative, I do not have a unique personality. So I'd better follow the leaders." This is what we in previous dispensations called "mechanization man" where people can even get to the point where they have lost their inbuilt creativity and they are just blindly following some kind of leader, almost like an automaton. This is of course what the fallen beings want to create. They want to create people who blindly follow them and accept that they are such unique individuals.

Now, you see, when you look at the dictators of the world, how they always make some kind of claim of why they are special, why they have special abilities, special powers. Look at what the people in North Korea believe about Kim Jong Un and his father and his Grandfather. Look at what people in the Soviet Union believed about Lenin, less about Stalin but still thought he was unique in certain ways. Look at Chairman Mao and how he is still revered as being a special person who was above and beyond any other human being. My beloved, where in Marxist ideology is there a place for the kind of idol worship that you see in China with regard to Chairman Mao? How can you reconcile this idolatry with Marxist philosophy? It boggles the mind that people can accept this, but it is again because of the hypnotic effect of the fallen beings.

Overcoming the need to be unique

Now, take everything I have told you here and do what we always tell our students, our direct students, to do. Look at yourself, look in the mirror. You say you are ascended master students, you say you want freedom. So many students throughout the ages have said to me: "Saint Germain, I want freedom, I want to be free." Okay, I will give you the key to freedom.

What is the key to being free? Stop wanting to be unique through the outer personality. Stop wanting to be unique in this world. It is your desire to be unique in this world that imprisons you. The key to freedom is to reconnect to the I AM Presence, to let go of that ego-based personality that thinks it is special, that wants to be special. *That* is the key to spiritual growth and spiritual freedom. Discover those separate selves that give you that desire to be unique in this world.

Those people on the planet who have given up their drive to be unique and are just following a leader and do not want to take responsibility for themselves, they do not become ascended master students. Who becomes ascended master students? Those who still have that original desire for self-expression. It can be avatars, it can be the original inhabitants of the earth but you have that desire for self-expression. That means you have a desire to be unique. So far, over many embodiments, you had attempted to create a sense of uniqueness by building an outer personality that is different, that you somehow think is special.

What do we see among ascended master students? We see it less in this dispensation, we saw it very, very clearly in previous dispensations. People come to the ascended master teachings, they recognize that there is value here. They all come with this drive to be recognized and validated by the ascended masters for being so special, so unique, so advanced, so sophisticated. We played upon this in the previous dispensation by saying you have the highest spiritual teaching on the planet. Well, my beloved, if you look at spiritual teachings, high and low are not really the best way to evaluate them. Because the best spiritual teaching for you is the one that helps you transcend your present level of consciousness, whatever that may be. Really, the highest spiritual teaching on the planet is a rather meaningless concept to anything but the linear, comparative, analytical mind that wants to always create a scale where it can compare everything.

Nevertheless, we saw how people latched on to this concept and thought that it must prove that when they can recognize the teaching, they must be the most advanced spiritual students on the planet. What was the effect of this? Look at what we talked about the other day (that the messenger read this book that you all have a chance to read, those of you who are staying in the hotel, about Buddhism). It is said that if you create a concept of enlightenment and think that with your present level of mind you can know what enlightenment is, then you are creating an obstacle to you attaining enlightenment.

Do you see that what has kept you from having a connection to your I AM Presence, after you fell into duality, is that you have built this outer self that wants to be unique in this world? As long as you have this outer self that wants to be unique in this world, you cannot connect to the uniqueness of your I AM Presence. What students did in previous dispensations is they took certain elements of the teachings and they created this concept of how special they were and this prevented them from overcoming the outer self. It reinforced, in some cases, the outer self where they were so eager to do something for the ascended masters that they actually came to feel more and more special: "Look at all the decrees I have given. Look at how I have been involved with the organization. I've been on staff, I have done all of these things, I must be really, really special." And they *were*—from a worldly perspective.

The unique self cannot ascend

How many times have we told you that the outer personality is not what ascends. Jesus said it 2,000 years ago: "Only he who descended from heaven can ascend back to heaven." What descended? The Conscious You with a point-like sense of identity, which is pure awareness. The Conscious You has created a vehicle for expression in this world, but this vehicle cannot ascend.

There were many, many people in previous dispensations, who believed that it was a matter of developing and refining their outer personality until it became so unique, so special, that it could ascend. This is what many, many religious people in other religions have believed throughout the ages. You will see Christians who are trying to be so good, according to a Christian definition, that they feel God simply has to let them into heaven because they are so good. You can see people in the Buddhist religion who are attempting to study and perform the practices religiously and they think this will bring them to a point where they are sure to go to heaven.

If you read the teachings of the Buddha, you will see he made it very clear that this outer personality that is dominated by the past will never reach Nirvana, will never become enlightened. He even said enlightenment is a concept that only exists because of ignorance. The self that is ignorant, when it becomes enlightened, ceases to exist because the self that is ignorant is the Conscious You colored by all of these outer selves. When the Conscious You realizes it is pure awareness, it is not the outer self, *then* it becomes enlightened. But then it merges back into the I AM Presence and becomes an entirely different being. It transcends the consciousness where there can be ignorance and enlightenment, this or that polarity. It transcends the pairs. What we see throughout the ages is that spiritual people have gone into this blind alley of seeking to force or bargain their way into heaven, by either creating a self that is so good that God has to let it in, or that it has the power to enter heaven by itself. Or they create a self that is so special that they make a bargain with God where they say: "God, if I do all of these things for you here on earth, then you will let me in, won't you?" Of course, the false gods created by the fallen beings will say: "Oh, yes, my beloved, you are so special, I will let you in, just do this thing for me here an earth and kill these other bad people who are working against my will. Then, you are sure to be let in, and there will be 70 virgins waiting for you."

Finding the absolute system

My beloved, so many times we have seen this. What we have also seen is something that is specific for avatars because avatars are not starting out, when they first embody on earth, with this point-like sense of identity. They have some identity with them from a natural planet and that means they have a stronger drive for being unique, a stronger drive for expressing their uniqueness here on earth. This means that many times avatars will be deceived by the fallen beings. The fallen beings will, when they expose you to the birth trauma, attempt to make you give up this quest to be unique because of course the fallen beings see this as a threat.

For most avatars, they cannot completely lose this drive. Therefore, the fallen beings then used Plan B, which is to get avatars to become so entangled with the fallen beings that they actually think that they can become as unique as the fallen beings are by doing what the fallen beings are doing. There are avatars that have been deceived into using black magic, for example. But there are more avatars who have been deceived into thinking that the way to become unique on earth is to find the absolute truth, the absolute system.

If you look back at, for example, medieval Europe, you will see that most countries in Europe had kings. The king would become a king, not by some violent revolution where he took power from an established dictator, but he inherited it from his father. What you see in many of the royal houses of Europe throughout the Middle Ages was that there was one person who was the king and he was a fallen being. But he had one or several sons who were avatars. There are examples of kings who were not fallen beings but who were avatars. Of course, growing up with a father who was a fallen being, they took over much of the mindset of that fallen being and usually this had been going on for many embodiments where the avatars had become so entangled with the fallen beings that they had taken over a lot of this mindset of thinking that they could somehow acquire the ability to define absolute truth, to define the absolute system.

There are also philosophers who have believed this. There are people who have been avatars who have been misled into thinking they could define the absolute religion or religious doctrine or religious system. You see this over and over again. This of course can be a real trap for avatars because it can be so difficult for an avatar to admit this. You can see that even the *My Lives* book kind of skirts the issue, does not really go into what happens when an avatar becomes closely involved with the fallen beings. There is a description of how the avatar is abused, killed or tortured by the fallen beings. But there is not really a description of what happens when the avatar becomes persuaded by the fallen beings into following the path that they are following and pursuing this ultimate quest for the absolute truth or the absolute system.

It can be very, very difficult for avatars to admit this. Nevertheless, if people will be honest about applying the tools we have given, you can actually come to see that all of this, whatever happened, whatever you may have done here on earth, it was just a separate self. It is not *you*, it never was you, it never will become you. You can actually come to see that the separate-self imprisons you in a certain approach to life that you feel is very restricting to you.

Therefore, you can see that the separate self is projecting that there is some problem that must be solved. For example, you have to find the ultimate truth. But this is what imprisons you. If you can let go of it, you will be free, and only *then* will you be free. When you see this, *that* is when you can come to look at that separate self, and spontaneously arises this desire, this drive: "I am not going to solve or try to solve the problem anymore, I am letting this self die."

Death is the key to freedom

Death is the key to freedom, not as the Christians believe that you have to die physically in order to be resurrected in a higher realm. The death of the separate self is the key to freedom, because the only prison that ever existed is the separate self. What does the *My Lives* book say in the very introduction, which is, in a sense, the most important teaching in the book? Everybody is having an entirely subjective experience and the only source of problems on earth is that some people are attempting to export their subjective experience to others and thereby trying to make their subjective experience universal.

This is what the fallen beings have been doing since they fell. This is what many human beings have been trying to do since they went into duality. As I said, many people are not trying to do this because they have given up trying to be creative. Those who have a certain creative drive, they have been trying to make their subjective experience universal, according to some criteria, they or some philosophy or authority figure have defined. They think that here on earth, you can define the criteria and when your outer-self lives up to these criteria, then you will enter heaven, you will be in Nirvana. Or, you will believe what the fallen beings believe: You will become immortal.

The fallen beings know that they are living on borrowed time but they are trying to make their fallen selves immortal. The way they can see immortality is that they try to prevent death. Look at the almost comical attempts that people have made of using current technology, current medical science, to first extend the life of the body and even to freeze the body down. Do you realize that some of these people who have had their bodies frozen, they have prevented their souls from re-embodying because they are so attached to the body that they cannot leave it? Many others who have had their bodies frozen down, have seen the folly of their ways once they were out of the body. Therefore, they have reincarnated again, and they do not need their body to be revived because the soul would not even want to come back into it.

Nevertheless, what people think is that the key to immortality is to prevent death. In reality, the key to immortality is to embrace death and allow the separate self, the mortal self, to die so that you return to your true sense of identity as an immortal spiritual being. *That* is freedom because when you ascend, then you will know what freedom truly is. I know because I have experienced it and I am experiencing it right now. I have radiated to you who are listening my experience, my Presence of Freedom, and I have used your chakras as broadcasting stations to radiate it into the collective consciousness.

My beloved, one of the real errors of Christianity is the concept of original sin that says that human beings are inherently flawed, that they were created flawed. One of the really profound aspects of Buddhism is that the Buddha made it very clear that everything is the Buddha nature, that every human being has the Buddha nature within it. No matter how low you have gone in this world, you cannot lose your Buddha nature. You can choose to rekindle it and therefore return to an awareness of the Buddha nature.

This is also what Jesus taught, even though he used other words, but it was perverted by Christianity. It has fortunately not been perverted to the same degree by Buddhism. The reality is that the Conscious You can never lose its ability to free itself from the separate selves it has created in this world. The Conscious You can never make a choice that it cannot free itself from by making a more aware choice.

The world is in an upward spiral

The world is in an upward spiral because the collective consciousness is being raised. This has created these pressures that we have talked about where there is a shift in awareness that is ready to break through. By your calls, and by you, yourselves, raising your consciousness, you can become the forerunners for creating many of these shifts where people suddenly wake up and they see what they have not seen before. They see that it is self-evident. It is, as it says in the Declaration of Independence: "We hold these truths to be self-evident." When the consciousness shifts, then at least the top 10% and gradually, more and more of the people will see that this is self-evident. This of course is the real value of you raising your consciousness, walking the spiritual path, but also giving the invocations and decrees whereby you radiate this into the collective consciousness.

For this, my beloved, we are very, very grateful. We want you to know and we want you to feel our gratitude for your efforts, for your willingness to look at yourself and raise your awareness. With this, my beloved, I have given you what I wanted to give you. I would like to stay with you much longer because I enjoy interacting with your beings. And I *will* stay with you, just not through a physical messenger, but I will anchor my Presence here for the rest of this conference, so you individually have a greater than normal opportunity to tune in to me if you are willing to do so. I will for that matter, also anchor my Presence in the recording of this dictation in the written version of this dictation and in the invocation that will be based on it so that whenever people listen to, read the dictation and give the invocation, they will have that opportunity to tune in to my Presence. This is my gift. It is my freely given gift that is in a sense a reward for your service. It is truly given just because I enjoy interacting with you and I would like to offer you the opportunity to feel the joy of interacting with me. With this, I set you free to be who you desire to be. "To be or not to be" is not the question for you anymore, for you have transcended the consciousness of Hamlet. It is not a matter of being or not being. It is a matter of: "What do I want to be?" We have talked about it before, you can come to that point where you are so free that you can say: "Who do I want to be today? What do I want to express today of my unique individuality?" *That* is freedom and it is possible to have that freedom while you are still in embodiment. I wish that for all of you.

15 | INVOKING FREEDOM FROM FEELING SPECIAL

In the name of the I AM THAT I AM, Jesus Christ, I use the authority that I have as a being in embodiment on earth to call upon Saint Germain to reinforce my calls and use my chakras to project the statements in this invocation into the collective consciousness and awaken people from the need to feel that they are special compared to others. Awaken people to the reality that we are spiritual beings and that we can co-create a new future by working with the ascended masters. I especially call for …

[Make your own calls here.]

Part 1

1. Saint Germain, shatter the energetic matrix that prevents people from seeing that we cannot understand why dictators see freedom as a threat unless we know about the fallen beings and their modus operandi.

> O Saint Germain, you do inspire,
> my vision raised forever higher,
> with you I form a figure-eight,
> your Golden Age I co-create.

O Saint Germain, what love you bring,
it truly makes all matter sing,
your violet flame does all restore,
with you we are becoming more.

2. Saint Germain, shatter the energetic matrix that prevents people from seeing that the fallen beings see freedom as a threat because they see individuality and individual creativity as a threat.

O Saint Germain, what Freedom Flame,
released when we recite your name,
acceleration is your gift,
our planet it will surely lift.

O Saint Germain, what love you bring,
it truly makes all matter sing,
your violet flame does all restore,
with you we are becoming more.

3. Saint Germain, shatter the energetic matrix that prevents people from seeing that we cannot be creative in a horizontal way. In order to be truly creative, we need to have a connection to our I AM Presences because it is through our intuitive faculties that we are creative.

O Saint Germain, in love we claim,
our right to bring your violet flame,
from you Above, to us below,
it is an all-transforming flow.

O Saint Germain, what love you bring,
it truly makes all matter sing,
your violet flame does all restore,
with you we are becoming more.

4. Saint Germain, shatter the energetic matrix that prevents people from seeing that in order to bring forth a new idea in a certain area, we need inspiration. In order to understand the deeper connections, we need a flash of inspiration.

O Saint Germain, I love you so,
my aura filled with violet glow,
my chakras filled with violet fire,
I am your cosmic amplifier.

**O Saint Germain, what love you bring,
it truly makes all matter sing,
your violet flame does all restore,
with you we are becoming more.**

5. Saint Germain, shatter the energetic matrix that prevents people from seeing that creativity is a matter of getting inspiration because the nature of creativity is that we get an idea we did not already have, we see something that we did not see before.

O Saint Germain, I am now free,
your violet flame is therapy,
transform all hang-ups in my mind,
as inner peace I surely find.

**O Saint Germain, what love you bring,
it truly makes all matter sing,
your violet flame does all restore,
with you we are becoming more.**

6. Saint Germain, shatter the energetic matrix that prevents people from seeing that the knowledge we already have sets certain parameters for how we think about any topic. Our minds normally will not go beyond those parameters.

O Saint Germain, my body pure,
your violet flame for all is cure,
consume the cause of all disease,
and therefore I am all at ease.

**O Saint Germain, what love you bring,
it truly makes all matter sing,
your violet flame does all restore,
with you we are becoming more.**

7. Saint Germain, shatter the energetic matrix that prevents people from seeing that we cannot bring forth a new idea with the awareness and the knowledge we currently have. We need something new and it must come from outside our present level of awareness, our present knowledge of the topic.

O Saint Germain, I'm karma-free,
the past no longer burdens me,
a brand new opportunity,
I am in Christic unity.

O Saint Germain, what love you bring,
it truly makes all matter sing,
your violet flame does all restore,
with you we are becoming more.

8. Saint Germain, shatter the energetic matrix that prevents people from seeing that most people are limited by their normal state of awareness and they cannot be creative within the parameters of that state of awareness.

O Saint Germain, we are now one,
I am for you a violet sun,
as we transform this planet earth,
your Golden Age is given birth.

O Saint Germain, what love you bring,
it truly makes all matter sing,
your violet flame does all restore,
with you we are becoming more.

9. Saint Germain, shatter the energetic matrix that prevents people from seeing that we can be creative and come up with a new idea only by reaching beyond our normal state of awareness.

O Saint Germain, the earth is free,
from burden of duality,
in oneness we bring what is best,
your Golden Age is manifest.

O Saint Germain, what love you bring,
it truly makes all matter sing,
your violet flame does all restore,
with you we are becoming more.

Part 2

1. Saint Germain, shatter the energetic matrix that prevents people from seeing that true creativity is that we establish a connection to our I AM Presences and receive ideas from our source or from an ascended master, not from a lower realm.

O Saint Germain, you do inspire,
my vision raised forever higher,
with you I form a figure-eight,
your Golden Age I co-create.

O Saint Germain, what love you bring,
it truly makes all matter sing,
your violet flame does all restore,
with you we are becoming more.

2. Saint Germain, shatter the energetic matrix that prevents people from seeing that the fallen beings cannot have this kind of creativity. Fallen beings in embodiment can be creative, but only when they receive ideas from fallen beings in the three other realms.

O Saint Germain, what Freedom Flame,
released when we recite your name,
acceleration is your gift,
our planet it will surely lift.

O Saint Germain, what love you bring,
it truly makes all matter sing,
your violet flame does all restore,
with you we are becoming more.

3. Saint Germain, shatter the energetic matrix that prevents people from seeing that the fallen beings are afraid of any human being who establishes a connection to their I AM Presence and the ascended realm.

O Saint Germain, in love we claim,
our right to bring your violet flame,
from you Above, to us below,
it is an all-transforming flow.

O Saint Germain, what love you bring,
it truly makes all matter sing,
your violet flame does all restore,
with you we are becoming more.

4. Saint Germain, shatter the energetic matrix that prevents people from seeing that when we do this, we can be the open door for bringing forth ideas that can overthrow the status quo. The status quo is what the fallen beings in the established power elite seek to maintain.

O Saint Germain, I love you so,
my aura filled with violet glow,
my chakras filled with violet fire,
I am your cosmic amplifier.

O Saint Germain, what love you bring,
it truly makes all matter sing,
your violet flame does all restore,
with you we are becoming more.

5. Saint Germain, shatter the energetic matrix that prevents people from seeing that there may be an aspiring power elite who are seeking to overthrow the established power elite. So many times in history, warfare and conflict has been between two groups of fallen beings who are fighting for who is going to be in control.

O Saint Germain, I am now free,
your violet flame is therapy,
transform all hang-ups in my mind,
as inner peace I surely find.

**O Saint Germain, what love you bring,
it truly makes all matter sing,
your violet flame does all restore,
with you we are becoming more.**

6. Saint Germain, shatter the energetic matrix that prevents people from seeing that this is the outcome of the duality consciousness, the epic mind-set. The fallen beings have managed to define an epic cause in such a way that it either keeps the established power elite in power, or that it seeks to overthrow the established elite because the aspiring elite claims they have the new truth.

O Saint Germain, my body pure,
your violet flame for all is cure,
consume the cause of all disease,
and therefore I am all at ease.

**O Saint Germain, what love you bring,
it truly makes all matter sing,
your violet flame does all restore,
with you we are becoming more.**

7. Saint Germain, shatter the energetic matrix that prevents people from seeing that there was an established power elite who had control of the Catholic church. The first scientists were seeking to bring forth genuinely creative ideas. Science quickly became dominated by materialism, which was an aspiring power elite seeking to take power from the church.

O Saint Germain, I'm karma-free,
the past no longer burdens me,
a brand new opportunity,
I am in Christic unity.

**O Saint Germain, what love you bring,
it truly makes all matter sing,
your violet flame does all restore,
with you we are becoming more.**

8. Saint Germain, shatter the energetic matrix that prevents people from seeing that since the fallen beings first embodied on earth, they have attempted to break the connection between people's conscious minds and their I AM Presences. They have attempted to stop the flow of creative ideas.

O Saint Germain, we are now one,
I am for you a violet sun,
as we transform this planet earth,
your Golden Age is given birth.

**O Saint Germain, what love you bring,
it truly makes all matter sing,
your violet flame does all restore,
with you we are becoming more.**

9. Saint Germain, shatter the energetic matrix that prevents people from seeing that the definition of freedom is that we have a conscious connection to our higher selves, to our I AM Presences, to the ascended realm.

O Saint Germain, the earth is free,
from burden of duality,
in oneness we bring what is best,
your Golden Age is manifest.

**O Saint Germain, what love you bring,
it truly makes all matter sing,
your violet flame does all restore,
with you we are becoming more.**

Part 3

1. Saint Germain, shatter the energetic matrix that prevents people from seeing that the essence of democracy is that there is a higher realm, there is a source in that realm that is the source of all people, and has therefore given all people certain rights.

O Saint Germain, you do inspire,
my vision raised forever higher,
with you I form a figure-eight,
your Golden Age I co-create.

**O Saint Germain, what love you bring,
it truly makes all matter sing,
your violet flame does all restore,
with you we are becoming more.**

2. Saint Germain, shatter the energetic matrix that prevents people from seeing that democracy has no meaning unless there is something beyond the material world that has given people rights that no power on earth should be allowed to take away.

O Saint Germain, what Freedom Flame,
released when we recite your name,
acceleration is your gift,
our planet it will surely lift.

**O Saint Germain, what love you bring,
it truly makes all matter sing,
your violet flame does all restore,
with you we are becoming more.**

3. Saint Germain, shatter the energetic matrix that prevents people from seeing that true creativity comes from beyond the material world. Intuition comes from beyond the material, so in the realm beyond the material, there must be some form of consciousness.

O Saint Germain, in love we claim,
our right to bring your violet flame,
from you Above, to us below,
it is an all-transforming flow.

**O Saint Germain, what love you bring,
it truly makes all matter sing,
your violet flame does all restore,
with you we are becoming more.**

4. Saint Germain, shatter the energetic matrix that prevents people from seeing that there is a higher form of consciousness, a higher self, that each individual has access to in a realm beyond the material. If each person was created from a source beyond the material, each person has a connection to a part of its own higher being that is beyond the material world.

O Saint Germain, I love you so,
my aura filled with violet glow,
my chakras filled with violet fire,
I am your cosmic amplifier.

O Saint Germain, what love you bring,
it truly makes all matter sing,
your violet flame does all restore,
with you we are becoming more.

5. Saint Germain, shatter the energetic matrix that prevents people who are into positive psychology or seeking to discover the higher potential of human beings from seeing that we must have a higher aspect of our beings.

O Saint Germain, I am now free,
your violet flame is therapy,
transform all hang-ups in my mind,
as inner peace I surely find.

O Saint Germain, what love you bring,
it truly makes all matter sing,
your violet flame does all restore,
with you we are becoming more.

6. Saint Germain, shatter the energetic matrix that prevents people from seeing that ultimate freedom is when we have a connection to our higher beings. Ultimate bondage, the ultimate anti-freedom, is when that connection is broken.

O Saint Germain, my body pure,
your violet flame for all is cure,
consume the cause of all disease,
and therefore I am all at ease.

O Saint Germain, what love you bring,
it truly makes all matter sing,
your violet flame does all restore,
with you we are becoming more.

7. Saint Germain, shatter the energetic matrix that prevents people from seeing that the value of having a source that is beyond the material is that it cannot be manipulated by any force on earth.

O Saint Germain, I'm karma-free,
the past no longer burdens me,
a brand new opportunity,
I am in Christic unity.

O Saint Germain, what love you bring,
it truly makes all matter sing,
your violet flame does all restore,
with you we are becoming more.

8. Saint Germain, shatter the energetic matrix that prevents people from seeing that throughout recorded history, people have been manipulated by a small elite. The major issue in history has been a small power elite attempting to take control of the population by manipulating them.

O Saint Germain, we are now one,
I am for you a violet sun,
as we transform this planet earth,
your Golden Age is given birth.

O Saint Germain, what love you bring,
it truly makes all matter sing,
your violet flame does all restore,
with you we are becoming more.

9. Saint Germain, shatter the energetic matrix that prevents people from seeing that the power elites have manipulated people by claiming that it is possible to create some system in this world, that is defined based on the knowledge we have in this world without any regard to a higher authority or a higher source.

O Saint Germain, the earth is free,
from burden of duality,
in oneness we bring what is best,
your Golden Age is manifest.

**O Saint Germain, what love you bring,
it truly makes all matter sing,
your violet flame does all restore,
with you we are becoming more.**

Part 4

1. Saint Germain, shatter the energetic matrix that prevents people from seeing that there is a tendency in the world of defining ideologies, religions, systems, political philosophies, that claim that we can know everything we need to know based on the knowledge that is available in this world.

O Saint Germain, you do inspire,
my vision raised forever higher,
with you I form a figure-eight,
your Golden Age I co-create.

**O Saint Germain, what love you bring,
it truly makes all matter sing,
your violet flame does all restore,
with you we are becoming more.**

2. Saint Germain, shatter the energetic matrix that prevents people from seeing that there is a certain level of consciousness where we believe that we have the power to define good and evil, truth and untruth. This is what has been done by most dictatorial systems.

O Saint Germain, what Freedom Flame,
released when we recite your name,
acceleration is your gift,
our planet it will surely lift.

**O Saint Germain, what love you bring,
it truly makes all matter sing,
your violet flame does all restore,
with you we are becoming more.**

3. Saint Germain, shatter the energetic matrix that prevents people from seeing that the world has two tendencies. One says that we human beings are capable of defining absolute truth in some system. The other says that we are not capable of defining absolute truth, we need to reach for a higher source.

O Saint Germain, in love we claim,
our right to bring your violet flame,
from you Above, to us below,
it is an all-transforming flow.

**O Saint Germain, what love you bring,
it truly makes all matter sing,
your violet flame does all restore,
with you we are becoming more.**

4. Saint Germain, shatter the energetic matrix that prevents people from seeing that a democracy is based on the concept of inalienable rights that are given by a source beyond anything on earth. If we take the approach that we human beings can define truth, this works against democracy.

O Saint Germain, I love you so,
my aura filled with violet glow,
my chakras filled with violet fire,
I am your cosmic amplifier.

**O Saint Germain, what love you bring,
it truly makes all matter sing,
your violet flame does all restore,
with you we are becoming more.**

5. Saint Germain, shatter the energetic matrix that prevents people from seeing that the very founding idea of democracy is that we human beings

are not capable of defining our own rights. We cannot allow a dictator or a government, or any other authority to define the rights of the population.

> O Saint Germain, I am now free,
> your violet flame is therapy,
> transform all hang-ups in my mind,
> as inner peace I surely find.

> **O Saint Germain, what love you bring,**
> **it truly makes all matter sing,**
> **your violet flame does all restore,**
> **with you we are becoming more.**

6. Saint Germain, shatter the energetic matrix that prevents people from seeing that the rights of the population are not defined by a small elite. They are not defined by the population. They are defined by an authority that is beyond the level where it can be manipulated either by the elite or by the people themselves.

> O Saint Germain, my body pure,
> your violet flame for all is cure,
> consume the cause of all disease,
> and therefore I am all at ease.

> **O Saint Germain, what love you bring,**
> **it truly makes all matter sing,**
> **your violet flame does all restore,**
> **with you we are becoming more.**

7. Saint Germain, shatter the energetic matrix that prevents people from seeing that our rights do not come from our present level of consciousness, they come from a higher level. That is why they are *rights,* that is why they should be *inalienable* because no authority on earth should take them away.

> O Saint Germain, I'm karma-free,
> the past no longer burdens me,
> a brand new opportunity,
> I am in Christic unity.

O Saint Germain, what love you bring,
it truly makes all matter sing,
your violet flame does all restore,
with you we are becoming more.

8. Saint Germain, shatter the energetic matrix that prevents people from seeing that if we do not acknowledge this, how can we hope to maintain democracy? How can we hope to create a true democracy, which we do not currently have in the highest potential?

O Saint Germain, we are now one,
I am for you a violet sun,
as we transform this planet earth,
your Golden Age is given birth.

O Saint Germain, what love you bring,
it truly makes all matter sing,
your violet flame does all restore,
with you we are becoming more.

9. Saint Germain, shatter the energetic matrix that prevents people from seeing that there has always been a tendency for a small elite to want to control the population and they do it by claiming that they have the ability to define absolute truth whereas the people do not have that ability.

O Saint Germain, the earth is free,
from burden of duality,
in oneness we bring what is best,
your Golden Age is manifest.

O Saint Germain, what love you bring,
it truly makes all matter sing,
your violet flame does all restore,
with you we are becoming more.

Part 5

1. Saint Germain, shatter the energetic matrix behind the lie that people cannot govern themselves, so they need an elite who has a higher ability to govern the people.

O Saint Germain, you do inspire,
my vision raised forever higher,
with you I form a figure-eight,
your Golden Age I co-create.

**O Saint Germain, what love you bring,
it truly makes all matter sing,
your violet flame does all restore,
with you we are becoming more.**

2. Saint Germain, shatter the energetic matrix that prevents people from seeing that the fallen beings first create a problem that results in chaos, and then they offer themselves as the solution to the problem.

O Saint Germain, what Freedom Flame,
released when we recite your name,
acceleration is your gift,
our planet it will surely lift.

**O Saint Germain, what love you bring,
it truly makes all matter sing,
your violet flame does all restore,
with you we are becoming more.**

3. Saint Germain, shatter the energetic matrix that prevents people from seeing that the fallen beings first manipulated people into the dualistic state of consciousness. They allowed the rising of chaos and anarchy, then they said that in order to avoid this, society needs a firm government, a strong leader.

O Saint Germain, in love we claim,
our right to bring your violet flame,

from you Above, to us below,
it is an all-transforming flow.

**O Saint Germain, what love you bring,
it truly makes all matter sing,
your violet flame does all restore,
with you we are becoming more.**

4. Saint Germain, shatter the energetic matrix that prevents people from seeing that we will not destroy ourselves because even though we are in the duality consciousness, we still have a basic humanity. Chaos is not created by the people but by the power elite of fallen beings who have no respect for life.

O Saint Germain, I love you so,
my aura filled with violet glow,
my chakras filled with violet fire,
I am your cosmic amplifier.

**O Saint Germain, what love you bring,
it truly makes all matter sing,
your violet flame does all restore,
with you we are becoming more.**

5. Saint Germain, shatter the energetic matrix that prevents people from seeing that the psychological effect of going into the duality consciousness is that we feel that we are not connected to anything outside ourselves. We have lost our basic sense of individuality, our basic sense of creativity.

O Saint Germain, I am now free,
your violet flame is therapy,
transform all hang-ups in my mind,
as inner peace I surely find.

**O Saint Germain, what love you bring,
it truly makes all matter sing,
your violet flame does all restore,
with you we are becoming more.**

6. Saint Germain, shatter the energetic matrix that prevents people from seeing that the basic driving force behind life is the desire for self-expression. This is the true source of creativity, the driving force of creativity.

> O Saint Germain, my body pure,
> your violet flame for all is cure,
> consume the cause of all disease,
> and therefore I am all at ease.

> **O Saint Germain, what love you bring,**
> **it truly makes all matter sing,**
> **your violet flame does all restore,**
> **with you we are becoming more.**

7. Saint Germain, shatter the energetic matrix that prevents people from seeing that the desire for self-expression causes us to define a self in this world that can give us a sense of being unique.

> O Saint Germain, I'm karma-free,
> the past no longer burdens me,
> a brand new opportunity,
> I am in Christic unity.

> **O Saint Germain, what love you bring,**
> **it truly makes all matter sing,**
> **your violet flame does all restore,**
> **with you we are becoming more.**

8. Saint Germain, shatter the energetic matrix that prevents people from seeing that the fallen beings have had such a long history of doing this that they have created this very strong outer personality that makes them feel special and better than the original inhabitants of the earth.

> O Saint Germain, we are now one,
> I am for you a violet sun,
> as we transform this planet earth,
> your Golden Age is given birth.

O Saint Germain, what love you bring,
it truly makes all matter sing,
your violet flame does all restore,
with you we are becoming more.

9. Saint Germain, shatter the energetic matrix that prevents people from seeing that after the fallen beings started embodying here, the majority of the people accepted: "Oh, I am not a unique being. I am not creative, I do not have a unique personality. So I'd better follow the leaders."

O Saint Germain, the earth is free,
from burden of duality,
in oneness we bring what is best,
your Golden Age is manifest.

O Saint Germain, what love you bring,
it truly makes all matter sing,
your violet flame does all restore,
with you we are becoming more.

Part 6

1. Saint Germain, shatter the energetic matrix that prevents people from seeing that this created "mechanization man" where people have lost their inbuilt creativity and are blindly following a leader, almost like automatons.

O Saint Germain, you do inspire,
my vision raised forever higher,
with you I form a figure-eight,
your Golden Age I co-create.

O Saint Germain, what love you bring,
it truly makes all matter sing,
your violet flame does all restore,
with you we are becoming more.

2. Saint Germain, shatter the energetic matrix that prevents people from seeing that the fallen beings want to create people who blindly follow them and accept that they are such unique individuals.

O Saint Germain, what Freedom Flame,
released when we recite your name,
acceleration is your gift,
our planet it will surely lift.

**O Saint Germain, what love you bring,
it truly makes all matter sing,
your violet flame does all restore,
with you we are becoming more.**

3. Saint Germain, shatter the energetic matrix that prevents people from seeing that the dictators of the world always make some kind of claim of why they are special, why they have special abilities, special powers.

O Saint Germain, in love we claim,
our right to bring your violet flame,
from you Above, to us below,
it is an all-transforming flow.

**O Saint Germain, what love you bring,
it truly makes all matter sing,
your violet flame does all restore,
with you we are becoming more.**

4. Saint Germain, shatter the energetic matrix that prevents people from seeing that everybody is having an entirely subjective experience and that the only source of problems on earth is that some people are attempting to export their subjective experience to others and thereby make their subjective experience seem universal.

O Saint Germain, I love you so,
my aura filled with violet glow,
my chakras filled with violet fire,
I am your cosmic amplifier.

O Saint Germain, what love you bring,
it truly makes all matter sing,
your violet flame does all restore,
with you we are becoming more.

5. Saint Germain, shatter the energetic matrix that prevents people from seeing that this is what the fallen beings have been doing since they fell. This is what many human beings have been trying to do since they went into duality.

O Saint Germain, I am now free,
your violet flame is therapy,
transform all hang-ups in my mind,
as inner peace I surely find.

O Saint Germain, what love you bring,
it truly makes all matter sing,
your violet flame does all restore,
with you we are becoming more.

6. Saint Germain, shatter the energetic matrix that prevents people from seeing that those who have a certain creative drive, they have been trying to make their subjective experience universal, according to some criteria they or some philosophy or authority figure have defined.

O Saint Germain, my body pure,
your violet flame for all is cure,
consume the cause of all disease,
and therefore I am all at ease.

O Saint Germain, what love you bring,
it truly makes all matter sing,
your violet flame does all restore,
with you we are becoming more.

7. Saint Germain, shatter the energetic matrix that prevents people from seeing that the key to immortality is *not* to prevent death, but to embrace death and allow the separate self to die so we can return to our true sense of identity as immortal spiritual beings.

O Saint Germain, I'm karma-free,
the past no longer burdens me,
a brand new opportunity,
I am in Christic unity.

**O Saint Germain, what love you bring,
it truly makes all matter sing,
your violet flame does all restore,
with you we are becoming more.**

8. Saint Germain, shatter the energetic matrix that prevents people from seeing that one of the real errors of Christianity is the concept of original sin that says human beings are inherently flawed, that they were created flawed.

O Saint Germain, we are now one,
I am for you a violet sun,
as we transform this planet earth,
your Golden Age is given birth.

**O Saint Germain, what love you bring,
it truly makes all matter sing,
your violet flame does all restore,
with you we are becoming more.**

9. Saint Germain, shatter the energetic matrix that prevents people from seeing that we can never lose our ability to free ourselves from the separate selves we have created in this world. We can never make a choice that we cannot free ourselves from by making a more aware choice.

O Saint Germain, the earth is free,
from burden of duality,
in oneness we bring what is best,
your Golden Age is manifest.

**O Saint Germain, what love you bring,
it truly makes all matter sing,
your violet flame does all restore,
with you we are becoming more.**

Sealing

In the name of the I AM THAT I AM, I accept that Archangel Michael, Astrea and Shiva form an impenetrable shield around myself and all constructive people, sealing us from all fear-based energies in all four octaves. I accept that the Light of God is consuming and transforming all fear-based energies that make up the dark forces working against ending the era of dictatorships on earth!

16 | OVERCOMING THE FEAR OF MAKING CHOICES

I AM the Ascended Master Shiva. Even though the millions of people in the Hindu religion who revere the name Shiva would object to that statement. They would say I am not an ascended master but a God. Nevertheless, I *am* an ascended master and I hold the office that is in the Hindu religion associated with the God Shiva. Truly, the God Shiva is a universal principle, one of the three creative principles: The creative, the principle that creates, the one that sustains and the one that breaks down.

You would see that if there was only creation and sustainment, then very quickly co-creators with a lack of experience would create things that would begin to limit themselves. How can you then break free of your previous creation? Well, that is where you need Shiva, where you need the principle that breaks down the structures that are not the highest. You see that truly what they often in the Hindu religion call destruction is not the best description of the principle behind Shiva. Truly, it would be better to talk about a liberating principle so that you can be set free from your previous creation.

Now, what is the true process that you go through as a co-creator? Well, it is that you set a process in motion through the four levels of your mind that over time creates a certain physical manifestation. This is where you use your co-creative abilities, the principle of Brahma. Then, the principle of Vishnu takes over and sustains your creation in the physical for some time. This is in order to give you an opportunity to experience your own creation and to evaluate your own creation.

What ideally happens is that you formulate a matrix in your mind, project it upon the Ma-ter light and manifest a physical circumstance. Then, as you see and experience that circumstance, you are raising your consciousness. This does not mean, in the ideal scenario, that you think you have done something wrong. In an ideal scenario, the concept of right and wrong has nothing to do with co-creation, they do not even come into the equation. You raise your awareness by creating something and experiencing what you have created. This means that now you could see how you can create something that is more. How can you create something more when you still have that physical manifestation that you already created? You can only do so if there is something that can break down what you have created and thereby liberate yourself from your own creation.

Death is an opportunity to move higher

You will see that the fallen beings attempt to pervert any spiritual teaching given to you. They have, even in the Hindu religion, created this idea that Shiva is the destroyer. They have created these fear-based images that you have all seen. Therefore, many people in the Hindu religion actually fear Shiva, as many people around the world fear death because they think death is a form of destruction.

My beloved, ask yourself this question. Would you want to be in your current physical body forever? Would you not rather reincarnate, with a higher level of consciousness that would then precipitate a physical body with better health, better looks, better abilities? In the current situation on earth, is death really a destructive process, or is it a liberating process? Is it not so that if you are on the path of raising your consciousness but you are not ready to make your ascension, then the death of one physical body is simply the breaking down of a body that was the result of a certain level of consciousness that you have now transcended. Therefore, you are set free to reincarnate in a higher body, of a higher stature.

You see that the fallen beings, because they are out of touch with the creative process, are not willing to be truly creative. They are manifesting a certain physical circumstance where they feel they are superior, they are in control and they want to maintain that forever—literally. Therefore, they are not so concerned about Brahma and Vishnu but the fallen beings are very concerned about Shiva. That is why they have created the perversion that Shiva is the destroyer.

Yet my beloved, am I a destructive force? You look at the fallen beings and the chaos and destruction they have created throughout the ages. There are some fallen beings who will say that they are just using the power of Shiva. They are even emissaries of Shiva because there needs to be destruction for there to be renewal. They are acting on the principle of Shiva by creating this destruction in the physical realm. Of course this is an untruth. The destruction created by the fallen beings is destruction, it is destructive. It breaks down what human beings have created. The fallen beings have broken down previous civilizations that were much more orderly than what you see today. The fallen beings brought war to this planet and that is certainly a destructive force, even though some fallen beings have glorified war, even glorified the destruction of war, even seen it as necessary for, as the saying goes, "culling the herd." Cutting down the unwanted human beings that are not beneficial for the survival of the race.

Shiva is the principle of liberation

You see that this entire consciousness of destruction is a perversion of the true aspect of Shiva. It has nothing to do with Shiva. I am not the destroyer because I work within the realms of free will. I do not break down what you do not want to have broken down unless we come to the point where you activate what we have called the second law of thermodynamics. If you seek to maintain a limited state indefinitely, then there is a law, which is an aspect of the Law of Free Will, that mandates that your creation will begin to self-destruct. This is not Shiva that comes in as a conscious ascended being and destroys. You are activating this destructive force. Your own creation destroys itself from within.

What then is the true nature of Shiva? It is that I stand ready to liberate human beings from their own creation when they invite me into action, when they call me into action. Indeed, I am inviting you who are ascended master students to call me into action by using the awareness that has been given you by the other masters who have spoken and who will speak at this conference. There will be invocations created that will invoke the fire of Shiva to consume the demons in the astral plane, the demons in the mental plane and the demons in the identity realm that are behind dictatorships on earth. You can call forth the judgment of the fallen beings, and as the law requires or allows me to do, they will be bound or consumed, whatever is appropriate.

Setting people free to choose a different government

By doing this, you can then provide the service that will free human beings from this hypnotic effect (that they are under) that blinds them so they cannot really see that they have a choice. They have a choice as to what kind of government they want. Do they want a dictatorship or do they want a democratic form of government? Do the people in the democratic nations want a world where there is still dictatorships? Or do they want a world that is free from dictatorships? By you making the calls for these dark forces, you are not interfering with the free will of the dark forces, for demons have no free will and fallen beings no longer have free will [their will is no longer free]. The human beings who are hypnotized by the fallen beings and the demons do not have free will either.

By freeing the human beings from the influence of these dark forces, you restore their freedom of will. This is the entire purpose of Shiva, to restore the freedom of people's will by restoring their awareness, their vision, that they actually have a choice. They have more than one option to choose from. What is one of the driving forces behind creating a dictatorship? It is setting up one person or a small group of people in a position of absolute authority where the people who are under that dictator have submitted their will to the dictator. They think there is no alternative to the dictator. They cannot free themselves, they cannot leave the nation, they cannot object to the dictator, they cannot criticize or they will be killed. They think they have no choice, they have no options. Of course they do! You always have options. You always have the option to shift your consciousness, to raise your consciousness.

This is what people do not realize. Many people in dictatorships do not realize it, even many people in the democratic world do not realize it. Why do you see, as we have said, that in some of the older democracies people are becoming dissatisfied with the government but they still feel powerless to change anything? They feel that the system is in a stalemate where they cannot really see how to change it. Well, the reason why they cannot see how to change their democracies is that they are not willing to change themselves, they are not willing to raise their consciousness.

Overcoming the human dilemma

When you do raise your consciousness, you can see what you cannot see now. This is the entire principle behind the spiritual path. What does it take to raise your consciousness? Is there some magical formula as so many people believe and as the false gurus controlled by the fallen beings promise people? Oh, do this meditation twenty minutes a day and you will one day be enlightened. Oh, do this mantra, do this chant, do this, do that and one day automatically you will be free. It is a complete lie, my beloved. There is only one way to be free and it is to raise your awareness by looking at yourself. By coming to recognize that you have created whatever you call it, matrices, selves, inner spirits in your own being, and that you created them as a result of situations on earth. Many of those situations you were manipulated into by the fallen beings so that you were in a situation where you thought you had no choice. Therefore, you created these selves to deal with the situation.

The way to overcome the self is to raise your awareness so you see that you do have a choice. You do have a choice to let the self go. You do have the choice to realize that the self projects that there is a problem you have to solve, but it is an unreal, a manipulated, an artificial problem. Therefore, you can choose to say: "I am no longer going to engage my attention and my energy in trying to solve this problem. I am giving up trying to solve the problem and I am letting the self die."

Saint Germain in his dictation mentioned the eternal question: "To be or not to be." You might find occasion to watch a movie about Hamlet because he is the archetype of what has happened as a result of the fallen beings manipulating people's free will. Hamlet was manipulated into a situation where he knew someone wanted to kill him. The question was: Did he strike first, or did he wait for them to strike first? Those were the only options he could see. This is an illustration inspired by Saint Germain, to show what could be called the human dilemma. The human dilemma is not really a *human* dilemma. It is an *artificial* dilemma created by the fallen beings.

In other words, it is not a dilemma that follows from human nature. It follows from the duality consciousness but the duality consciousness is not human nature. With all the teachings we have given you, you are able to make that distinction. Duality is not human nature and therefore the problems that spring from duality are not human nature. They are not inevitable, you are not created in a dualistic state. It is something you have taken on and that you can take off again.

The fallen beings have manipulated people into situations where you think you have limited choices. You are, as the saying goes: "Damned if you do and damned if you don't." Whether you act or whether you refuse to act, it creates unpleasant consequences. The reason why you see it that way is that your vision is limited so you do not see more than two or a few options. You think you have to either do this or do nothing. You do not see the alternative and the alternative is of course always raising your consciousness.

We have given the illustration before that raising your consciousness is like starting at the ground level and walking up through an observation tower that gives you a view over the entire landscape. At the ground level you can only see the forest, or rather you can only see the trees, for you cannot see the forest for the trees. Once you ascend to the top of the tower, you can see what is beyond the trees. At a certain level of consciousness you see only problems, you see no solutions. You see only the options that the fallen beings want you to see. Once you rise to a higher level of consciousness, you see beyond these dualistic options, the dualistic polarities, and you see that there is always an alternative.

You may say: "But there is one self that is prompting me to do something. There is another self that is prompting me to do nothing. What is there besides doing something or doing nothing? What choices do I have?" Well, this is the entire concept of the Middle Way as taught by the Buddha. There is an alternative to doing or not doing. Now, where modern Buddhism (and for that matter throughout history) has deviated from the Buddha's teachings, is that they often think that the alternative to doing something in the world that leads to undesirable consequences, is to withdraw to a monastery and perform Buddhist practices and rituals. What the Buddha really meant with the concept of the Middle Way is that you transcend the pairs, the dualistic polarities. Therefore, you see that there are more options than doing, or doing nothing. You can come to a state of consciousness where you are not acting based on duality. Therefore, you see that you can do something that is not the dualistic option manipulated by the fallen beings. There are other ways to act.

Karma is not inevitable

The Hindu religion is very focused on Karma and they think that any action you take creates karma. Many people around the world, even many New Age people, think that an action always creates karma. It can be good karma, it can be bad karma but whenever you take an action, it creates karma. The way they look at karma is actually not in accordance with reality. We have given teachings about karma that are at a higher level. Karma is not something that you inevitably create because part of the karma is your own state of consciousness. It is that when you take a certain action, you are actually basing that action on a particular separate self. By taking the action and even seeing the consequence mirrored back by the cosmic mirror, you are reinforcing that self. What happens is, you are colored by a certain separate self, you take an action through that separate self, this reinforces the self. Then, when the reaction comes back from the Cosmic Mirror, you are evaluating the reaction through the same separate self (or through another separate self) and that reinforces that separate self. This is really karma. It is not something that you send out and that then some mysterious force in the universe or law sends back to you. It is something you create internally.

Truly, what comes back to you is something that you have continued to create by continuing to allow yourself to act through that separate self. When you come to a point where you have overcome your birth trauma or earth trauma, where you have let go of these separate selves, then you can act in the world without making karma. The actions you take are not taken through a separate self, they are not reinforcing that separate self. When a reaction comes back to you, you are not evaluating that reaction through another separate self. Therefore, you are not reinforcing your separate selves when you take action. This means that you can take action without limiting your freedom because you are not attached to the fruits of action, as the Buddha taught.

Non-attachment can only be achieved by shedding the separate selves because it is the separate selves that generate the attachments. We might not say that a separate self has an attachment but the attachment is the result of the programming of the separate self. The separate self wants to reinforce its programming and therefore, when you evaluate what comes back to you through a separate self, it will seem to reinforce the programming of that separate self. When you let go of the separate selves, you can evaluate what comes back in a completely neutral manner.

Therefore, you are simply saying: "Was this what I really wanted? Do I want more *of* this, or do I want more *than* this?" If you decide that this was not what you really wanted, you want more than this, then you simply shift your consciousness. In other words, when you let go of the separate selves, you are back in the true co-creative process. You are taking an action, you are sending an impulse into the Cosmic Mirror. When it is returned to you as a physical circumstance, you are not even evaluating: "Was it good or bad, right or wrong, should I feel guilty about this, should I feel bad about this, does this show I am inadequate." You simply say: "What can I learn from this." You learn from it and then you send a new impulse that then manifests a higher circumstance.

Overcoming the fear of acting

You are not going from one karmic return to another. You are not damned if you do and damned if you don't. You are not afraid of acting, you are not afraid of making choices because you realize that any choice you make is an opportunity to learn that empowers you to make a higher choice. So many people, even many ascended master students, are afraid of doing something because they are afraid of making bad karma, they are afraid of making a mistake. They are afraid of being condemned by others, being condemned by the ascended masters, being condemned by themselves.

You are not condemned by yourself but by your selves—your separate selves. When you let go of them, there is no fear associated with the creative process. There is no unwillingness, reluctance to make decisions. You simply make decisions. This does not mean that you always make a snap decision in any situation. You may in many situations say that there is a need to just step back. People will say: "I need to think about this" but you are not really thinking about it with the analytical mind. You are actually going into a neutral state of mind, looking at the situation, formulating a question, you are sending that question to your I AM Presence and then you just wait until an impulse comes back from the Presence. It does not tell you what to do. It just gives you a certain vibration, a certain vibrational matrix, that gives you a frame of reference so it suddenly becomes obvious: "Oh yes, this is what I am going to do." There is no fear, there is no reluctance. You can come to a point where co-creation becomes a joyful process.

This is what all of us in the ascended realm want to see for our students. That is why I, Shiva, will offer you that I am willing to work with you, if you are willing to come to see your separate selves, see these structures and beliefs you have in your mind. Then, call me to come and consume them so you can be set free to have more choices, more options, instead of standing there like Hamlet wondering "to be or not to be" "to do or not to do" "to do this, to do that, to not do this, to not do that." "What will I do, God help me," you cry out. "God, come down here and tell me what to do so that I do not have to make a choice."

Well, my beloved, why are so many people subject to dictators? Because they have cried out: "Someone tell me what to do, I do not want to choose for myself." The fallen beings have said: "Aha, we will send you a dictator who will tell you what to do. Just follow us." People follow them until they experience disaster after disaster and somehow there is an impulse in their beings that says: "Perhaps I could actually do better by making my own choices than by following these dictators? Perhaps there would be less consequences by me making my own choices than by following Adolph Hitler on his insane quest?"

Rising above the dictator

When people then come to that point, then they can very gradually, very slowly, begin to grow. It does not take that long after people make that decision before their next embodiment will be in a democratic nation where they then have the option to make more decisions on their own without wanting some absolute authority to tell them what to do. Look today, look today, my beloved, in many democratic nations where the nation itself is free in a political sense. You still have many people who although they are in a democratic nation and although they have opinions about this or that, although they go to the polling stations and vote for their representatives, they still belong to one of these religions that are also set up by the fallen beings to tell people what to do, at least in a certain aspect of life.

You see that it is not only a political dictator that tells people what to do but also the religious dictators that tell people what to do. This is also something you can make calls for so that people will be cut free from this, so that they take responsibility for themselves. They realize: "I am willing to make my own choices." Why is it important to realize this? Well, it is simply an outcome of the Law of Free Will. Each human being is an individual. As we have said, each human being has a unique I AM Presence. It is always better for the growth of that human being, regardless of what level of consciousness they are at, that they make their own choices. *That* is what can help them grow.

When you put your willingness to choose on pause and blindly follow a dictator, you are not growing. You cannot grow. Therefore, it is always better to make your own choices. It is always better because what is the process I have described? You make a choice, you see the consequence, you evaluate: "How can I raise my consciousness?" Then, you can make a better choice. You can only do this when you make your own decisions. They may be of course partially affected by whatever you have been exposed to on earth. But by making decisions, you have the opportunity to raise your consciousness. You do not have that when you are not making decisions. You cannot grow when you are not making decisions.

Many people will say: "But if I am in a lower state of consciousness, isn't it better that I do not make decisions, so that I do not make negative karma?" No, it is not better because whatever state of consciousness you are at, when you make a decision from that state of consciousness, this will be reflected back to you by the Cosmic Mirror. What does that give you an opportunity to do? To see the limitations of that state of consciousness so you can transcend it.

Setting people free to make their own choices

Therefore, what you realize here is that when you, as the spiritual people, call for other people to be cut free from all these demons, the burdens, the illusions of the fallen beings, you are not violating their free will or the Law of Free Will. You are restoring the freedom of their will and you are giving them an opportunity to grow. You need to be completely non-attached as to whether they take that opportunity or not. You are content with giving them the opportunity. You have no intent about what they should do with their lives.

This is especially important when you make calls for loved ones. You need to go into that neutral frame of mind. You give them the freedom to choose and you allow them to choose. You do not even have an opinion about what they should choose. You do not try to influence them, blame them or whatever. You allow them to choose without having an opinion. You are in a neutral state of mind. Otherwise, you can actually make what you traditionally call karma because you have that intent to influence other people's choices. Be neutral. When you are in a neutral state of mind, you are not violating people's free will by calling for them to be set free from what limits their free will.

This concludes my remarks. I want to express my gratitude to all of you for your willingness to be here, to broadcast this message through your auras and chakras into the collective consciousness. I am grateful to those who will take the invocations we give and use them to also broadcast into the collective consciousness that there is a real choice. There is always a choice, a *real* choice. Thus, SHIVA I AM.

17 | INVOKING FREEDOM TO CHOOSE WITHOUT FEAR

In the name of the I AM THAT I AM, Jesus Christ, I use the authority that I have as a being in embodiment on earth to call upon Shiva to reinforce my calls and use my chakras to project the statements in this invocation into the collective consciousness and restore people's freedom to choose. Awaken people to the reality that we are spiritual beings and that we can co-create a new future by working with the ascended masters. I especially call for ...

[Make your own calls here.]

Part 1

1. Shiva, shatter the energetic matrix that prevents people from seeing that we are co-creators. We co-create by setting a process in motion through the four levels of our minds that over time creates a certain physical manifestation.

> O Shiva, God of Sacred Fire,
> It's time to let the past expire,

I want to rise above the old,
a golden future to unfold.

O Shiva, clear the energy,
O Shiva, bring the synergy,
O Shiva, make all demons flee,
O Shiva, bring back peace to me.

2. Shiva, shatter the energetic matrix that prevents people from seeing that we ideally learn from what we have manifested and thereby raise our consciousness.

O Shiva, come and set me free,
from forces that do limit me,
with fire consume all that is less,
paving way for my success.

O Shiva, clear the energy,
O Shiva, bring the synergy,
O Shiva, make all demons flee,
O Shiva, bring back peace to me.

3. Shiva, shatter the energetic matrix that prevents people from seeing that in order to create something based on our higher consciousness, we need something that can break down what we have created and thereby liberate ourselves from our own creation.

O Shiva, Maya's veil disperse,
clear my private universe,
dispel the consciousness of death,
consume it with your Sacred Breath.

O Shiva, clear the energy,
O Shiva, bring the synergy,
O Shiva, make all demons flee,
O Shiva, bring back peace to me.

4. Shiva, shatter the energetic matrix that prevents people from seeing that some fallen beings say that they are emissaries of Shiva because there needs to be destruction for there to be renewal.

O Shiva, I hereby let go,
of all attachments here below,
addictive entities consume,
the upward path I do resume.

O Shiva, clear the energy,
O Shiva, bring the synergy,
O Shiva, make all demons flee,
O Shiva, bring back peace to me.

5. Shiva, shatter the energetic matrix that prevents people from seeing that this is an untruth because the destruction created by the fallen beings is destructive. It breaks down what human beings have created.

O Shiva, I recite your name,
come banish fear and doubt and shame,
with fire expose within my mind,
what ego seeks to hide behind.

O Shiva, clear the energy,
O Shiva, bring the synergy,
O Shiva, make all demons flee,
O Shiva, bring back peace to me.

6. Shiva, shatter the energetic matrix that prevents people from seeing that the fallen beings brought war to this planet and that it is a destructive force, even though some fallen beings have glorified war, even glorified the destruction of war, even seen it as necessary for "culling the herd."

O Shiva, I am not afraid,
my karmic debt hereby is paid,
the past no longer owns my choice,
in breath of Shiva I rejoice.

O Shiva, clear the energy,
O Shiva, bring the synergy,
O Shiva, make all demons flee,
O Shiva, bring back peace to me.

7. Shiva, shatter the energetic matrix that prevents people from seeing that the true nature of Shiva is to liberate human beings from their own creation when they invite this into action.

O Shiva, show me spirit pairs,
that keep me trapped in their affairs,
I choose to see within my mind,
the spirits that you surely bind.

O Shiva, clear the energy,
O Shiva, bring the synergy,
O Shiva, make all demons flee,
O Shiva, bring back peace to me.

8. Shiva, I use the authority I have as an ascended master student to call you into action for removing the energies and the lies behind dictatorships on earth.

O Shiva, naked I now stand,
my mind in freedom does expand,
as all my ghosts I do release,
surrender is the key to peace.

O Shiva, clear the energy,
O Shiva, bring the synergy,
O Shiva, make all demons flee,
O Shiva, bring back peace to me.

9. Shiva, I call forth the judgment of Christ upon the fallen beings, and I call for you to bind or consume them as the Law allows you to do.

O Shiva, all-consuming fire,
with Parvati raise me higher,

when I am raised your light to see,
all men I will draw onto me.

O Shiva, clear the energy,
O Shiva, bring the synergy,
O Shiva, make all demons flee,
O Shiva, bring back peace to me.

Part 2

1. I invoke the fire of Shiva to consume the demons in the astral plane that are behind dictatorships on earth.

O Shiva, God of Sacred Fire,
It's time to let the past expire,
I want to rise above the old,
a golden future to unfold.

O Shiva, clear the energy,
O Shiva, bring the synergy,
O Shiva, make all demons flee,
O Shiva, bring back peace to me.

2. I invoke the fire of Shiva to consume the beings in the mental plane that are behind dictatorships on earth.

O Shiva, come and set me free,
from forces that do limit me,
with fire consume all that is less,
paving way for my success.

O Shiva, clear the energy,
O Shiva, bring the synergy,
O Shiva, make all demons flee,
O Shiva, bring back peace to me.

3. I invoke the fire of Shiva to consume the beings in the identity realm that are behind dictatorships on earth.

> O Shiva, Maya's veil disperse,
> clear my private universe,
> dispel the consciousness of death,
> consume it with your Sacred Breath.

> **O Shiva, clear the energy,**
> **O Shiva, bring the synergy,**
> **O Shiva, make all demons flee,**
> **O Shiva, bring back peace to me.**

4. Shiva, shatter the energetic matrix and free human beings from the hypnotic effect that blinds them so they cannot see that they have a choice as to what kind of government they want, a dictatorship or a democratic government.

> O Shiva, I hereby let go,
> of all attachments here below,
> addictive entities consume,
> the upward path I do resume.

> **O Shiva, clear the energy,**
> **O Shiva, bring the synergy,**
> **O Shiva, make all demons flee,**
> **O Shiva, bring back peace to me.**

5. Shiva, shatter the energetic matrix and free human beings from the hypnotic effect that blinds them so they cannot see that they have a choice as to whether they want a world where there is still dictatorships or a world that is free from dictatorships.

> O Shiva, I recite your name,
> come banish fear and doubt and shame,
> with fire expose within my mind,
> what ego seeks to hide behind.

O Shiva, clear the energy,
O Shiva, bring the synergy,
O Shiva, make all demons flee,
O Shiva, bring back peace to me.

6. Shiva, shatter the energetic matrix and free people from the influence of dark forces so their freedom of will is restored.

O Shiva, I am not afraid,
my karmic debt hereby is paid,
the past no longer owns my choice,
in breath of Shiva I rejoice.

O Shiva, clear the energy,
O Shiva, bring the synergy,
O Shiva, make all demons flee,
O Shiva, bring back peace to me.

7. Shiva, shatter the energetic matrix that prevents people from seeing that the entire purpose of Shiva is to restore the freedom of people's will by restoring their awareness that they actually have a choice. They have more than one option to choose from.

O Shiva, show me spirit pairs,
that keep me trapped in their affairs,
I choose to see within my mind,
the spirits that you surely bind.

O Shiva, clear the energy,
O Shiva, bring the synergy,
O Shiva, make all demons flee,
O Shiva, bring back peace to me.

8. Shiva, shatter the energetic matrix that prevents people from seeing that one of the driving forces behind creating a dictatorship is setting up one person or a small group of people in a position of absolute authority where the people who are under that dictator have submitted their will to the dictator.

O Shiva, naked I now stand,
my mind in freedom does expand,
as all my ghosts I do release,
surrender is the key to peace.

O Shiva, clear the energy,
O Shiva, bring the synergy,
O Shiva, make all demons flee,
O Shiva, bring back peace to me.

9. Shiva, shatter the energetic matrix that prevents people from seeing that there is an alternative to the dictator. They can free themselves and their nation by shifting their consciousness, by raising their consciousness.

O Shiva, all-consuming fire,
with Parvati raise me higher,
when I am raised your light to see,
all men I will draw onto me.

O Shiva, clear the energy,
O Shiva, bring the synergy,
O Shiva, make all demons flee,
O Shiva, bring back peace to me.

Part 3

1. Shiva, shatter the energetic matrix that prevents people in the older democracies from seeing that they are not powerless. They can change their democracies if they are willing to change themselves, if they are willing to raise their consciousness.

O Shiva, God of Sacred Fire,
It's time to let the past expire,
I want to rise above the old,
a golden future to unfold.

O Shiva, clear the energy,
O Shiva, bring the synergy,
O Shiva, make all demons flee,
O Shiva, bring back peace to me.

2. Shiva, shatter the energetic matrix that prevents people from seeing that when we do raise our consciousness, we can see what we cannot see now. This is the entire principle behind the spiritual path.

O Shiva, come and set me free,
from forces that do limit me,
with fire consume all that is less,
paving way for my success.

O Shiva, clear the energy,
O Shiva, bring the synergy,
O Shiva, make all demons flee,
O Shiva, bring back peace to me.

3. Shiva, shatter the energetic matrix that prevents people from seeing that the only way to be free is to raise our awareness by looking at ourselves.

O Shiva, Maya's veil disperse,
clear my private universe,
dispel the consciousness of death,
consume it with your Sacred Breath.

O Shiva, clear the energy,
O Shiva, bring the synergy,
O Shiva, make all demons flee,
O Shiva, bring back peace to me.

4. Shiva, shatter the energetic matrix that prevents people from seeing that we have created matrices, selves, inner spirits in our own beings as a result of situations on earth.

O Shiva, I hereby let go,
of all attachments here below,

addictive entities consume,
the upward path I do resume.

O Shiva, clear the energy,
O Shiva, bring the synergy,
O Shiva, make all demons flee,
O Shiva, bring back peace to me.

5. Shiva, shatter the energetic matrix that prevents people from seeing that the way to overcome the self is to raise our awareness so we see that we do have a choice to let the self go.

O Shiva, I recite your name,
come banish fear and doubt and shame,
with fire expose within my mind,
what ego seeks to hide behind.

O Shiva, clear the energy,
O Shiva, bring the synergy,
O Shiva, make all demons flee,
O Shiva, bring back peace to me.

6. Shiva, shatter the energetic matrix that prevents people from seeing that the self projects that there is a problem we have to solve, but it is an unreal, a manipulated, an artificial problem.

O Shiva, I am not afraid,
my karmic debt hereby is paid,
the past no longer owns my choice,
in breath of Shiva I rejoice.

O Shiva, clear the energy,
O Shiva, bring the synergy,
O Shiva, make all demons flee,
O Shiva, bring back peace to me.

7. Shiva, shatter the energetic matrix that prevents people from seeing that we have the option to say: "I am no longer going to engage my attention

and my energy in trying to solve this problem. I am giving up trying to solve the problem and I am letting the self die."

O Shiva, show me spirit pairs,
that keep me trapped in their affairs,
I choose to see within my mind,
the spirits that you surely bind.

O Shiva, clear the energy,
O Shiva, bring the synergy,
O Shiva, make all demons flee,
O Shiva, bring back peace to me.

8. Shiva, shatter the energetic matrix that prevents people from seeing that the human dilemma is not really a *human* dilemma. It is an *artificial* dilemma created by the fallen beings.

O Shiva, naked I now stand,
my mind in freedom does expand,
as all my ghosts I do release,
surrender is the key to peace.

O Shiva, clear the energy,
O Shiva, bring the synergy,
O Shiva, make all demons flee,
O Shiva, bring back peace to me.

9. Shiva, shatter the energetic matrix that prevents people from seeing that the human dilemma is not a dilemma that follows from human nature. It follows from the duality consciousness but the duality consciousness is not human nature.

O Shiva, all-consuming fire,
with Parvati raise me higher,
when I am raised your light to see,
all men I will draw onto me.

O Shiva, clear the energy,
O Shiva, bring the synergy,

O Shiva, make all demons flee,
O Shiva, bring back peace to me.

Part 4

1. Shiva, shatter the energetic matrix that prevents people from seeing that the problems that spring from duality are not human nature. They are not inevitable, we are not created in a dualistic state. It is something we have taken on and that we can take off again.

> O Shiva, God of Sacred Fire,
> It's time to let the past expire,
> I want to rise above the old,
> a golden future to unfold.

> **O Shiva, clear the energy,**
> **O Shiva, bring the synergy,**
> **O Shiva, make all demons flee,**
> **O Shiva, bring back peace to me.**

2. Shiva, shatter the energetic matrix that prevents people from seeing that the fallen beings have manipulated us into situations where it seems that whether we act or refuse to act, it creates unpleasant consequences.

> O Shiva, come and set me free,
> from forces that do limit me,
> with fire consume all that is less,
> paving way for my success.

> **O Shiva, clear the energy,**
> **O Shiva, bring the synergy,**
> **O Shiva, make all demons flee,**
> **O Shiva, bring back peace to me.**

3. Shiva, shatter the energetic matrix that prevents people from seeing that the reason we see it that way is that our vision is limited so we do not see

more than a few options. We think we have to either do this or do nothing. We do not see the alternative, which is to raise our consciousness.

> O Shiva, Maya's veil disperse,
> clear my private universe,
> dispel the consciousness of death,
> consume it with your Sacred Breath.

> **O Shiva, clear the energy,**
> **O Shiva, bring the synergy,**
> **O Shiva, make all demons flee,**
> **O Shiva, bring back peace to me.**

4. Shiva, shatter the energetic matrix that prevents people from seeing that through the duality consciousness we see only the options that the fallen beings want us to see. Once we raise our consciousness, we see beyond these dualistic options and we see that there is always an alternative.

> O Shiva, I hereby let go,
> of all attachments here below,
> addictive entities consume,
> the upward path I do resume.

> **O Shiva, clear the energy,**
> **O Shiva, bring the synergy,**
> **O Shiva, make all demons flee,**
> **O Shiva, bring back peace to me.**

5. Shiva, shatter the energetic matrix that prevents people from seeing that they are subject to dictators because they are afraid to make decisions. They have cried out: "Someone tell me what to do, I do not want to choose for myself."

> O Shiva, I recite your name,
> come banish fear and doubt and shame,
> with fire expose within my mind,
> what ego seeks to hide behind.

O Shiva, clear the energy,
O Shiva, bring the synergy,
O Shiva, make all demons flee,
O Shiva, bring back peace to me.

6. Shiva, shatter the energetic matrix that prevents people from seeing that the fallen beings have sent dictators and said: "Just follow us."

O Shiva, I am not afraid,
my karmic debt hereby is paid,
the past no longer owns my choice,
in breath of Shiva I rejoice.

O Shiva, clear the energy,
O Shiva, bring the synergy,
O Shiva, make all demons flee,
O Shiva, bring back peace to me.

7. Shiva, shatter the energetic matrix that prevents people from seeing that we follow the fallen beings until we experience disaster after disaster and say: "Perhaps we could do better by making our own choices than by following these dictators?"

O Shiva, show me spirit pairs,
that keep me trapped in their affairs,
I choose to see within my mind,
the spirits that you surely bind.

O Shiva, clear the energy,
O Shiva, bring the synergy,
O Shiva, make all demons flee,
O Shiva, bring back peace to me.

8. Shiva, shatter the energetic matrix that prevents people from seeing that there are political dictators and religious dictators that tell us what to do.

O Shiva, naked I now stand,
my mind in freedom does expand,

as all my ghosts I do release,
surrender is the key to peace.

**O Shiva, clear the energy,
O Shiva, bring the synergy,
O Shiva, make all demons flee,
O Shiva, bring back peace to me.**

9. Shiva, shatter the energetic matrix that prevents people from taking responsibility for themselves and realizing: "I am willing to make my own choices."

O Shiva, all-consuming fire,
with Parvati raise me higher,
when I am raised your light to see,
all men I will draw onto me.

**O Shiva, clear the energy,
O Shiva, bring the synergy,
O Shiva, make all demons flee,
O Shiva, bring back peace to me.**

Part 5

1. Shiva, shatter the energetic matrix that prevents people from seeing that we only grow by making choices. When we put our willingness to choose on pause and blindly follow a dictator, we are not growing.

O Shiva, God of Sacred Fire,
It's time to let the past expire,
I want to rise above the old,
a golden future to unfold.

**O Shiva, clear the energy,
O Shiva, bring the synergy,
O Shiva, make all demons flee,
O Shiva, bring back peace to me.**

2. Shiva, shatter the energetic matrix that prevents people from seeing that it is always better to make our own choices. We make a choice, we see the consequence, we evaluate: "How can I raise my consciousness?" Then, we can make a better choice.

> O Shiva, come and set me free,
> from forces that do limit me,
> with fire consume all that is less,
> paving way for my success.

> **O Shiva, clear the energy,**
> **O Shiva, bring the synergy,**
> **O Shiva, make all demons flee,**
> **O Shiva, bring back peace to me.**

3. Shiva, shatter the energetic matrix that prevents people from seeing that by making decisions, we have the opportunity to raise our consciousness. We cannot grow when we are not making decisions.

> O Shiva, Maya's veil disperse,
> clear my private universe,
> dispel the consciousness of death,
> consume it with your Sacred Breath.

> **O Shiva, clear the energy,**
> **O Shiva, bring the synergy,**
> **O Shiva, make all demons flee,**
> **O Shiva, bring back peace to me.**

4. Shiva, shatter the energetic matrix that prevents people from seeing that when we make a decision from any state of consciousness, this will be reflected back to us by the cosmic mirror. This gives us an opportunity to see the limitations of our state of consciousness so we can transcend it.

> O Shiva, I hereby let go,
> of all attachments here below,
> addictive entities consume,
> the upward path I do resume.

O Shiva, clear the energy,
O Shiva, bring the synergy,
O Shiva, make all demons flee,
O Shiva, bring back peace to me.

5. Shiva, cut people free from the demons, the burdens, the illusions of the fallen beings and restore the freedom of their will, thereby giving them an opportunity to grow.

O Shiva, I recite your name,
come banish fear and doubt and shame,
with fire expose within my mind,
what ego seeks to hide behind.

O Shiva, clear the energy,
O Shiva, bring the synergy,
O Shiva, make all demons flee,
O Shiva, bring back peace to me.

6. Shiva, help me be completely non-attached as to whether people take that opportunity or not. Help me be content with giving them the opportunity without having any intent about what they should do with their lives.

O Shiva, I am not afraid,
my karmic debt hereby is paid,
the past no longer owns my choice,
in breath of Shiva I rejoice.

O Shiva, clear the energy,
O Shiva, bring the synergy,
O Shiva, make all demons flee,
O Shiva, bring back peace to me.

7. Shiva, help me go into that neutral frame of mind when I make calls for loved ones so I can give them the freedom to choose. Help me to not have an opinion about what they should choose.

O Shiva, show me spirit pairs,
that keep me trapped in their affairs,

I choose to see within my mind,
the spirits that you surely bind.

**O Shiva, clear the energy,
O Shiva, bring the synergy,
O Shiva, make all demons flee,
O Shiva, bring back peace to me.**

8. Shiva, help me be in a neutral frame of mind so I do not try to influence or blame others but allow them to choose without having an opinion.

O Shiva, naked I now stand,
my mind in freedom does expand,
as all my ghosts I do release,
surrender is the key to peace.

**O Shiva, clear the energy,
O Shiva, bring the synergy,
O Shiva, make all demons flee,
O Shiva, bring back peace to me.**

9. Shiva, help me overcome all intent to influence other people's choices. Help me be in a neutral state of mind, so I am not violating people's free will by calling for them to be set free from what limits their free will.

O Shiva, all-consuming fire,
with Parvati raise me higher,
when I am raised your light to see,
all men I will draw onto me.

**O Shiva, clear the energy,
O Shiva, bring the synergy,
O Shiva, make all demons flee,
O Shiva, bring back peace to me.**

Sealing

In the name of the I AM THAT I AM, I accept that Archangel Michael, Astrea and Shiva form an impenetrable shield around myself and all constructive people, sealing us from all fear-based energies in all four octaves. I accept that the Light of God is consuming and transforming all fear-based energies that make up the dark forces working against ending the era of dictatorships on earth!

18 | EXPOSING THE DARK FORCES BEHIND DICTATORS

I AM the Ascended Master Jesus Christ. What does it mean when we ask you to call forth the Judgment of Christ on some phenomenon, some occurrence, on earth, as you have done in this invocation you have given? Well, it means that we are asking you to suspend human judgment and let the mind of Christ bring forth the judgment that is needed according to the vision of that mind.

So many times people have human judgments, and they of course come from external selves that are created in reaction to some condition on earth. Can you see, as I am sure many of you who are ascended master students can, that when a self is created as a result of some condition that is manifest on earth already, then that self cannot see beyond the condition, it cannot see the deeper reason behind that condition, it cannot see the higher vision of Christ? Therefore, the self then can only make a human judgment, and this is at a level where it does not bring the judgment of the phenomenon or the dark forces behind it.

Human judgment brings only conflict

What is the most common thing you see on earth as the source of conflict between human beings? It is that one person has one opinion on an issue, the other person has the opposite opinion or at least a different opinion.

But they are both *human* opinions. Of course, both people might claim that theirs is not a human opinion, it is the absolute truth, and therefore the other person's opinion is the absolute lie.

Can you not see throughout the ages how conflict after conflict after conflict has been generated by this phenomenon: One human opinion against another human opinion, both of them claiming not to be human opinions, but having some higher authority, some higher truth. Yet, what has that led to? It has led only to conflict and chaos. You can see that neither of the two can be a higher truth. They are just human opinions, and therefore one human judgment against another human judgment is not going to bring change. The Judgment of Christ is from a higher level, a higher vision.

That is why I said 2,000 years ago: "Judge not that ye be not judged." Because when you judge from the level of human opinion, then you are sending an impulse into the cosmic mirror, and what must the mirror do? Reflect back to you according to what you are sending out. How does the cosmic mirror reflect something back to you? Well, if you have a strong human judgment on a particular issue, the cosmic mirror will send you another human being who has the opposite human judgment and now the two can clash.

Now my beloved, consider this. We have told you about the duality consciousness where there is always a polarization towards two extremes. What you can learn from the teachings of Buddhism is that what the Buddha called "the pairs," are created simultaneously. They are created in polarity. They cannot exist one without the other. What human beings believe on earth is that their opinion, their judgment, is the higher truth that exists at first and then the opposite opinion came later when perhaps the devil himself opposed the truth. They think that the truth came first and the opposite came later. Therefore, they fail to see that the two human opinions arose simultaneously out of the duality consciousness.

Pure science does not oppose pure religion

Now, you have of course some situations where a society for a long time has been dominated by one particular philosophy, perhaps one particular religion. Therefore, people have been conditioned to believe that this religion represents truth and that any other religion (or any other viewpoint) represents error. Perhaps the opposite opinion has been suppressed, the opposite dualistic polarity has been suppressed by the one dualistic polarity that attained dominance. Therefore, people no longer see that the two are just like two sides of the coin—one cannot exist without the other.

For example, you will see how the Catholic church for a thousand years suppressed all sources of knowledge other than Catholic doctrine. They claimed that Catholic doctrine represented the only truth and many people were programmed to believe this over many lifetimes. Then, when science comes in and starts questioning Catholic doctrine, then naturally people tend to believe that doctrine is the truth, and therefore science must be the error when it questions doctrine.

The reality is that pure scientific observation – *neutral* scientific observation – is beyond dualistic polarities. The earth does revolve around the sun, it is not the center of the universe. This is not a matter of human opinion. It is reality. What you need to recognize here is that throughout the ages, you see how there has been a tendency for the emergence of some thought system, a religion, a political ideology, a philosophy, that claims to have an absolute truth. It also claims that all divergent viewpoints are the error. What you see throughout history is that this absolute truth has then been in conflict with the people who have the opposite viewpoint, and the result has been a conflict that has often been ongoing for a long time. In some cases, as you see with the Catholic church, one particular version, one particular side, took over and dominated for a time.

Look at the fact that the Catholic church dominated Europe for almost a thousand years. Did this bring peace? Did the dominance of one supposedly absolute truth bring peace to earth? No, it did not. Even in those thousand years there was conflict after conflict where the Catholic church fought groups of Christians within themselves, like the Cathars. They fought the Muslims, they had the Inquisition and the witch hunts, there was always some enemy that needed to be fought.

You see, if you have a higher truth, an absolute truth, then that truth is not dualistic. That means it does not have an opposite polarity. Therefore, if that truth actually managed to dominate a society, it would not generate conflict. By the very fact that the Catholic church and Catholic doctrine did not create peace but created conflict after conflict, you can know that it was not a higher truth. It was a dualistic polarity that therefore must have one or several opposites.

How fallen logic distorts everything

Now, you do realize, I am sure, that human logic is *human* logic and this is what the fallen beings used time and time and time again to confuse people. Take what I just said. There was a time when Catholic doctrine said that the earth is the center of the universe. The sun and all the other planets, all the stars in the firmament, revolved around the earth because the earth is so important to God that he put it in the center of his creation. Human beings are so important to God that he put them in the center of his creation.

Then comes science, which is, as we have explained, based on neutral observation. How does the world actually work? How do the planets move relative to the earth and what does that show about the earth? This is neutral observation. Do you see that the fallen beings do not want people to have such a neutral, we might say objective, truth, a higher truth? They use this dualistic logic to create an opposition. In fact, they have already created the opposition by establishing Catholic doctrine based on a faulty observation of the universe. It is not so much the faulty observation that was the problem. It was not really a problem that people believed the earth was the center of the universe. The problem was the claim that this was an infallible doctrine of this infallible organization that was the only representative of Christ on earth.

By making the claim that this is an absolute truth, authorized by some higher unquestionable authority, the fallen beings have already set up the potential for conflict. Therefore, when science comes up with a neutral observation of how the world works, it is very easy for them to take the scientific observation and overlay it with this materialistic philosophy that now puts itself in opposition to the religious authority. You now have your religious authority, which has been dominating for a while—the established power elite. You have a "scientific" authority, which claims that it now has the absolute truth. What was actually a neutral scientific observation has now become a dualistic polarity in the ongoing dualistic conflict created by the fallen beings.

Science was hijacked by the fallen beings. This is also, as we have explained, what happened with religion or spirituality where mysticism is as neutral as scientific observation. Mysticism in its pure form simply is a matter of experiencing the spiritual reality, instead of having theories and doctrines about the spiritual reality. It is not a matter of how you think that the spiritual realm is, it is a matter of experiencing it yourself. As a true mystic, you also realize that even though you may have an experience where the conscious you steps outside of your four lower bodies, that experience may not be absolute.

Mystical experiences and their claim to truth

We have talked about the 144 levels of consciousness. What we can say is that if you are at the 96th level of consciousness, the Conscious You has a normal state of awareness at the 96th level, but it is not the highest level. You still have filters and illusions that you are seeing through. The Conscious You may step outside of that state of consciousness, have a mystical experience that feels absolutely real. As soon as the Conscious You comes back into its four lower bodies, it now immediately interprets that experience through that level of consciousness and the illusions that it still has left.

For that matter, you could also set up a scale where you have the 144 levels of consciousness here, and then in the higher realms, starting with the emotional, mental, and identity, and even going into the spiritual, you have 144 different levels of experiences you can have. If you are at a particular level of consciousness, the Conscious You can still step outside of its normal state of consciousness, but it cannot go to the highest level of the spiritual realm. Say you are at the 12th level of consciousness possible on earth. You can go outside of that and have a mystical experience, but you are not going to go to the highest level of the 144 levels of mystical experiences possible for people in embodiment.

You see, there is a correspondence. Throughout the ages, mystics have had various visions that have been genuine mystical visions, but they have not necessarily been the highest. That particular person who is at the 12th level of consciousness, may have a mystical experience at a fairly low level. Nevertheless, because it is different from the person's normal consciousness, the person experiences it as real. This is why you can see throughout the ages that there are mystics who will claim (even people who are not considered mystics, but who have had a near-death experience) that they have had an experience of the spiritual realm. It felt so real to them that they are convinced that this was the highest possible vision, and that they saw the highest possible level of the spiritual realm. A person at the 12th level may be able to see a mystical vision at the 12th level of mystical consciousness possible, but it certainly will not be the highest possible. Then, when the person comes back, it interprets that vision through the 12th level of consciousness. As soon as it starts communicating, the vision is communicated at that level.

That, my beloved, is why you can go and find literature, as many of you have read spiritual books, that claim, for example, that there is a civilization inside the earth, there is *this* phenomenon there is *that* phenomenon, there is *this* world and *that* world. They are, many of them, the result of this mystical experience where the Conscious You stepped outside of its normal level of consciousness but the level of that experience on the 144 levels of mystical experiences possible on earth was not necessarily the highest. You will see that throughout the ages there are mystics who have been able to step outside their normal state of consciousness and have a mystical experience but they may have gone to the emotional realm. I am not saying the astral realm because the astral plane is the lower level of the emotional realm.

When you have what I call a genuine mystical experience, it is because the Conscious You goes outside of your normal state of consciousness. Now, you will see, if you look at these kinds of experiences, that this can happen in various ways. Sometimes it happens as a result of a very violent experience, for example, an accident or the like. This shocks the person out of their normal state of conscious. There are also people who take drugs and thereby force an out-of-normal consciousness experience. When you force it, that is when you can go to the astral plane, and that is when you can have these experiences that may seem very real and very frightening, but they are not the highest level of mystical experiences.

When you have what I call a genuine mystical experience, it is not the result of you deliberately forcing it. It is something that happens through a different process that is not as force-based. You may still have such an experience and go to the higher levels of the emotional realm and have an experience of what exists there, the structures, the beings that exist there. It may feel very real to you. You may also have an experience where you go to the mental realm, and you there meet beings that you experience as having a higher level of consciousness than you do, and they might very well have that. Therefore, you think they are real, or you think they give you some ultimate truth.

There are many, many spiritual books out there that have resulted from people having a mystical experience, but they go into some level of the mental realm where they have been given instructions that come from that mental realm. Then, there are a few people who are able to go to the identity realm, the lower levels of the identity realm, and they receive something from the beings who reside there. As we have explained to you, there are fallen beings even in the lower levels of the identity realm. There are also beings there who are not fallen beings, and who do not have evil intentions as such, but they of course can only give you what they have seen based on their level of consciousness. It may feel very real to you when you are embodiment, and you have this experience of going outside your normal state of consciousness and you contact these beings in the identity realm that seem very advanced compared to you.

This is why you will see that there are so many people who have had these different experiences, there are so many channelers who can channel various beings, some in the emotional, some in the mental, a few in the identity realm. There are many people who cannot tell where they are coming from. They cannot tell: Is it true or is it not true? Many people believe that they are getting some higher truth, maybe even an absolute truth, from beings in the emotional realm. Many more believe they are getting an absolute truth from beings in the mental realm because they do not have the discernment.

Science and its claim to truth

Now, we can go to the area of science and we can say, well, there was a time where people believed that the earth was the center of the universe. Now, science has discovered that the earth revolves around the Sun, and the Sun is just one sun among many and they are all revolving around the center of the galaxy. The galaxy is one among many galaxies that are revolving around something else that they do not even know where it is or what is. But is what science has discovered now an absolute truth?

When Isaac Newton was hit by the apple and discovered, supposedly, the force of gravity, did he discover an absolute truth? Well, my beloved, in a sense you would say that the idea that the earth has created this attractive force called the gravitational force is a valid idea. It is a possible, and in some ways constructive, way to describe what you can observe on earth—that things fall down. Apples fall off the trees and hit the ground or whomever is sitting under the tree. It is not an invalid description but is it the *only* description? Nay, because in 1905, Albert Einstein came up with a new theory and according to the theories of relativity, the general and the specific, there is another explanation of gravity. It is not necessarily a force but a result of the geometry of what Einstein called space-time. Well, even though he has gotten the Nobel Prize and is considered one of the greatest geniuses, is that the absolute truth now? Nay, because quantum physics has gone beyond it already.

My beloved, look at the amazing developments of science in the last hundred years. Then, project 500 years into the future. Do you really think science is going to stand still? There was a time in the 1800s where leading scientists claimed that all the major discoveries have been made but look how many discoveries have been made since. Do you really think that scientists have now made all the major discoveries and science will not make progress in the next 500 years? I can assure you that they will.

What is it that is right now holding back scientific progress? It is the claim made by materialism that science has discovered some absolute truth, namely that there is nothing beyond the material universe and that everything that takes place in the material universe can be explained as effects of causes that are also in the material universe. What materialism has done is to impose a certain human interpretation on pure scientific observation, just as the Catholic church imposed a purely human interpretation on the example and the teachings that I gave 2,000 years ago. The Catholic church created "infallible" doctrines. Materialism has created "infallible" scientific doctrines. When you have a doctrine that you believe is infallible, it immediately stops growth because those who accept the infallibility claim will not look beyond the doctrine. Therefore, how can progress happen?

We make karma through the separate selves

Again, the judgment of Christ is that when you make a call for the judgment of Christ upon some phenomenon, you are saying: "I am calling the judgment on this phenomenon, but not my own human judgment, but the higher judgment of the Christ mind." This is why we have you do this so that you do not make the karma of letting your invocations be driven by a human judgment, perhaps a human anger or human resentment.

I wish to give you here a deeper understanding of karma. Let us say that you will become aware that there is a particular phenomenon and let us just use the example of pedophilia. You obviously reason that this is not right, that this should not be going on. Let us say you now become very angry because this is happening. You become angry at the pedophiles, for example, the Catholic priests who have abused children. It is a normal human reaction. You decide that you are now going to give some invocation or some decrees to bring forth the judgment of this. As you are giving these decrees, you are colored by the human anger you are feeling.

Now, in previous ascended master dispensations, we would have said that if you allow your decrees, prayers or calls to be colored by human anger, you are making karma. It is just one way of explaining what is happening. What we can give you today is a higher explanation of this because why do you have that human anger? Why do you have the human judgment? Well, as I said, because you have a separate self. What is karma? When you do something and you are making karma, what is actually happening? Well, if you are making decrees against pedophilia, but you are doing it because you are angry, then it is not so much that you create this karma that is outside yourself. The real problem is that you are reinforcing the separate self. If you are looking at a particular phenomenon through a separate self, you cannot be the Christ in action concerning that phenomenon. You are not the Living Christ in embodiment with regard to pedophilia if you are looking at it through a human self and you are colored by human anger.

The Living Christ in embodiment is completely neutral towards any human phenomenon. I know you might say: "Well Jesus, you seemed pretty angry at the money changers when you overturned their tables." But did I ever claim to be perfect? Nay. The Catholic church claimed I was perfect. *I* never made that claim. You see that you can learn from my example in both ways: both what to do and what *not* to do.

The reality is that you can look at my trial and how I was not angry with the authorities. I let them do what they wanted to do because I was in that neutral state of mind. It is when you are in the neutral state of mind that you become the instrument for the judgment of Christ. For your own protection's sake, we are asking you to say: "I call forth the judgment of Christ upon…" When you actually reach a certain level of Christ consciousness, you do not need to say this. You in fact do not even always need to make a call. It is enough that you put your attention on a certain phenomenon and you go into that neutral state of mind, and you are just observing. There is no human analysis. There is no human evaluation, no human judgment. You are just observing the phenomenon from that completely neutral state of mind.

Manipulation through extreme emotions

Cyclopea talked about the fact that in the emotional, mental and identity realms, the fallen beings have created this entire apparatus, this machine, aimed at deception. The goal of this entire machinery is of course to influence human beings in embodiment and get them to do things they normally would not do. Those things serve the cause of the fallen beings and their agenda on earth. You will see that in the emotional realm, there are beings that we have often called demons that are very aggressive, very forceful, and they will attempt to take over the emotional bodies of people in embodiment.

When you look at one of these rallies where Adolf Hitler was speaking to a group of people and they were all screaming "Heil Hitler," you can see in their eyes that they were taken over by these demons—demons of hatred. You can see modern-day Muslims, who are part of the more extremist Muslim movements, and they are again having this anger shining from their eyes because their emotional bodies are taken over by demons. You have seen throughout history many times where you had battles between two groups of people or two armies, and they would run towards each other screaming, and again, they were driven by this hatred towards the enemy.

This is how the false hierarchy (as we have often called it) in the emotional realm attempt to influence people. They take over their emotional bodies and they have such strong emotions. It can be fear, total panic, it can be anger, and it can be an even stronger version of anger that we call hatred. It can also be jealousy, it can be greed, it can be lust. It is the point where suddenly people suspend what they all know from experience, namely that in the physical octave, everything you do has a consequence. There is a price tag on everything you do. You may do something that feels good now, but there is a price to be paid later. You may eat that extra cake at the cafe, but there is a price to be paid when you come back and jump on the scale and see that you have once again gained weight. You realize that everybody who is in embodiment has learned the hard way that whatever you do has a consequence.

What the false hierarchy in the emotional realm are so good at doing is stirring up people's emotional bodies. The emotions are so turbulent that it draws the focus of the Conscious You down into the emotional body and the Conscious You loses its connection to the mental body. The mental body can evaluate: But if you do this, the consequence will be this and is that really what you want? Now, that evaluation is gone and people just act without any thought of consequence. This is how the fallen beings have so many times caused people to go into war where you know if you go into battle, you might very well get hurt or killed. But it does not matter anymore because you *have* to kill the enemy. You have to defend your nation, you have to defend the Christian faith. "So even if I'm killed, it's worth it because I will get some better position in heaven."

Manipulation through thoughts

Where does the idea that you will get a better position in heaven come from? Well, it comes to the mental realm, not from the emotional. Emotional is raw emotion, acting without any thought of consequence. Even the thought that I will get seventy virgins in heaven for killing the non-believers is at the mental level. This is how you see that the false hierarchy at the mental level manage to influence people.

They also make people suspend their knowledge that everything you do in the physical has a physical consequence. They do it by making people think that there is a greater reward that can outweigh the physical consequence. Or it makes people think that somehow there is this magical way to avoid the consequence. If you look at the Catholics of the Middle Ages, there were people who strongly believed in hell. These people in many cases did believe that if you killed another human being, you could go to hell for doing so. Now, you see those same people put on armor, put on a white shirt with a red cross on the front. They take their sword, they ride into a village in the Middle East, and they chop the heads off men, women and children because those men, women, and children are not Christians. They are Muslims. If you kill a Christian, you go to hell, but if you kill a Muslim, you go to heaven.

Now, how did that ever become logical to anybody? Well, only because they suspended normal logic. Normal logic would say, based on observation of how the world works, if I throw something up into the air, it will fall back down. If I throw a rock into the air and it falls down, it might hit me on the head. You know that this will always be the case. No matter what you throw up into the air, it is going to come down and hit you on the head. Once you have experienced that a certain number of times, you stop throwing things into the air. Here are people who believe that: If I kill other human beings, it has a consequence. They know that any human being they kill, it will have a consequence. But here comes the false hierarchy and they manage to insert this serpentine logic that says, thou shalt not *surely* go to hell for killing another human being because if you kill the wrong kind, the bad people, the people who oppose God, then you will not go to hell, you will be rewarded by going to heaven. This is how they once again manage to get people to suspend that scientific observation on how the universe works: there is always a consequence.

People's vulnerability to dark forces

They also managed to get people to suspend their intuitive sense, which will tell anybody that if you live by the sword, you will die by the sword. Because if you are in that human state of consciousness, that lower state of consciousness, you will not be able to go to heaven.

What you can do here is to set up a scale of the human levels of consciousness, the 144 levels. You can see that at the lower levels of consciousness people are very, very vulnerable to having their emotional bodies taken over by demons from the astral plane. At certain higher levels of consciousness people have more control over their emotional bodies but they are very vulnerable to the mental realm. At an even higher level, people are better at using logic and applying logic and they also become more intuitive but now they become vulnerable to the false hierarchy in the identity realm.

Now, how does the false hierarchy in the identity realm work? Well, much the same way as what you see in the mental realm and the emotional. Again, you have normal observation: For every action there is an opposite and equal reaction, as Newton formulated it. This is also a description of the Law of Karma. Whatever you do, you create karma, there is a consequence. Now, we have said before that this is because if you could do something that did not have a consequence, how would you know you had done something? How would you know you had made a choice? How can you exercise free will if there is no consequence?

What the false hierarchy is trying to do, even at the identity level, is suspend this common observation. At the identity level they are also very concerned about destroying, obscuring, falsifying people's intuitive visions, people's intuitive sense of what is right. In other words, you could express this in different ways. You can say, for example, that there is a level of intuition that applies to the material universe. There is a level of intuition that applies beyond the material universe. One of the scientific principles is that you make certain observations. You throw a rock into the air, it falls down. You throw another rock, it falls down. You do this a number of times, but there comes a point where now you are going to make the conclusion that you can keep doing this indefinitely and every time you throw something into the air, it is going to fall down. Therefore, you do not have to spend the rest of your life throwing things into the air. You can reason, you can draw the conclusion, you can make the inductive reasoning that this is the way it is. You might explain it as a law of nature or you might just say: "Okay, I've had enough of throwing things into the air, let me get on to something else."

This is in a way intuition. You have not observed that you can keep on for the rest of your life throwing things in the air and they will fall down. You cannot theoretically know that there could not be some anomaly some time where you threw something into the and it did not fall back down. You might throw your lunch sandwich into the air and a seagull might come by and grab it and it would not fall back down. Or there might be some quantum tunneling effect where the sandwich went into a black hole and emerged in another universe. Nevertheless, you do not have to continue to throw things into the air because you can use your intuitive faculties to say, to project: "Oh this will continue to happen."

Intuition beyond physical consequences

The other aspect of intuition is that you use your intuitive faculties to know something that cannot be observed by the physical senses because it does not necessarily have a physical consequence. This is what allows you to know, to simply know from within, the truth that what you do to others will be returned to you. If you harm others, something will happen to you. There will be a consequence, not right now necessarily, but in the future. This is what allows you to know that there is a certain state of consciousness that will tie you to earth. It is only by going beyond that state of consciousness that you can rise and ascend from earth. This is how human beings throughout the ages have been able to say, to reason, to know that they do not want to continue indefinitely experiencing the pleasures or the suffering on earth. They want to rise above it and they can then know that the only way to rise above it is to change their own consciousness. How do the beings in the false hierarchy in the identity realm distort or pervert this kind of judgment? Well, they do it in two ways. First of all, you have the knowledge that if you do something, it will have a consequence. But they have throughout the ages created this concept that there are certain people who are in a special category. Because of the identity of these people, they are so special that they can do things that enable them to not have the consequence it has for the majority of the population. In other words, they can get away with things. There are no free lunches for the people but there are free lunches for the elite, so they claim.

You can see throughout the ages how there have been these privileged elites. You can see how the Catholic priests of the Middle Ages were in this privileged position where they could get away with certain things that ordinary people could not get away with. You can even see today how Catholic priests have, for a long time, been getting away with pedophilia because they were protected by the church. You have seen in previous ages how there was a noble class and there was a law in society. If you stole something, you would have your hand cut off. But the noble class could do whatever they wanted and they were not punished. You can see societies today all around the world where you have created a privileged elite who through corruption can get away with things or gain privileges for themselves, that the ordinary population cannot have. You see how the fallen beings have distorted people's sense of identity to make certain people feel: "Oh, I am in a special category, I am above the law. I am not an ordinary human being. Therefore, I can do things and there will not be a consequence."

Fallen beings can dodge karma

This of course is complete nonsense because the laws of nature work the same for everyone. The law of karma works the same for everyone, you *will* make karma. However, there is an exception to this in the sense that, take a dictator such as Adolf Hitler. He is not forcing (at least not all) the German people to follow him and accept his ideology. You will see, as we have said, that there were people, even highly educated people, who believed in the Nazi ideology. They actually believed it was fully justified to kill the Jews because they were a danger to some higher plan for the universe. It was their duty to purify the race of these inferior human beings. They actually believed this. You might say that Adolf Hitler was the one who initiated this entire madness so he should be the one who made the karma. When people come to believe in the dictator, they take upon themselves some of the karma.

Therefore, you see many examples throughout history where there has been a certain elite of fallen beings who have initiated some horrendous atrocity. The people have voluntarily, without knowing it consciously, but they have by believing and following the leaders taken on part of the karma. This does not mean that these people will ultimately get away with things. It does mean that they have spread it out. You can see how even today the Catholic priests are making karma for violating children, but in fact all Catholics who are truly believing in the church and the importance and sanctity of the institution, are taking on themselves part of that karma. The Catholics believe that preserving the church is so important that it can either excuse the pedophilia, or at least that it should not result in the demise of the church. Therefore, even though this maybe needs to be exposed, maybe needs to be dealt with, the infallibility, the sanctity or the importance of the church must not be questioned by these acts.

Therefore, Catholics will not say: "Something is rotten in Rome. We need to make systemic changes in the Catholic church." No, they will say: "Oh, well, here's a little problem. We just deal with it without questioning the importance and the infallibility of the church." That is how they take on karma that actually should be the karma of the fallen beings.

Of course, the priests are not acting alone, they have their emotional bodies taken over by demons in the astral realm. That is why the priests are able to reason that even though they know that it is wrong to have sex with children, there is some excuse they can come up with where they believe they will not suffer the consequences. Or in some cases, they are just so taken over that they do not think about the consequences. Then, when they are no longer taken over by demons in the emotional realm, they go into the mental body and now they realize they have done something. That is when the beings in the mental realm start giving them this reasoning that: "Oh it is not so bad or you can get away with it because the church will protect you." There are even those in the identity realm that will make them feel that, well, because I am a priest who belongs to the most important church, then somehow this is acceptable behavior.

There is this, as we have said, almost hypnotic state that people go into. The priests who are abusing children are in this hypnotic state. The bishops and the cardinals who are becoming aware of this problem are also in a hypnotic state because nothing must question the sanctity of the church. The ordinary Catholics who are becoming aware of this are also in this hypnotic state because again they are so loyal to the outer institution. Well, how about being loyal to Christ and realizing what I said: "Inasmuch as ye have done it unto the least of these my little ones, you have done it unto me." Is it more important to preserve an earthly institution than to be loyal to the Christ principle, the Christ reality that is beyond anything on earth?

What do you want? Do you want your reward on earth by feeling superior as members of the highest church, the highest representative of Christ on earth? Or do you want your reward in heaven by being here with me? You cannot have both. What do you want?

Manipulation through the desire to feel special

My beloved, you see how there is this entire false hierarchy in the emotional, mental and identity realms who will take advantage of people. The Conscious You or person steps outside its four lower bodies. It goes to whatever level it can go to on the scale. It has a mystical experience, it is contacted, or comes in contact with these beings in these three realms and they manage to make the person believe that it has now had some ultimate experience.

This of course very much ties in with what Saint Germain was talking about, that the fallen beings used this desire to be special. Look at how many people throughout the ages have had this desire to be special. They have had some kind of unusual experience, and now (when they come back to their normal state of awareness), they use the experience and the reality of that experience, the sense of reality of that experience, to go out and tell other people. What they are basically saying is: "Look how special I am that I was given this experience. It must mean that I'm so special." You see this over and over again throughout the ages. You see it today.

Look at how many channelers feel special. Look at how many people who had an out-of-body experience feel special. Look at all of this that is going on. You who are ascended master students, you can use the tools we have given you to rise above this. I know that many of you will look back at your lives and you will see how: "Well, I read that book or I was following that guru or I was in that organization." And this is all part of your path. But now you are at a point of your path where you do not need to look back at this and blame yourself for being involved with this teaching that you now realize was not the highest possible. You use it constructively to say: "I clearly didn't have good discernment back then. What do I need to do to get that discernment of Christ so I can know what comes from the false hierarchy in the three higher realms and what comes from the ascended realm?"

How to get the discernment of Christ

How do I get that discernment, as one of you asked earlier? Again, the ultimate way to get discernment is to dissolve the primal self, to dissolve these other selves. Then, when you have dissolved the selves, you are not pulled into a reactionary pattern. What does that mean? It means that you can now go into this neutral state of mind. When you are in a neutral state of mind and have suspended all of these human opinions and judgments, *that* is when you have discernment, and only *then* will you have discernment.

There are many people who in certain situations and regarding certain issues, they are able to go into a neutral state of mind, and therefore they have good discernment in these areas. There are other areas of life where they are pulled into a reactionary pattern, and now they do not have discernment on that particular aspect of life. If you see that in yourself, you just realize: "But the fact that I have discernment in some areas means that I have overcome some of my separate selves. But when I do not have the discernment, when I do have a certain reaction in a certain area, it is because I still have some separate selves left. And now I just go to work on it."

The desire to be special aborts spiritual progress

You see my beloved, this is how the desire to be special can distort, even *abort,* your spiritual progress. What has happened to many ascended master students and many other spiritual and religious people is that you grow up in a certain state of confusion. You know you have not found the truth or what you need to find, but then you suddenly find something. Now, you have a conversion experience and you enter a Christian church, the Muslim religion, the Buddhist religion or some New Age movement or an ascended master teaching. You suddenly feel: "Now, I have found what I was meant to find. And now I am superior, I am special because of this." As we have said, many ascended master students reacted to the statement:

"You have the highest spiritual teaching on the planet" by feeling: "We are now the most advanced spiritual students on the planet." Well, where did that feeling come from? It came from the false hierarchy in the identity realm who distorted people's emotional, mental and identity bodies so that they suddenly felt: "Because I'm an ascended master student, that's why I'm special." Or because I have that particular experience, I am special.

When you have this desire to be special, you cannot have discernment because you are not going into a neutral state of mind. Everything you do is personal. Just as with the Catholics, their overall concern is not to destroy the sanctity of the church. Your overall concern is not to destroy the sense that "I'm special." So everything you do, even everything you do on the spiritual path, you look at it through that filter: "I must not destroy the sense that I now have of being special."

That is why you see so many people who come into an ascended master teaching. They sit there, they listen to our dictations, they read our dictations, they study it. They understand it intellectually, but it does not go to the identity realm, through the identity bodies. It stays at the mental level. Many of these students are tied into the false hierarchy at the mental level that are telling them that all you need to do is understand it intellectually. But what you need to do as a spiritual student, an ascended master student, is you first look at your physical actions and you reform those physical actions so you do not do things that are detrimental to your spiritual growth. You do not take drugs. You do not drink yourself unconscious with alcohol. You do not violate or harm other people or steal from them. You reform your physical actions.

Then, you take command over your emotional body. This is how you can use our decrees and invocations. Call to Archangel Michael, call to Astrea to be cut free from ties to the astral plane so you restore some level of calm in your emotional body. Then, you use the teachings we have given you to take command over your mental body by understanding the teachings, by understanding the difference between truth and error. But it cannot stop there. You can see that there are certain students who have studied ascended master teachings and other spiritual teachings for many years and have a vast knowledge and a vast intellectual understanding but their psychology has not changed. They still have certain aspects of their psychology that they have not even started to change—they have not touched them. The reason is that these students have not taken the process into the identity level where you can now shift your sense of identity. When you overcome the birth trauma, when you let go of that primal self and certain other selves, that is when you can shift your sense of identity. You can shift away from being a reactionary being that is so focused on what happens here on earth.

That is when you can come to see that this desire to be special is just coming from a separate self and you can see how your desire to be special has distorted your spiritual path. You can see how it has caused you to tie knots on yourself to avoid being proven wrong. You can see how it is causing an enormous tension in you because constantly you are evaluating: "Could I do something wrong? Could I be proven wrong? Could I perhaps follow a false teaching or a false guru? Am I doing something wrong?" You are always in a state where you are at risk because the sense of being right by being superior is always threatened by the possibility that you could be proven wrong.

Depersonalizing your path

When you see this tension, you can see that this all comes from several separate selves. When you let them go, you have done what we have said. You have depersonalized your life. You have depersonalized the spiritual path. That is when you can then do what will take you to the higher levels. You can take our teachings and you can look in the mirror and say: "How does that apply to me? What does that show me I need to overcome, what separate selves I have I need to overcome?" When you are still in this state of mind of feeling superior, feeling special and not wanting to have that feeling destroyed by being proven wrong, you cannot really look at our teachings. You can understand them intellectually, but the intellectual mind can always find some reasoning why it does not apply to you. You can see how other people are having that particular problem but: "It doesn't apply to me. I've already overcome this."

This very mechanism is what makes it possible for people to study the teaching for decades, but there is a certain aspect of their psychology that has not changed because they have not seen it. They have not seen it because they are so intent on being special that they think that if they see something in their psychology that needs to change, it will be proven wrong: "I was not perfect after all, and therefore I'm not special. Maybe the masters won't like me anymore." As if they think that we could not see through this whole charade of wanting to be special. We love you, even if you have this desire to be special, but you cannot feel our love. You can only feel it when you overcome this desire to be special because that is when you can connect to us and actually accept what we have said: We accept you unconditionally for who you are. When you depersonalize your path, you get to the point where you are not afraid to look at yourself—because if you see something, you know it is a limitation and getting rid of it will make you feel more free, more at peace.

This messenger, himself, is perfectly willing to admit that for the first twenty years he was on the spiritual path he was completely colored by this desire to feel special, to be validated. Much of his eagerness to do the decrees for hours and hours and hours was springing from this desire to reinforce the sense that he was so special. But there came a point where he was able to see it, to step outside of it and see it. That was when he could be trained by me to be a messenger. Ever since then he has gone through these phases of depersonalizing his service and his life more and more, which means that he has come to a point where there is no resistance in him to seeing another separate self. He has accepted that he is not ascended, he is not at the 144thlevel. He has accepted that how does he get from where he is at to the 144th level? By letting go of the remaining separate selves that correspond to those levels of consciousness.

Letting go of a self with the help of Jesus

How can you let go of a self? Only when you see it. So how do you make progress? By overcoming the resistance to seeing something. You can do this only, my beloved, *only* when you overcome that need, that desire to be special that blocks you from looking at yourself and saying: "Is what the master is saying really applying to me?"

Be honest, just for one moment here.

You are sitting here. You have chosen to sit here, wherever you are sitting, whether you are hearing or reading this, you have voluntarily chosen to take in a teaching that comes from the Ascended Master Jesus Christ. So be honest with yourself.

Is what I am saying applying to you? Look in the mirror. Be neutral and be willing to see how it applies to you. Because it applies to each and every one of you. How can I say this? Are you not in physical embodiment? Therefore, you have not ascended. Therefore, you are not at the 144th level. Therefore, you still have some separate selves that you need to let go of. So be willing to look at: "What is the separate self that I am dealing with right now, that is preventing me from going to the next level of consciousness?" Then say: "Jesus, help me see it." *And I will.*

So my beloved, you *are* special but you are not special in a worldly sense. You are not special in the way the false hierarchy wants you to feel special. You are special because you are open to the truth of Christ. You see my beloved, what is it that is going to help you see a separate self? It is the mind of Christ, the truth of Christ, the higher perspective of Christ that is beyond the separate self. *That* is the only way to see it.

When you are inside the separate self, you cannot see it—only when you step outside of it, and you can only step outside of it through the mind of Christ. If you are not open to that, if you are not open to seeing it, you cannot see it, you cannot step outside of it, you cannot have that perspective of the Christ mind. For each of the 144 levels, there is an aspect of the Christ mind that can help you see the separate self that corresponds to that level. Get to the point where you are willing to go through that process and that is when you escape the influence of the false hierarchy.

False hierarchy impostors

Now, an aspect of the false hierarchy that we have mentioned before is of course that aspect that we have called the false hierarchy impostors. You will see if you look at, for example, the channelers that are out there that some of them have channeled some being that has a name that nobody has really heard of before. This may be a being that claims to be from some other planetary system or some other galaxy or whatever. But it just has a name that is neutral to people on earth, and it gives forth a teaching. That being, we may say, is in the mental realm and it is, in a sense, completely honest. It is just saying: "Here I am, I am the being I am, and this is the teaching I am giving you." The being is not necessarily claiming that this is the highest possible teaching. It is still part of the false hierarchy in a sense that it is not an ascended being, but it is not really being dishonest.

Then, there are other beings in the three realms that will claim to have some kind of name known to people on earth or some kind of position. There is, for example, a series of books called *Conversations with God.* They are channeled from a being in the mental realm that claims to be God, the ultimate God. It is a false hierarchy impostor because it is not the ultimate God. Because, as we have said, the Creator is at such a high level of consciousness that it cannot speak directly to a human being. It may be able to give something through the ascended hierarchy of ascended beings. This is possible, but certainly not as an isolated event.

Then, you have of course (after the concept of ascended masters was released) beings who claim to be ascended masters but they are in the mental realm, they are in the lower identity realm. You have throughout the ages various beings in the mental and identity realm who have claimed to be some kind of deity, some kind of god that has influenced people. You can go out there and you can find books that are channeled, and they claim to be from ascended masters. But if you look at this carefully, you can see that there are certain outer points you can use to evaluate this. Really, how do you know? These beings in the mental realm are so good at presenting intellectual teachings and intellectual reasonings and arguments that your intellectual mind cannot easily sort out what is right and not right. It can be done but it is difficult many times, and that is why many of you have been drawn to these books at an earlier stage of your path.

How do you sort this out? Well, you do it through the Christ mind. You do it through what I call the higher intuitive faculty that reaches beyond the material universe. You do it by reading the vibration, you read the intent and you can ask yourself: "Do these beings who claim to be ascended masters, do they want something from me? Do they want my energy? Do they want to be worshiped or admired? Do they want to be obeyed? Do they want me to blindly do what they say?" These are sort of outer measures, but really it all comes down to this: Can you read the vibration? You cannot read vibration through a separate self. When you get rid of these separate selves and the primal self, then you will be able to read vibration. Therefore, you can know, am I the Ascended Master Jesus Christ, or am I a false hierarchy impostor? You can know by reading the vibration. Do I want anything from you? Or do I only desire to set you free?

Dictators claim to be special

What is the basis for dictatorships on earth? Well, it is that the dictator claims to be special and have something, some ability, that you do not have. It can be the raw violence, the willingness to kill that you saw in Stalin and Mao, or it can be some intellectual ability that you saw in Lenin, or it can be other things. The most insidious, the most dangerous form of dictatorships on earth are those who claim that they stand between you and

God—between you and the spiritual realm. That is the most dangerous form of dictatorship that we naturally look for you to make the calls on. Because you are in a position where you can read the vibration of ascended masters, you are in a position to bring the judgment of Christ upon those who are the false hierarchy impostors who imposture some spiritual being but are not ascended. Therefore, they still have some agenda, they still have something they need.

You see my beloved, beings in the emotional, mental and identity realms that are approaching human beings on earth, they need something from human beings. They need energy. Why do they need this energy? *I* do not need your energy because I am an ascended being. I am getting all the energy I could ever need from the hierarchy of ascended beings above me, reaching all the way to the Creator. Why would I need energy from a lower realm? I do not. But you see, when a being (whether it is a fallen being or just a non-ascended being in the emotional, mental and identity realms) have gone into duality, well, they are cut off from that flow of energy from above and that is why they need energy from your level.

This is another measure you can use to expose what they are and what they are about. I do not need your energy and if you have discernment, you can feel it. I am not taking anything from you and have not taken anything from you during this dictation. I have given. I have released to you. You will have absorbed it if you have been open to it. If you have not been open to it, you may not have felt it. But anyone who listens to or reads this dictation for the indefinite future will be able to activate the flow of energy that I have put into this dictation and they can absorb it at any time because I will always be there to release that flow.

This is proof, for those who can read it, that I am an ascended being, and therefore, I do not need any energy from any realm below myself. I do not need it from any source outside myself, because I am connected inside myself to the flow of energy from my source, my Creator.

We have, from the very beginning, made it clear that this messenger does not stand between you and the ascended masters. He is the open door for speaking in the physical, which most people cannot do. But he does not need you to worship him, to obey him, and he does not need you to think that he is special or that he is between you and the masters. The reason he is still a messenger is that he has never inserted himself between any person and the ascended masters. Therefore, you look at the messenger, and for you he is simply a tool that you use to promote your personal growth.

You take the teachings—but the entire purpose of the teachings given through this messenger is to help you establish your own direct contact within to the ascended masters. As the messenger is fully aware, the ultimate success of his work is that you no longer need him. He is perfectly willing to serve in that capacity and to set you free. If there was a point where you who are here now had all gone out to fulfill aspects of your Divine plan that you have come to see, and there was no one sitting here, the messenger would not have a problem with that. He would just ascend, or he would serve in other ways where we can give other teachings for people who are not necessarily ready to come here and attend a conference like this, which after all requires a certain willingness to go away from your normal daily activities, and to focus your attention on this activity, which we know can be quite demanding.

I have spoken for a long time now. I do not feel it, the messenger does not feel it, many of you do not feel it, but nevertheless, it is demanding to sit there and listen for so long. We honor the fact that you have been willing to set aside your daily lives, to come here, to be physically here, to serve as the broadcast stations. Those of you who are sensitive can feel how you have received energy from me. But if you are at a certain level of consciousness, you have not absorbed it all yourself, you have allowed your chakras to broadcast it into the collective consciousness. This is one of the real advantages of having people come together because you multiply each other and you multiply what we can broadcast through you.

I can assure you that this conference has provided a very, very powerful surge of energy that has radiated into the collective consciousness. It has had tremendous effect here in Korea, in North Korea, but far beyond it to the entire world. All of these topics of the various aspects of dictatorships that we have exposed and will expose—this has had a major impact and it has shifted something and created an upward trend that will be reinforced as people use these tools. Therefore, it will spread like rings on the water's surface into the emotional, mental and identity realms until there is that shift that we have talked about so many times where people suddenly see it. They see with the Christ mind and therefore they see that the false hierarchy impostors have nothing on.

19 | JUDGING THE DARK FORCES BEHIND DICTATORS (PART 1)

In the name of the I AM THAT I AM, Jesus Christ, I use the authority that I have as a being in embodiment on earth to call upon Jesus to reinforce my calls and use my chakras to project the statements in this invocation into the collective consciousness and bring about the judgment of all dark forces behind dictators. Awaken people to the reality that we are spiritual beings and that we can co-create a new future by working with the ascended masters. I especially call for …

[Make your own calls here.]

Part 1

1. Jesus, help me suspend human judgment and let the mind of Christ bring forth the judgment that is needed according to the vision of that mind.

O Jesus, blessed brother mine,
I walk the path that you outline,

a great example to us all,
I follow now your inner call.

**O Jesus, let the Fire of Joy,
consume the devil's subtle ploy,
transfigured is our planet earth,
the golden age is given birth.**

2. I call forth the judgment of Christ upon the dark forces that prevent people from seeing that the most common source of conflict between human beings is that one person has one opinion, the other person has the opposite opinion. They are both *human* opinions but both people claim their opinion is the absolute truth.

O Jesus, open inner sight,
the ego wants to prove it's right,
but this I will no longer do,
I want to be all one with you.

**O Jesus, let the Fire of Joy,
consume the devil's subtle ploy,
transfigured is our planet earth,
the golden age is given birth.**

3. I call forth the judgment of Christ upon the dark forces that prevent people from seeing that throughout the ages conflict after conflict has been generated by one human opinion against another human opinion, both of them claiming not to be human opinions but having some higher authority.

O Jesus, I now clearly see,
the Key of Knowledge given me,
my Christ self I hereby embrace,
as you fill up my inner space.

**O Jesus, let the Fire of Joy,
consume the devil's subtle ploy,
transfigured is our planet earth,
the golden age is given birth.**

4. I call forth the judgment of Christ upon the dark forces that prevent people from seeing that this has led only to conflict and chaos. One human judgment against another human judgment is not going to bring change. The Judgment of Christ is from a higher vision.

> O Jesus, show me serpent's lie,
> expose the beam in my own eye,
> as Christ discernment you me give,
> in oneness I forever live.

> **O Jesus, let the Fire of Joy,**
> **consume the devil's subtle ploy,**
> **transfigured is our planet earth,**
> **the golden age is given birth.**

5. I call forth the judgment of Christ upon the dark forces that prevent people from seeing that when we judge from the level of human opinion, we are sending an impulse into the cosmic mirror, and the mirror must reflect back to us according to what we are sending out.

> O Jesus, I am truly meek,
> and thus I turn the other cheek,
> when the accuser attacks me,
> I go within and merge with thee.

> **O Jesus, let the Fire of Joy,**
> **consume the devil's subtle ploy,**
> **transfigured is our planet earth,**
> **the golden age is given birth.**

6. I call forth the judgment of Christ upon the dark forces that prevent people from seeing that if we have a strong human judgment on a particular issue, the cosmic mirror will send us another human being who has the opposite human judgment and now the two can clash.

> O Jesus, ego I let die,
> surrender ev'ry earthly tie,
> the dead can bury what is dead,
> I choose to walk with you instead.

O Jesus, let the Fire of Joy,
consume the devil's subtle ploy,
transfigured is our planet earth,
the golden age is given birth.

7. I call forth the judgment of Christ upon the dark forces that prevent people from seeing that in the duality consciousness there is always a polarization, and both extremes are created simultaneously. They cannot exist one without the other.

O Jesus, help me rise above,
the devil's test through higher love,
show me separate self unreal,
my formless self you do reveal.

O Jesus, let the Fire of Joy,
consume the devil's subtle ploy,
transfigured is our planet earth,
the golden age is given birth.

8. I call forth the judgment of Christ upon the dark forces that prevent people from seeing that so many believe that their opinion, their judgment, is the higher truth that was created first, and then the opposite opinion came later when perhaps the devil himself opposed the truth.

O Jesus, what is that to me,
I just let go and follow thee,
with this I do pass ev'ry test,
to find with you eternal rest.

O Jesus, let the Fire of Joy,
consume the devil's subtle ploy,
transfigured is our planet earth,
the golden age is given birth.

9. I call forth the judgment of Christ upon the dark forces that prevent people from seeing that when we think that the truth came first and the opposite came later, we fail to see that the two human opinions arose simultaneously out of the duality consciousness.

O Jesus, fiery master mine,
my heart now melting into thine,
I love with heart and mind and soul,
the God who is my highest goal.

O Jesus, let the Fire of Joy,
consume the devil's subtle ploy,
transfigured is our planet earth,
the golden age is given birth.

Part 2

1. I call forth the judgment of Christ upon the dark forces that prevent people from seeing that a society can be dominated by one particular philosophy, so people have been conditioned to believe that it represents truth and that any other system represents error.

O Jesus, blessed brother mine,
I walk the path that you outline,
a great example to us all,
I follow now your inner call.

O Jesus, let the Fire of Joy,
consume the devil's subtle ploy,
transfigured is our planet earth,
the golden age is given birth.

2. I call forth the judgment of Christ upon the dark forces that prevent people from seeing that throughout the ages, there has been a tendency for the emergence of some thought system, a religion, political ideology or philosophy that claims to have an absolute truth. It also claims that all divergent viewpoints are in error.

O Jesus, open inner sight,
the ego wants to prove it's right,
but this I will no longer do,
I want to be all one with you.

O Jesus, let the Fire of Joy,
consume the devil's subtle ploy,
transfigured is our planet earth,
the golden age is given birth.

3. I call forth the judgment of Christ upon the dark forces that prevent people from seeing that this absolute truth has then been in conflict with the people who have the opposite viewpoint, and the conflict has often been ongoing for a long time.

O Jesus, I now clearly see,
the Key of Knowledge given me,
my Christ self I hereby embrace,
as you fill up my inner space.

O Jesus, let the Fire of Joy,
consume the devil's subtle ploy,
transfigured is our planet earth,
the golden age is given birth.

4. I call forth the judgment of Christ upon the dark forces that prevent people from seeing that the fact that the Catholic church dominated Europe for almost a thousand years did not bring peace. The dominance of one supposedly absolute truth does not bring peace to earth.

O Jesus, show me serpent's lie,
expose the beam in my own eye,
as Christ discernment you me give,
in oneness I forever live.

O Jesus, let the Fire of Joy,
consume the devil's subtle ploy,
transfigured is our planet earth,
the golden age is given birth.

5. I call forth the judgment of Christ upon the dark forces that prevent people from seeing that if we have a higher truth, it is not dualistic and does not have an opposite polarity. If that truth managed to dominate a society, it would not generate conflict.

O Jesus, I am truly meek,
and thus I turn the other cheek,
when the accuser attacks me,
I go within and merge with thee.

O Jesus, let the Fire of Joy,
consume the devil's subtle ploy,
transfigured is our planet earth,
the golden age is given birth.

6. I call forth the judgment of Christ upon the dark forces that prevent people from seeing that by the very fact that a certain thought system does not create peace but creates conflict after conflict, we can know that it is not a higher truth. It is a dualistic polarity that must have one or several opposites.

O Jesus, ego I let die,
surrender ev'ry earthly tie,
the dead can bury what is dead,
I choose to walk with you instead.

O Jesus, let the Fire of Joy,
consume the devil's subtle ploy,
transfigured is our planet earth,
the golden age is given birth.

7. I call forth the judgment of Christ upon the dark forces that prevent people from seeing that human logic is human logic and this is what the fallen beings have used many times in order to confuse people.

O Jesus, help me rise above,
the devil's test through higher love,
show me separate self unreal,
my formless self you do reveal.

O Jesus, let the Fire of Joy,
consume the devil's subtle ploy,
transfigured is our planet earth,
the golden age is given birth.

8. I call forth the judgment of Christ upon the dark forces that prevent people from seeing that the fallen beings do not want people to have a neutral truth, a higher truth. They use dualistic logic to create an opposition.

O Jesus, what is that to me,
I just let go and follow thee,
with this I do pass ev'ry test,
to find with you eternal rest.

O Jesus, let the Fire of Joy,
consume the devil's subtle ploy,
transfigured is our planet earth,
the golden age is given birth.

9. I call forth the judgment of Christ upon the dark forces that prevent people from seeing that by making the claim that this is an absolute truth, authorized by some higher unquestionable authority, the fallen beings have already set up the potential for conflict.

O Jesus, fiery master mine,
my heart now melting into thine,
I love with heart and mind and soul,
the God who is my highest goal.

O Jesus, let the Fire of Joy,
consume the devil's subtle ploy,
transfigured is our planet earth,
the golden age is given birth.

Part 3

1. I call forth the judgment of Christ upon the dark forces that prevent people from seeing that the fallen beings took scientific observations and overlaid them with the materialistic philosophy that put itself in opposition to the religious authority.

O Jesus, blessed brother mine,
I walk the path that you outline,
a great example to us all,
I follow now your inner call.

O Jesus, let the Fire of Joy,
consume the devil's subtle ploy,
transfigured is our planet earth,
the golden age is given birth.

2. I call forth the judgment of Christ upon the dark forces that prevent people from seeing that we now have a religious authority, the established power elite, and an opposing scientific authority, the aspiring power elite.

O Jesus, open inner sight,
the ego wants to prove it's right,
but this I will no longer do,
I want to be all one with you.

O Jesus, let the Fire of Joy,
consume the devil's subtle ploy,
transfigured is our planet earth,
the golden age is given birth.

3. I call forth the judgment of Christ upon the dark forces that prevent people from seeing that science was hijacked by the fallen beings. This also happened with religion. In reality mysticism is as neutral as scientific observation.

O Jesus, I now clearly see,
the Key of Knowledge given me,
my Christ self I hereby embrace,
as you fill up my inner space.

O Jesus, let the Fire of Joy,
consume the devil's subtle ploy,
transfigured is our planet earth,
the golden age is given birth.

4. I call forth the judgment of Christ upon the dark forces that prevent people from seeing that mysticism in its pure form is a matter of experiencing the spiritual reality, instead of having theories and doctrines about the spiritual reality. Science in its pure form is a matter of observing how the world works instead of having man-made theories.

O Jesus, show me serpent's lie,
expose the beam in my own eye,
as Christ discernment you me give,
in oneness I forever live.

**O Jesus, let the Fire of Joy,
consume the devil's subtle ploy,
transfigured is our planet earth,
the golden age is given birth.**

5. I call forth the judgment of Christ upon the dark forces that prevent people from seeing that both mystical experiences and scientific observations will correspond to our level of consciousness and we will interpret them though our present level of consciousness. Therefore, they are not the absolute truth.

O Jesus, I am truly meek,
and thus I turn the other cheek,
when the accuser attacks me,
I go within and merge with thee.

**O Jesus, let the Fire of Joy,
consume the devil's subtle ploy,
transfigured is our planet earth,
the golden age is given birth.**

6. I call forth the judgment of Christ upon the dark forces that prevent people from seeing that both true spirituality and true science are open-ended processes that are not pursuing absolute truth but a progressively higher understanding.

O Jesus, ego I let die,
surrender ev'ry earthly tie,

the dead can bury what is dead,
I choose to walk with you instead.

O Jesus, let the Fire of Joy,
consume the devil's subtle ploy,
transfigured is our planet earth,
the golden age is given birth.

7. I call forth the judgment of Christ upon the dark forces that prevent people from seeing that what is right now holding back scientific progress is the claim made by materialism that science has discovered some absolute truth, namely that there is nothing beyond the material universe and that everything that takes place in the material universe can be explained as effects of causes that are also in the material universe.

O Jesus, help me rise above,
the devil's test through higher love,
show me separate self unreal,
my formless self you do reveal.

O Jesus, let the Fire of Joy,
consume the devil's subtle ploy,
transfigured is our planet earth,
the golden age is given birth.

8. I call forth the judgment of Christ upon the dark forces that prevent people from seeing that materialism has imposed a human interpretation on pure scientific observation, just as the Catholic church imposed a purely human interpretation on the example and the teachings that Jesus gave 2,000 years ago.

O Jesus, what is that to me,
I just let go and follow thee,
with this I do pass ev'ry test,
to find with you eternal rest.

O Jesus, let the Fire of Joy,
consume the devil's subtle ploy,

**transfigured is our planet earth,
the golden age is given birth.**

9. I call forth the judgment of Christ upon the dark forces that prevent people from seeing that the Catholic church created "infallible" doctrines and materialism has created "infallible" scientific doctrines. When we have a doctrine that we believe is infallible, it stops growth because we will not look beyond the doctrine.

O Jesus, fiery master mine,
my heart now melting into thine,
I love with heart and mind and soul,
the God who is my highest goal.

**O Jesus, let the Fire of Joy,
consume the devil's subtle ploy,
transfigured is our planet earth,
the golden age is given birth.**

Part 4

1. I call forth the judgment of Christ upon the fallen beings in the emotional, mental and identity realms who have created an apparatus, a machine, aimed at getting people to do things that serve the cause of the fallen beings and their agenda on earth.

O Jesus, blessed brother mine,
I walk the path that you outline,
a great example to us all,
I follow now your inner call.

**O Jesus, let the Fire of Joy,
consume the devil's subtle ploy,
transfigured is our planet earth,
the golden age is given birth.**

2. I call forth the judgment of Christ upon the demons in the emotional realm that are very aggressive, very forceful, and attempt to take over the emotional bodies of people in embodiment.

O Jesus, open inner sight,
the ego wants to prove it's right,
but this I will no longer do,
I want to be all one with you.

O Jesus, let the Fire of Joy,
consume the devil's subtle ploy,
transfigured is our planet earth,
the golden age is given birth.

3. I call forth the judgment of Christ upon all demons of hatred who have taken over the minds of members of the more extremist Muslim movements.

O Jesus, I now clearly see,
the Key of Knowledge given me,
my Christ self I hereby embrace,
as you fill up my inner space.

O Jesus, let the Fire of Joy,
consume the devil's subtle ploy,
transfigured is our planet earth,
the golden age is given birth.

4. I call forth the judgment of Christ upon all demons of hatred who have taken over people's emotional bodies and caused them to fight battles that were driven by hatred towards the enemy.

O Jesus, show me serpent's lie,
expose the beam in my own eye,
as Christ discernment you me give,
in oneness I forever live.

O Jesus, let the Fire of Joy,
consume the devil's subtle ploy,

**transfigured is our planet earth,
the golden age is given birth.**

5. I call forth the judgment of Christ upon the false hierarchy in the emotional realm who attempt to take over people's emotional bodies through fear, panic, anger, hatred, jealousy, greed or lust.

O Jesus, I am truly meek,
and thus I turn the other cheek,
when the accuser attacks me,
I go within and merge with thee.

**O Jesus, let the Fire of Joy,
consume the devil's subtle ploy,
transfigured is our planet earth,
the golden age is given birth.**

6. I call forth the judgment of Christ upon the false hierarchy in the emotional realm who get people to suspend what they all know from experience, namely that everything we do has a consequence.

O Jesus, ego I let die,
surrender ev'ry earthly tie,
the dead can bury what is dead,
I choose to walk with you instead.

**O Jesus, let the Fire of Joy,
consume the devil's subtle ploy,
transfigured is our planet earth,
the golden age is given birth.**

7. I call forth the judgment of Christ upon the false hierarchy in the emotional realm who are stirring up people's emotional bodies so they act without any thought of consequence.

O Jesus, help me rise above,
the devil's test through higher love,
show me separate self unreal,
my formless self you do reveal.

**O Jesus, let the Fire of Joy,
consume the devil's subtle ploy,
transfigured is our planet earth,
the golden age is given birth.**

8. I call forth the judgment of Christ upon the false hierarchy in the emotional realm who have caused people to go into war, feeling they *have* to kill the enemy, they have to defend their nation, they have to defend their faith.

O Jesus, what is that to me,
I just let go and follow thee,
with this I do pass ev'ry test,
to find with you eternal rest.

**O Jesus, let the Fire of Joy,
consume the devil's subtle ploy,
transfigured is our planet earth,
the golden age is given birth.**

9. I call forth the judgment of Christ upon the false hierarchy in the mental realm who have defined the idea that people will get a better position in heaven by killing those who oppose their religion.

O Jesus, fiery master mine,
my heart now melting into thine,
I love with heart and mind and soul,
the God who is my highest goal.

**O Jesus, let the Fire of Joy,
consume the devil's subtle ploy,
transfigured is our planet earth,
the golden age is given birth.**

Sealing

In the name of the I AM THAT I AM, I accept that Archangel Michael, Astrea and Shiva form an impenetrable shield around myself and all constructive people, sealing us from all fear-based energies in all four octaves. I accept that the Light of God is consuming and transforming all fear-based energies that make up the dark forces working against ending the era of dictatorships on earth!

20 | JUDGING THE DARK FORCES BEHIND DICTATORS (PART 2)

In the name of the I AM THAT I AM, Jesus Christ, I use the authority that I have as a being in embodiment on earth to call upon Jesus to reinforce my calls and use my chakras to project the statements in this invocation into the collective consciousness and bring about the judgment of all dark forces behind dictators. Awaken people to the reality that we are spiritual beings and that we can co-create a new future by working with the ascended masters. I especially call for …

[Make your own calls here.]

Part 1

1. I call forth the judgment of Christ upon the false hierarchy in the mental realm who get people to suspend their knowledge that everything has a physical consequence by making them think that there is a greater reward that can outweigh the physical consequence.

O Jesus, blessed brother mine,
I walk the path that you outline,
a great example to us all,
I follow now your inner call.

**O Jesus, let the Fire of Joy,
consume the devil's subtle ploy,
transfigured is our planet earth,
the golden age is given birth.**

2. I call forth the judgment of Christ upon the false hierarchy in the mental realm who make people think that there is this magical way to avoid the consequence. For example, if you kill a Christian, you go to hell, but if you kill a Muslim, you go to heaven.

O Jesus, open inner sight,
the ego wants to prove it's right,
but this I will no longer do,
I want to be all one with you.

**O Jesus, let the Fire of Joy,
consume the devil's subtle ploy,
transfigured is our planet earth,
the golden age is given birth.**

3. I call forth the judgment of Christ upon the false hierarchy in the mental realm who use serpentine logic that says, thou shalt not *surely* go to hell for killing another human being because if you kill the wrong kind, the bad people, the people who oppose God, then you will be rewarded in heaven.

O Jesus, I now clearly see,
the Key of Knowledge given me,
my Christ self I hereby embrace,
as you fill up my inner space.

**O Jesus, let the Fire of Joy,
consume the devil's subtle ploy,
transfigured is our planet earth,
the golden age is given birth.**

4. I call forth the judgment of Christ upon the false hierarchy in the mental realm who get people to suspend their intuitive sense, which will tell them that if they live by the sword, they will die by the sword.

O Jesus, show me serpent's lie,
expose the beam in my own eye,
as Christ discernment you me give,
in oneness I forever live.

O Jesus, let the Fire of Joy,
consume the devil's subtle ploy,
transfigured is our planet earth,
the golden age is given birth.

5. I call forth the judgment of Christ upon the false hierarchy in the identity realm who are trying to get people to suspend the common observation that actions have consequences by destroying, obscuring or falsifying people's intuitive sense of what is right.

O Jesus, I am truly meek,
and thus I turn the other cheek,
when the accuser attacks me,
I go within and merge with thee.

O Jesus, let the Fire of Joy,
consume the devil's subtle ploy,
transfigured is our planet earth,
the golden age is given birth.

6. I call forth the judgment of Christ upon the false hierarchy in the identity realm who have created the concept that there are certain people who are in a special category.

O Jesus, ego I let die,
surrender ev'ry earthly tie,
the dead can bury what is dead,
I choose to walk with you instead.

**O Jesus, let the Fire of Joy,
consume the devil's subtle ploy,
transfigured is our planet earth,
the golden age is given birth.**

7. I call forth the judgment of Christ upon the false hierarchy in the identity realm who claim that some people are so special that they can do things that enable them to not have the consequence it has for the majority of the population. They can get away with things. There are no free lunches for the people but there are free lunches for the elite.

O Jesus, help me rise above,
the devil's test through higher love,
show me separate self unreal,
my formless self you do reveal.

**O Jesus, let the Fire of Joy,
consume the devil's subtle ploy,
transfigured is our planet earth,
the golden age is given birth.**

8. I call forth the judgment of Christ upon the false hierarchy in the identity realm who have set up these privileged elites, such as a privileged elite who through corruption can get away with things or gain privileges for themselves that the ordinary population cannot have.

O Jesus, what is that to me,
I just let go and follow thee,
with this I do pass ev'ry test,
to find with you eternal rest.

**O Jesus, let the Fire of Joy,
consume the devil's subtle ploy,
transfigured is our planet earth,
the golden age is given birth.**

9. I call forth the judgment of Christ upon the false hierarchy in the identity realm who have distorted people's sense of identity to make certain people feel: "Oh, I am in a special category, I am above the law. I am not

an ordinary human being. Therefore, I can do things and there will not be a consequence."

O Jesus, fiery master mine,
my heart now melting into thine,
I love with heart and mind and soul,
the God who is my highest goal.

O Jesus, let the Fire of Joy,
consume the devil's subtle ploy,
transfigured is our planet earth,
the golden age is given birth.

Part 2

1. I call forth the judgment of Christ upon the dark forces that prevent people from seeing that when people come to believe in a dictator, they take upon themselves some of the karma he creates.

O Jesus, blessed brother mine,
I walk the path that you outline,
a great example to us all,
I follow now your inner call.

O Jesus, let the Fire of Joy,
consume the devil's subtle ploy,
transfigured is our planet earth,
the golden age is given birth.

2. I call forth the judgment of Christ upon the false hierarchy who have initiated various atrocities and have made the people take on part of the karma without knowing it consciously.

O Jesus, open inner sight,
the ego wants to prove it's right,
but this I will no longer do,
I want to be all one with you.

O Jesus, let the Fire of Joy,
consume the devil's subtle ploy,
transfigured is our planet earth,
the golden age is given birth.

3. I call forth the judgment of Christ upon the dark forces that prevent people from seeing that even though Catholic priests are making karma for violating children, all Catholics who are truly believing in the church and the importance and sanctity of the institution, are taking on themselves part of that karma.

O Jesus, I now clearly see,
the Key of Knowledge given me,
my Christ self I hereby embrace,
as you fill up my inner space.

O Jesus, let the Fire of Joy,
consume the devil's subtle ploy,
transfigured is our planet earth,
the golden age is given birth.

4. I call forth the judgment of Christ upon the dark forces that prevent people from seeing that Catholics believe that preserving the church is so important, it can either excuse the pedophilia, or at least that it should not result in the demise of the church.

O Jesus, show me serpent's lie,
expose the beam in my own eye,
as Christ discernment you me give,
in oneness I forever live.

O Jesus, let the Fire of Joy,
consume the devil's subtle ploy,
transfigured is our planet earth,
the golden age is given birth.

5. I call forth the judgment of Christ upon the dark forces that prevent people from seeing that this prevents Catholics from saying: "Something is rotten in Rome. We need to make systemic changes in the Catholic

church." By not saying this, they take on karma that should be the karma of the fallen beings.

> O Jesus, I am truly meek,
> and thus I turn the other cheek,
> when the accuser attacks me,
> I go within and merge with thee.

> **O Jesus, let the Fire of Joy,**
> **consume the devil's subtle ploy,**
> **transfigured is our planet earth,**
> **the golden age is given birth.**

6. I call forth the judgment of Christ upon the demons in the astral plane who have taken over the emotional bodies of the priests, causing them to reason that even though they know that it is wrong to have sex with children, there is some excuse so they will not suffer the consequences.

> O Jesus, ego I let die,
> surrender ev'ry earthly tie,
> the dead can bury what is dead,
> I choose to walk with you instead.

> **O Jesus, let the Fire of Joy,**
> **consume the devil's subtle ploy,**
> **transfigured is our planet earth,**
> **the golden age is given birth.**

7. I call forth the judgment of Christ upon the false hierarchy in the mental realm who make priests believe that they can get away with it because the church will protect them.

> O Jesus, help me rise above,
> the devil's test through higher love,
> show me separate self unreal,
> my formless self you do reveal.

> **O Jesus, let the Fire of Joy,**
> **consume the devil's subtle ploy,**

**transfigured is our planet earth,
the golden age is given birth.**

8. I call forth the judgment of Christ upon the false hierarchy in the identity realm who make priests believe that because they belong to the most important church, then this is acceptable behavior.

O Jesus, what is that to me,
I just let go and follow thee,
with this I do pass ev'ry test,
to find with you eternal rest.

**O Jesus, let the Fire of Joy,
consume the devil's subtle ploy,
transfigured is our planet earth,
the golden age is given birth.**

9. I call forth the judgment of Christ upon the false hierarchy who have produced the hypnotic state that blinds the priests who are abusing children, the bishops and cardinals who think nothing must question the sanctity of the church and the ordinary Catholics who are loyal to the outer institution.

O Jesus, fiery master mine,
my heart now melting into thine,
I love with heart and mind and soul,
the God who is my highest goal.

**O Jesus, let the Fire of Joy,
consume the devil's subtle ploy,
transfigured is our planet earth,
the golden age is given birth.**

Part 3

1. I call forth the judgment of Christ upon the dark forces that prevent Catholics from seeing that they must be loyal to Christ instead of seeking to preserve an earthly institution.

> O Jesus, blessed brother mine,
> I walk the path that you outline,
> a great example to us all,
> I follow now your inner call.

> **O Jesus, let the Fire of Joy,**
> **consume the devil's subtle ploy,**
> **transfigured is our planet earth,**
> **the golden age is given birth.**

2. I call forth the judgment of Christ upon the false hierarchy who have used the desire to be special so that people who have had an unusual experience feel they have to go out and tell other people and what they are basically saying is: "Look how special I am that I was given this experience. It must mean that I'm so special."

> O Jesus, open inner sight,
> the ego wants to prove it's right,
> but this I will no longer do,
> I want to be all one with you.

> **O Jesus, let the Fire of Joy,**
> **consume the devil's subtle ploy,**
> **transfigured is our planet earth,**
> **the golden age is given birth.**

3. I call forth the judgment of Christ upon the dark forces that prevent ascended master students from seeing that we need to overcome all desire to be special so we can be in a neutral state of mind and therefore achieve the discernment of the Christ mind.

O Jesus, I now clearly see,
the Key of Knowledge given me,
my Christ self I hereby embrace,
as you fill up my inner space.

**O Jesus, let the Fire of Joy,
consume the devil's subtle ploy,
transfigured is our planet earth,
the golden age is given birth.**

4. I call forth the judgment of Christ upon the dark forces that prevent ascended master students from seeing that the desire to be special can distort, even abort our spiritual progress by making us feel superior to those who are not in our teaching.

O Jesus, show me serpent's lie,
expose the beam in my own eye,
as Christ discernment you me give,
in oneness I forever live.

**O Jesus, let the Fire of Joy,
consume the devil's subtle ploy,
transfigured is our planet earth,
the golden age is given birth.**

5. I call forth the judgment of Christ upon the dark forces that prevent people from seeing that the feeling of being better than others always comes from the false hierarchy in the identity realm who distort our emotional, mental and identity bodies so that we feel: "Because I'm in this group, that's why I'm special." Or: "Because I had that particular experience, I am special."

O Jesus, I am truly meek,
and thus I turn the other cheek,
when the accuser attacks me,
I go within and merge with thee.

**O Jesus, let the Fire of Joy,
consume the devil's subtle ploy,**

**transfigured is our planet earth,
the golden age is given birth.**

6. I call forth the judgment of Christ upon the dark forces that prevent people from seeing that when we have this desire to be special, we cannot have discernment because we are not going into a neutral state of mind. Everything we do is personal and our overall concern is to not destroy the sense that "I'm special."

O Jesus, ego I let die,
surrender ev'ry earthly tie,
the dead can bury what is dead,
I choose to walk with you instead.

**O Jesus, let the Fire of Joy,
consume the devil's subtle ploy,
transfigured is our planet earth,
the golden age is given birth.**

7. I call forth the judgment of Christ upon the false hierarchy impostors who claim to be God or ascended masters or who use names known to people on earth in order to gain a position of authority.

O Jesus, help me rise above,
the devil's test through higher love,
show me separate self unreal,
my formless self you do reveal.

**O Jesus, let the Fire of Joy,
consume the devil's subtle ploy,
transfigured is our planet earth,
the golden age is given birth.**

8. I call forth the judgment of Christ upon the beings in the mental and identity realm who have claimed to be some kind of deity, some kind of god that has influenced people.

O Jesus, what is that to me,
I just let go and follow thee,

with this I do pass ev'ry test,
to find with you eternal rest.

**O Jesus, let the Fire of Joy,
consume the devil's subtle ploy,
transfigured is our planet earth,
the golden age is given birth.**

9. I call forth the judgment of Christ upon the false hierarchy impostors who are seeking to confuse or destroy people's Christ discernment by producing teachings that contain some truth but also many errors.

O Jesus, fiery master mine,
my heart now melting into thine,
I love with heart and mind and soul,
the God who is my highest goal.

**O Jesus, let the Fire of Joy,
consume the devil's subtle ploy,
transfigured is our planet earth,
the golden age is given birth.**

Part 4

1. I call forth the judgment of Christ upon the dark forces that prevent people from seeing that the basis for dictatorships on earth is that the dictator claims to be special and have something, some ability, that people do not have.

O Jesus, blessed brother mine,
I walk the path that you outline,
a great example to us all,
I follow now your inner call.

**O Jesus, let the Fire of Joy,
consume the devil's subtle ploy,**

transfigured is our planet earth,
the golden age is given birth.

2. I call forth the judgment of Christ upon the dark forces that prevent people from seeing that the most insidious, the most dangerous form of dictatorships on earth are those who claim that they stand between people and God—between us and the spiritual realm.

O Jesus, open inner sight,
the ego wants to prove it's right,
but this I will no longer do,
I want to be all one with you.

O Jesus, let the Fire of Joy,
consume the devil's subtle ploy,
transfigured is our planet earth,
the golden age is given birth.

3. I call forth the judgment of Christ upon the false hierarchy impostors who claim that people in embodiment can only reach God or the spiritual realm through them, whether they are in physical embodiment or in the emotional, mental or identity realms.

O Jesus, I now clearly see,
the Key of Knowledge given me,
my Christ self I hereby embrace,
as you fill up my inner space.

O Jesus, let the Fire of Joy,
consume the devil's subtle ploy,
transfigured is our planet earth,
the golden age is given birth.

4. I call forth the judgment of Christ upon the false hierarchy impostors who imposture some spiritual being but are not ascended, and therefore they still have some agenda, they still have something they need.

O Jesus, show me serpent's lie,
expose the beam in my own eye,

as Christ discernment you me give,
in oneness I forever live.

O Jesus, let the Fire of Joy,
consume the devil's subtle ploy,
transfigured is our planet earth,
the golden age is given birth.

5. I call forth the judgment of Christ upon the false hierarchy in the emotional, mental and identity realms who are behind the dictatorship of the Catholic church.

O Jesus, I am truly meek,
and thus I turn the other cheek,
when the accuser attacks me,
I go within and merge with thee.

O Jesus, let the Fire of Joy,
consume the devil's subtle ploy,
transfigured is our planet earth,
the golden age is given birth.

6. I call forth the judgment of Christ upon the false hierarchy in the emotional, mental and identity realms who are behind the dictatorship of Islam.

O Jesus, ego I let die,
surrender ev'ry earthly tie,
the dead can bury what is dead,
I choose to walk with you instead.

O Jesus, let the Fire of Joy,
consume the devil's subtle ploy,
transfigured is our planet earth,
the golden age is given birth.

7. I call forth the judgment of Christ upon the false hierarchy in the emotional, mental and identity realms who are behind the dictatorship in North Korea.

O Jesus, help me rise above,
the devil's test through higher love,
show me separate self unreal,
my formless self you do reveal.

O Jesus, let the Fire of Joy,
consume the devil's subtle ploy,
transfigured is our planet earth,
the golden age is given birth.

8. I call forth the judgment of Christ upon the false hierarchy in the emotional, mental and identity realms who are behind the dictatorship in communist China.

O Jesus, what is that to me,
I just let go and follow thee,
with this I do pass ev'ry test,
to find with you eternal rest.

O Jesus, let the Fire of Joy,
consume the devil's subtle ploy,
transfigured is our planet earth,
the golden age is given birth.

9. I call forth the judgment of Christ upon the false hierarchy in the emotional, mental and identity realms who are behind the dictatorship in Vladimir Putin's Russia.

O Jesus, fiery master mine,
my heart now melting into thine,
I love with heart and mind and soul,
the God who is my highest goal.

O Jesus, let the Fire of Joy,
consume the devil's subtle ploy,
transfigured is our planet earth,
the golden age is given birth.

Sealing

In the name of the I AM THAT I AM, I accept that Archangel Michael, Astrea and Shiva form an impenetrable shield around myself and all constructive people, sealing us from all fear-based energies in all four octaves. I accept that the Light of God is consuming and transforming all fear-based energies that make up the dark forces working against ending the era of dictatorships on earth!

21 | YOU CANNOT CHANGE YOURSELF BY SEEKING TO CHANGE OTHERS

I AM the Ascended Master Kuan Yin, and I will give you the perspective of the Divine Mother on some issues that we have determined can be of value for you. First of all, I want to speak about the situation in Korea. I know that you who are from Korea have been very gracious in inviting this conference here, even though we are not specifically focused on Korea. Given that you have a neighbor to the North, then it is of course all of relevance to you, even of special relevance to you.

Now, we have given you at previous conferences many dictations specifically on the situation in Korea. They are naturally all still relevant and it is not our intention to say that these are the only issues you need to work on. Naturally, you are free to look at your nation, determine that there are certain issues you would like to make calls on, and then you use our decrees and invocations to call for action on those issues. The reason we have chosen the issues we have spoken about at the previous conferences was that we see the complex geometry that will bring forth change in Korea, and we have given you the topics that based on this will have the most impact on the future of Korea.

Korean business conglomerates

There is however one topic that I want to talk about here and it is the situation that you have in Korea allowed the creation of these large business conglomerates, which we have talked about before. What we would like you to realize is that this has created sort of a special situation. You understand that there was a practical necessity to rebuild Korea after the war and therefore the government took what it saw as a practical realist measure for accomplishing this as quickly as possible. It created these business entities, gave them very much a free rein without much oversight from the government and their only charge was: "rebuild the country, create jobs."

Now, it is clear that this was a practical necessity, although of course not the only way it could have been done, but it was one way and it was relatively efficient. There was a certain element of force here involved with these business conglomerates. They started relatively quickly competing amongst each other. There was a certain power game for establishing the supremacy of one or a couple of these business conglomerates. What has been created through this process is certain, what we might call, collective beasts or even collective demons.

Each of the business conglomerates has created a particular beast that exists in the emotional realm, in the mental, and even in the lower identity realm. It is not a conscious being, as we have described to you that there are demons and entities that are not conscious, they are not self-aware. It is a programmed being that will mindlessly carry out its programming, and the programming is of course to expand this particular business conglomerate and to preserve it almost at all cost.

The people behind these business conglomerates were very much enveloped in the consciousness that the end can justify the means, and they still are for the most part. There was a certain attitude that anything goes—whatever we can do to rebuild the country regardless of the human cost, regardless of any considerations for the individual, needs to be done. This then shifted into anything we can do to grow the corporation, to preserve the corporation and destroy the competition is also acceptable to be done. What this has created is of course a situation where the business conglomerates have used their privileged position to influence the collective consciousness of Korea to the point where most people think that these business conglomerates are necessary, are beneficial, and that Korea and the Korean economy could not survive without them. In other words, they have created a mindset that this is the only way to do business in

Korea. This is the only way for the economy to survive and thrive. There are of course (as we have said before) alternatives, but most people are not even open to looking for them because they think this is the Korean model, and it has worked so far, so why should it not it work in the future? There is a certain loyalty that has been created in the Korean population towards these business conglomerates.

The need for a new business model in Korea

What you need to realize here is that for Korea to truly thrive and for the Korean economy to grow in the future, you need to gradually open up so there is more of an awareness of different business models. Also, so that the government gradually starts making it easier for other businesses to be established, and to even come up and compete with the large conglomerates. Otherwise, the Korean economy will not remain vital in the future and it will not be able to deal with the burden of a reunification of Korea.

In order to create this shift in consciousness, you can make the calls that people will be set free from the hypnotic effect of these huge demons or beasts that have been created and that demand the loyalty and the special treatment of these conglomerates. You can see, my beloved, if you think about this, that in Korea there is a special awareness of, for example, Samsung. There is a certain sense in the population that we should buy Samsung products or at least Korean made products. Here is a Korean housewife who needs to buy a new washing machine, and she thinks: "Oh, I should be a good Korean citizen and buy a Samsung washing machine." But you need to recognize that Samsung as it is today is so large a corporation that it could not survive by just selling washing machines and other products in Korea.

Samsung is a huge multinational corporation that sells washing machines in almost every country around the world. The Korean attitude towards Samsung, the loyalty, the sense that Samsung is entitled to special privileges and special treatment by the government cannot ensure the survival of Samsung. Samsung's future depends on people in other countries buying their products. If you look at a housewife in Denmark, for example, who needs to buy a new washing machine, she does not have that loyalty towards Samsung. She does not feel the need to buy Korean products. If something shifts in the international perception of Samsung, it does not take very much for there to be a wave in the collective consciousness internationally where people suddenly become aware, for example, that workers are not paid fairly or not treated well, and they say: "Why should I buy a Samsung washing machine when there is another company that treats its employees better or pays them better? Let me choose that product instead."

You can see that the Korean attitude towards Samsung cannot ensure the survival of Samsung, or Hyundai, or any other corporation in Korea. Therefore, there is a need for you who are the spiritual people to make the calls that there will be a shift in the Korean consciousness towards these business conglomerates so that people will adopt a more international awareness and therefore realize that the businesses in Korea need to look at what is happening in the world at large, what is happening in the attitude and awareness of consumers in the world.

The need to treat employees well

They therefore need to start adapting to this so that they look at how Western corporations are treating their employees, how well they are paying them. How much, for example, of the earnings of a corporation are going to the shareholders and how big of a percentage is going to the employees. They need to make these adjustments so that Korean corporations follow the trends in the international business climate and are not staying in this hypnotic bubble created by these large beasts. In other words, you can make the calls that the Korean business climate is freed from these beasts, and even that the large corporations are freed from it, so they can grow and adapt to the changing times, and even start adopting a Golden Age business model. For unless they do begin to make the transition into a Golden Age model, how can they survive in the Golden Age?

We of the ascended masters would like to see Korea be an example of a nation that transitions into the Golden Age, not just in the area of business of course but also in other areas. These are calls that you can make and that will have an important impact.

Now, you can also make calls for the exposure of anything that is hidden, both in the government and in these large business conglomerates. You will see that in Korea since the war there has been created almost the sense that you have an upper class, a special class of Korean people who are the rich people, the leaders of these big business conglomerates. There has arisen in the population almost a sense that these very rich and powerful people are in a special class, that they are almost perfect or that they are beyond criticism. You can make the calls for the exposure of any inappropriate actions, any illegal actions, any corruption, any special dealings. It is necessary in order for Korea to transition into this new business model that the idolatry of these seemingly all-powerful business leaders is broken down. It may necessitate that there is an exposure of personal failings or wrongdoings on the part of some of these leaders so that the Korean people can awaken and have a shift where they realize that they are still human beings and they are still as fallible as other human beings. Therefore, they do not deserve special treatment or privileges, and they do not deserve to be looked up to as if they were some kind of gods walking around on earth. I can assure you that God does not wear business suits, my beloved. These are some issues for you to make calls on in the nation of Korea.

Students of the masters in Korea

I would also like to briefly address the issue that has come up at this conference of the ascended master student community in Korea. Naturally, we are very happy, very joyful to see the enormous progress you have made in such a short period of time. The amount of teachings that have been translated, the amount of books that have been translated and published, the groups you have created, the amount of invocations you have given, and the conferences you have organized. We are very joyful to see this change and you all, who have been part of this, deserve credit. We do not as ascended masters praise or elevate specific individuals. All of you have been a part of this and all of you deserve to feel that you are part of something that will make a difference, and it *is* making a difference.

Now, you also need to be aware that what you have been doing in terms of all this work, all your invocations, all your group activities, your translations, and your organizing these conferences, is a major threat, and is seen as a major threat, by the dark forces, both on a planetary level, but of course specifically here in Korea and in North Korea. You need to be aware that the dark forces will do what they always do. They will try to find an inroad into your activity, into your group, and they will try to create inharmony. How do they do it? By creating division. Divide and conquer is their eternal, or at least very old, strategy. When you look at spiritual, religious, New Age, even ascended master communities, you see that it still works. We have in previous ascended master dispensations seen this tendency that divisions are created, different groups spring up, they polarize, and this can always lead to division. It can lead to a movement not fulfilling its potential. I am not trying to create any kind of fear-based reaction in you. We are not looking to have you approach this from a fear-based sense that: "Oh we are under threat and we need to keep out any kind of division, and therefore we need to suppress any kind of criticism or free discussion." In past ascended master organizations they have attempted to suppress criticism and avoid free discussion, and it only creates more pressure. What we are asking you to do is of course to use the teachings that you have been given in this dispensation.

My beloved, in order to create an ascended master organization that can sustain itself against the divide-and-conquer strategy of the fallen beings and the dark forces, it is necessary that all of the members of this organization dedicate themselves to walking the spiritual path. As we have described, the spiritual path is essentially about one thing: overcoming your separate selves, and especially about going down there to the very bottom of this structure of separate selves and identifying the primal self. Whether you are an avatar or an original inhabitant, you have a primal self, created in reaction to the fallen beings. Do you see, my beloved, the simple logic here? If you have an organization that is under attack by the dark forces, and they are attempting to use divide-and-conquer, what is their inroad? It is the separate selves and especially the primal self.

The primal self was created in reaction to the fallen beings. The self that can only react to the fallen beings can never help you free yourself from the influence of the fallen beings. It can never help you transcend the consciousness of the fallen beings. This is very, very simple logic.

The only realistic way for an ascended master student organization to survive in the long run is that as many people as possible among the members, and certainly among the leaders, dedicate themselves to resolving the primal self. Once you overcome your primal self, as we have described and as the messenger described last night, you depersonalize your path. This means that you can now be in an ascended master organization, working with other people, and whenever there is any kind of difference of opinion, or various disagreements, you can avoid taking it personally.

Saving the world in five minutes

What have we seen in previous ascended master organizations? We have seen people who were driven by what Saint Germain and Jesus talked about, this desire to be special. They have come into an organization, as even this messenger admitted he did as a young man coming into his first ascended master organization, with this desire to reinforce their sense of being special by doing something special, something decisive. This leads to a certain impatience. As the messenger has said, he wanted as a young man to save the world in five minutes. Of course, it cannot be done. We are not asking you to do it. We never have.

You need to realize here that when these differences of opinion happen, then when you take things personally, the different views become the source of tension. This means that people (often on both sides, but always on at least one side) start accumulating energy in their emotional bodies. They start accumulating energy that gradually builds in intensity so that they start feeling agitated, they start feeling that they have been rejected, people are not listening to them. They feel angry and they sometimes get into these discussion groups where they reinforce this emotional energy. Then, in their mental bodies they also start building a certain energy, and now they start going into these intellectual arguments and reasonings: This should not be done that way, these people are not doing the right thing. The master said this so therefore we should do this. It all stays at this intellectual level. What happens here is that now, what was really a difference of opinion becomes a source of polarization, opposition, personal conflict, and even personal power plays.

We have seen this so many times in ascended master organizations that if ascended masters were able to become nauseated and throw up, then we would have done so many times. Naturally, we are non-attached and we love you and we accept you, regardless of what you are going through. On the other hand, we also many times must step back because once you go into this state of accumulating energy, you shut off your intuitive faculties and therefore we cannot reach you—you cannot reach us. In many cases, students actually go into a state of mind where they are subconsciously saying to us: "Oh, stay away, masters, I have this all figured out. I have taken your teachings that you said ten years ago, and I have interpreted it so that I am right and the other people are wrong. And do not come and tell me anything different, I do not want to hear it right now, because I want to fight with other people and prove that I'm right." We still love you, my beloved. But we must love you from a distance because you have said: "Do not come too close."

Expressing your unique creativity

What this all comes down to is what we have said previously: Each of you has an I AM Presence that is an absolutely unique being, a unique facet in the diamond of God. Your greatest desire, your greatest drive, is to express your individuality by being a co-creator with your I AM Presence. So here you are, for many lifetimes that creativity might have been suppressed. Now, you find an ascended master teaching that resonates with you and you are thinking: "Here is my opportunity to be creative and to express my individuality."

It *could* be that way. But you see, as Saint Germain and Jesus explained, so often the desire to be special in this world and be special through the separate self, distorts your creative efforts. If you take these two dictations by Saint Germain and Jesus, you can receive essential keys for overcoming this whole dynamic and actually fulfilling your highest potential and the highest potential of any ascended master organization. You see, my beloved, it is necessary to first clear out the separate selves and the primal self before you can be truly creative. When you do this, you can come to a point where you have depersonalized your life.

Now, you can see that each of you has a certain unique personality, individuality. You have a unique I AM Presence and a unique creative expression. Instead of seeing your differences as being the source of conflict, tension and opposition, you can see that your differences can actually complement each other. Therefore, you can do something together that none of you can do alone. This cannot happen until a critical mass of the people in a group have gone through this process of overcoming the primal self and these other selves. You must have depersonalized your spiritual path, your personal life, your personal psychology. You must come to that point where, as Jesus described, you are always willing to look at a separate self that comes up. You are not seeking to defend the separate self. You are open to seeing it. When you see it, you are not condemning yourself in any way, you are just saying: "Oh, there you are. Now you're dead."

My beloved, when you are in that state, the fallen beings have no idea what to do. They can only say: "What happened? How did these people suddenly slip out of our grasp? How can it be that all the arrows we send at them pass right through? They do not create a reaction, they do not create an effect. If we can't make people fight each other, what can we do?" So they stand there, and for once they are not in control, and they realize they are not in control. There can come a point where you no longer need to worry about them because you have transcended the level of consciousness that is vulnerable to them. It is like Jesus said: "The prince this world cometh and has nothing in me." He has no self in me whereby he can force me to react to him. This of course is the goal we see not only for you here in Korea, but for the student body worldwide. We would love to see it happen for previous ascended master organizations, but how can it if they are not open to these deep psychological teachings we have given through this dispensation, and that could not be brought forth through previous dispensations?

My beloved, these are some important thoughts for you. It is important for you to take these dictations that have been given and really understand the mechanism, and come to that point that Jesus described where you are willing to look at: "How does this apply to me? What is my separate self?"

Cliques in ascended master organizations

What we have seen in previous ascended master organizations is a tendency that there were certain people (who perhaps were among the early ones to find the organization) who started feeling that because they had been in the organization for so long, they were now more advanced than new students. I am not saying this is a big problem here in Korea. I am just saying that this is the pattern that we have seen and that you need to be aware of.

There could come a certain point where these people feel that others should listen to them, others should obey them, others should not object, or should not come with suggestions. We have seen in past organizations how a clique or various cliques formed in the organization, of certain members who felt that anyone who did not submit to them was being critical. You realize here that the human consciousness can take anything we of the ascended master say and use it to justify itself or to invalidate other people. You can always, as I said, come up with reasonings and arguments why these other people are wrong. What we have seen in previous dispensations is that people have gone into these—almost what you see among fundamentalist Christians who are slinging Bible quotes at each other. Ascended master students have taken selected quotes from ascended master dictations out of context and said: "Well, El Morya has said this, and therefore, you are wrong, and you should do what I say." This of course is something we are telling you: You have the teachings, you have the tools, you can avoid this. You can set a pattern for how spiritual movements can function in the Aquarian Age. Obviously, they cannot function in the Aquarian Age the way they did in the Piscean Age, let alone the fact that they largely did not function in the Piscean Age because of the influence of the fallen beings and the dark forces and people's egos.

You have the opportunity to avoid this reaction. It is very simple. As the messenger has said himself, he realized that as long as he is in embodiment, he is going to have separate selves. The challenge of a separate self is always to come to see it. If you are aware of this, and you accept this fact, then you are always open to seeing something in yourself. If someone comes and points something out, you listen to what they are saying. You say: "Does this relate to me? Is there a separate self I haven't seen?" You may even ask us: "Help me see this separate self." You are just open, you are just neutral, you receive what people tell you in a neutral frame of mind. If you see that there is some reality to it, then you work on that separate self. If you do not see any reality, or if you do not feel any reaction in you, well, then you move on.

You allow these people to be in whatever frame of mind they are in. If they get angry with you, well, what can you do about that? In fact, if you have been willing to look at yourself, you do not need to do anything. You do not need to persuade them, you do not need to try to make them see that they are wrong or that you are right. You do not need to defend yourself. You can just say: "I have considered what you have told me, but I do not see anything in me. And so, I'm going to move on." Then, you allow them to have whatever reaction they have.

What I am saying is this, my beloved: Any organization based on these teachings, both the members and the leaders should be aware that as long as you are in physical embodiment, you have separate selves. Therefore, you are not above learning something from other people. You are not above having to look at yourself in any situation where you are dealing with other people. The first thing to look at is always: "Do I have a reaction? Do I feel some kind of emotion? Do I feel threatened? Do I start building tension, building energy? Do I want to refute what the other person is saying? Am I defending myself?" These things you can look at, and if you see that reaction, as the messenger has been willing to do many times, you know there is a separate self behind the reaction because where else would the reaction come from? It does not come from your I AM Presence. And as we have tried to help you see, it does not actually come from the Conscious You because the Conscious You is a neutral observer, and it is only through the separate selves that you react.

A group can be a source of joy

My beloved, if you just take these tools, if you just make that shift of depersonalizing your path, then you will find that your involvement with an ascended master activity, your involvement with a group, becomes a source of joy, a source of growth. You do not feel threatened, you do not feel vulnerable, you do not feel under attack, you do not feel criticized, you do not feel you are rejected, that you have to criticize others. There is no struggle. There *is* no struggle. When you rise above the primal self and the other selves that are always reacting, then your work together can be a source of joy. I know it has already been for many of you in the Korean community. I am simply saying you can continue to work on whatever separate selves you have left and you will find that your joy will be more and more full, and you will be more and more at peace.

This messenger has realized himself that when he was new in an ascended master teaching, he was very eager to do something because he wanted to prove that he was special. He wanted to prove that he was a good student. Many, many people have had the same drive, and we are not saying that this is wrong. It is simply a stage on the path, and we are always glad to see students who are eager. We are not so glad to see when their eagerness somehow runs into this pattern of conflict that in many cases causes people to become discouraged or angry and leave an ascended master organization, or even leave the teachings behind.

We have seen people who became so angry over a conflict with other people that they left the spiritual path for the rest of that lifetime. In some cases, they had the potential to ascend after that lifetime, but the conflict with one other person (with whom they also had conflicts in many past lifetimes) caused them to leave the path towards the ascension. Of course, we do not desire to see that repeated.

Letting nothing come between you and the masters

Now, this messenger had, even when he was very young, one realization that can help you. He realized very early on that the uniqueness of the ascended masters and an ascended master teaching, or an ascended master organization, is that we of the ascended masters are in a higher level of consciousness, a fundamentally higher level of consciousness. He realized that this meant that he could not know with his present level of consciousness how ascended masters would act or react in a particular situation. He did not understand fully back then that we would never react but he knew that in order for him to grow, he could never allow himself to think that he knew what the ascended masters would do or say. He always had to be open to a higher understanding. He realized that in order for him to be on the path, in order for him to attune to the ascended masters, he had to be willing to look beyond his present level of consciousness. He also realized that because we are beyond the human level of consciousness, he could never allow anything on earth to come between himself and the ascended masters.

When he had conflicts with particular individuals, he realized that he could not allow those people to come between him and his attunement with the masters. He realized that if he became angry or went into disharmony, he could not at the same time have attunement with the ascended masters. Therefore, he had to choose: Would he continue to try and prove himself right and prove these other people wrong? Or would he let the whole thing go and tune in to the ascended masters, as he did one time when he experienced, then, the love, the very pink love, of El Morya for a student who is willing to let the ego go because the student understands what Jesus meant when he said: "What is that to thee—follow thou me."

This is something you can all cultivate, and you can begin to say: "I cannot allow anything on earth to stand between me and the ascended masters and my attunement, my inner attunement, with the ascended masters. I cannot allow an outer organization to stand between me and the ascended masters." This messenger was a member of an organization and as we have explained, that organization was created specifically for people in the Piscean mindset. This messenger was not part of that target group.

He had transcended most of the Piscean mindset and was already into the Aquarian mindset. He saw some of these elements of this organization, but he also said to himself: "I cannot allow myself to let this stand between me and the masters. I cannot start fighting this, trying to change the organization to the point where it takes away my inner attunement and my harmony." He even looked at the previous messenger and saw certain things that he could not understand, even things that he intuitively knew were not the only way to do things, but he also said: "I cannot allow the messenger to stand between me and my attunement with the ascended masters."

This is what you can all learn from and adopt that same attitude: to not let anything stand between you and your attunement with the ascended masters. What does it mean that something stands between you and the ascended masters? It means that something takes you out of attunement. Where do we have attunement, my beloved? Inside, in your heart, in your heart chakra. What does it take to have attunement? As we have said, you need to be in a neutral frame of mind. If your attention is pulled outwards, and is pulled into disharmony and conflict and arguing and this and that, you cannot have attunement at the same time.

You have in various cultures around the world, various statements of this. You have the saying in the United States: "You cannot have your cake and eat it too." You have in the messenger's country the saying that you cannot have flour in your mouth, and at the same time whistle. Because you will of course blow it out of your mouth. You have in many other cultures similar sayings that simply emphasize the fact that in the physical octave on planet earth, you always have to make a choice. You cannot, when there are, for example, two options, you cannot have both. You cannot direct your attention outwards, into some kind of conflict with other people or in an attempt to change the world, and at the same time direct it inward towards the ascended masters.

I am not saying you always need to direct your attention inward—you obviously have things to take care of in your practical life. What I am saying is that many students have gone into this state of being in an agitated state of mind, always thinking about this problem they are having or this conflict they are having, and their attention is pulled outwards. They never have a moment to go within and if they did go within, what would happen? Well, as we have said, it is not that we suddenly appear as some booming voice from heaven that says: "Do this! Do not do that!" What we do is, we manifest our Presence with you so that you can sense our vibration. You can then sense the difference in the vibration of an ascended master, and the energy you have allowed to accumulate as a result of this conflict you have with another person. Then, you can say: "Oh, I do not want that energy. I want the energy I'm sensing from Kuan Yin." Then, you can choose. Now, you have a frame of reference. You have experienced something outside of the separate self and that is the first step of separating yourself from it. Then, you keep working on it until you come to the point where now you see the belief behind that separate self, you see the problem that the separate self thinks it has to solve.

Making karma for abusing a spiritual teaching

In many cases in these personality conflicts it is that you have a separate self that thinks that an organization should be run this particular way and it cannot be run any other way—*that* is wrong. When you see people doing things differently, it suddenly becomes of this epic importance for you to change these people's minds. They resist it and so the tension builds and now you are in the spiral. You are caught in the spiral and the separate self can never get out of it. The only way out of it is that you experience an alternative vibration.

We have seen ascended master students, my beloved, who went into these conflicts or into these attempts to change something, even attempt to change things in the world, and they become so focused in this consciousness that they always need to look for what is wrong. They always need to be critical of every situation because they know better as ascended master students, and they always need to go out there and try to make the world conform to their vision. This all comes from a separate self. What do all their efforts do, my beloved? It reinforces that separate self, it feeds the separate self with energy but it also convinces you that the separate self must be right.

What have we said? The key to your ascension is to overcome the separate self so anything that reinforces the separate self is actually how you make karma. We have seen ascended master students who have taken our teachings and used them, or a specific interpretation of them, to reinforce their separate selves and actually make a special kind of karma. They do not make the karma you make for going out and killing somebody, but they are making a special form of karma by abusing a spiritual teaching. You are using a spiritual teaching as a weapon against others. It is not as severe as taking a physical weapon and using it against others, but it is by no means innocent either.

The effect of it is that it reinforces your separate self and that is why, as Jesus explained, you cannot see that here is an aspect of the teaching that reveals a specific problem in psychology and it applies to you. You are so focused on changing something outside of yourself that you think all this applies to these other people: "I see that that person and that person have the exact problem that Saint Germain was talking about and if I get the chance, I am certainly going to tell them!" You forget to look in the mirror and see that: "Oops, I have that problem, I have that kind of a self and if I want to be free and make progress, then I need to let go of that self. I need to let it die."

My beloved, we have seen in ascended master organizations how there was a group of people that came in at an early stage. They applied the teachings, they served the organization, and they grew from it. They grew very quickly to a certain level. Now, they suddenly became concerned about maintaining their position in the organization and they stopped growing. We have seen in organizations how new students came in, they took the teachings, they applied them to themselves and they actually went beyond the level of consciousness of the previous group. This created a special resentment where the old guard, so to speak, felt that the new students had gone beyond them, but they resented this fact. Instead of making the shift to saying: "Well, perhaps I should look in the mirror too," they wanted to in some ways hold back and restrict the new students. This is a pattern we do not want to repeat.

We also do not want new students to use this teaching to say: "Oh, this is exactly what has happened to our leaders and that's why we need to criticize them and make them change!" You see again, the human consciousness can take anything we say and use it to justify itself. But my beloved, you cannot have your cake and eat it too. You cannot point the finger at someone else and at the same time point the finger at yourself and look in the mirror. It does not matter how wrong another person is. It does not matter how right you are in seeing what they are doing wrong—you will never grow.

I am pointing my finger at YOU, my beloved, for I am an ascended master. *You* will never grow, you will never grow by pointing the finger at someone else! You will never grow by attempting to change someone else. You will only grow by looking at yourself and changing yourself.

That, my beloved, was what I wanted to give you. I hope you will accept it as a gift of love from my heart. Truly, getting to that neutral state of mind where you are not trying to change others, you are not taking them personally, taking yourself too seriously, that is the ultimate state of mercy that you can show to other people.

22 | INVOKING CHANGE IN KOREAN BUSINESSES

In the name of the I AM THAT I AM, Jesus Christ, I use the authority that I have as a being in embodiment on earth to call upon Kuan Yin to reinforce my calls and use my chakras to project the statements in this invocation into the collective consciousness and awaken people to the need for Korean society and business to move into a Golden Age mindset. Awaken people to the reality that we are spiritual beings and that we can co-create a new future by working with the ascended masters. I especially call for …

[Make your own calls here.]

Part 1

1. Kuan Yin, shatter the energetic matrix that prevents people from seeing that the creation of large business conglomerates in Korea after the war generated a special situation.

> O Kuan Yin, what sacred name,
> fill me now with Mercy's Flame.
> In giving mercy I am free,
> forgiving all is magic key.

In Kuan Yin's sweet melody,
I am set free my Self to be.
In Kuan Yin's vitality,
I claim my immortality.

2. Kuan Yin, shatter the energetic matrix that prevents people from seeing that there was a certain element of force involved with these business conglomerates.

O Kuan Yin, I now let go,
of all attachments here below.
All pent-up feelings I release,
free from emotional disease.

In Kuan Yin's sweet melody,
I am set free my Self to be.
In Kuan Yin's vitality,
I claim my immortality.

3. Kuan Yin, shatter the energetic matrix that prevents people from seeing that the business conglomerates started competing amongst each other, generating a power game for establishing the supremacy of one or a couple of these conglomerates.

O Kuan Yin, why must I feel,
that life falls short of my ideal?
All expectations I give up,
my mind is now an empty cup.

In Kuan Yin's sweet melody,
I am set free my Self to be.
In Kuan Yin's vitality,
I claim my immortality.

4. I call forth the judgment of Christ upon the collective beasts and collective demons created through this process.

O Kuan Yin, transcend the past,
as all resentment gone at last.

From future nothing I expect,
eternal now I won't reject.

In Kuan Yin's sweet melody,
I am set free my Self to be.
In Kuan Yin's vitality,
I claim my immortality.

5. I call forth the judgment of Christ upon the beasts in the emotional realm, in the mental, and even in the lower identity realm that have been created by each of the business conglomerates.

O Kuan Yin, uplifting me,
beyond Samsara's raging sea.
All safe inside your Prajna boat,
the farther shore no more remote.

In Kuan Yin's sweet melody,
I am set free my Self to be.
In Kuan Yin's vitality,
I claim my immortality.

6. Kuan Yin, shatter the energetic matrix that prevents people from seeing that these beasts are not conscious beings, they are programmed beings that will mindlessly carry out their programming, and the programming is to expand this particular business conglomerate and to preserve it at any cost.

O Kuan Yin, your alchemy,
with miracles you set me free.
As I forgive, I am forgiven,
by guilt I am no longer driven.

In Kuan Yin's sweet melody,
I am set free my Self to be.
In Kuan Yin's vitality,
I claim my immortality.

7. Kuan Yin, shatter the energetic matrix that prevents people from seeing that the people behind these business conglomerates were enveloped in the consciousness that the end can justify the means, and they still are for the most part.

O Kuan Yin, all worries gone,
with nothing done, no thing undone.
Through separate self I will not do,
and thus I rest, all one with you.

In Kuan Yin's sweet melody,
I am set free my Self to be.
In Kuan Yin's vitality,
I claim my immortality.

8. Kuan Yin, shatter the energetic matrix that prevents people from seeing that there was an attitude that anything goes. We must do whatever we can do to rebuild the country regardless of the human cost, regardless of any considerations for the individual.

O Kuan Yin, your sanity,
now sets me free from vanity.
For truly, what is that to me;
I just let go and follow thee.

In Kuan Yin's sweet melody,
I am set free my Self to be.
In Kuan Yin's vitality,
I claim my immortality.

9. Kuan Yin, shatter the energetic matrix that prevents people from seeing that this shifted into the belief that we must do anything we can do to grow the corporation, to preserve the corporation and destroy the competition.

O Kuan Yin, so sweet the sound,
that emanates from holy ground.
As I let go of ego's chore,
I find myself on farther shore.

In Kuan Yin's sweet melody,
I am set free my Self to be.
In Kuan Yin's vitality,
I claim my immortality.

Part 2

1. Kuan Yin, shatter the energetic matrix that prevents people from seeing that this has created a situation where the business conglomerates have used their privileged position to influence the collective consciousness of Korea to the point where most people think that these business conglomerates are necessary, beneficial, and that Korea and the Korean economy could not survive without them.

O Kuan Yin, what sacred name,
fill me now with Mercy's Flame.
In giving mercy I am free,
forgiving all is magic key.

In Kuan Yin's sweet melody,
I am set free my Self to be.
In Kuan Yin's vitality,
I claim my immortality.

2. Kuan Yin, shatter the energetic matrix that prevents people from seeing that the conglomerates have created a mindset that this is the only way to do business in Korea. This is the only way for the economy to survive and thrive.

O Kuan Yin, I now let go,
of all attachments here below.
All pent-up feelings I release,
free from emotional disease.

In Kuan Yin's sweet melody,
I am set free my Self to be.

In Kuan Yin's vitality,
I claim my immortality.

3. Kuan Yin, shatter the energetic matrix that prevents people from seeing that most people are not looking for alternatives because they think this is the Korean model, and it has worked so far, so why should it not it work in the future? There is a certain loyalty that has been created in the Korean population towards these business conglomerates.

O Kuan Yin, why must I feel,
that life falls short of my ideal?
All expectations I give up,
my mind is now an empty cup.

In Kuan Yin's sweet melody,
I am set free my Self to be.
In Kuan Yin's vitality,
I claim my immortality.

4. Kuan Yin, shatter the energetic matrix that prevents people from seeing that for Korea to truly thrive and for the Korean economy to grow in the future, we need to open up for different business models.

O Kuan Yin, transcend the past,
as all resentment gone at last.
From future nothing I expect,
eternal now I won't reject.

In Kuan Yin's sweet melody,
I am set free my Self to be.
In Kuan Yin's vitality,
I claim my immortality.

5. Kuan Yin, shatter the energetic matrix that prevents people from seeing that the government must make it easier for other businesses to be established, and to even come up and compete with the large conglomerates. Otherwise, the Korean economy will not remain vital in the future and it will not be able to deal with the burden of a reunification of Korea.

O Kuan Yin, uplifting me,
beyond Samsara's raging sea.
All safe inside your Prajna boat,
the farther shore no more remote.

In Kuan Yin's sweet melody,
I am set free my Self to be.
In Kuan Yin's vitality,
I claim my immortality.

6. Kuan Yin, shatter the energetic matrix so that people will be set free from the hypnotic effect of these huge demons or beasts that have been created and that demand loyalty towards and the special treatment of these conglomerates.

O Kuan Yin, your alchemy,
with miracles you set me free.
As I forgive, I am forgiven,
by guilt I am no longer driven.

In Kuan Yin's sweet melody,
I am set free my Self to be.
In Kuan Yin's vitality,
I claim my immortality.

7. Kuan Yin, shatter the energetic matrix that prevents people from seeing that there is a loyalty towards some of these conglomerates. There is a certain sense in the population that we should buy Korean made products.

O Kuan Yin, all worries gone,
with nothing done, no thing undone.
Through separate self I will not do,
and thus I rest, all one with you.

In Kuan Yin's sweet melody,
I am set free my Self to be.
In Kuan Yin's vitality,
I claim my immortality.

8. Kuan Yin, shatter the energetic matrix that prevents people from seeing that the loyalty towards these corporations and the special treatment by the government cannot ensure their survival.

O Kuan Yin, your sanity,
now sets me free from vanity.
For truly, what is that to me;
I just let go and follow thee.

In Kuan Yin's sweet melody,
I am set free my Self to be.
In Kuan Yin's vitality,
I claim my immortality.

9. Kuan Yin, shatter the energetic matrix that prevents people from seeing that the future of Korean corporations depends on people in other countries buying their products.

O Kuan Yin, so sweet the sound,
that emanates from holy ground.
As I let go of ego's chore,
I find myself on farther shore.

In Kuan Yin's sweet melody,
I am set free my Self to be.
In Kuan Yin's vitality,
I claim my immortality.

Part 3

1. Kuan Yin, shatter the energetic matrix that prevents people from seeing that it does not take very much for there to be a wave in the collective consciousness internationally where people suddenly become aware, for example, that workers are not paid fairly or not treated well, and they stop buying Korean products.

O Kuan Yin, what sacred name,
fill me now with Mercy's Flame.
In giving mercy I am free,
forgiving all is magic key.

**In Kuan Yin's sweet melody,
I am set free my Self to be.
In Kuan Yin's vitality,
I claim my immortality.**

2. Kuan Yin, shatter the energetic matrix so there will be a shift in the Korean consciousness towards these business conglomerates so that people will adopt a more international awareness and therefore realize that the businesses in Korea need to look at what is happening in the world at large, what is happening in the attitude and awareness of consumers in the world.

O Kuan Yin, I now let go,
of all attachments here below.
All pent-up feelings I release,
free from emotional disease.

**In Kuan Yin's sweet melody,
I am set free my Self to be.
In Kuan Yin's vitality,
I claim my immortality.**

3. Kuan Yin, shatter the energetic matrix that prevents people from seeing that Korean corporations need to look at how Western corporations are treating their employees, how well they are paying them, how much of the earnings of a corporation is going to the shareholders and how big of a percentage is going to the employees.

O Kuan Yin, why must I feel,
that life falls short of my ideal?
All expectations I give up,
my mind is now an empty cup.

**In Kuan Yin's sweet melody,
I am set free my Self to be.
In Kuan Yin's vitality,
I claim my immortality.**

4. Kuan Yin, shatter the energetic matrix that prevents people from seeing that Korean corporations need to follow the trends in the international business climate instead of staying in the hypnotic bubble created by these large beasts.

O Kuan Yin, transcend the past,
as all resentment gone at last.
From future nothing I expect,
eternal now I won't reject.

**In Kuan Yin's sweet melody,
I am set free my Self to be.
In Kuan Yin's vitality,
I claim my immortality.**

5. Kuan Yin, shatter the energetic matrix and set the Korean business climate free from these beasts. Set the large corporations free so they can grow and adapt, even start adopting a Golden Age business model. For unless they begin to make the transition into a Golden Age model, how can they survive in the Golden Age?

O Kuan Yin, uplifting me,
beyond Samsara's raging sea.
All safe inside your Prajna boat,
the farther shore no more remote.

**In Kuan Yin's sweet melody,
I am set free my Self to be.
In Kuan Yin's vitality,
I claim my immortality.**

6. Kuan Yin, shatter the energetic matrix that prevents people from making Korea an example of a nation that transitions into the Golden Age, not just in the area of business but also in other areas.

O Kuan Yin, your alchemy,
with miracles you set me free.
As I forgive, I am forgiven,
by guilt I am no longer driven.

In Kuan Yin's sweet melody,
I am set free my Self to be.
In Kuan Yin's vitality,
I claim my immortality.

7. Kuan Yin, shatter the energetic matrix that prevents the exposure of anything that is hidden, both in the government and in these large business conglomerates.

O Kuan Yin, all worries gone,
with nothing done, no thing undone.
Through separate self I will not do,
and thus I rest, all one with you.

In Kuan Yin's sweet melody,
I am set free my Self to be.
In Kuan Yin's vitality,
I claim my immortality.

8. Kuan Yin, shatter the energetic matrix that prevents people from seeing that since the war there has been created the sense that there is an upper class, a special class of Korean people who are the rich people, the leaders of these big business conglomerates.

O Kuan Yin, your sanity,
now sets me free from vanity.
For truly, what is that to me;
I just let go and follow thee.

In Kuan Yin's sweet melody,
I am set free my Self to be.
In Kuan Yin's vitality,
I claim my immortality.

9. Kuan Yin, shatter the energetic matrix that prevents people from seeing that the population has a sense that these very rich and powerful people are in a special class, that they are almost perfect or that they are beyond criticism.

> O Kuan Yin, so sweet the sound,
> that emanates from holy ground.
> As I let go of ego's chore,
> I find myself on farther shore.

> **In Kuan Yin's sweet melody,**
> **I am set free my Self to be.**
> **In Kuan Yin's vitality,**
> **I claim my immortality.**

Part 4

1. Kuan Yin, shatter the energetic matrix that prevents the exposure of any inappropriate actions, any illegal actions, any corruption, any special dealings on the part of the elite.

> O Kuan Yin, what sacred name,
> fill me now with Mercy's Flame.
> In giving mercy I am free,
> forgiving all is magic key.

> **In Kuan Yin's sweet melody,**
> **I am set free my Self to be.**
> **In Kuan Yin's vitality,**
> **I claim my immortality.**

2. Kuan Yin, shatter the energetic matrix that prevents people from seeing that in order for Korea to transition into this new business model, the idolatry of these seemingly all-powerful business leaders must be broken down.

O Kuan Yin, I now let go,
of all attachments here below.
All pent-up feelings I release,
free from emotional disease.

In Kuan Yin's sweet melody,
I am set free my Self to be.
In Kuan Yin's vitality,
I claim my immortality.

3. Kuan Yin, shatter the energetic matrix that prevents the exposure of personal failings or wrongdoings on the part of some of these leaders so that the Korean people can realize that they are still human beings and they are as fallible as other human beings.

O Kuan Yin, why must I feel,
that life falls short of my ideal?
All expectations I give up,
my mind is now an empty cup.

In Kuan Yin's sweet melody,
I am set free my Self to be.
In Kuan Yin's vitality,
I claim my immortality.

4. Kuan Yin, shatter the energetic matrix that prevents people from seeing that the elite do not deserve special treatment or privileges, and they do not deserve to be looked up to as if they were some kind of gods walking on earth.

O Kuan Yin, transcend the past,
as all resentment gone at last.
From future nothing I expect,
eternal now I won't reject.

In Kuan Yin's sweet melody,
I am set free my Self to be.
In Kuan Yin's vitality,
I claim my immortality.

5. Kuan Yin, shatter the energetic matrix that prevents people from overcoming the taboo, so they will feel free to talk about the elite and make the necessary changes.

O Kuan Yin, uplifting me,
beyond Samsara's raging sea.
All safe inside your Prajna boat,
the farther shore no more remote.

In Kuan Yin's sweet melody,
I am set free my Self to be.
In Kuan Yin's vitality,
I claim my immortality.

6. Kuan Yin, shatter the energetic matrix that prevents people from seeing that there are many taboos in Korean society and culture, and that Korea cannot transition into the Golden Age unless people become willing to talk about these things.

O Kuan Yin, your alchemy,
with miracles you set me free.
As I forgive, I am forgiven,
by guilt I am no longer driven.

In Kuan Yin's sweet melody,
I am set free my Self to be.
In Kuan Yin's vitality,
I claim my immortality.

7. Kuan Yin, shatter the energetic matrix that prevents people from overcoming the taboo of the relationship between men and women, so they can feel free to talk about a new role for women in Korean society.

O Kuan Yin, all worries gone,
with nothing done, no thing undone.
Through separate self I will not do,
and thus I rest, all one with you.

In Kuan Yin's sweet melody,
I am set free my Self to be.
In Kuan Yin's vitality,
I claim my immortality.

8. Kuan Yin, shatter the energetic matrix that prevents people from overcoming the taboo of the relationship between young people and the older generation, so they will feel free to talk about how young people can fulfill their potential to bring needed change.

O Kuan Yin, your sanity,
now sets me free from vanity.
For truly, what is that to me;
I just let go and follow thee.

In Kuan Yin's sweet melody,
I am set free my Self to be.
In Kuan Yin's vitality,
I claim my immortality.

9. Kuan Yin, shatter the energetic matrix that prevents people from overcoming the taboo of the hierarchical structure of Korean society, so they will feel free to talk about how to create a more egalitarian society that allows all people to express their potential.

O Kuan Yin, so sweet the sound,
that emanates from holy ground.
As I let go of ego's chore,
I find myself on farther shore.

In Kuan Yin's sweet melody,
I am set free my Self to be.
In Kuan Yin's vitality,
I claim my immortality.

Sealing

In the name of the I AM THAT I AM, I accept that Archangel Michael, Astrea and Shiva form an impenetrable shield around myself and all constructive people, sealing us from all fear-based energies in all four octaves. I accept that the Light of God is consuming and transforming all fear-based energies that make up the dark forces working against ending the era of dictatorships on earth!

23 | THE FINGER-POINTING DISCOURSE

I AM the Ascended Master Gautama Buddha. When you experience a discourse as the one you have experienced from Kuan Yin, you realize why there is absolute equality between male and female in the ascended realm. You realize why there should be absolute equality between men and women on earth. As Kuan Yin has provided the omega half of our combined discourse, I will give you the alpha. I would like to pick up on what she gave you, and dedicate this discourse as the "Finger-Pointing Discourse."

What is it that the fallen beings have used as their primary weapon for controlling humankind? It is pointing the finger. You have the sentence in the Book of Revelation from the New Testament that says that there were those who "accused our brethren before our God, day and night." And when the accuser of the brethren was cast down, there was rejoicing in heaven. This of course is inaccurate in the sense that it does not refer to heaven, but it does refer to that first sphere where beings first fell. Before they fell, they were indeed accusing everyone around them, pointing the finger at everyone else and at God. Because they had decided that it could not be them who had to change, their only option left was that everyone else had to change, and the universe had to change, and God had to change, and the weather had to change.

My beloved, what you realize here is that in a sense you could say that the essence of the fallen mindset is pointing the finger at someone else because one is unwilling to look at oneself. You see that we have talked about a structure, a machine, in the emotional, mental, and identity realms that is aimed at controlling humankind, deceiving humankind. This is the foundation for all dictatorships you have seen throughout history and that you see today. The very core of this structure is this very consciousness of pointing the finger outside oneself.

There is always a justification for hurting others

You may find this difficult to believe when you see how there are demons in the astral plane that are taking over people's minds and causing them to kill indiscriminately. You realize that even the worst psychopath or narcissist who goes into a shopping mall and starts firing a gun still has to have some rudimentary level of reasoning and justification for doing it. Where does that justification come from? You may look at it, and many people do look at it, from a normal state of human consciousness, a common-sense perspective, you might say, and find it completely unreasonable, illogical, and absolutely crazy. But there is some rudimentary reasoning, some level of justification. It all boils down to this: There is something wrong somewhere. Something has gone wrong in this person's life, or other people have done something wrong. It is never the person himself or herself, who is at fault.

Again, the principle of pointing the finger outside oneself can justify absolutely any human behavior. Ponder that sentence for a moment. *Pointing the finger outside oneself can justify absolutely any human behavior.* Then, look at history and see how horrendous atrocities have been committed by people—but they could always justify it. The way they justified it was to point that something had gone wrong outside themselves, and that is why they had to do what they did.

You see, my beloved, how pointing the finger can so easily result in a bending of the finger around the trigger that fires at someone else and kills them. The pointing finger and the trigger finger are just a short movement apart from each other. The fallen beings are experts at first getting someone to point the finger and then getting them to put the finger on the trigger and pull, over and over and over and over and over and over—need I go on? They have repeated this pattern, and people fall for it again, and again and again and again—need I repeat myself?

Why there is suffering in the world

What can break the spiral? What can break it? The Buddha nature can break it, for even those who have gone completely insane and are pointing the finger and pulling the trigger have the Buddha nature within them. What can cause them to connect to that Buddha nature and start pointing the finger at themselves instead of pointing it somewhere else? Well, that is why there is suffering in the world.

Once people have gone into duality and started pointing the finger outside themselves, they will suffer. Why will they suffer, my beloved? Because when you think that the cause of the problem (that the fault, that the error) is outside yourself, you have instantly made yourself powerless to change yourself. Once you go into creating these separate selves that see themselves as separate from the Buddha nature, you *will* suffer. The separate self can only suffer. Even if the separate self attains absolute power on earth and feels it can do anything it wants, it still suffers because there is still tension. Even if you have all power on earth, there could still be more power to be had. There could still be a threat that could cause you to lose your power. You might be momentarily elated, but you can never really be free of suffering.

Once you go into suffering, you lose that contact with the Buddha nature. You lose your intuitive faculties very quickly because how can you have discernment when you are pointing the finger at somebody else? Therefore, what can awaken you? We of the ascended masters cannot reach you. A spiritual teaching cannot reach you. As my beloved brother Jesus has just explained, when you go into this state of mind, you lose your intuition. You lose your ability to reason and to make neutral observations. You are always looking through that separate self that is defining the problem as being out there, and therefore defining that it is someone else that has to change in order for you to be at peace.

What did I teach 2,500 years ago? What did Jesus teach 2,000 years ago? That the key to avoid suffering is to go into yourself and change the condition in there that causes your suffering. What happens when you point the finger? You think the cause of your suffering is outside yourself, in these external conditions or these other people. You cannot see that your experience of suffering does not reside out there, on top of a mountain or among those other people that you think are your enemies. Your suffering is an *internal* experience, and an internal experience can only have an internal cause. This internal cause may be triggered by an external circumstance, but the cause is not the external circumstance. The cause is internal.

You see that once you start pointing the finger, you are looking in the wrong direction. You think that in order to escape suffering, you have to change something out there. In the beginning, you might think you have to just change one person. Perhaps you even can come to the extreme where you think that if you kill one person, your suffering will end. The fallen beings have gone through a very long process of attempting to alleviate their suffering by changing something outside themselves. They have transcended – long ago – the personal level. Now, they think that the only way to alleviate their suffering is to change everything around them in their environment. They think that in order to change everything around them, they need to have power over everything around them, they need to be able to control everything around them. The fallen beings are always blindly driven to attempt to gain control, to gain power, and thereby force their external circumstances to change.

The ultimate dictator on earth

What happens whenever a fallen being rises to a position, such as being a dictator, like Hitler, Stalin, or Mao? Well, he experiences that his suffering does not go away. This may cause insanity in that lifetime. What happens after that lifetime is that often that fallen being cannot even come back into embodiment. It may for a while go into the astral plane and act out its anger there. Some fallen beings have risen above that raw anger of the astral plane, and they have risen to the mental realm or lower identity realm. From there, they are also seeking to control, thinking that: "If I just get one step up in my level of control, then my suffering will go away." Or if they get the ultimate control, as they are able to see it in their environment, then their suffering will go away. Or if they are able to even gain control over God and change God and God's giving of free will, then their suffering will go away.

What you see is that behind this entire machinery in the emotional, mental and identity realms (that is aimed at controlling humankind) there is this very limited number of fallen beings in those three realms who are working towards this end of controlling humankind, and controlling every aspect of life on earth.

We have not emphasized this teaching before, but in the *My Lives* book [*My Lives with Lucifer, Satan, Hitler and Jesus*] we do give the concept that at the top of this structure is one particular fallen being, whom the book calls the Dark Master. When you follow the structure of fallen beings, you see that there is indeed this one being at the top of this structure. What is the ultimate dictator on earth? Well, it is this Dark Master. He is in control of the other fallen beings in the identity realm, those in the mental, and those in the astral, and of course those in the physical. He is ultimately in control.

Now, you may think: Why has this person, this being, risen to this state of being in ultimate control of all the fallen beings associated with earth? Was he particularly powerful? Did he have specific abilities? Was he particularly wise or intelligent? Well, you might say that he was, but how is he then controlling the other fallen beings?

You do realize, I assume, that there is no true cooperation among fallen beings. We of the ascended masters on a regular basis have council meetings where a group of us get together. In perfect harmony, and with equality among us, respecting our positions in hierarchy, we can cooperate freely. Fallen beings, even though they may have council meetings, cannot create the atmosphere that we have. They are not actually cooperating. They may have a common goal, but they are not truly cooperating. There always has to be one who is on top and who is controlling the others. How does he control them? By getting them to point the finger at each other. How does he do that? By him pointing the finger at all the rest.

Authority in the fallen community

You may say that, as Kuan Yin said, I can point the finger at you because I am an ascended master. That means I have no judgment of you. Therefore, I am not pointing the finger at you to project that the problem is outside of myself. I am pointing the finger at you to help you look at yourself and thereby free yourself. You might even go a step further and ask: Why can an ascended master point the finger at you without at the same time refusing to look at himself? First of all, you have already looked at yourself in order to become an ascended master, but nevertheless as an ascended master I do not see all of you as being separate from myself. I see an expanded self that encompasses all human beings on earth. When I am pointing the finger at you, I am at the same time pointing the finger at myself, and myself, and myself, and myself, and myself. The fallen beings do not do this. They are pointing the finger at others in order to avoid looking at themselves. The Dark Master who is controlling the other fallen beings is pointing the finger at all of them. Now, why are they not responding in kind and pointing their fingers at him? Because he has gone into such a state of denial that he will never, ever accept anyone pointing the finger at him. What is his claim to authority in the "fallen community?" It is that his denial is greater than the denial of the other fallen beings.

From an earthly perspective you would say it is absolute, in the sense that he believes that absolutely nothing that could come from earth is something he needs to look at. There is nothing on earth that could ever point the finger at him and make him look at himself because every being on earth is lower than him, even every fallen being is lower than him. You can imagine how much lower he considers human beings to be. That is why you could not possibly persuade such a being to look at itself. You see that at the very top of the pyramid of the fallen beings associated with earth is this state of absolute denial, absolute refusal to look at oneself.

Why dictators are above criticism

Now, follow this down, and look at the dictators you have seen on earth. The "greater" the dictator, the more powerful the dictator, do you not see that behind their power is denial? The more powerful they seem, the more denial they have of themselves. As we have said, there have been many people throughout the ages who have been in a dictatorial position but nevertheless have not been in total denial. There is a difference between denial and delusion.

Delusion means that you are believing in something that is false, but if you were somehow made to see that it was false, you would change. Denial means that nothing could make you see that what you believe is wrong because you would refuse to look at it. You would deny its existence, its reality, its validity. There are dictators who have been in a state of delusion but not that absolute denial. That is why they, in rare cases, can actually change.

We have said that the leader of Kazakhstan has at least made some changes. He was not in a state of denial, although he is still in a state of delusion, as most people in the country can see by his attempts to glorify himself. Likewise, Kim Jong Un is not in a state of complete denial. He is in a state of very strong delusion, but there is a potential that it could change. The "great" Chairman Mao was in a state of delusion, but his denial was also very, very strong. The same with Hitler and Stalin and Lenin. You see that the biggest, the most severe, atrocities committed by these dictators throughout history have been committed because of this state of denial, pointing the finger outside oneself.

Why people are overpowered by a dictator

Now, consider that no dictator can rule a nation alone. There needs to be people who are willing to do his bidding, people who follow him and who accept that he has something that they do not have, that he is either right or that he is more powerful than they are. What causes people to believe a dictator is right, as there were people who thought Chairman Mao and Marxism were right? Or they thought that Lenin was right. Or they thought that Hitler's ideology was right. It is because the dictator is in a very strong state of delusion and has managed to export that delusion to others so they believe that the delusionary state of the dictator is based on reality. It is not delusion, it is reality.

What makes people believe that the dictator has some ultimate power? Well, that is the dictator's denial. He is acting as if he is perfect or beyond criticism or absolutely right because that is what he believes, and that is what he projects out. Those who are weak in themselves, and do not dare to think that they could possibly know the truth, can be overpowered by this power, this absolute denial. They come to believe that it is not denial. They think it is some mysterious power that this dictator has.

There were people who met Mao or Hitler and were overpowered by what they felt emanating from these people, and it was because the denial was so absolute that they could sense it. It was such a contrast to their own inner insecurity that they submitted themselves to this "great powerful man." You see this with many of the so-called powerful people throughout the ages. It was simply the intensity of their denial that made it possible for them to overpower other people so they submitted themselves without any critical evaluation.

Again, how is this achieved? How do the dictators on earth even rule? Well, they do not always rule by themselves, or rather they do not rule alone. They are open doors for the fallen beings in the identity, mental, and emotional realms. Again, this is all based on everybody pointing the finger at everybody else unless they are submitting themselves to that hierarchy, the false hierarchy that the fallen beings have created.

We could say, from that perspective, that the Dark Master is pointing the finger at everybody else. There is a group of beings beneath him who are never pointing their finger at him, but they are pointing the finger at each other and everyone below them. You can see this repeated in the human dictators. Nobody dared to point the finger at Hitler. Even when it became clear to some of his generals that the war was irrevocably lost, nobody dared to say this because the Führer had declared that the war would be won. Contradicting the Führer would be criticizing the Führer and pointing the finger at the Führer. Everyone knew that if you pointed the finger at the Führer, well, he would take the whole hand and the rest of you too so nobody dared to make Hitler aware of what was going on.

There was a group of people who were below him, at the step right below him in the Nazi hierarchy, and they were of course pointing the finger at everybody below them. But they were also pointing a finger at each other, competing amongst each other about who would be the most powerful and who would be favored by the great man at the top. If you actually examined this entire hierarchy created by the Nazi forces, you would see that everybody was pointing the finger at everybody because everybody had one overriding fear.

The fear of not fitting in

That is, that they would not fit into this matrix defined by the Nazis as the people who were right, the master race. You see my beloved, in a sense, you might say that the Nazis helped people feel superior because they were part of the master race. The price people paid was that the ultimate fear was that you could be excluded from the master race by being proven wrong in some way. Once you accepted that you were part of the master race, there was constantly a finger pointing at you, looking for any weakness, any wavering in your beliefs, any doubts, any unwillingness to carry out orders and to mindlessly do what those above you told you to do. If that pointing finger (that was constantly moving around looking for fault) happened to stop, pointing at you, then the worst thing that could possibly happen to you, would happen. You would be excluded from the master race. You see that everybody was constantly in this fear of being found wrong. What did it cause? It caused that the population in general needed a scapegoat. They needed someone outside themselves (that was clearly defined as being outside themselves) that they could point the finger at and say: "Well, we may not be completely perfect according to Nazi ideology, but at least we are Germans and not Jews." Again, the pointing finger needs to point at somebody.

Now, look at the communist hierarchy created during Lenin. Lenin was the one that was in absolute denial, he thought he was completely right. He thought that every word that he ever spoke, or ever wrote, was perfect. Do you know, my beloved, that during Soviet times, after the death of Lenin, they had entire teams of people who were reading through the writings of Lenin, trying to weed out contradictions, trying to weed out instances where Lenin contradicted something that he had said earlier. Because it could not be allowed that there were any contradictions that might cast doubt upon the absolute rightness of Lenin. Yet, if you look at the people below him, there was again this criticism, the constant pointing the finger, looking for fault.

What happened when Stalin took over? Well, he did not have that claim to superiority because he was not in a total state of denial. He realized that he was not as smart as Lenin, and by the way he was not as smart as most of the people around him but he was the most ruthless. That is why he created a climate again where everybody was constantly looking at everybody else, trying to find fault and avoid that they were found fault with.

You see in communist societies where they did not dare to talk freely with anyone, except perhaps a few close family members, because they never knew when anybody would report them to the authorities. Then again, they would be excluded from the Club, those who were right, those who were true believing communists, true Soviet citizens. Of course, it was unpleasant to be sent to the Gulag, but there were many people that had bought into this fear of being excluded from the group. You saw the same in Mao's China, you have seen the same in others of these dictatorships.

The hierarchy of the Catholic church

Now, look at what we have called one of the worst dictatorships ever to emerge on earth, the Catholic church. At the top of the structure was the Pope and it was again considered that he was infallible. His word, at least when he spoke under the power of God, was infallible. Nobody in the

Catholic church dared to point the finger at the Pope and hardly anyone today dares to do so. You saw in the Middle Ages how there was this one person at the top, nobody could point the finger at him. Below him was a level of the higher leaders of the church, the Cardinals and others. They were all pointing the finger at each other in a power play to assume the top position under the Pope. They were also pointing the finger at everyone below them. This went all the way to the Catholic priest in his local parish who was serving as the one who was supposedly pointing the finger of God at everybody in the community. It went to the point where most people would again be pointing the finger at each other, looking for any signs that the neighbors are not good Catholics, they did not go to Mass last Sunday, or they are not devout enough, or they ate this, or they did that.

You see how, during the Middle Ages, especially at the heyday (so to speak) of the Catholic dictatorship, everybody was pointing the finger at everybody else. The fear they had was even greater than the fear of those in the Soviet Union. Sure, it is unpleasant to be sent to the Gulag, it is unpleasant to be killed. But the fear of being killed or the fear of being sent to Siberia is nothing compared to the fear that was generated by the Catholic church. For when you fear eternal torment in hell, what fear could be greater? You see that the very dictatorship that claimed to represent Christ on earth, that claimed to be a force for good, had actually generated the greatest fear seen in recorded history. Who can see the logic in that?

Well, nobody can, but of course nobody who is inside the hypnotic trance generated by the Catholic church could even see the problem, the discrepancy, the contradiction. For they had suspended their logical, analytical, observatory abilities. They were not looking at the church and saying: "Does this make sense? Should we really be treating each other this way? Is this the way Jesus wanted us to treat each other? If so, why did he tell us not to judge? Why he did he tell us to love your neighbor as yourself? Are we loving our neighbor by constantly looking for fault in our neighbor?" They would actually say: "Oh, yes, we are. Because by looking for fault in our neighbor, we are preventing them from going to hell." Therefore, they could not see that they were already in hell. The fiery hell they imagined does not even exist. Therefore, there is no hell worse than what they had here on earth. Well, you might argue that some of the levels of the astral plane are worse, but still you get my point. They thought they were on the road to heaven but in reality they were in hell.

Nobody, either, could use their intuitive faculties to tune in to the living Ascended Master Jesus Christ. Jesus ascended 2,000 years ago so for the entire time of the Catholic church during the Middle Ages, Jesus was there as an ascended master, willing to work with anyone who was able to tune in to him. He was willing to give them the vibration that was the ultimate frame of reference that would allow anyone to look at the Catholic church and say: "But this is not in alignment with Christ. This is not in alignment with the vibration of Christ, it is not in alignment with the words of Christ, with the actions of Christ. This is simply madness."

People are ready to see through finger-pointing

Again, a pressure has been built over a long time, by many, many, many measures taken by the ascended masters. This goes back centuries. We have very carefully, one small step at a time, worked with human beings who were open and therefore created these impulses, these initiatives, that would release certain ideas that have shifted the collective consciousness upwards. This has built that tension. There is a tension built to the point where at least the more aware people are ready to come to see this mechanism, of how pointing the finger is such a destructive force in human life. It is a destructive force in the psychology of the individual. It is a destructive force in families, in any kind of group, in entire nations and in humanity as a whole.

As Kuan Yin attempted to help you see, we hope that we can create communities of ascended master students where you will not point the finger at each other, for you will be willing to look at yourselves. As we have said, in previous dispensations they had the exact same mechanism. You think you are special because you are inside, you are good ascended master students. The price you pay for this sense of superiority, the sense of being special, as Saint Germain exposed to you, is that you have a constant fear of being excluded from the inner circle by there being some fault in you. You saw ascended master students going around pointing the finger at each other, always being critical and judgmental of each other.

I can assure you that there were certain fallen beings who thought this was pretty near their ultimate triumph in their work with earth. They could get even ascended master students to go into this finger-pointing game. They thought: "If we can get even the students who recognize ascended masters to do this, then we can counteract anything the ascended masters can come up with." They are wrong of course because we have come up with many other things that they have not been able to counteract. But it is certainly something to ponder that even ascended master students can fall into this pattern of finger-pointing.

Communities that do not point the finger

We have given you the tools, we have given you the teachings, to avoid this. It is really a matter of applying the teachings but it is also a matter of just pausing, just stopping. As Jesus said, being willing to consider: "Does this apply to me? Do I have an element in myself of pointing the finger at others. If I do, then I know now that it is not me who is pointing the finger." So you do not need to do this double action that the fallen beings always try to get you into where when you realize: "I have pointed the finger at others, now I need to start pointing the finger at myself. And as judgmental as I have been at others, now I need to be equally judgmental towards myself for having pointed the finger at others."

My beloved, just skip that whole scenario and realize what we have told you. It is not *you* pointing the finger, it is a separate self. Do not point the finger at the separate self. Just look at it. See the belief behind it. What is the belief behind it? Well, it is this desire to be special by somehow defining some criteria on earth that creates a division between those who are inside and those who are outside. Those who are inside are special and those who are outside are not special. Once you accept this kind of view of life, once you go into it, yes, the benefit you get is that you feel special, the price you pay is that you always have the fear of falling out of being special.

Staying in a group by excluding someone else

You may go into this state where at the conscious level, you are pointing the finger at everybody else. But at the unconscious level (subconscious level), you are actually constantly pointing the finger at yourself. The fallen beings have managed to get you to point the finger at yourself. Why are you not seeing this at the conscious level? Because the fallen beings have one more trick up their sleeve. They know that once people go into this state of pointing the finger, the way to control them is to get people to point the finger at themselves. You are afraid of being found wanting. You are afraid that you do not fit the mold, the standard for being inside the group and this is unbearable. This is an unbearable state of mind to be in. The fallen beings know that they need to offer people a way out of this unbearable state, or they will not be able to stand it and they will not be able to keep them inside the group once they are in it. There are two ways of giving people relief from this. The one way is to divert attention, to divert the energies by getting you to point the finger at somebody else. They have done this by creating this very subtle mindset that you will scarcely ever see anyone on earth who has picked up on or who has written about. It is a very subtle idea that if you see a fault in yourself, then if you can find a worse fault in someone else, then you can still stay inside the group because the other person will be the one who is excluded. In other words, even though you realize you are not perfect, if you can find someone who is more imperfect than you, then *they* can be excluded. If you have been a tool for excluding someone else, you can still stay in the group.

Take the extreme example of this. A German soldier who has been assigned to work at the Auschwitz concentration camp and his job is to get people who are coming out of the cattle carts to go into the gas chamber. He knows what is going to happen to these people once they release the gas. He has heard their screams even over the noise created to mask them. He knows what is happening. Why does he not object to this? Because he wants to stay inside the group. In order to save his own position in the group, he is willing to exclude someone else and kill them. This is what you see time and time again where people, in order to preserve their own position in a group, are willing to exclude someone else. This then gives you the illusion that you can stay in the group, even though you are not perfect.

Do you see the mechanism behind this? The fallen beings, as we have said before, have created a standard of perfection. They have created many. They create a certain standard of perfection. This standard defines that here is a group, and those who live up to this standard can be in the group. This does not work if there were people who could actually see: "But I am perfect and therefore, I deserve to be part of the group." It works only when you define an impossible standard so that the people who are in the group realize they do not fully live up to the standard. Because it is only then that they have the fear that they could be excluded and that is why they go into the mindset of diverting attention from their own imperfections by pointing out the imperfections of others and getting them excluded from the group.

Denying your own imperfections

Now, there is of course one more way that the fallen beings can relieve this unbearable state of being in these very disharmonious critical environments, and it is through denial. They have always managed to get some people to go into denial where they can deny their own imperfections. There were some of those below Hitler who were almost convinced that they fit the model of the true Aryan—*almost* convinced because they still realized that it was possible that the Führer could one day point his finger at them, and they would be out just like that.

There are people throughout the ages who have gone into such a state of denial that they have been absolutely sure, or at least almost sure, that they were beyond blame—that they were beyond reproach. Those are the ones you see in all of these privileged groups you see around the world, whether it is the leaders of the business conglomerates in Korea today, whether it is the top communist officials under Mao, or the noble class of the European kingdoms, or the Cardinals of the Catholic church. You still see Cardinals of the Catholic church who are in this state of mind today and therefore believe that their assessment of the church is correct. They just need to continue to resist change and refuse to adapt to society, for that is the only way they think that the church will survive. It is of course the only sure way that the church will *not* survive, but they cannot see it.

The highest potential for the conference

My beloved, we have given you many, many tools during this conference, much information that can help you make a decisive difference in starting the process that will end the era of dictatorships on earth. For this, we are grateful. We are grateful for your willingness to come together. The fact that so many of you have come together in one place, that you have been willing to focus your attention and by focusing your attention, you have become of one accord in one place, at least for brief periods of time. There are times during these dictations where almost all of you in this room, and those on the broadcast, have been of one accord. This has set a very powerful forcefield that we have been able to use as broadcasting stations.

We have also been able to release more teachings than we had originally planned to do as the lowest potential for this conference. Therefore, I am happy to tell you that we have reached the highest potential for this conference. We have therefore released what we wanted to release, at least in this portion, about the topic.

My beloved, with this I want to express the gratitude of all of us, not just those masters who have spoken, but all of us who are working with the earth for the victory of this conference. With this, I seal you in the love of all of us, the love that is the ultimate key to avoiding the finger-pointing game.

Love is the anti-dote to finger-pointing

What is it, my beloved, that is the real key to escaping this game? I have said you need to tune in to the vibration of an ascended master. Well, yes, but what is the vibration of an ascended master? It is ultimately love. It can be expressed through the seven rays or in other ways, but it is love—and love that is unconditional.

You see people who have been in this judgmental mind, this judgmental environment, where everybody is judging everybody else. Well, as you cannot point the finger at somebody else and point at yourself at the same time, you cannot judge somebody else and love them at the same time. You cannot judge yourself and love yourself at the same time. This means that when you are in this judgmental frame of mind, you cannot feel loved so you are trapped in judgment.

You think perhaps even (as the ultimate deception of the fallen beings) that it is only by judging yourself and judging others and living up to the standard of perfection that God will allow you into heaven. But it is the judgmental mindset that causes you to resist heaven. The only way to get to heaven is to let go of the judgmental mindset, which means letting go of the separate selves that are the source of judgment. How can you do this? You must see that there is something more. You must experience that there is something more. You must experience that there is something you love more than the judgmental self.

What can make you feel that there is something you love more than this judgmental self that you think is so right and so necessary? Well, it is the pure, unconditional love of the ascended masters. What is it that the judgmental mindset makes people think, and that is the fallen ones' ultimate deception? It makes people think that God is a judgmental God, that the Creator, that God, is an angry, judgmental God who will judge them harshly for any imperfection. They think that a standard defined on earth is what God will judge them by. How can you escape this illusion? By experiencing that God's love is without judgment, without conditions. When you experience this, you can realize, my beloved, that no matter how perfect you are according to an earthly standard, no matter how perfect you are according to your own judgment or the judgment of anyone else on earth, it will not get you to heaven. Judgment will only push you away from heaven. The more you judge, the more you push yourself away.

The key to going into heaven is *not* to live up to some condition defined on earth. The key to going to heaven is to transcend all conditions defined on earth, and the consciousness that has defined them. The key to transcending this consciousness is to experience the unconditional love of God so you can finally accept that the self you were created as, was from the very beginning worthy to return to God.

God did not cast you out of the Garden of Eden. You went out in order to have experiences in this world, but no matter what you have done in this world, no matter how much you have judged yourself or judged others, it has not made you unworthy to return. As Jesus said, only the man who descended from heaven can ascend back to heaven. It is not the "man," it is the self, the Conscious You. The Conscious You has no conditions in its pure awareness—non-judgmental awareness. When you return to that, you are free to go into heaven.

As long as you still have conditions and judgments, well, you yourself do not think you are worthy to enter heaven or ready to enter heaven. Therefore, you yourself are keeping yourself out. God never kept anyone out of heaven. People do that all by themselves, admittedly with the help of the fallen beings.

Unconditional love is the ultimate key. It is the ultimate frame of reference that allows you to look at all of this finger-pointing game and the finger-pointing hierarchy and say: "But the Dark Master has nothing on. He certainly has nothing on me."

With this, my beloved, I do seal you—this time.

24 | INVOKING FREEDOM FROM FINGER-POINTING (PART 1)

In the name of the I AM THAT I AM, Jesus Christ, I use the authority that I have as a being in embodiment on earth to call upon Gautama Buddha to reinforce my calls and use my chakras to project the statements in this invocation into the collective consciousness and set people free from the obsession with pointing the finger at others instead of changing ourselves. Awaken people to the reality that we are spiritual beings and that we can co-create a new future by working with the ascended masters. I especially call for ...

[Make your own calls here.]

Part 1

1. Gautama, shatter the energetic matrix that prevents people from seeing that the primary weapon used by the fallen beings for controlling humankind is pointing the finger.

Gautama, show my mental state
that does give rise to love and hate,
your exposé I do endure,
so my perception will be pure.

**Gautama, Flame of Cosmic Peace,
unruly thoughts do hereby cease,
we radiate from you and me
the peace to still Samsara's Sea.**

2. Gautama, shatter the energetic matrix that prevents people from seeing that the essence of the fallen mindset is pointing the finger at someone else because one is unwilling to look at oneself.

Gautama, in your Flame of Peace,
the struggling self I now release,
the Buddha Nature I now see,
it is the core of you and me.

**Gautama, Flame of Cosmic Peace,
unruly thoughts do hereby cease,
we radiate from you and me
the peace to still Samsara's Sea.**

3. I call forth the judgment of the Buddha upon the machine in the emotional, mental, and identity realms that is aimed at controlling humankind and that forms the foundation for all dictatorships we have seen throughout history and that we see today.

Gautama, I am one with thee,
Mara's demons do now flee,
your Presence like a soothing balm,
my mind and senses ever calm.

**Gautama, Flame of Cosmic Peace,
unruly thoughts do hereby cease,
we radiate from you and me
the peace to still Samsara's Sea.**

4. Gautama, shatter the energetic matrix that prevents people from seeing that the very core of this machine is this consciousness of pointing the finger outside oneself.

Gautama, I now take the vow,
to live in the eternal now,
with you I do transcend all time,
to live in present so sublime.

Gautama, Flame of Cosmic Peace,
unruly thoughts do hereby cease,
we radiate from you and me
the peace to still Samsara's Sea.

5. Gautama, shatter the energetic matrix that prevents people from seeing that even the worst psychopath or narcissist has to have some rudimentary level of reasoning and justification for their actions.

Gautama, I have no desire,
to nothing earthly I aspire,
in non-attachment I now rest,
passing Mara's subtle test.

Gautama, Flame of Cosmic Peace,
unruly thoughts do hereby cease,
we radiate from you and me
the peace to still Samsara's Sea.

6. Gautama, shatter the energetic matrix that prevents people from seeing that this justification comes from the sense that there is something wrong. Something has gone wrong in this person's life, or other people have done something wrong. It is never the person himself or herself who is at fault.

Gautama, I melt into you,
my mind is one, no longer two,
immersed in your resplendent glow,
Nirvana is all that I know.

**Gautama, Flame of Cosmic Peace,
unruly thoughts do hereby cease,
we radiate from you and me
the peace to still Samsara's Sea.**

7. Gautama, shatter the energetic matrix that prevents people from seeing that the principle of pointing the finger outside oneself can justify any human behavior. History is filled with horrendous atrocities that people could always justify by saying that something had gone wrong outside themselves, and that is why they had to do what they did.

Gautama, in your timeless space,
I am immersed in Cosmic Grace,
I know the God beyond all form,
to world I will no more conform.

**Gautama, Flame of Cosmic Peace,
unruly thoughts do hereby cease,
we radiate from you and me
the peace to still Samsara's Sea.**

8. Gautama, shatter the energetic matrix that prevents people from seeing that pointing the finger can so easily result in bending the finger around the trigger that fires at someone else and kills them. The fallen beings are experts at first getting someone to point the finger and then getting them to put the finger on the trigger.

Gautama, I am now awake,
I clearly see what is at stake,
and thus I claim my sacred right
to be on earth the Buddhic Light.

**Gautama, Flame of Cosmic Peace,
unruly thoughts do hereby cease,
we radiate from you and me
the peace to still Samsara's Sea.**

9. Gautama, shatter the energetic matrix that prevents people from seeing that once people have gone into duality and started pointing the finger

outside themselves, they will suffer. When you think that the cause of the problem is outside yourself, you have instantly made yourself powerless to change yourself.

> Gautama, with your thunderbolt,
> we give the earth a mighty jolt,
> I know that some will understand,
> and join the Buddha's timeless band.

> **Gautama, Flame of Cosmic Peace,**
> **unruly thoughts do hereby cease,**
> **we radiate from you and me**
> **the peace to still Samsara's Sea.**

Part 2

1. Gautama, shatter the energetic matrix that prevents people from seeing that the key to avoiding suffering is to go into ourselves and change the condition in there that causes our suffering.

> Gautama, show my mental state
> that does give rise to love and hate,
> your exposé I do endure,
> so my perception will be pure.

> **Gautama, Flame of Cosmic Peace,**
> **unruly thoughts do hereby cease,**
> **we radiate from you and me**
> **the peace to still Samsara's Sea.**

2. Gautama, shatter the energetic matrix that prevents people from seeing that when we point the finger, we think the cause of our suffering is outside ourselves, in these external conditions or other people.

> Gautama, in your Flame of Peace,
> the struggling self I now release,

the Buddha Nature I now see,
it is the core of you and me.

Gautama, Flame of Cosmic Peace,
unruly thoughts do hereby cease,
we radiate from you and me
the peace to still Samsara's Sea.

3. Gautama, shatter the energetic matrix that prevents people from seeing that suffering is an internal experience, and an internal experience can only have an internal cause. This internal cause may be triggered by an external circumstance, but the cause is not the external circumstance. The cause is internal.

Gautama, I am one with thee,
Mara's demons do now flee,
your Presence like a soothing balm,
my mind and senses ever calm.

Gautama, Flame of Cosmic Peace,
unruly thoughts do hereby cease,
we radiate from you and me
the peace to still Samsara's Sea.

4. Gautama, shatter the energetic matrix that prevents people from seeing that once we start pointing the finger, we are looking in the wrong direction. We think that in order to escape suffering, we have to change something out there.

Gautama, I now take the vow,
to live in the eternal now,
with you I do transcend all time,
to live in present so sublime.

Gautama, Flame of Cosmic Peace,
unruly thoughts do hereby cease,
we radiate from you and me
the peace to still Samsara's Sea.

5. Gautama, shatter the energetic matrix that prevents people from seeing that the fallen beings think that the only way to alleviate their suffering is to change everything around them. The fallen beings are blindly driven to attempt to gain control, to gain power, and thereby force their external circumstances to change.

Gautama, I have no desire,
to nothing earthly I aspire,
in non-attachment I now rest,
passing Mara's subtle test.

Gautama, Flame of Cosmic Peace,
unruly thoughts do hereby cease,
we radiate from you and me
the peace to still Samsara's Sea.

6. Gautama, shatter the energetic matrix that prevents people from seeing that whenever a fallen being rises to a position of being a dictator, like Hitler, Stalin, or Mao, he experiences that his suffering does not go away and this may cause insanity.

Gautama, I melt into you,
my mind is one, no longer two,
immersed in your resplendent glow,
Nirvana is all that I know.

Gautama, Flame of Cosmic Peace,
unruly thoughts do hereby cease,
we radiate from you and me
the peace to still Samsara's Sea.

7. I call forth the judgment of the Buddha upon the fallen beings behind the machinery in the emotional, mental, and identity realms that is working towards the end of controlling humankind, and controlling every aspect of life on earth.

Gautama, in your timeless space,
I am immersed in Cosmic Grace,

I know the God beyond all form,
to world I will no more conform.

Gautama, Flame of Cosmic Peace,
unruly thoughts do hereby cease,
we radiate from you and me
the peace to still Samsara's Sea.

8. I call forth the judgment of the Buddha upon the Dark Master who is at the top of this structure and who is the ultimate dictator on earth.

Gautama, I am now awake,
I clearly see what is at stake,
and thus I claim my sacred right
to be on earth the Buddhic Light.

Gautama, Flame of Cosmic Peace,
unruly thoughts do hereby cease,
we radiate from you and me
the peace to still Samsara's Sea.

9. I call forth the judgment of the Buddha upon the Dark Master who is in control of the other fallen beings in the identity realm, those in the mental, those in the astral, and those in the physical.

Gautama, with your thunderbolt,
we give the earth a mighty jolt,
I know that some will understand,
and join the Buddha's timeless band.

Gautama, Flame of Cosmic Peace,
unruly thoughts do hereby cease,
we radiate from you and me
the peace to still Samsara's Sea.

Part 3

1. I call forth the judgment of the Buddha upon the Dark Master who is controlling the other fallen beings by getting them to point the finger at each other, himself pointing the finger at all the rest.

> Gautama, show my mental state
> that does give rise to love and hate,
> your exposé I do endure,
> so my perception will be pure.
>
> **Gautama, Flame of Cosmic Peace,**
> **unruly thoughts do hereby cease,**
> **we radiate from you and me**
> **the peace to still Samsara's Sea.**

2. I call forth the judgment of the Buddha upon the fallen beings who are pointing the finger at others in order to avoid looking at themselves.

> Gautama, in your Flame of Peace,
> the struggling self I now release,
> the Buddha Nature I now see,
> it is the core of you and me.
>
> **Gautama, Flame of Cosmic Peace,**
> **unruly thoughts do hereby cease,**
> **we radiate from you and me**
> **the peace to still Samsara's Sea.**

3. I call forth the judgment of the Buddha upon the Dark Master who has gone into such a state of denial that he will never accept anyone pointing the finger at him. Therefore, his claim to authority in the "fallen community" is that his denial is greater than the denial of the other fallen beings.

> Gautama, I am one with thee,
> Mara's demons do now flee,
> your Presence like a soothing balm,
> my mind and senses ever calm.

**Gautama, Flame of Cosmic Peace,
unruly thoughts do hereby cease,
we radiate from you and me
the peace to still Samsara's Sea.**

4. I call forth the judgment of the Buddha upon the Dark Master who believes that absolutely nothing that could come from earth is something he needs to look at. There is nothing on earth that could ever point the finger at him and make him look at himself because every being on earth is lower than him, even every fallen being is lower than him.

Gautama, I now take the vow,
to live in the eternal now,
with you I do transcend all time,
to live in present so sublime.

**Gautama, Flame of Cosmic Peace,
unruly thoughts do hereby cease,
we radiate from you and me
the peace to still Samsara's Sea.**

5. I call forth the judgment of the Buddha upon the consciousness of absolute denial, of absolute refusal to look at oneself, that is at the very top of the pyramid of the fallen beings associated with earth.

Gautama, I have no desire,
to nothing earthly I aspire,
in non-attachment I now rest,
passing Mara's subtle test.

**Gautama, Flame of Cosmic Peace,
unruly thoughts do hereby cease,
we radiate from you and me
the peace to still Samsara's Sea.**

6. Gautama, shatter the energetic matrix that prevents people from seeing that the more powerful the dictators, the more denial they have of themselves. Denial means that nothing could make you see that what you believe is wrong because you would refuse to look at it.

Gautama, I melt into you,
my mind is one, no longer two,
immersed in your resplendent glow,
Nirvana is all that I know.

Gautama, Flame of Cosmic Peace,
unruly thoughts do hereby cease,
we radiate from you and me
the peace to still Samsara's Sea.

7. Gautama, shatter the energetic matrix that prevents people from seeing that the most severe atrocities committed by dictators throughout history have been committed because of this state of denial, pointing the finger outside oneself.

Gautama, in your timeless space,
I am immersed in Cosmic Grace,
I know the God beyond all form,
to world I will no more conform.

Gautama, Flame of Cosmic Peace,
unruly thoughts do hereby cease,
we radiate from you and me
the peace to still Samsara's Sea.

8. Gautama, shatter the energetic matrix that prevents people from seeing that no dictator can rule a nation alone. What causes people to follow a dictator is that the dictator is in a very strong state of delusion and has managed to export that delusion to others so they believe that the delusionary state of the dictator is based on reality.

Gautama, I am now awake,
I clearly see what is at stake,
and thus I claim my sacred right
to be on earth the Buddhic Light.

Gautama, Flame of Cosmic Peace,
unruly thoughts do hereby cease,

**we radiate from you and me
the peace to still Samsara's Sea.**

9. Gautama, shatter the energetic matrix that prevents people from seeing that what makes people believe that the dictator has some ultimate power is the dictator's denial. He is acting as if he is absolutely right and those who are weak in themselves can be overpowered by this absolute denial.

Gautama, with your thunderbolt,
we give the earth a mighty jolt,
I know that some will understand,
and join the Buddha's timeless band.

**Gautama, Flame of Cosmic Peace,
unruly thoughts do hereby cease,
we radiate from you and me
the peace to still Samsara's Sea.**

Part 4

1. Gautama, shatter the energetic matrix that prevents people from seeing that some people met Mao or Hitler and were overpowered by the denial that was such a contrast to their own insecurity that they submitted themselves to this "great powerful man."

Gautama, show my mental state
that does give rise to love and hate,
your exposé I do endure,
so my perception will be pure.

**Gautama, Flame of Cosmic Peace,
unruly thoughts do hereby cease,
we radiate from you and me
the peace to still Samsara's Sea.**

2. Gautama, shatter the energetic matrix that prevents people from seeing that many of the so-called powerful people throughout the ages had such

an intensity of their denial that they could overpower other people, so they submitted themselves without any critical evaluation.

> Gautama, in your Flame of Peace,
> the struggling self I now release,
> the Buddha Nature I now see,
> it is the core of you and me.

> **Gautama, Flame of Cosmic Peace,**
> **unruly thoughts do hereby cease,**
> **we radiate from you and me**
> **the peace to still Samsara's Sea.**

3. Gautama, shatter the energetic matrix that prevents people from seeing that dictators on earth do not rule alone. They are open doors for the fallen beings in the identity, mental, and emotional realms.

> Gautama, I am one with thee,
> Mara's demons do now flee,
> your Presence like a soothing balm,
> my mind and senses ever calm.

> **Gautama, Flame of Cosmic Peace,**
> **unruly thoughts do hereby cease,**
> **we radiate from you and me**
> **the peace to still Samsara's Sea.**

4. Gautama, shatter the energetic matrix that prevents people from seeing that dictatorship is based on everybody pointing the finger at everybody else, unless they are submitting themselves to the false hierarchy that the fallen beings have created.

> Gautama, I now take the vow,
> to live in the eternal now,
> with you I do transcend all time,
> to live in present so sublime.

> **Gautama, Flame of Cosmic Peace,**
> **unruly thoughts do hereby cease,**

**we radiate from you and me
the peace to still Samsara's Sea.**

5. Gautama, shatter the energetic matrix that prevents people from seeing that the Nazis helped people feel superior because they were part of the master race. The price people paid was the ultimate fear that they could be excluded from the master race by being proven wrong in some way.

Gautama, I have no desire,
to nothing earthly I aspire,
in non-attachment I now rest,
passing Mara's subtle test.

**Gautama, Flame of Cosmic Peace,
unruly thoughts do hereby cease,
we radiate from you and me
the peace to still Samsara's Sea.**

6. Gautama, shatter the energetic matrix that prevents people from seeing that once you accept that you are part of the master race, there is constantly a finger pointing at you, looking for any weakness. If that finger is pointing at you, you would be excluded from the master race.

Gautama, I melt into you,
my mind is one, no longer two,
immersed in your resplendent glow,
Nirvana is all that I know.

**Gautama, Flame of Cosmic Peace,
unruly thoughts do hereby cease,
we radiate from you and me
the peace to still Samsara's Sea.**

7. Gautama, shatter the energetic matrix that prevents people from seeing that those who submit to a dictator live in constant fear of being found wrong.

Gautama, in your timeless space,
I am immersed in Cosmic Grace,

I know the God beyond all form,
to world I will no more conform.

Gautama, Flame of Cosmic Peace,
unruly thoughts do hereby cease,
we radiate from you and me
the peace to still Samsara's Sea.

8. Gautama, shatter the energetic matrix that prevents people from seeing that this causes people to need a scapegoat. They needed someone outside that they could point the finger at and say: "Well, we may not be completely perfect but we are better than those other people."

Gautama, I am now awake,
I clearly see what is at stake,
and thus I claim my sacred right
to be on earth the Buddhic Light.

Gautama, Flame of Cosmic Peace,
unruly thoughts do hereby cease,
we radiate from you and me
the peace to still Samsara's Sea.

9. Gautama, shatter the energetic matrix that prevents people from seeing that whether it was the Nazi regime, the communist regime or the Catholic regime, there is always one person at the top who is considered infallible so no one can point the finger at him.

Gautama, with your thunderbolt,
we give the earth a mighty jolt,
I know that some will understand,
and join the Buddha's timeless band.

Gautama, Flame of Cosmic Peace,
unruly thoughts do hereby cease,
we radiate from you and me
the peace to still Samsara's Sea.

Sealing

In the name of the I AM THAT I AM, I accept that Archangel Michael, Astrea and Shiva form an impenetrable shield around myself and all constructive people, sealing us from all fear-based energies in all four octaves. I accept that the Light of God is consuming and transforming all fear-based energies that make up the dark forces working against ending the era of dictatorships on earth!

25 | INVOKING FREEDOM FROM FINGER-POINTING (PART 2)

In the name of the I AM THAT I AM, Jesus Christ, I use the authority that I have as a being in embodiment on earth to call upon Gautama Buddha to reinforce my calls and use my chakras to project the statements in this invocation into the collective consciousness and set people free from the obsession with pointing the finger at others instead of changing ourselves. Awaken people to the reality that we are spiritual beings and that we can co-create a new future by working with the ascended masters. I especially call for …

[Make your own calls here.]

Part 1

1. Gautama, shatter the energetic matrix that prevents people from seeing that in all dictatorships, everybody is pointing the finger at everybody else.

> Gautama, show my mental state
> that does give rise to love and hate,

your exposé I do endure,
so my perception will be pure.

**Gautama, Flame of Cosmic Peace,
unruly thoughts do hereby cease,
we radiate from you and me
the peace to still Samsara's Sea.**

2. I call forth the judgment of the Buddha upon the fallen beings behind the
Catholic church, who claimed to represent Christ on earth, who claimed to
be a force for good, but who generated the greatest fear seen in recorded
history, the fear of burning forever in hell.

Gautama, in your Flame of Peace,
the struggling self I now release,
the Buddha Nature I now see,
it is the core of you and me.

**Gautama, Flame of Cosmic Peace,
unruly thoughts do hereby cease,
we radiate from you and me
the peace to still Samsara's Sea.**

3. Gautama, shatter the energetic matrix that prevents people from escaping the hypnotic trance generated by the Catholic church, so they can again
use their logical, analytical, observatory abilities.

Gautama, I am one with thee,
Mara's demons do now flee,
your Presence like a soothing balm,
my mind and senses ever calm.

**Gautama, Flame of Cosmic Peace,
unruly thoughts do hereby cease,
we radiate from you and me
the peace to still Samsara's Sea.**

4. Gautama, shatter the energetic matrix that prevents people from seeing
that Jesus did not want Christians to point the finger at each other.

Gautama, I now take the vow,
to live in the eternal now,
with you I do transcend all time,
to live in present so sublime.

Gautama, Flame of Cosmic Peace,
unruly thoughts do hereby cease,
we radiate from you and me
the peace to still Samsara's Sea.

5. Gautama, shatter the energetic matrix that prevents people from using their intuitive faculties to tune in to the living Ascended Master Jesus Christ.

Gautama, I have no desire,
to nothing earthly I aspire,
in non-attachment I now rest,
passing Mara's subtle test.

Gautama, Flame of Cosmic Peace,
unruly thoughts do hereby cease,
we radiate from you and me
the peace to still Samsara's Sea.

6. Gautama, shatter the energetic matrix that prevents people from tuning in to Jesus, looking at the Catholic church and saying: "This is not in alignment with the vibration of Christ, it is not in alignment with the words of Christ, with the actions of Christ, this is simply madness."

Gautama, I melt into you,
my mind is one, no longer two,
immersed in your resplendent glow,
Nirvana is all that I know.

Gautama, Flame of Cosmic Peace,
unruly thoughts do hereby cease,
we radiate from you and me
the peace to still Samsara's Sea.

7. Gautama, shatter the energetic matrix that prevents the more aware people from seeing this mechanism of how pointing the finger is such a destructive force in human life. It is a destructive force in the psychology of the individual. It is a destructive force in families, in any kind of group, in entire nations and in humanity as a whole.

> Gautama, in your timeless space,
> I am immersed in Cosmic Grace,
> I know the God beyond all form,
> to world I will no more conform.

> **Gautama, Flame of Cosmic Peace,**
> **unruly thoughts do hereby cease,**
> **we radiate from you and me**
> **the peace to still Samsara's Sea.**

8. Gautama, shatter the energetic matrix that prevents people from seeing that when we are pointing the finger at everybody else at the conscious level, we are at the unconscious level pointing the finger at ourselves.

> Gautama, I am now awake,
> I clearly see what is at stake,
> and thus I claim my sacred right
> to be on earth the Buddhic Light.

> **Gautama, Flame of Cosmic Peace,**
> **unruly thoughts do hereby cease,**
> **we radiate from you and me**
> **the peace to still Samsara's Sea.**

9. Gautama, shatter the energetic matrix that prevents people from seeing that the fallen beings have managed to get us to point the finger at ourselves. We are not seeing this at the conscious level because we are afraid of being excluded from the group and this is an unbearable state of mind to be in.

> Gautama, with your thunderbolt,
> we give the earth a mighty jolt,

I know that some will understand,
and join the Buddha's timeless band.

Gautama, Flame of Cosmic Peace,
unruly thoughts do hereby cease,
we radiate from you and me
the peace to still Samsara's Sea.

Part 2

1. Gautama, shatter the energetic matrix that prevents people from seeing that the fallen beings offer us two ways out of this unbearable state. One way is to divert attention by getting us to point the finger at somebody else.

Gautama, show my mental state
that does give rise to love and hate,
your exposé I do endure,
so my perception will be pure.

Gautama, Flame of Cosmic Peace,
unruly thoughts do hereby cease,
we radiate from you and me
the peace to still Samsara's Sea.

2. Gautama, shatter the energetic matrix that prevents people from seeing that this is based on the very subtle idea that if we see a fault in ourselves, then if we can find a worse fault in someone else, then we can still stay inside the group because the other person will be the one who is excluded.

Gautama, in your Flame of Peace,
the struggling self I now release,
the Buddha Nature I now see,
it is the core of you and me.

Gautama, Flame of Cosmic Peace,
unruly thoughts do hereby cease,

we radiate from you and me
the peace to still Samsara's Sea.

3. Gautama, shatter the energetic matrix that prevents people from seeing that even though we realize we are not perfect, if we can find someone who is more imperfect than us, then they can be excluded. If we have been a tool for excluding someone else, we can still stay in the group.

Gautama, I am one with thee,
Mara's demons do now flee,
your Presence like a soothing balm,
my mind and senses ever calm.

Gautama, Flame of Cosmic Peace,
unruly thoughts do hereby cease,
we radiate from you and me
the peace to still Samsara's Sea.

4. Gautama, shatter the energetic matrix that prevents people from seeing that the fallen beings have created a standard of perfection and it defines that here is a superior group, and those who live up to the standard can be in the group.

Gautama, I now take the vow,
to live in the eternal now,
with you I do transcend all time,
to live in present so sublime.

Gautama, Flame of Cosmic Peace,
unruly thoughts do hereby cease,
we radiate from you and me
the peace to still Samsara's Sea.

5. Gautama, shatter the energetic matrix that prevents people from seeing that this only works when you define an impossible standard so that the people who are in the group realize they do not fully live up to the standard. They have the fear that they could be excluded, and that is why they go into the mindset of diverting attention from their own imperfections by pointing out the imperfections of others.

Gautama, I have no desire,
to nothing earthly I aspire,
in non-attachment I now rest,
passing Mara's subtle test.

**Gautama, Flame of Cosmic Peace,
unruly thoughts do hereby cease,
we radiate from you and me
the peace to still Samsara's Sea.**

6. Gautama, shatter the energetic matrix that prevents people from seeing that the other way that the fallen beings can relieve the unbearable state is through denial. They get some people to deny their own imperfections.

Gautama, I melt into you,
my mind is one, no longer two,
immersed in your resplendent glow,
Nirvana is all that I know.

**Gautama, Flame of Cosmic Peace,
unruly thoughts do hereby cease,
we radiate from you and me
the peace to still Samsara's Sea.**

7. Gautama, shatter the energetic matrix that prevents people from seeing that throughout the ages some people have gone into a state of denial, and they are the ones we see in all of the privileged groups around the world, those who think they are fit to lead the population.

Gautama, in your timeless space,
I am immersed in Cosmic Grace,
I know the God beyond all form,
to world I will no more conform.

**Gautama, Flame of Cosmic Peace,
unruly thoughts do hereby cease,
we radiate from you and me
the peace to still Samsara's Sea.**

8. Gautama, shatter the energetic matrix that prevents people from seeing that the key to escaping the finger-pointing game is a love that is unconditional.

> Gautama, I am now awake,
> I clearly see what is at stake,
> and thus I claim my sacred right
> to be on earth the Buddhic Light.

> **Gautama, Flame of Cosmic Peace,**
> **unruly thoughts do hereby cease,**
> **we radiate from you and me**
> **the peace to still Samsara's Sea.**

9. Gautama, shatter the energetic matrix that prevents people from seeing that we cannot judge somebody else and love them at the same time. We cannot judge ourselves and love ourselves at the same time.

> Gautama, with your thunderbolt,
> we give the earth a mighty jolt,
> I know that some will understand,
> and join the Buddha's timeless band.

> **Gautama, Flame of Cosmic Peace,**
> **unruly thoughts do hereby cease,**
> **we radiate from you and me**
> **the peace to still Samsara's Sea.**

Part 3

1. Gautama, shatter the energetic matrix that prevents people from seeing that when we are in the judgmental frame of mind, we cannot feel loved so we are trapped in judgment.

> Gautama, show my mental state
> that does give rise to love and hate,

your exposé I do endure,
so my perception will be pure.

**Gautama, Flame of Cosmic Peace,
unruly thoughts do hereby cease,
we radiate from you and me
the peace to still Samsara's Sea.**

2. Gautama, shatter the energetic matrix that prevents people from seeing that the ultimate deception of the fallen beings is the idea that only by judging ourselves, judging others and living up to the standard of perfection, will God allow us into heaven.

Gautama, in your Flame of Peace,
the struggling self I now release,
the Buddha Nature I now see,
it is the core of you and me.

**Gautama, Flame of Cosmic Peace,
unruly thoughts do hereby cease,
we radiate from you and me
the peace to still Samsara's Sea.**

3. Gautama, shatter the energetic matrix that prevents people from seeing that it is the judgmental mindset that causes us to resist heaven. The only way to get to heaven is to let go of the judgmental mindset, which means letting go of the separate selves that are the source of judgment.

Gautama, I am one with thee,
Mara's demons do now flee,
your Presence like a soothing balm,
my mind and senses ever calm.

**Gautama, Flame of Cosmic Peace,
unruly thoughts do hereby cease,
we radiate from you and me
the peace to still Samsara's Sea.**

4. Gautama, shatter the energetic matrix that prevents people from experiencing that there is something more, there is something they love more than the judgmental self.

> Gautama, I now take the vow,
> to live in the eternal now,
> with you I do transcend all time,
> to live in present so sublime.

> **Gautama, Flame of Cosmic Peace,**
> **unruly thoughts do hereby cease,**
> **we radiate from you and me**
> **the peace to still Samsara's Sea.**

5. Gautama, shatter the energetic matrix that prevents people from seeing that what can make us feel that there is something we love more than this judgmental self is the pure, unconditional love of the ascended masters.

> Gautama, I have no desire,
> to nothing earthly I aspire,
> in non-attachment I now rest,
> passing Mara's subtle test.

> **Gautama, Flame of Cosmic Peace,**
> **unruly thoughts do hereby cease,**
> **we radiate from you and me**
> **the peace to still Samsara's Sea.**

6. Gautama, shatter the energetic matrix that prevents people from seeing that the ultimate deception of the fallen beings is to make people think that God is a judgmental God, that God is an angry God who will judge them harshly for any imperfection. They think that a standard defined on earth is what God will judge them by.

> Gautama, I melt into you,
> my mind is one, no longer two,
> immersed in your resplendent glow,
> Nirvana is all that I know.

**Gautama, Flame of Cosmic Peace,
unruly thoughts do hereby cease,
we radiate from you and me
the peace to still Samsara's Sea.**

7. Gautama, shatter the energetic matrix that prevents people from experiencing that God's love is without judgment, without conditions.

Gautama, in your timeless space,
I am immersed in Cosmic Grace,
I know the God beyond all form,
to world I will no more conform.

**Gautama, Flame of Cosmic Peace,
unruly thoughts do hereby cease,
we radiate from you and me
the peace to still Samsara's Sea.**

8. Gautama, shatter the energetic matrix that prevents people from seeing that no matter how perfect we are according to an earthly standard, no matter how perfect we are according to our own judgment or the judgment of anyone else on earth, it will not get us to heaven.

Gautama, I am now awake,
I clearly see what is at stake,
and thus I claim my sacred right
to be on earth the Buddhic Light.

**Gautama, Flame of Cosmic Peace,
unruly thoughts do hereby cease,
we radiate from you and me
the peace to still Samsara's Sea.**

9. Gautama, shatter the energetic matrix that prevents people from seeing that judgment will only push us away from heaven. The more we judge, the more we push ourselves away.

Gautama, with your thunderbolt,
we give the earth a mighty jolt,

I know that some will understand,
and join the Buddha's timeless band.

**Gautama, Flame of Cosmic Peace,
unruly thoughts do hereby cease,
we radiate from you and me
the peace to still Samsara's Sea.**

Part 4

1. Gautama, shatter the energetic matrix that prevents people from seeing that the key to going to heaven is *not* to live up to some condition defined on earth.

Gautama, show my mental state
that does give rise to love and hate,
your exposé I do endure,
so my perception will be pure.

**Gautama, Flame of Cosmic Peace,
unruly thoughts do hereby cease,
we radiate from you and me
the peace to still Samsara's Sea.**

2. Gautama, shatter the energetic matrix that prevents people from seeing that the key to going to heaven is to transcend all conditions defined on earth, and the consciousness that has defined them.

Gautama, in your Flame of Peace,
the struggling self I now release,
the Buddha Nature I now see,
it is the core of you and me.

**Gautama, Flame of Cosmic Peace,
unruly thoughts do hereby cease,
we radiate from you and me
the peace to still Samsara's Sea.**

3. Gautama, shatter the energetic matrix that prevents people from seeing that the key to transcending this consciousness is to experience the unconditional love of God.

Gautama, I am one with thee,
Mara's demons do now flee,
your Presence like a soothing balm,
my mind and senses ever calm.

Gautama, Flame of Cosmic Peace,
unruly thoughts do hereby cease,
we radiate from you and me
the peace to still Samsara's Sea.

4. Gautama, shatter the energetic matrix that prevents people from accepting that the self we were created as was, from the very beginning, worthy to return to God.

Gautama, I now take the vow,
to live in the eternal now,
with you I do transcend all time,
to live in present so sublime.

Gautama, Flame of Cosmic Peace,
unruly thoughts do hereby cease,
we radiate from you and me
the peace to still Samsara's Sea.

5. Gautama, shatter the energetic matrix that prevents people from seeing that God did not cast us out of the Garden of Eden. We went out in order to have experiences in this world.

Gautama, I have no desire,
to nothing earthly I aspire,
in non-attachment I now rest,
passing Mara's subtle test.

Gautama, Flame of Cosmic Peace,
unruly thoughts do hereby cease,

we radiate from you and me
the peace to still Samsara's Sea.

6. Gautama, shatter the energetic matrix that prevents people from seeing that no matter what we have done in this world, no matter how much we have judged ourselves or judged others, it has not made us unworthy to return.

Gautama, I melt into you,
my mind is one, no longer two,
immersed in your resplendent glow,
Nirvana is all that I know.

Gautama, Flame of Cosmic Peace,
unruly thoughts do hereby cease,
we radiate from you and me
the peace to still Samsara's Sea.

7. Gautama, shatter the energetic matrix that prevents people from seeing that only the self who descended from heaven can ascend back to heaven. The Conscious You has no conditions in its pure awareness—non-judgmental awareness. When we return to that, we are free to go into heaven.

Gautama, in your timeless space,
I am immersed in Cosmic Grace,
I know the God beyond all form,
to world I will no more conform.

Gautama, Flame of Cosmic Peace,
unruly thoughts do hereby cease,
we radiate from you and me
the peace to still Samsara's Sea.

8. Gautama, shatter the energetic matrix that prevents people from seeing that as long as we still have conditions and judgments, we do not think we are worthy to enter heaven or ready to enter heaven. Therefore, we are keeping ourselves out. God never kept anyone out of heaven. People do that all by themselves, with the help of the fallen beings.

Gautama, I am now awake,
I clearly see what is at stake,
and thus I claim my sacred right
to be on earth the Buddhic Light.

Gautama, Flame of Cosmic Peace,
unruly thoughts do hereby cease,
we radiate from you and me
the peace to still Samsara's Sea.

9. Gautama, shatter the energetic matrix that prevents people from seeing that unconditional love is the ultimate key. It is the ultimate frame of reference that allows us to look at the finger-pointing game and the finger-pointing hierarchy and say: "But the Dark Master has nothing on. He certainly has nothing on me."

Gautama, with your thunderbolt,
we give the earth a mighty jolt,
I know that some will understand,
and join the Buddha's timeless band.

Gautama, Flame of Cosmic Peace,
unruly thoughts do hereby cease,
we radiate from you and me
the peace to still Samsara's Sea.

Sealing

In the name of the I AM THAT I AM, I accept that Archangel Michael, Astrea and Shiva form an impenetrable shield around myself and all constructive people, sealing us from all fear-based energies in all four octaves. I accept that the Light of God is consuming and transforming all fear-based energies that make up the dark forces working against ending the era of dictatorships on earth!

26 | PROTECTING YOURSELF FROM THE FALLEN BEINGS

The Ascended Master Mother Mary: I know very well that our teachings can encourage some students to become unbalanced. You become so "fired up," so to speak, about doing what you came here to do. Some people feel that they have wasted a big part of their lives by not having found the teachings. When they finally find the teachings, they want to compensate for this by throwing themselves at it and making calls all day and neglecting other parts of life. I am not asking you to do this.

I know that this book deals with an extreme condition on earth. I know that when you are a soldier in war, you are in a very extreme state. I am not asking you, as an ascended master student, to go into a warlike mindset and put other aspects of your life aside and think that now you have to live some unbalanced, extreme lifestyle in order to bring the judgment of the fallen beings. I am asking you to live a balanced spiritual life, but to still find time to make the calls and give us the authority and the energy to multiply so that we can do our work.

Yes, we are dealing with an extreme condition. Yes, it needs to be removed, but do you not see that what the fallen beings are doing by creating conflict and war is that they are forcing human beings in embodiment to go towards greater and greater extremes to defeat the enemy?

Do you not also see that for everything that happens in the physical, there is a parallel in consciousness? When you see people take extreme physical actions, you know that they have gone into a parallel extreme in their emotional, mental and identity bodies. Do you not also see that it is this unbalance in the three higher bodies that leads to the imbalance at the physical level? Why would you think that you going into an imbalanced state would help remove an extreme condition from the earth?

You would actually contribute to the imbalance on earth, even though you are a spiritual student following a spiritual teaching. There are ascended master students who have found our teachings, given in past dispensations, and who have used them to become so unbalanced that they have actually contributed to the survival of war and conflict on earth through their imbalance. They have also become so angry with the fallen beings, or with certain human beings from another political system, that they have contributed to the misqualified energy that feeds the entire machine. This I am asking you to *not* do.

I am asking you to take our teachings, and the many other teachings we have given about balance, and to walk a balanced path, to live a balanced life. I am not asking you to go to war against darkness. I am asking you to fight darkness by finding your own personal inner balance, by finding your personal inner peace and, from that state of peace, making the calls that give us the authority to go in and do the dirty work, so to speak, of cleaning up the astral pit and the mental and identity realms. This is *our* job. This is *our* task. This is *our* joy. We are perfectly capable of doing this without going into a state of imbalance. Archangel Michael is absolutely unbending when he is dealing with the fallen beings, but he is not angry with them. He is not in his mind fighting a battle against them. He is simply doing his work, being completely centered in the peace of God.

For you to be most efficient in making the calls for the removing of the forces of darkness, you need to transcend the consciousness that you want to see removed. This we have given you the tools to do, both in this book and in our other books. I would consider it important for those who are using this book in order to make the calls that you also study the book *Healing Your Spiritual Traumas* and other books in that series. Certainly, you should be familiar with the teachings about fallen beings, and you may find them in a concentrated form in the book *Cosmology of Evil.*

If a critical mass of people take this book, take the tools and teachings, and make use of them, then we can make an incredibly significant step towards removing darkness from this planet. If a critical mass of people took and used the tools and teachings we have given in this book, then we could start a process that would quickly become irreversible and would lead to the complete removal of darkness from planet earth.

It is possible that, within a few decades, people would look back and would scarcely be able to understand that such dramatic changes could happen in such a short time. They would look at the specter of darkness as it has been hanging over humankind for thousands of years and they would say: "How could it disappear so quickly?" Probably, official society would never recognize the importance of spiritual people making the calls. If a critical mass of people would embrace the teachings and tools in this book, then I can assure you that darkness could become an impossibility in the lifetimes of many of you. Would this not be a great joy to your heart? Would it not give you a sense that you have fulfilled an important part of your purpose for coming to this planet? Would it not make you feel that it was worthwhile, even though this is such a difficult and dense planet upon which to embody?

I know many of you have gone through many hardships, many sufferings, but if you could feel that you had made an important contribution to the removal of darkness, would it not all have been worth it? Would you not feel this connection to the River of Life and a sense that, even though one human lifetime may seem insignificant, it can still be part of the cosmic purpose, the cosmic upward movement that is the River of Life?

Overcoming the recoil from the fallen beings

I know that if you start making the calls on darkness, you will go through a period where you might feel burdened by the energies you are dealing with. You should be able to realize by now that, when you start using the tools in this book, the fallen beings will throw everything they have at you in all four levels. They will attempt to manipulate you. They will attempt to burden you in all ways. They might even attempt to do this with the people in your circle of influence. That is why you need to make the calls for the protection not only of yourself but of all people around you.

Again, I am not asking you to go into a state of fear or a sense of being at war or fighting the fallen beings. I am just asking you to make the calls so that we can do the work of protecting you. I am also asking you to be aware that when you feel burdened, when you feel you are under attack, it is because there is something, some illusion, in your consciousness that the fallen beings are using to burden you. I am asking you to look at that beam in your own eye and to use our teachings and tools to remove it so that you can transcend it and become even more efficient.

What I am telling you here is this: If you make the decision to seriously start using the tools and teachings in this book, you might go through an initial period where you will feel, perhaps, even more burdened than you feel today. You will feel you are being attacked. You should know that this is the fallen beings throwing everything at you in order to discourage you from doing the work that will lead to their removal from the earth. You should not be surprised that they would do this. They will do absolutely anything they can to prevent anyone from using the teachings and tools of the ascended masters because it will lead to their own removal from the earth. For them, it is seen as a life-and-death battle.

I am asking you to *not* see it this way but to simply be aware of what is happening and what will be happening. Then make the calls for it. Then look at yourself and overcome the illusion that gives them an inroad into your consciousness. If you do this knowingly, you will be surprised at how quickly you can work through this period. You will come out the other side feeling that you have now raised yourself to a point where the fallen beings cannot reach you as they used to be able to do. You have accelerated yourself. You have accelerated your consciousness beyond the reach of those fallen beings who were attacking you in the past. This is a great sense of freedom, a great sense of inner knowing.

You cannot awaken by remaining blind

My beloved, do you begin to see here that even though they say "ignorance is bliss," ignorance is *not* bliss? There are spiritual people who feel that all they need to do is to be positive and send out positive vibrations. There are those who say that you should not put your mind on anything dark or evil because even by making the calls or the invocations we are giving you, you are, they say, giving your energy to the dark forces. I can assure you that these invocations are designed in such a way that they will not give your energy to the dark forces, unless you give them from a state of extreme imbalance. If you give them with non-attachment, centered in peace, knowing that *we* will do the work, then you will not give your energies to the dark forces.

What I am pointing out to you is that the spiritual path is a path of awakening. You do not awaken by remaining blind. There are spiritual people who refuse to look at the existence of dark forces, and they think they can still walk the spiritual path, but you cannot walk the path beyond a certain level. The real path is that, as you begin to awaken yourself, you must look at the planet you are on. You must look at what is going on here. You must acknowledge the presence of fallen beings because they are such an intricate part of planet earth and have been for so long. You cannot walk the spiritual path on a planet like earth without becoming aware of the fallen beings. I am not asking you to fight them or give them energy. I am not asking you to be afraid of them. I am asking you to be aware.

Do you understand what I am saying? You cannot walk the spiritual path towards a higher state of consciousness by remaining unaware. You cannot walk the path by refusing to look at something just because it is inconvenient or unpleasant to you. You walk the path by being willing to look at *everything*.

First, you must look at the fallen beings. Then you will be disturbed when you begin to acknowledge the things we talk about in this book. As you keep rising, you will come to a point where you have now transcended the fallen beings. Now you can look at them and acknowledge their existence with complete non-attachment and inner peace.

Looking at darkness while maintaining harmony

Some spiritual students think that it is so important to be at peace and maintain their inner harmony that they will not look at anything that might disturb that harmony. As long as there is *anything* that can disturb your inner harmony, you have not reached a high level of spiritual attainment. You have only created the outer impression of having spiritual attainment because you are supposedly always able to maintain this state of inner harmony and balance. This is not true spiritual attainment. This is not mastery.

The Buddha did not enter nirvana by ignoring the demons of Mara. The last test he faced was that he had to look at all the demons of Mara, and he had to allow them to do anything and everything they could think of to get him to react. He had to sit there and see it all and remain non-attached so that he did not react. *Then,* he could enter nirvana. You cannot enter your own personal nirvana until you are able and willing to look at everything the fallen beings can throw at you and simply look at it all and say: "I am not this."

You cannot walk the spiritual path by being unaware of what is happening on the planet where you have taken embodiment. You must see everything, and then you must see beyond it. You see that, behind all the demons of Mara, everything is still the Buddha nature. Everything is still one. You look at everything here on earth and you say: "I am not this." Then, you look at the oneness of the spiritual realm and you say: "I AM this. I am that 'I AM' up there, not the separate 'I am' down here." Then you can enter nirvana.

Be here below all that you are Above

I will be the first to greet you. I am asking you to consider that your goal for taking embodiment on earth in this lifetime was not primarily to enter nirvana. It was to do some work while you are in embodiment on this planet. You came here to make a difference because you saw how critical this time is for the evolution of the earth. You set aside your personal entering of nirvana in order to do the work of raising the earth and setting free the billions of lifestreams that embody upon it.

With this, I simply want to welcome you into the ranks of those who consider themselves not only ascended master students but who are also beginning to consider themselves the extensions of the ascended masters on earth. You are among those who are beginning to realize that the highest potential of earth is to be "as Above, so below." This will happen only when you become as Above, so below. Will you become here below all that you already are Above? I AM Mother Mary Above. Will *you* be Mother Mary below?

27 | PROTECTION FROM DARK FORCES

In the name of the I AM THAT I AM, Jesus Christ, I call upon Mother Mary, Archangel Michael, Astrea and Saint Germain to help us accelerate ourselves beyond the reach of the dark forces. Awaken people to the reality that we are spiritual beings and that we can co-create a new future by working with the ascended masters. I especially call for ...

[Make your own calls here.]

Part 1

1. Archangel Michael, I accept your total protection for myself and all people in my circle of influence from any backlash from the fallen beings in the form of physical accidents, mishaps or acts of violence.

> Archangel Michael, light so blue,
> my heart has room for only you.
> My mind is one, no longer two,
> your love for me is ever true.

Archangel Michael, you are here,
your light consumes all doubt and fear.
Your Presence is forever near,
you are to me so very dear.

2. Archangel Michael, I accept your total protection for myself and all people in my circle of influence from any backlash from the fallen beings in the form of disease or problems with the physical body.

Archangel Michael, I will be,
all one with your reality.
No fear can hold me as I see,
this world no power has o'er me.

Archangel Michael, you are here,
your light consumes all doubt and fear.
Your Presence is forever near,
you are to me so very dear.

3. Archangel Michael, I accept your total protection for myself and all people in my circle of influence from any backlash from the fallen beings in the form of emotional projections causing erratic or insane behavior.

Archangel Michael, hold me tight,
shatter now the darkest night.
Clear my chakras with your light,
restore to me my inner sight.

Archangel Michael, you are here,
your light consumes all doubt and fear.
Your Presence is forever near,
you are to me so very dear.

4. Archangel Michael, I accept your total protection for myself and all people in my circle of influence from any backlash from the fallen beings in the form of emotional projections causing depression or a sense of discouragement.

Archangel Michael, now I stand,
with you the light I do command.
My heart I ever will expand,
till highest truth I understand.

Archangel Michael, you are here,
your light consumes all doubt and fear.
Your Presence is forever near,
you are to me so very dear.

5. Archangel Michael, I accept your total protection for myself and all people in my circle of influence from any backlash from the fallen beings in the form of mental projections causing confusion or mental instability.

Archangel Michael, in my heart,
from me you never will depart.
Of hierarchy I am a part,
I now accept a fresh new start.

Archangel Michael, you are here,
your light consumes all doubt and fear.
Your Presence is forever near,
you are to me so very dear.

6. Archangel Michael, I accept your total protection for myself and all people in my circle of influence from any backlash from the fallen beings in the form of mental projections causing fanaticism or closed-mindedness.

Archangel Michael, sword of blue,
all darkness you are cutting through.
My Christhood I do now pursue,
discernment shows me what is true.

Archangel Michael, you are here,
your light consumes all doubt and fear.
Your Presence is forever near,
you are to me so very dear.

7. Archangel Michael, I accept your total protection for myself and all people in my circle of influence from any backlash from the fallen beings in the form of identity projections causing attachments to certain belief systems.

> Archangel Michael, in your wings,
> I now let go of lesser things.
> God's homing call in my heart rings,
> my heart with yours forever sings.

> **Archangel Michael, you are here,**
> **your light consumes all doubt and fear.**
> **Your Presence is forever near,**
> **you are to me so very dear.**

8. Archangel Michael, I accept your total protection for myself and all people in my circle of influence from any backlash from the fallen beings in the form of identity projections causing an identity crisis or fanaticism.

> Archangel Michael, take me home,
> in higher spheres I want to roam.
> I am reborn from cosmic foam,
> my life is now a sacred poem.

> **Archangel Michael, you are here,**
> **your light consumes all doubt and fear.**
> **Your Presence is forever near,**
> **you are to me so very dear.**

9. Archangel Michael, I accept your total protection for myself and all people in my circle of influence from any backlash from the fallen beings in the form of any opposition to our spiritual growth.

> Archangel Michael, light you are,
> shining like the bluest star.
> You are a cosmic avatar,
> with you I will go very far.

Archangel Michael, you are here,
your light consumes all doubt and fear.
Your Presence is forever near,
you are to me so very dear.

Part 2

1. Beloved Astrea, I accept that you are cutting free myself and all people in my circle of influence from any fallen beings in embodiment or any people controlled by fallen beings in the three higher octaves.

> Astrea, loving Being white,
> your Presence is my pure delight,
> your sword and circle white and blue,
> the astral plane is cutting through.

> **Astrea, come accelerate,**
> **with purity I do vibrate,**
> **release the fire so blue and white,**
> **my aura filled with vibrant light.**

2. Beloved Astrea, I accept that you are cutting free myself and all people in my circle of influence from any fallen beings, demons or entities in the astral plane.

> Astrea, calm the raging storm,
> so purity will be the norm,
> my aura filled with blue and white,
> with shining armor, like a knight.

> **Astrea, come accelerate,**
> **with purity I do vibrate,**
> **release the fire so blue and white,**
> **my aura filled with vibrant light.**

3. Beloved Astrea, I accept that you are cutting free myself and all people in my circle of influence from any fallen beings or demons in the mental realm.

> Astrea, come and cut me free,
> from every binding entity,
> let astral forces all be bound,
> true freedom I have surely found.

> **Astrea, come accelerate,**
> **with purity I do vibrate,**
> **release the fire so blue and white,**
> **my aura filled with vibrant light.**

4. Beloved Astrea, I accept that you are cutting free myself and all people in my circle of influence from any fallen beings or demons in the identity octave.

> Astrea, I sincerely urge,
> from demons all, do me purge,
> consume them all and take me higher,
> I will endure your cleansing fire.

> **Astrea, come accelerate,**
> **with purity I do vibrate,**
> **release the fire so blue and white,**
> **my aura filled with vibrant light.**

5. Beloved Astrea, I accept that you are binding and consuming the demons and fallen beings in the astral plane who are attacking myself or any people in my circle of influence as an act of revenge for me making the calls for putting a stop to their activities.

> Astrea, do all spirits bind,
> so that I am no longer blind,
> I see the spirit and its twin,
> the victory of Christ I win.

Astrea, come accelerate,
with purity I do vibrate,
release the fire so blue and white,
my aura filled with vibrant light.

6. Beloved Astrea, I accept that you are binding and consuming the demons and fallen beings in the mental realm who are attacking myself or any people in my circle of influence as an act of revenge for me making the calls for putting a stop to their activities.

Astrea, clear my every cell,
from energies of death and hell,
my body is now free to grow,
each cell emits an inner glow.

Astrea, come accelerate,
with purity I do vibrate,
release the fire so blue and white,
my aura filled with vibrant light.

7. Beloved Astrea, I accept that you are binding and consuming the demons and fallen beings in the identity realm who are attacking myself or any people in my circle of influence as an act of revenge for me making the calls for putting a stop to their activities.

Astrea, clear my feeling mind,
in purity my peace I find,
with higher feeling you release,
I co-create in perfect peace.

Astrea, come accelerate,
with purity I do vibrate,
release the fire so blue and white,
my aura filled with vibrant light.

8. Beloved Astrea, I accept that you are binding and consuming the demons and fallen beings who are aggressively seeking to discourage me from doing the work that will lead to their removal from the earth.

Astrea, clear my mental realm,
my Christ self always at the helm,
I see now how to manifest,
the matrix that for all is best.

Astrea, come accelerate,
with purity I do vibrate,
release the fire so blue and white,
my aura filled with vibrant light.

9. Beloved Astrea, I accept that you are binding and consuming the demons and fallen beings who are seeking to prevent anyone from using the teachings and tools of the ascended masters that will lead to their removal from the earth.

Astrea, with great clarity,
I claim a new identity,
etheric blueprint I now see,
I co-create more consciously.

Astrea, come accelerate,
with purity I do vibrate,
release the fire so blue and white,
my aura filled with vibrant light.

Part 3

1. Mother Mary, I accept that you are helping myself and all people in my circle of influence see and transcend all physical habits that are making us vulnerable to the attacks of the demons and fallen beings in all for octaves.

O blessed Mary, Mother mine,
there is no greater love than thine,
as we are one in heart and mind,
my place in hierarchy I find.

O Mother Mary, generate,
the song that does accelerate,
the earth into a higher state,
all matter does now scintillate.

2. Mother Mary, I accept that you are helping myself and all people in my circle of influence see and transcend all emotional patterns that are making us vulnerable to the attacks of the demons and fallen beings in all for octaves.

I came to earth from heaven sent,
as I am in embodiment,
I use Divine authority,
commanding you to set earth free.

O Mother Mary, generate,
the song that does accelerate,
the earth into a higher state,
all matter does now scintillate.

3. Mother Mary, I accept that you are helping myself and all people in my circle of influence see and transcend all mental illusions that are making us vulnerable to the attacks of the demons and fallen beings in all for octaves.

I call now in God's sacred name,
for you to use your Mother Flame,
to burn all fear-based energy,
restoring sacred harmony.

O Mother Mary, generate,
the song that does accelerate,
the earth into a higher state,
all matter does now scintillate.

4. Mother Mary, I accept that you are helping myself and all people in my circle of influence see and transcend all false sense of identity that is making us vulnerable to the attacks of the demons and fallen beings in all for octaves.

Your sacred name I hereby praise,
collective consciousness you raise,
no more of fear and doubt and shame,
consume it with your Mother Flame.

O Mother Mary, generate,
the song that does accelerate,
the earth into a higher state,
all matter does now scintillate.

5. Mother Mary, I accept that you are helping myself and all people in my circle of influence see and transcend any tendency to think we are in opposition to the fallen beings or other people.

All darkness from the earth you purge,
your light moves as a mighty surge,
no force of darkness can now stop,
the spiral that goes only up.

O Mother Mary, generate,
the song that does accelerate,
the earth into a higher state,
all matter does now scintillate.

6. Mother Mary, I accept that you are helping myself and all people in my circle of influence see and transcend any tendency to think we have to live an extremist or unbalanced lifestyle in order to fulfill our Divine plans.

All elemental life you bless,
removing from them man-made stress,
the nature spirits are now free,
outpicturing Divine decree.

O Mother Mary, generate,
the song that does accelerate,
the earth into a higher state,
all matter does now scintillate.

7. Mother Mary, I accept that you are helping myself and all people in my circle of influence see and transcend any tendency to go into a mindset where we produce inharmonious energies that actually feed the dark forces.

I raise my voice and take my stand,
a stop to war I do command,
no more shall warring scar the earth,
a golden age is given birth.

O Mother Mary, generate,
the song that does accelerate,
the earth into a higher state,
all matter does now scintillate.

8. Mother Mary, I accept that you are helping myself and all people in my circle of influence see and transcend the intent of the fallen beings to force us to go towards greater and greater extremes in order to defeat an enemy.

As Mother Earth is free at last,
disasters belong to the past,
your Mother Light is so intense,
that matter is now far less dense.

O Mother Mary, generate,
the song that does accelerate,
the earth into a higher state,
all matter does now scintillate.

9. Mother Mary, I accept that you are helping myself and all people in my circle of influence see and transcend any imbalance in the three higher bodies that leads to imbalances at the physical level.

In Mother Light the earth is pure,
the upward spiral will endure,
prosperity is now the norm,
God's vision manifest as form.

O Mother Mary, generate,
the song that does accelerate,
the earth into a higher state,
all matter does now scintillate.

Part 4

1. Saint Germain, send oceans of violet flame into the lives of myself and all people in my circle of influence. Transmute any karmic vulnerability to physical accidents, mishaps or other events that block our Divine plans.

O Saint Germain, you do inspire,
my vision raised forever higher,
with you I form a figure-eight,
your Golden Age I co-create.

O Saint Germain, what love you bring,
it truly makes all matter sing,
your violet flame does all restore,
with you we are becoming more.

2. Saint Germain, send oceans of violet flame into the physical bodies of myself and all people in my circle of influence. Transmute any karmic vulnerability to physical diseases or bodily imbalances that block our Divine plans.

O Saint Germain, what Freedom Flame,
released when we recite your name,
acceleration is your gift,
our planet it will surely lift.

O Saint Germain, what love you bring,
it truly makes all matter sing,
your violet flame does all restore,
with you we are becoming more.

3. Saint Germain, send oceans of violet flame into the emotional bodies of myself and all people in my circle of influence. Transmute any karmic ties to any beings in the emotional octave and any tendency for depression or emotional instability.

> O Saint Germain, in love we claim,
> our right to bring your violet flame,
> from you Above, to us below,
> it is an all-transforming flow.

> **O Saint Germain, what love you bring,**
> **it truly makes all matter sing,**
> **your violet flame does all restore,**
> **with you we are becoming more.**

4. Saint Germain, send oceans of violet flame into the mental bodies of myself and all people in my circle of influence. Transmute any karmic ties to any beings in the mental octave and any tendency for confusion or lack of clarity.

> O Saint Germain, I love you so,
> my aura filled with violet glow,
> my chakras filled with violet fire,
> I am your cosmic amplifier.

> **O Saint Germain, what love you bring,**
> **it truly makes all matter sing,**
> **your violet flame does all restore,**
> **with you we are becoming more.**

5. Saint Germain, send oceans of violet flame into the identity bodies of myself and all people in my circle of influence. Transmute any karmic ties to any beings in the identity octave and any tendency for fanaticism or closed-mindedness.

> O Saint Germain, I am now free,
> your violet flame is therapy,
> transform all hang-ups in my mind,
> as inner peace I surely find.

O Saint Germain, what love you bring,
it truly makes all matter sing,
your violet flame does all restore,
with you we are becoming more.

6. Saint Germain, send oceans of violet flame into the lives of myself and all people in my circle of influence. Transmute any karmic vulnerability that prevents us from walking a balanced path and living a balanced life.

O Saint Germain, my body pure,
your violet flame for all is cure,
consume the cause of all disease,
and therefore I am all at ease.

O Saint Germain, what love you bring,
it truly makes all matter sing,
your violet flame does all restore,
with you we are becoming more.

7. Saint Germain, send oceans of violet flame into the lives of myself and all people in my circle of influence. Transmute any karmic vulnerability that prevents us from finding the personal inner balance that allows us to make the calls that give the ascended masters the authority to remove the dark forces from the earth.

O Saint Germain, I'm karma-free,
the past no longer burdens me,
a brand new opportunity,
I am in Christic unity.

O Saint Germain, what love you bring,
it truly makes all matter sing,
your violet flame does all restore,
with you we are becoming more.

8. Saint Germain, send oceans of violet flame into the lives of myself and all people in my circle of influence. Transmute any illusion in our own consciousness that makes us vulnerable to the energies and attacks from the dark forces.

O Saint Germain, we are now one,
I am for you a violet sun,
as we transform this planet earth,
your Golden Age is given birth.

O Saint Germain, what love you bring,
it truly makes all matter sing,
your violet flame does all restore,
with you we are becoming more.

9. Saint Germain, send oceans of violet flame into the lives of myself and all people in my circle of influence. Transmute any karmic vulnerability and energies so that the fallen beings can no longer hurt us because we have accelerated our consciousness beyond their reach.

O Saint Germain, the earth is free,
from burden of duality,
in oneness we bring what is best,
your Golden Age is manifest.

O Saint Germain, what love you bring,
it truly makes all matter sing,
your violet flame does all restore,
with you we are becoming more.

Sealing

In the name of the I AM THAT I AM, I accept that Archangel Michael, Astrea and Shiva form an impenetrable shield around myself and all constructive people, sealing us from all fear-based energies in all four octaves. I accept that the Light of God is consuming and transforming all fear-based energies that make up the dark forces!